EDWARD PETERS

University of Pennsylvania

EUROPE
AND
THE MIDDLE AGES

PRENTICE-HALL, INC., Englewood Cliffs, New Jersey 07632

Library of Congress Cataloging in Publication Data

PETERS, EDWARD [date]
    Europe and the Middle Ages.

    Abridged ed. of: Europe, the world of the Middle Ages.
c1977.
    Bibliography: p. 303
    Includes index.
    1. Middle Ages—History.   2. Civilization, Medieval.
I. Title.
D118.P452 1983   940.1   82-3717
ISBN 0-13-291914-1   AACR2

Editorial supervision and interior design: Serena Hoffman
Cover design: Sue Behnke
Cover art courtesy of the Metropolitan Museum of Art.
Gift of J. Pierpont Morgan, 1917.
Copyright © 1966 by the Metropolitan Museum of Art.
Manufacturing buyer: Edmund W. Leone

PRINTED IN THE UNITED STATES OF AMERICA

10 9 8 7 6 5 4 3

ISBN 0-13-291914-1

PRENTICE-HALL INTERNATIONAL, INC., *London*
PRENTICE-HALL OF AUSTRALIA PTY. LIMITED, *Sydney*
PRENTICE-HALL OF CANADA, LTD., *Toronto*
PRENTICE-HALL OF INDIA PRIVATE LIMITED, *New Delhi*
PRENTICE-HALL OF JAPAN, INC., *Tokyo*
PRENTICE-HALL OF SOUTHEAST ASIA PTE. LTD., *Singapore*
WHITEHALL BOOKS LIMITED, *Wellington, New Zealand*

To my brother Jack,
and to Ann, Heather, and John,
in memory of

EDWARD LOUIS PETERS
(1964–1981)

Contents

9 Europe Emerges   113

PART IV: CHRISTENDOM: AUTHORITY AND ENTERPRISE, 950–1150   127

10 Material Civilization   129

11 Power and Society   141

12 Christendom East and West   152

PART V: CULTURE AND SOCIETY IN THE HIGH MIDDLE AGES   171

13 The New Learning   173

Preface

As individual human beings, we have not lived, and cannot remember, very much of the past. As participants in a culture, however, we share the artificial memory of that culture, and as the character of our culture changes, we make different demands upon its artificial memory—the study of history. Each generation or two, we require that history be made intelligible in a different way and that this intelligibility relate in some way to our own lives, experience, and image of ourselves. At one time in our past, the artificial memory was expected to produce lists and adventures of important folk—kings, generals, heroes, and other sorts of "great men." By their actions, it was thought, as if by the actions of a kind of social spark plug, the "historical events" of an age were ignited. Somewhat later—in fact relatively recently—our culture required us to know not so much about great men as about ordinary men, women, and children—how they lived, what their values were, how they fared economically, how they felt themselves members of larger communities and whole cultures. Today we make rather extensive demands of the study of history, and because that history has been put to such different uses, there are many different methods for finding out about—and explaining—the past.

Different methods of historical investigation and explanation came into existence precisely because of the different questions about the past that people asked. In the late fourteenth century, as the last chapter of this book will tell, a number of literary moralists asked why the great power of the Roman Empire collapsed around A.D. 500, or, as the greatest successor they ever had, Edward Gibbon, put it, why the Roman Empire "declined and fell.'' These men themselves thought that in their own time they had managed to revive, or give rebirth to, many of the values of ancient Rome. They came to call their own age (from about the year 1350 or so) the period of rebirth, ''the Renaissance'' of Roman and, later, Greek values. With the glories of ancient Rome at one end, and the perceived glories of revived Roman and Greek culture at the other, the period from 500 to 1350 acquired a kind of negative shape. What seemed to be conspicuous about it was its ''un-Romanness,'' between two periods of ''Romanness.'' And so people took to calling it ''Middle''—middle between two more admirable periods of human energy, order, and achievement.

Religious reformers in the early sixteenth century added to this picture their accusations that at the end of the Roman Empire a kind of true, evangelical Christianity had been perverted and was not purified until their own time. This view reinforced the first definition of the Middle Ages. It was reinforced in the late sixteenth and seventeenth centuries by thinkers who sensed that even if their age had not quite re-created ancient Greece and Rome, it had done something even better—it had created a greater civilization.

None of these three points of view had much good to say about—or reason to change the name of—the Middle Ages. By the criteria of Romanness, reformed Christian values, and the idea of progress, the Middle Ages were indeed the middle—or, as many others called the period, rusty, monkish, leaden, dull, and barbarous.

On the other hand, the thinkers who seemed to defend some of the values of the Middle Ages appeared to represent precisely those elements in early modern European culture that resisted improvement and progress—the forces of royalism, ecclesiastical coercion, aristocratic privilege, or, as the first American medieval historian, Henry Charles Lea, once called them, ''Superstition and Force.''

The questions that eighteenth- and nineteenth-century Europeans and Americans asked about the past were: How did political liberty grow out of savage repression? How did toleration and freedom of conscience grow out of ecclesiastical intolerance and narrow-minded superstition? How did backwardness change to progress? None of these questions did anything to improve the image of the Middle Ages, although the process of answering some of them—and arguing against the answers of others—produced some good history and, even more important, some critical historical methodology.

By the end of the eighteenth century a large mass of historical materials, from physical ruins to documents, had accumulated in Europe, and the methods for using these materials to gain a clearer picture of the past had developed, often independently of the value judgments that had shaped historical questions. With the growth of historical research and teaching as a profession in the early years of the nineteenth century, a subtle change came over the nature of the questions people asked about the past. People did not immediately change the values with which they framed their questions, but they did not let those values dictate the methods they used to find their answers. Moreover, some of the values of the period between the fourteenth and the nineteenth centuries were under attack. Both of these conditions permitted freer investigation of a thousand-year period that had come to seem too long and too full of important events and foundations of later history to be ignored or scorned as cavalierly as before.

By the mid nineteenth century three events had taken place that made this question even more pressing. First, a series of political revolutions from 1756 to 1848 had made even the political world of early modern Europe—a world ruled by kings and aristocrats—seem remote and oppressive. Political questions came to include such nonpolitical elements as national or ethnic character, and common language and history—collective identity. The answers to these questions clearly lay in the very period when historical Europe, with its historical peoples, came into existence—the Middle Ages.

Second, the two industrial revolutions of the nineteenth century seemed to change the lives of more people so drastically, to increase wealth on such an immense scale, and to change the very nature of economic experience so thoroughly, that the differences between the Middle Ages and the period that followed seemed to shrink, especially in comparison with the great changes caused by industrialization and "modernization." Social thinkers began to speak of *preindustrial* and *industrial* societies, reducing the differences between shorter periods to virtual insignificance.

Third, by the nineteenth century Europeans had discovered just how large the world was and how diverse its peoples and cultures and religions were. This knowledge confronted them with two choices: either they could assume that the family of humans was hopelessly fragmented, with many peoples barely qualifying as "human" at all, or they could find some scale by which to measure the different kinds of humanity they encountered. The first choice led to a particular kind of outright racism, the second to anthropology. Nineteenth-century ideas of progress, genetic evolution, and the comparative study of culture types produced a model of world human society that accounted for the size and diversity of the world's cultures.

Using "developed," "industrialized," politically "liberal," and religiously "rational" Europe as their measure, thinkers began to classify other societies as "developed" or "underdeveloped" according to the degree to which they resembled Europe—or some earlier stage of European development. Here too the Middle Ages became important; it was part of the measuring scale by which Europeans judged the rest of the world.

Neither the opposition of thinkers between the fourteenth and nineteenth centuries nor the interest of thinkers of the nineteenth and early twentieth centuries was entirely free from bias. In the first group, literary, moral, and religious values distorted the assessment of the historical evidence. In the work of the second group, a Euro-centrism that seemed to patronize contemporary "underdeveloped" peoples and peoples in the past often shaped the questions and answers about human society that scholars asked. Romantic readers of Sir Walter Scott's historical novels that were set in the Middle Ages, and aesthetes who insisted upon having medieval ruins in their gardens even when this meant building ruins on purpose, trivialized medieval culture by their uncritical admiration of it, just as social scientists distorted it by using it illegitimately as a scale for measuring other cultures.

Throughout this process of changing cultural demand, historical scholars had slowly, and sometimes painfully, improved their techniques for handling evidence, from the reading of ancient languages and difficult documents to the realization that what people called "politics," "economics," "social class," and "religion" often meant different things in the past, and touched different areas of life and thought. The discipline of historical study—and historical criticism based on a professional methodology—had come into its own. History, the artificial memory of a culture, could no longer be turned quite so easily to the service of fashionable ideas, ideology, or confessional wrangling.

But history has never entirely freed itself from the undisciplined uses to which cultures often still wish to put it. Supporters of one modern ideology or another still insist that "history" proves them right and everyone else wrong. For nonhistorical reasons, others deny the historicity of events whose factual character is massively documented—most recently, the truth of the Holocaust, but generally anything that might be embarrassing, inconsistent with their view of the world, or merely inconvenient. Still others, in a timid and bland ignorance of historical differences, deny the use of the rich detail of the historical past, claiming that critical history is merely "names and dates." Instead they wish to homogenize all human history to the point at which important differences and the richness of different cultural traditions vanish entirely into a vague and timeless world in which "structures" and "models" and "statistical measurement" replace human beings as history's characters. In the twentieth century the discipline of history had become almost an art of intellectual self-defense; if we do not use it properly, others will use it, usually against us.

The history of historical study and method has produced a particular kind of knowledge—historical knowledge—that can be tested rationally and critically and yet still respond to the questions that our culture asks it, even if it must sometimes insist that the questions be rephrased and that it cannot produce the kind of knowledge the questioner insists upon. Any discipline must recognize those questions it cannot answer and the kind of knowledge it is unable to produce. This sense of the limits of historical knowledge is also a defense against the misuse of history by those who do not respect its critical and disciplined character. And that observation leads us to the character of historical knowledge—in this case medieval historical knowledge—as our culture understands it today.

Like other situations in which professionals inform nonprofessionals, the configuration of historical study must range between two poles: the detailed research of the specialist, about which few nonspecialists care to know in detail, and the "living past," the common received opinion of the past that most members of a culture have at any particular time in their own lives. In that part of the human past with which this book deals, the first is represented by a host of complex techniques for dating and authenticating manuscripts, reconstructing population figures, and interpreting many kinds of sources that are no longer produced by modern societies, such as saints' lives and local diocesan liturgical calendars. The second is represented by the "popular" ideas about knights and ladies, the predominance of ecclesiastical institutions over many aspects of daily life, and perhaps—to lay the term out and have done with it—"the Dark Ages." There is always a vast distance between the two poles in any culture, but the Middle Ages in general has suffered most because of it.

For its name has stuck. In spite of the entirely new picture of the Middle Ages in Europe that historical study has created in the last century, popular imagination and scholarly convenience have preserved the name "Middle" for a period that witnessed the beginning of a distinctive European civilization, created out of old and new elements by people who arrived and settled in Europe in its early stages and whose descendants are still there. Modern Europeans and Americans are *not* the only cultural descendants of ancient Greece and Rome, but we are the *only* descendants of medieval Europe.

We cannot remember that past, but the discipline of historical study permits us to know about it all that is possible to know. Human beings live in time, but, as novelists and physicists continually remind us, we perceive our own passage through time in subjective and distorted ways. Perhaps there is no other way to live through time. But historical study has created an intellectual tool that permits us to observe other people living in time without the distortion that prevented them, and often prevents us, from perceiving what living in time means. At one level, perhaps the most important, we are able to experience time and to understand, however incompletely, that our experience of time may be measured in other ways, and that the study of history sharpens that awareness and elaborates our individual and collective self-consciousness.

The study of any period of history will do this, for this is what historical study does best. In this book a particular segment of the intelligible past, isolated from early value judgments based on nonhistorical criteria, as well as from ideology, confessionalism, and the reductionism and blandness of static social science, is described in terms that have been tested, criticized, and required to be intelligible to interested readers in the last quarter of the twentieth century. The description will constitute a part of artificial memory, cultural memory. Its aim is to bridge the gap between specialized historical research and "the living past" that this culture maintains. The author—and the professional readers who have looked over his shoulder, kindly critical—have done their homework. It is time for the readers to get on with theirs.

ACKNOWLEDGMENTS

This is a shortened and considerably rewritten version of my earlier book, *Europe: The World of the Middle Ages,* which Prentice-Hall published in 1977. Fortunately many readers passed on to me their thoughts about that text, and this work has benefited immeasurably from their efforts. I am grateful to those teachers who used the earlier book and commented on the experience of teaching it. I am also grateful to several students who read closely enough to spot errors and inconsistencies and were kind enough to inform me of them.

I also wish to thank the anonymous readers who considered the manuscript for Prentice-Hall: Professor James M. Muldoon of Rutgers University at Camden, Professor Jeremy DuQuesnay Adams of Southern Methodist University, Professor Charles W. Connell of West Virginia University, Professor Barbara A. Hanawalt of Indiana University at Bloomington, and Professor Bernard W. Scholz of Seton Hall University. I thank those readers whose comments were such as to instill humility into egos far greater than mine; favorable reviews are a joy, but hostile ones send the writer back to work, disgruntled, but determined.

Professor R. Dean Ware and Professor Archibald R. Lewis, both of the University of Massachusetts, Amherst, commented extensively on the first version. Their comments have, I hope, made this book much better than it would have been without them. Much of this book has been inflicted in conversational form upon Professor James Muldoon and Dr. Thomas G. Waldman of Philadelphia, who also read the entire manuscript and commented extensively upon it, not for Prentice-Hall, but for me—an act of great scholarly courtesy and friendship.

The book is dedicated in memory of my nephew to my brother and sister-in-law and their children.

EDWARD PETERS

PART

I

EUROPE AND

THE WORLD OF ANTIQUITY

1

The Beginning and End
of the Roman Peace

GREECE, ROME, AND THE MEDITERRANEAN WORLD

Between 750 and 550 B.C. the city-states and kingdoms of Greece and Phoenicia situated along the eastern edge of the Mediterranean basin began to send out settlers and found colonies westward across the Mediterranean Sea. By 400 B.C. the coast of the Mediterranean from Morocco and Spain to Syria was dotted with city-states, each linked to its cultural homeland by well-traveled sea routes, and each widening the world that Greeks and Phoenicians regarded as their own. Because the Mediterranean is a sea with similar coastal areas, its shores were relatively easy to colonize. The colonization movement produced two great results. First, the former Phoenician colony of Carthage in North Africa became the center of a prosperous seaborne empire. Second, the Greek and Carthaginian colonies encountered and influenced the other Mediterranean societies: the Etruscans and Latins in Italy; the tribal Celts in southern Gaul and Spain; the Berbers, Numidians, and Egyptians in North Africa.

This colonial and cultural expansion widened the social horizons of the Greek world. No longer did the *polis* (city-state) claim the full attention and loyalty of the individual Greek thinker; Greeks in the late fourth century B.C. began to speak of the *oikumene,* the human world, as the natural community. The philosopher Isocrates (436–338 B.C.) urged Philip of Macedon, the father of Alexander the Great, to extend his

Greek Colonial World

☐ Areas of Greek settlement

power over all peoples so that "the nations are delivered from barbaric despotism and are brought under the protection of Hellas." In Isocrates' eyes, living under Greek rule and adopting Greek culture would make the Mediterranean world a single community, "for Hellene means a kind of intelligence, not a race."

Alexander the Great (356–323 B.C.) allied the forces of his Macedonian kingdom with those of the weakened Greek city-states and marched against the rest of the known world, hoping to turn the idea of *oikumene* into a political reality. Although Alexander's great empire was divided among his generals after his death, the culture of the states carved out of that empire was predominantly Greek, and the Greek cultural survival and its spread lasted in the Mediterranean world for more than six hundred years. From 300 B.C. until A.D. 500 Greek-speaking kings, administrators, and social elites gave a high degree of cultural homogeneity to the ruling classes of the Mediterranean world. The spread of Greek schools where the classic Greek poets were studied and Greek religious ideas circulated gave these ruling classes a common educational background that carried into their later careers.

But no power directly succeeded Alexander the Great in the political sphere until the slow rise of Rome in the third century B.C. Located in the west-central coastal region of the Italian peninsula, the small, agricultural city-state of Rome lay between two strong cultures that were far more developed. In the north of Italy, the civilization of the Etruscans long overshadowed and influenced that of Rome. To the south, the colonial Greek city-states (modern Naples, Syracuse, and Agrigento) brought Rome into contact with Hellenistic culture and mainland Greece. The hilly location of Rome was easily defended, and the Tiber River was easily bridged. Thus, trade routes passed through Roman territory, and Roman military strength, based on an army of tough, well-disciplined peasant soldiers, was exercised in small wars against neighbors. Intervention

4

in the quarrels of neighboring peoples was Rome's first step to power in the Mediterranean world.

By 275 B.C. Rome controlled the southern and central parts of the Italian peninsula and extended its interests into the central Mediterranean, where it encountered the power of Carthage. From the third century to the middle of the second century B.C., Rome and Carthage struggled in a series of wars (the Punic Wars) in which the power of Carthage was finally broken and Rome gained extensive territory in North Africa and Spain. During the second and first centuries B.C. Rome was drawn into the affairs of Greece and Asia Minor, and by the end of the first century B.C. Rome had accomplished what even Alexander had failed to do: Roman armies and administrators ruled the entire Mediterranean basin and had begun to extend their power into the Mediterranean hinterlands. After three centuries of virtually unceasing war, Romans imposed upon the *oikumene* the realities of a Roman peace.

Since the Roman "Empire" had been put together piecemeal, its "frontiers" were at first the frontiers of the territories Rome had conquered. In the light of imperial policy, however, some of these required adjustment. When Romans conquered Spain, for example, they recognized the importance of Gaul as a land route between Spain and Italy. After defeating a confederation of Celtic Gauls in 125 B.C., Romans founded the town of Aquae Sextiae (Aix-en-Provence) in 123. Between 123 and 118 B.C. southern Gaul became a Roman province, *Gallia Narbonensis,* and two characteristic Roman institutions were quickly introduced: a city (*Narbo Martius,* modern Narbonne) and a road, the *Via Domitia,* connecting Roman Italy with Roman Spain by a province that was rapidly becoming Roman Gaul. Other Roman towns in Gaul, such as Arelate (modern Arles) and Massilia (modern Marseilles) followed.

The settling of southern Gaul brought Rome into close contact with the tribal Celtic world of Gaul and northern Italy. Thus, Roman colonists and soldiers had to secure the new province from attack from the north, and the needs of defense required the frontier of Gaul to move northwards to strategically defensible ground. Elsewhere in the Mediterranean world Rome encountered similar problems. The Romans' eastern conquests in Asia Minor brought the edge of their territories into contact with the Parthian Empire of Persia, which had been founded in 248 B.C. and lasted until A.D. 224, when it was succeeded by the strong and hostile Sasanid Persian Empire. The conquest of Egypt drew Roman forces far up the Nile River. The conquest of Numidia brought them to the edge of the Sahara Desert. The search for coherent and manageable frontiers consumed the thought and energies of many Roman rulers, administrators, and soldiers for the next century.

GOVERNMENT AND SOCIETY IN THE ROMAN EMPIRE

The Romans imposed political and military institutions upon a world that was already materially and culturally homogeneous, at least among its prosperous and ruling classes. The Latin language spread nearly as widely as Greek, and Latin literature flowered in the new cosmopolitan atmosphere of the empire, although Greek remained the language of philosophy. Even for Romans, Greek remained the language of daily life in most of the eastern part of the empire.

The creation of the empire, however, imposed great stresses upon Roman society and political institutions. Rome had been a republic, ruled by elected officials called con-

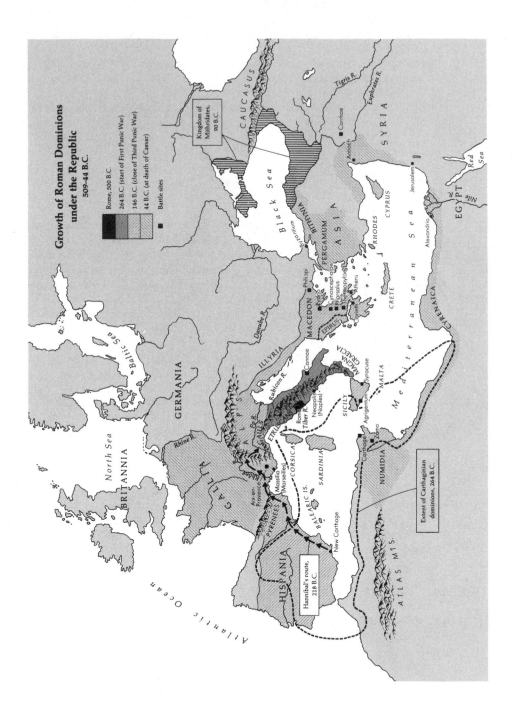

**Growth of Roman Dominions
under the Republic
509–44 B.C.**

Rome, 500 B.C.
264 B.C. (start of First Punic War)
146 B.C. (close of Third Punic War)
44 B.C. (at death of Caesar)
Battle sites

Kingdom of
Mithridates,
90 B.C.

Extent of Carthaginian
dominions, 264 B.C.

Hannibal's route,
218 B.C.

CAUCASUS

Tigris R.

Euphrates R.

Carrhae

Antioch

SYRIA

Red Sea

Jerusalem

EGYPT

Nile

Alexandria

CYPRUS

RHODES

CRETE

Black Sea

Byzantium

BITHYNIA

PERGAMUM

ASIA

Mediterranean Sea

CYRENAICA

Philippi

Cynoscephalae

Pharsalus

Thermopylae

Actium

Athens

MACEDON

EPIRUS

ILLYRIA

Danube R.

MAGNA GRAECIA

Cannae

Rubicon R.

Tiber R.

Rome

Neapolis
(Naples)

ETRURIA

Syracuse

SICILY

Agrigentum

MALTA

Zama

Carthage

NUMIDIA

SARDINIA

CORSICA

New Carthage

BALEARIC IS.

Massilia
(Marseilles)

Aix-en-
Provence

Rhone R.

GAUL

PYRENEES

HISPANIA

ATLAS MTS.

ALPS

Rhine R.

GERMANIA

BRITANNIA

North Sea

Baltic Sea

Atlantic Ocean

suls, who represented the interests of the ruling landowning classes, and by an assembly of powerful men called the Senate. The military successes of the second century B.C., however, caused social unrest, and programs of reform were never entirely successful. The first century B.C. witnessed a struggle for power among different factions of Roman society, some Romans urging a rigid adherence to the older patrician ways, others seeking change in broadening the political participation of middling classes. In addition, the immense wealth that poured into Rome from the conquered territories and the opportunities for personal gain that provincial administratorships offered quickly changed the character of Roman society. The stern agrarian morality, simple piety, and tribal institutions of a small city-state proved no match for the power, wealth, and distractions of a worldwide empire.

In spite of social pressures, Romans proved reluctant to give up the republican form of government, even though that form could not contain the conflicting forces of the first century B.C. Several Romans offered constitutional reforms, the most influential of them being Gaius Julius Caesar (102–44 B.C.). Caesar rose from a provincial governorship in Gaul to the head of a political conspiracy and seemed ready to seize absolute power in the Roman state when he was assassinated by political rivals. Caesar's death plunged the empire into a series of civil wars that ended with the triumph of his adopted son, Octavian Augustus (63 B.C.–A.D. 14).

Augustus adopted the facade of republican officeholding, calling himself merely the *princeps,* or "first citizen" of Rome, but he thoroughly dominated the Senate and the armies. The leading Romans were satisfied that the form of republican government had been preserved, even though it became clear that Augustus was, in fact, the sole ruler of the Roman "Empire." Augustus' genius, ruthlessness, and vast power and wealth established for three centuries the constitution of the Roman Empire. Within Rome itself the emperor was technically the holder of several key republican offices, the direct ruler of key provinces, and the commander of the armies. Outside Rome the Roman emperor was looked upon as a world-king, and later, as other world-kings had been, as a god. By the end of the first century A.D., the Roman emperor was regarded as a god by his own Roman subjects, too.

During the first century A.D. emperors and senatorial aristocrats, imperial civil servants, and military leaders established a workable administration of the empire. They also achieved a temporary social peace internally, since the riches of the Mediterranean world, distributed by the emperor to all of his subjects in the form of free food supplies, public shows, and frequent donations of money, quieted some of the turmoil of the preceding century. Romans were exhausted by the civil wars, many of the most vociferous and dangerous opponents of Augustus were dead, and even the discharged soldiers of the Roman armies were amply provided with lands upon which they could live a life of retirement.

So successful did Rome's internal and external affairs appear in the first and second centuries A.D., and so little were the frontiers troubled, that this period has often been called the *Pax Romana*—the Roman Peace. Cicero (106–43 B.C.), an opponent of Caesar but a man who appreciated the spread of Roman power and did much to popularize Greek philosophy in Rome, remarked that under Roman rule *orbis terrarum est civitas*—"the whole world has been turned into a single Roman city-state." To Cicero and to others, the *orbis terrarum,* "the circle of the lands," was the Mediterranean and its shores and hinterlands. Poets, philosophers, and historians praised Rome's rule and recognized that they lived in a cultural and political world the like of which had never been seen before.

In spite of Augustus' success, however, the empire was never as stable as its admirers believed. Part of Augustus' success depended upon the elimination of his enemies and the enormous wealth he strategically distributed throughout Roman society. But the benefits of empire went chiefly to the ruling elite of the empire—a thin level of senators and high administrators, imperial relatives and favorites—and to the inhabitants of central Italy. Most people in the empire lived a characteristic Mediterranean life—always on the margin of starvation and having little opportunity for economic development. Slavery flourished, thus preventing a free labor economy from emerging, and very little liquid capital was invested in trade or manufacturing. The prosperous appearance of the first two centuries of the Roman Empire was the result of conquest, but Rome developed few other economic resources. The empire was governed chiefly with the well-being of Roman citizens in mind.

Inhabitants of the provinces and conquered client states had military peace and systematic government, but they shared little of the fruits of Roman triumph. Restrictive laws prevented a lively economy from developing, and a high degree of localism in administration and imagination, together with a rudimentary agricultural technology, imposed further brakes on growth and economic vitality. Imperial public works and services, the public donations of powerful and wealthy families, and army payrolls were the basis of economic well-being in too many cities. Although the Romans built marvelously engineered roads to link the nerve centers of the empire, they received primarily military and administrative use; the permission required to travel on them was rarely given to commercial entrepreneurs. Although the Roman land frontier grew longer and longer, sea transportation always remained the fastest and cheapest way to move about the Mediterranean world.

In the hinterlands and the remoter provinces, Romanization and Hellenization touched smaller elites. Classical towns and villas (country estates) appeared first in Gaul, North Africa, and Syria, later in Britain, the Rhineland, and the valley of the Danube. Private and public largesse decorated these remote towns and villas with the attributes of classical Mediterranean civilization—great amphitheaters and public baths, sculpture and monuments, paved streets and Roman-style houses. But the cities, especially in the western part of the empire, were centers of administration rather than production, consumers of revenue rather than producers of income. Aside from the first flood of wealth that was widely distributed by Augustus, the empire benefited only its ruling elite. For them, however, it was a privileged and secure existence, homogeneous throughout a larger and larger world. The historian Peter Brown has illustrated this world:

For a short time an officer's mess modelled on an Italian country villa faced the Grampians in Scotland. A checkerboard town, with amphitheater, library, and statues of classical philosophers, looked out over the Hodna range, at Timgad, in what are now the bleak southern territories of Algeria. At Dura-Europos, on the Euphrates, a garrison-town observed the same calendar of public festivals as at Rome. . . . One of the main problems of the period from 200 to 700 was how to maintain, through a vast empire, a style of life and a culture based originally on a slender coastline studded with classical city states.[1]

Besides the fragile and uneven economic and social fabric of the Roman Empire, the political fabric too proved unstable. Caesar's and Augustus' practice of adopting their

[1] Peter Brown, *The World of Late Antiquity* (reprint, New York: W. W. Norton, 1978), p. 11.

successors gave each emperor the legitimacy of a personal relationship with his divine predecessor, but dynasticism was not really compatible with republican constitutionalism. Moreover, several of the emperors made bad choices of successors. Augustus' own successor, Tiberius (A.D. 14–37) proved psychologically unequal to the demands of ruling, and his successors proved little better. When some of the early emperors, notably Caligula (37–41) and Nero (54–68), weakened the Senate by their purges and aroused outrage at their behavior, the administration of the empire fell into the hands of the imperial civil service, and power threatened to fall into the hands of the armies. The great flaw in Augustus' constitutional settlement was the problem of succession to the unique office he had created.

From 64 to 96, rival contenders for the imperial throne raised armies and fought each other, until the accession of the elderly senator Nerva (96–98) inaugurated a revival of senatorial influence and a series of able and diplomatic emperors, the Antonines, who ruled through most of the second century. It is not surprising that the Age of the Antonines (96–180) has long been regarded by historians as the golden age of the Roman Empire. It was so regarded by the wealthy, privileged, and powerful classes of the empire themselves; the world seemed to them to be ruled by conscientious, considerate, talented rulers who adopted promising protégés and trained them in imperial duties. Trajan (98–117), a Spaniard and Nerva's immediate successor, extended the frontiers of the em-

A Scene from Trajan's Column. This detailed scene showing a battle at a wall is typical of the extraordinary wealth of pictorial display commemorating the triumphs of the emperor.

pire to their farthest limits. The Roman view of the empire and its military success is illustrated in the great column that Trajan dedicated in 113 to commemorate his victory over the Dacians. In a spiral frieze, 3 feet high and 670 feet long, climbing a 100-foot column, Trajan's artists skillfully illustrated the military triumph of the conquering emperor. Under Trajan the internal peace of the empire was restored. The reign of his successor, Hadrian, is an ideal point from which to survey both the full extent of the empire and some of the fundamental changes that the existence of the Empire had brought about.

HADRIAN'S TRAVELS

Hadrian (117–38) was also a Spaniard. By the end of the first century A.D., membership in the senatorial aristocracy had widened to include the elites of the old provinces. Just as Italy no longer exclusively provided senators, the reigns of Trajan and Hadrian proved that it no longer exclusively provided emperors. Indeed, one of the chief results of imperial history was the slow process of transforming Rome from being the head of subordinate territories to becoming the center of an association of provinces, the oldest of which—Spain, Gaul, and North Africa—considered themselves as venerable as Rome itself. By Trajan's reign 40 percent of the senatorial class was made up of provincials, and by the end of the second century, the Senate represented the upper classes of the whole empire. One reason for the success of the Antonine emperors was that they, like the Senate, were cosmopolitans who moved easily throughout the empire. They were traditionally educated and were as comfortable speaking Greek as Latin. More and more, they thought of the empire as a whole, not simply as an appurtenance of the city of Rome.

Nor did they remain exclusively in Rome. Trajan was a widely traveled aristocratic general, Hadrian a widely traveled scholar and administrator. Both these rulers probably knew the empire from personal experience and inclination better than had any of their predecessors. By Trajan's reign the Roman Empire stretched 1,600 miles north to south, from northern Britain to the edge of the Sahara Desert, and 2,800 miles west to east, from northern Spain to the Caucasus Mountains. The empire held 70 million inhabitants, 1.5 million in the city of Rome itself. It was nearly the size of the United States. Its population was about the same as that of medieval Europe in 1300, and about one-third that of the population of the United States today. The haphazard frontiers had in a century been transformed into a well-marked and well-guarded border. The Romans called the frontier the *limes,* a term that had originally meant the boundary of a farm but was applied by Tiberius in the Rhineland to a zone of military occupation. Trajan had pursued a policy of expansion with his conquest of Dacia, but he and Hadrian after him were very concerned about the nature of the frontier and how defensible it really was. Within the *limes* the Roman provinces had attained nearly equal footing with the capital of the empire, and the imperial administration achieved a certain uniformity throughout the empire without destroying all signs of local culture and tradition.

One of the most remarkable features of Hadrian's reign was his travels. It has been estimated that Hadrian spent nearly twelve of his twenty-three-year rule moving about the empire, accompanied by officials, architects, and cultural and artistic advisers. Part of Hadrian's purpose was practical; he wanted to know at firsthand how his administrators worked, how efficient or oppressive they were, how good the defenses were, what his subjects wanted and needed, and also to give immediate impetus to change where he thought it necessary. On the other hand, Hadrian had an insatiable curiosity about the varieties of life and thought and religious beliefs in the empire. He was bilingual in Latin and Greek, well read, and had excellent artistic taste, as his villa at Tivoli and his tomb in Rome, now the Castel Sant' Angelo, illustrate. When he traveled, he inquired about local customs, religious beliefs, and history. This side of his character was well known, and a generation after his death the Christian apologist Tertullian labeled him, certainly not in a complimentary sense, *omnium curiositatum explorator*—a seeker-out of every kind of trivial curiosity. Some historians have said that Hadrian was able, perhaps for the first time in imperial history, to view the empire as a whole.

Hadrian's travels informed the emperor about everything, but they informed him most about administration and defense. His legal reforms gave the empire a uniform code of law. Much of his travel resulted in a pulling back and tightening of frontiers. Perhaps its best known legacy is Hadrian's Wall, which the emperor ordered built on his visit to Britain in 122. From Wallsend on the mouth of the River Tyne to Bowness on the Solway Firth, Hadrian and his architects personally surveyed the seventy-three-mile distance across the width of northern Britain and helped design the long stone wall linking sixteen forts and many small guard posts and watchtowers. Although the wall was not intended primarily to keep the invading northern Picts out, it divided hostile peoples in the north and made an impressive display of Roman might on the far northern edge of the empire. From Bowness the Roman frontier stretched eastward along the wall to the North Sea, and then, in a chain of frontier towns and forts, down the Rhine and Danube rivers to the Black Sea. It then ran south from the Black Sea coast, down the valleys of the Tigris and Euphrates rivers, and turned west across Palestine, Arabia, Egypt, and North Africa, all the way to Morocco on the North African Atlantic coast.

Hadrian's visits to the provinces increased the sense of community among the provincial ruling classes, as did Hadrian's commissioning statues of the personified pro-

Hadrian's Wall. Looking westward across northern Britain, the course and fabric of the wall suggest the achievement of the emperor-engineer after whom it is named. (Courtesy of the British Tourist Authority)

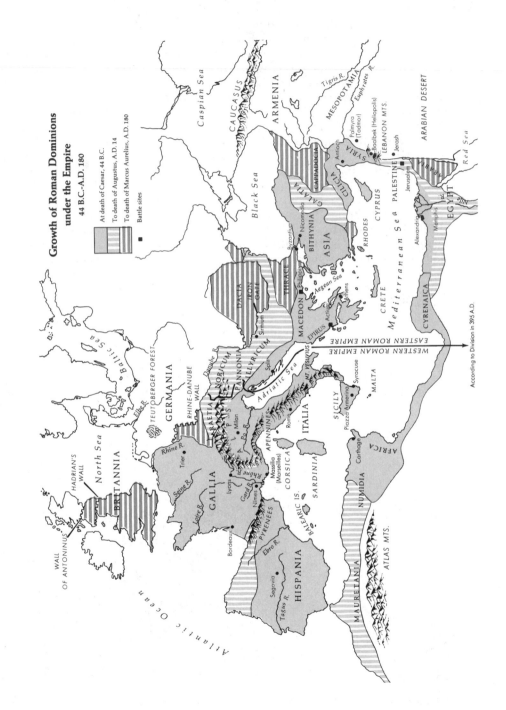

Growth of Roman Dominions under the Empire
44 B.C.–A.D. 180

At death of Caesar, 44 B.C.

To death of Augustus, A.D. 14

To death of Marcus Aurelius, A.D. 180

Battle sites

vinces for his museum, the Hadrianeum in Rome, and his issue of coinage depicting twenty-five different provinces and cities. All these acts suggest the cosmopolitan character of the emperor and the empire just before the middle of the second century A.D. Hadrian's two successors, Antoninus Pius (138–61) and Marcus Aurelius (161–80) continued both Hadrian's administrative concerns and his personal learning. Indeed, Marcus Aurelius has been claimed as the last classical Greek philosopher. But the events of his reign suggest that the golden world of Trajan and Hadrian was already coming to an end.

THE THIRD-CENTURY CRISIS

For the first time in nearly two centuries a Roman emperor, Marcus Aurelius, had to fight three major defensive wars—one against the Parthian Empire of Persia (161–80) and two against large confederations of barbarian armies on the Danube River (167–75 and 177–80). In addition, a great plague struck the empire in 166. Marcus Aurelius completed his book of philosophical reflections, the *Meditations,* in a military camp and died on the Danube near Vienna in 180. His incompetent son and successor Commodus (180–92) ended the Danube wars only by making an excessively generous treaty with the invaders. He displayed utter indifference, however, to both the provinces and the armies. His lenient treatment of the barbarians certainly stimulated barbarian interest in making war on Rome again, and his indifferent treatment of the army stimulated revolt. Commodus' assassination in 192 was followed by a period of civil wars.

At the end of the civil wars, the North African general Septimius Severus defeated his rivals and ascended the imperial throne with the backing of the Danube army. Septimius Severus did not come from the provincial senatorial elite that had produced the Antonines, nor did he possess universal interests. He was married to Julia Domna, a wealthy Syrian whose intelligence and wide religious interests mark her as the first consort of a Roman emperor who was intellectually distinguished in her own right. Unlike Commodus, Septimius Severus strove to retain military support. He restored the frontier defenses (including Hadrian's Wall), increased the size of the army to around 400,000 men, increased the army's pay by half, and threw the imperial service open to favorites from all corners of the empire. His greatest concern was to secure the imperial succession within his own family. He eroded the authority of the senatorial aristocracy and began the process of militarization and bureaucratization that quickly influenced government and finance. He died in 211 in a military camp near York, in northern Britain.

But in spite of Septimius Severus' favoring of the army, the frontiers remained troubled. Neither Severus' son Caracalla (211–17) nor Caracalla's son Alexander Severus (222–35) was able to guarantee the security of the frontiers. An army revolt led to Alexander Severus' assassination in 235, and from that year on the army created the emperors. Until nearly 270, with most of the empire's frontiers under attack, no emperor ascended the throne without the support of his army; when a stronger candidate, backed by a stronger army, challenged his rule, civil war decided the issue. Thus, after 235 neither the Senate nor an imperial dynasty, the traditional sources of successful emperors, played a significant role in the rule of Rome. Not only did the army make the emperor, but the emperor was usually a soldier himself, sometimes a soldier who had been born in a remote province and been a peasant farmer before joining the military. Working his way up through the ranks, where talent, rather than social status, was rewarded by promotion, a peasant soldier might become a general, and a successful and popular general who made the right promises to his troops had a ready-made faction to support his imperial candidacy. Sometimes generals were compelled to revolt because their very success and popularity made them threats to the current regime. The first of these peasant generals to become emperor was Maximinus Thrax (235–38), whose surname tells of his reputed place of origin—Thrace, a remote and backward province. After his ascent to military and then imperial power, Maximinus doubled the army's salary, thus imposing even heavier burdens on the fragile imperial finances.

A successful imperial candidate had to reward his troops; to do this and maintain the frontiers he had to raise more and more money from the population of the empire. He also had to spend more and more money on administration—even raising money cost money. Armies, imperial bureaucrats, and heavier and heavier taxes were the chief features of public life inside the empire during the third century. With them went debased coinage, inflation, and heavier and heavier burdens on those citizens who were forced to pay the taxes. Having imposed harsh financial burdens, the new emperor had to be ruthless in enforcing the law. Lacking the social and educational training of earlier emperors, he substituted instead the grim discipline of the army and borrowed the ceremonial trappings of the kings of the Persian East. From the mid third century on, the figure of the emperor in documents, sculpture, and court ceremonial grew more remote, godlike, forbidding, and capricious. Dressed either in military uniform or elaborate ceremonial robes, the third- and fourth-century Roman emperors were far different figures from Trajan, Hadrian, and Marcus Aurelius. Within a century the core of the empire, the imperial office, had been drastically transformed.

Between 235 and 270, however, emperor after emperor went down to military defeat or assassination. Decius (249–51) was lost with his army fighting on the Danube. Valerian (255–60) was defeated in battle and captured by the great king Shapur II of Persia. Between 260 and 268 most of Gaul was seized by an imperial pretender, Postumus, who claimed to establish a "Gallic Empire." From 267 to 270 the great caravan city of Palmyra, under its queen Zenobia, declared the independence of a vast stretch of the Persian frontier, including Syria, the Levant, and northern Arabia. Even the inner provinces of the empire felt the impact of these disasters, and not only in a financial way. In 271 the emperor Aurelian built a fortified wall around the city of Rome itself—a grim reminder of just how deeply the empire was threatened.

Even the empire's enemies had changed from the second century. In 224 the decaying Parthian monarchy was overthrown by the vigorous dynasty of the Sasanids. The Sasanid kings created a powerful, highly centralized state with a common religion (Zoroastrianism) and developed strong armies. Under the greatest of its kings, Shapur II (241–72), the Roman emperor Valerian was captured in battle, as we have seen, and led in Shapur's triumphal march to his capital at Ctesiphon, where the great victory was commemorated in large and beautifully executed relief sculptures. From Shapur's reign until the end of the Persian Empire in 626, Persia proved the most formidable and threatening of Rome's enemies. No emperor could rule or deal with a crisis elsewhere in the empire without covering the Persian front.

The societies of the Germanic invaders of the Rhine and Danube had also changed. Instead of tribes and small peoples on raiding parties, the Germans beyond the frontier tended from the late second century on to assemble into larger confederations. Armed and trained by fighting either in or against the Roman army, they were geared to a predominantly military way of life. The confederation of the Marcomanni fought Marcus Aurelius. In the third and fourth centuries the confederations of the Alamanni (not an

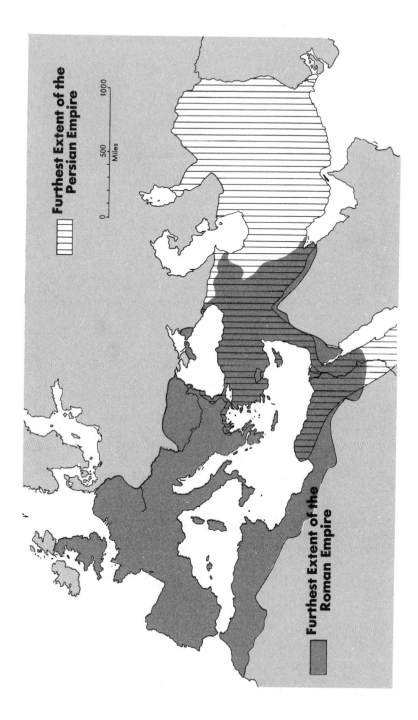

Furthest Extent of the
Persian Empire

Furthest Extent of the
Roman Empire

1000

500

0

Miles

ethnic designation, but a term meaning "all men") and the Franks (a term meaning "the free men") threatened the Danube and Rhine frontiers. Migrating eastern Germanic peoples, such as the Goths, also broke through the Danube frontier in the third century. It is not surprising, with the kinds of pressures on the Danube frontier in the third century, that Roman armies on the Danube, comprised of tough Balkan peasants, provided the core of Rome's defenses. Nor is it surprising that a series of talented generals from those armies succeeded each other on the imperial throne from 235 to 305, reformed the army, and saved the empire.

The military crisis was hastened because one kind of challenge that earlier emperors had never foreseen—major wars on two or more fronts—suddenly broke out early in the third century. The army had no strategic reserves to send quickly from a safe province to a threatened one, and the old Roman legions tended to be too cumbersome to perform the battle tactics required for fighting two major and new enemies. The Romans needed more heavy cavalry and archers to fight the speedy and skillful Persians and Germans, and they needed supply and command bases located at strategic points behind the battle lines from which troops could be deployed and directed quickly to deal with trouble from many directions. The stationary frontier line of forts, walls, and earthworks, staffed by resident provincial soldiers, was less valuable than the ability to put armies with proper equipment and experienced leaders where they were needed when they were needed. The great military base camps of the Danube valley, such as Carnuntum and Sirmium, and such cities as Milan and Aquileia in northern Italy, grew rapidly in their roles as command and supply bases.

The size of the Roman army increased to around 600,000 men, a 50-percent increase over the army of Septimius Severus. Barbarians as well as provincials were permitted to serve in the army, and the command of the army was placed in the hands of professional soldiers. After 260 the members of the Senate were excluded from military command. As the old Roman legion disappeared, the army was divided into two new kinds of troops. The *limitanei,* as their name suggests, were stationed permanently on the frontiers and were expected to hold off an invasion, if only for a short time. The *comitatenses,* a mobile field army made up of heavy cavalry, specially trained infantry, and archers, were stationed at the new command bases behind the *limitanei.* The *comitatenses* were elite troops; they could be deployed rapidly, and at their best they were certainly the equals and often the superiors of their enemies.

Changes in the structure of the Roman armies paralleled changes in the structure of Roman society. Beneath the rank of senator Roman society consisted of two broad groups, the *honestiores* and the *humiliores.* The *honestiores* constituted a kind of professional middle class, consisting of city officials, army officers, teachers, physicians, and the civil servants of the imperial administration. They were the salaried managers of society who, when they could afford to, bought land and aimed at achieving senatorial rank. Beneath the *honestiores* were the *humiliores,* the merchants and traders, craftsmen, and small farmers. And beneath these two social groups were the slaves. Slaves, however, were used somewhat less frequently under the empire, partly because the conquest of foreign peoples—the chief source of slaves—ceased once the empire had ceased to expand, and partly because after the second century A.D. mines, fields, and industries tended to use more free labor. Slaves predominated in domestic service, however, down to the level even of the households of *humiliores.* Besides, barbarians had found new careers in the empire after the second century. Instead of becoming slaves, they could enroll in the army of Rome or lease agricultural land in the provinces.

The composition of the senatorial class changed in the third and fourth centuries, but the wealth and privileges of that class did not. The financial burdens of the state fell more and more upon the *honestiores* and *humiliores*. The economic decline of the third century, therefore, must be regarded chiefly in terms of its effect upon the lower ranks of society—the men and women whose ability to lighten the new economic burdens of taxation and inflation was strictly limited.

Three general reasons for the decline stand out: the expensive century and a half of war between 161 and 313; the generic limitations of the Roman economy; and the possibility of a general decrease in population, particularly in the western part of the empire. In addition, new migrations and confederations of people beyond the Roman imperial frontiers, the rivalry of army leaders for the imperial throne, and the increasing use of soldiers in all aspects of civil administration imposed increasing economic strains upon Roman society from the mid second to the fourth century.

DIOCLETIAN'S REFORMS
AND THE FOURTH-CENTURY RECOVERY

The military, economic, and administrative crisis of the third century was reversed by the reform of imperial government by the emperor Diocletian (284–305) and his successor Constantine. Although these reforms produced another century of general stability for the empire, in the long run they proved immensely expensive. During the fourth and fifth centuries the eastern part of the empire, with its many prosperous cities, strong commercial economy, productive peasantry, and greater population survived better than the western part of the empire. The west felt the consequences of having fewer people, less productive and fewer cities, a less-developed economy, and more frequently attacked frontiers that were closer to the main centers of government. The cities of the western Roman Empire had developed chiefly as centers of administration of provinces, and they did not have the resilience that eastern cities did, nor the economic base. The western peasantry grew more and more oppressed by powerful large landholders. In short, the response to the crisis of the third century produced a transformed empire in which the eastern parts fared far better than the western.

The 270s and 280s produced a series of military victories that for a time pacified the frontiers and allowed the emperors to turn to the pressing need for internal reforms in finance and governmental organization. One of the military emperors, Diocletian, turned out to be an immensely skillful reformer. Diocletian's reforms touched all levels of society. He regularized the new and heavy taxes. He attempted to "freeze" the structure of society by legislating that laborers and their children remain in key trades and professions. He attempted to set strict price controls on all goods sold in the empire. He increasingly bureaucratized imperial government. His close supervision of the law courts extended imperial governmental institutions and officials deeper and deeper into the daily life of most of the empire's population. The new competence and ruthlessness of imperial officials carried out the emperor's reforms so that, by Diocletian's retirement in 305, the Roman Empire had been subjected to the most complete overhaul of governmental institutions the ancient world had ever seen.

Although not all of Diocletian's reforms took root, many had a quick and enduring influence. Not only did he reform society, but Diocletian even took on the dramatic reform of imperial governance. He created a second Augustus, a partner-emperor for himself, and announced the division of the empire into two halves, the *pars orientalis,* or eastern half, and the *pars occidentalis,* or western half. One Augustus was to rule in each. Each *pars* was in turn broken into two parts: in one the Augustus ruled, and in the other a Caesar, the Augustus' assistant and prospective successor, ruled. The tetrarchy, or rule of four—two *Augusti* and two *Caesares*—proposed to solve the two perennial problems of Roman imperial rule: the question of succession and the needs of government and defense. Each Augustus was to rule for twenty years.

In 305 Diocletian retired to Split (in modern Yugoslavia), having arranged, or so he thought, the appointment of the next four rulers. Diocletian's arrangements, however, foundered upon the equally perennial problem of dynasticism. Maxentius and Constantine, the sons of the first two Caesars, had been passed over in the succession, and their armies revolted and proclaimed them emperors. Constantine eliminated Maxentius in 312, and his other rivals and a large part of his own family over the next twenty years. Diocletian's reforms, which had been partially discontinued during the wars, survived, however, in Constantine's redivision of the empire and in his creation of a new army and civil service.

Constantine also continued the administrative redivision of the empire. Each *pars*

The Majesty of Emperors. This colossal head of Constantine the Great, nine times life size, was once part of a gigantic statue of the emperor that stood in the Basilica of Constantine in Rome. The size and imperial facial expression suggest the remoteness and majesty of late imperial portraiture. (Hirmer Fotoarchiv, Munich)

was subdivided into prefectures. The four imperial prefectures were those of the east and Illyricum (for the *pars orientalis*) and those of the Gauls (Britain, Gaul, and Spain) and Italy (Italy and Africa) for the *pars occidentalis.* Rome and Constantine's new city of Constantinople each had its own urban prefect. Constantine also transformed the army high command, creating a master of infantry (*magister peditum*) and a master of cavalry (*magister equitum*). The highest command levels were now open to barbarians as well as provincials, and by the mid fourth century barbarian *magistri* commanded Roman armies. Finally, Constantine continued and completed Diocletian's restructuring of society. Members of the class of municipal officials were forbidden to leave their towns for the country or the army; free farmers were legally tied to the soil they cultivated; membership in the trade corporations in the towns was made hereditary.

Diocletian's and Constantine's reforms have been called the earliest and most complete form of state socialism the West has ever seen. Certainly the price that most of Roman society had to pay for protection and government was excessive. Diocletian and Constantine had succeeded in turning each class in society into an instrument for the survival of the apparatus of government and defense. If these changes pressed most severely on the lower classes of society, they did not leave the aristocracy untouched. Increased government efficiency began to encroach even upon aristocratic privilege. Although the Roman aristocracy remained immensely wealthy and largely untouched by the demands of taxation, it faced the threat of a flood of ''new aristocrats'' in the imperial service and the willingness of even the most respectful emperors to take drastic steps to preserve the life of the state. As long as the peace of the frontiers and the inner world of the empire was maintained, the emperor and the aristocracy could avoid coming to blows. Before the third quarter of the fourth century, though, new invasions subjected that relationship in the west to a strain that it was not to survive.

FURTHER READING

On the expansion of Rome, see Fergus Millar, *The Roman Empire and Its Neighbors* (London: Weidenfeld & Nicolson, 1967), and R. E. M. Wheeler, *Rome Beyond the Imperial Frontiers* (1954; reprint ed., Westport, Conn.: Greenwood Press, 1971). A brilliant short treatment of the whole period covered by Parts I and II of this book is Peter Brown, *The World of Late Antiquity* (reprint, New York: W. W. Norton, 1978). Longer and more detailed are H. St. L. B. Moss, *The Birth of the Middle Ages, 395–814* (New York: Oxford University Press, 1964), and Joseph Vogt, *The Decline of Rome* (London: Weidenfeld & Nicolson, 1968).

On Trajan and Hadrian, see Lino Rossi, *Trajan's Column and the Dacian Wars* (Ithaca, N.Y.: Cornell University Press, 1971), and A. D. Divine, *Hadrian's Wall* (Boston: Gambit, 1969).

On the crisis and Rome's response, see Ramsay MacMullen, *The Roman Government's Response to Crisis, A. D. 235–337* (New Haven: Yale University Press, 1976), and idem, *Constantine* (New York: Harper & Row, 1971).

2

Religion and Society
in Late Antiquity

FROM GODS OF THE HOUSE TO GODS OF THE STATE

The oldest and most deeply revered deities of the Greco-Roman world were the domestic and local gods who protected the house, the family, the fields, woods, and groves. These ''little gods'' were the closest that the ancient world came to personal deities, although they paled beside the cult of the Olympian gods—powerful deities of the heroic age of Greece whose worship survived and prospered in the Greek city-states. The family of Olympian gods, headed by Zeus, the Jupiter of the Romans, were very different from the older local gods. They were eternal, but otherwise resembled superhuman beings, immensely more powerful than even the greatest human heroes and supremely beautiful. The proper human attitude toward them was awe and deference.

Besides their cults and temples, however, the gods lived on in poems, especially those of Homer and Hesiod, written in the ninth and eighth centuries B.C. By the sixth century B.C. the gods' conduct in these literary works had begun to offend religious thinkers, whose sensibilities recoiled at tales of the gods' lusts, jealousies, and petty human vanity. The culture of the city-states developed strongly in the direction of ethical thought and metaphysics, and the Olympian gods came to seem somewhat old-fashioned and gross to the philosophers. Some of these produced elaborate explanations of the gods' behavior in Homer and Hesiod, arguing that Homer's text was not to be understood literally but figuratively; it concealed higher truths from uninitiated human minds. Although cult worship of the Olympian gods survived in Greece and Rome, most sophisticated religious thinkers after the fourth century B.C. speculated upon the possibility of a transcendent deity, a single god whose actions could account for the complexity of life.

By the first century B.C., the approaches to religion by representatives of different philosophical schools determined the personal religious beliefs of most educated Greeks and Romans. Publicly, the official cults of Greece and Rome still paid homage to the Olympians, still sought the gods' advice about the future through divination, omens, and prophecies, and prayed for the well-being of whole communities. To a large extent the corporate welfare, rather than the personal connection between an individual and a god, occupied a prominent place in paganism. Roman state religious cults operated to bring the gods' favor to the community as a whole, and thus the impersonal character of the pagan gods was perpetuated.

With the rise of Rome to Mediterranean-wide power, much of the worship of the Greek and non-Greek worlds turned to Rome itself and to the figure of the Roman emperor. *Dea Roma,* "Goddess Rome," was worshiped in conquered provinces, although this cult did not reach Rome itself until the second century A.D. As we have seen, Roman emperors too were worshiped as divine, first in the provinces and later in Rome and Italy. The expansion of Roman power also brought new religions and new gods to Rome, some of them from very remote corners of the world.

The officials of Rome usually permitted many cults in the city, although some features of these cults—particularly human sacrifice, ritual prostitution, and other repugnant elements—had to be toned down or eliminated outright for Roman approval. From the late Republic on, the state cults of Rome remained highly formal and impersonal: they invoked the gods' protection for Roman rule and prosperity, but offered little solace to the individual and had no relevance to personal conduct, spiritual life, or hope for the afterlife. The Olympians, the philosophers' gods, and the character of Roman public cults suggest some of the variety—and some of the limitations—of pagan religion in the first centuries of the empire. Ethnic religions such as Judaism, mystery cults, and Christianity were some of the alternatives that the world of late antiquity offered.

JUDAISM IN PALESTINE AND THE DIASPORA

In 37 B.C. Palestine was conquered by the Romans and became a Roman province. The century-old monarchy of the Maccabees was destroyed, and a Roman-appointed Jewish king, Herod, assumed the rule of Palestine. In spite of religious and cultural resistance and several bitter revolts in the periods A.D. 66–70 and 131–35, Palestine remained a Roman province until Persian conquest in the early seventh century and Moslem conquest in the eighth. It proved to be somewhat different from other Roman provinces, however. Not only did the majority of the Palestinian population possess great ethnic solidarity, but they professed a monotheistic religion that contrasted sharply with those around them. Although by the first century Jews lived in many parts of the Mediterranean and Persian worlds, the Temple of Solomon at Jerusalem provided a physical center for Judaism. With a few exceptions, such as Alexandria in Egypt and parts of Persia, Jewish life was more vigorous in Palestine than in Jewish communities elsewhere. The land of Palestine and the temple at Jerusalem were the literal location of Jewish history, and the Jews refused to permit their land to be profaned by the customary rites of Roman occupation.

By the first century B.C., Judaism contained a wide variety of practices and beliefs, opposing schools of legal and scriptural interpretation, and many sects. Among these groups, the Pharisees insisted upon the observance of the Mosaic law to the letter, strict observance of the laws of purity and tithes, and resistance to outside religious and philosophical influences. Another group, the Sadducees, tended to accept Greek philosophical thought. Others practiced cults of personal holiness, individual devotion to God, and an emphasis upon the mystical interpretation of the Psalms rather than strict and literal observance of the law. Thinkers in Alexandria attempted to join Greek philosophical speculation with the observance of the law. Philo Judaeus (25 B.C.–A.D. 41), devised a complex system of interpreting the Old Testament (which in Alexandria was read in Greek, rather than Hebrew) according to which the literal interpretation of what Scripture said was simply the first of several levels of meaning. To seek higher levels, the devout scholar had to be trained in philosophy and figurative interpretation. Philo's technique later exerted an immense influence upon both Jewish and Christian biblical scholarship and theology.

In addition to groups such as these, smaller groups pursued the worship of Yahweh in other forms. (The discovery in 1947 of the Dead Sea Scrolls, the literature of a hitherto unknown Jewish sect at Qumran on the Dead Sea, revealed one such group.) Individual holy men certainly formed others. Some groups focused their devotions upon the expectation of a Messiah, which could mean either a messenger from God or a new king. Early in the first century A.D., a group of men and women in Galilee claimed that their master, Jesus of Nazareth, who had been tried and executed by the Romans, had been just such a Messiah. He had brought a new law to the Jews and was, in fact, the son of God, who had returned to life after his execution and continued his teaching, commissioning his followers in the name of God to preach the necessity of baptism for the forgiveness of old sins and for a spiritual rebirth.

Christian beliefs spread slowly throughout the Jewish world, sometimes carried by exiles from Palestine. In the Syrian city of Antioch, Jesus' followers were first called "Christians." In Asia Minor a Pharisee named Saul, a persecutor of the new sect, was converted to Christian beliefs by a vision of Jesus, after which he changed his name to Paul and preached enthusiastically in the cities of the Mediterranean not only to Jews but to gentiles (non-Jews) as well. In his Epistles Paul developed a new universal appeal of Christianity. Conflicting Jewish and Christian interpretations of Scripture, their differing attitudes toward the observance of the Mosaic law, and Christians' insistence upon the divinity of Jesus slowly separated the early Christians from their Jewish origins and from the contemporary Jewish community.

The emergence of Christianity marks one aspect of first-century Judaism, but there are other important aspects as well. A Jewish revolt against Roman rule in A.D. 66 brought Roman retaliation. Jerusalem was captured and the temple destroyed in A.D. 70. With the destruction of the temple, teachers of the law emerged as the chief guides to worship, and during the first and second centuries A.D. the figure of the rabbi (teacher) emerged as the chief official of the Jewish community. A second revolt against Roman rule occurred in some of the North African provinces and Cyprus in A.D. 115–17, but it was put down with great severity. Finally, in A.D. 131–35 a leader named Simon bar-Kosiba led an unsuccessful revolt in Palestine, which resulted in the virtual annihilation of Judaism in that province. Since political resistance had been crushed and the party of rabbis who had opposed the war had triumphed, the rabbinic office emerged as the most important organizational force in Jewish life.

In the late second century A.D., a revised law code called the Mishnah was established by a rabbinical court. Subsequent commentaries on the Mishnah by scholars in Palestine and Mesopotamia produced the Talmud, the great guide to rabbinical Judaism that formed, with Scripture, the backbone of later medieval Judaism. A second great achievement of the rabbinical period was the final establishing of the canon of authentic scriptural books, which also occurred in the late first and the second centuries A.D.

Although the Romans had given Judaism legal toleration, designating it a *religio licita,* ''a legal religion,'' the revolts, the destruction of the temple, and the annihilation of priests and other leaders by Roman repression drastically transformed the Jewish community after the first century. Scattered throughout the Greco-Roman world, possessing only Scripture and Mishnah, the Jewish communities, led by rabbis, preserved the great religion of law and prayer in the face of increasing indifference on the part of pagans and increasing hostility on the part of Christians.

MYSTERY RELIGIONS

Religions such as Judaism probably never attracted large numbers of converts, chiefly because of their ethnic orientation. Although Paul encountered both Jews and Gentiles in the synagogue at Athens when he went there to preach, and although many Romans showed great interest in the ethical and monotheistic tenets of Judaism, few conversions took place after the first century. Those Romans who were not satisfied with state cults, who felt no love for the Olympian gods, and were not philosophers or Christians turned to other religious cults, most widely to the mystery religions.

Rome's conquest of the Mediterranean world brought other deities besides the Olympians and Yahweh to Romans' attention. From the first century B.C. these new cults arrived in the city of Rome itself. The dynasty of Septimius Severus, for example, brought the worship of the Syrian sun god Elgabal to Rome, thus lending the prestige of the imperial title to the practice of importing religions. We have already seen Hadrian's curiosity about different religions, and Septimius Severus' son, Alexander Severus, paid homage to many different gods, including, it is said, the god of the Christians. During the late third century other religions also appeared and attracted many followers.

One reason for the proliferation of religious cults in the third century was that the state cult of Rome was not exclusive—one could be a devotee of several gods without violating one's obligation to the state religion. Only Jews were exempt from observing the state cults. As we shall see, Christians lost the protection of Jewish status when their beliefs made it clear that they were not part of the Jewish community, or protected any longer by its legal privileges.

Two new cults, that of the Persian god Mithras and that of *Sol Invictus*—the unconquered sun—appealed especially to the army and the emperors. Other cults worshiped personified abstractions, such as *Fortuna* and *Victoria.* Third-century emperors also revived the worship of some of the Olympian gods, particularly Jove and Hercules, by associating themselves with these beings. The third century may also have witnessed the increased frequency of the public and professional practice of magic.

EARLY CHRISTIANITY

The first Christian communities were to be found in the Jewish communities scattered throughout the eastern part of the Roman Empire. The slow separation of Christians from Jews, however, deprived the Christians of protected Jewish status, although "Judaizing" sects of Christians survived for several centuries. Even when separated from their Jewish origins, however, Christian communities were modeled upon Jewish communities. Their leaders were prestigious teachers who interpreted Scripture and the law and directed liturgical services—in short, Christian rabbis. What bound these communities together was loyalty to the person and teachings of Jesus.

Besides oral tradition, several literary texts preserved that teaching. Shortly after A.D. 66 several texts recounting episodes in Jesus' life appeared. In Greek these were called *evangelion,* or "good news"—the Gospels. The four canonical Gospels, those of Matthew, Mark, Luke, and John, were not the only ones written. There were at least three others, traditionally designated Q, L, and M. Paul's letters, the Epistles, were widely circulated, and they too were later accepted as divinely inspired. A few other letters attributed to Jesus' followers, the Apostles—a narrative historical account of early Christian proselytizing called the Acts of the Apostles and a prophetic account of the end of the world and the last judgment that was deeply colored by contemporary Jewish revolutionary imagery and violently anti-Roman, the Revelation of John—all gained increasing recognition as Christian canonical scripture. The formal canon of Christian Scripture was defined at the Council of Carthage in 397.

The first and second centuries knew other scripture as well. In 1945 a discovery was made at Nag Hammadi in Egypt that was as important for the early history of Christianity as that of the Dead Sea Scrolls at Qumran. The fifty-two texts of Nag Hammadi constitute a library of Christian writings, much of it purporting to be scriptural, that reveals the widely held differences that had emerged by the late first and early second centuries among Christians. Although scholars had long known that the earliest writings of churchmen against dissidents within the Christian communities were written against such divergent beliefs, the Nag Hammadi manuscripts revealed the full extent of the variety of those beliefs for the first time.

The religious ideas they describe were called Gnosticism. A religious movement that probably predated Christianity, Gnosticism flowered when it was combined with selected texts of the Christian Scriptures and the story of Jesus. Gnosticism, as its name implies, offered *gnosis,* "knowledge," to its initiates, specifically a more important kind of knowledge than the normal Scriptures professed and one that was concealed from the average Christian. The Gnostic initiate, after studying highly selective versions of authentic Scripture and other texts such as those found at Nag Hammadi, discovered that the Christian story was a veil of myth concealing the "true" story of the imprisonment of the spirit in the material world and containing instructions as to how the spirit might free itself and rejoin the divinity. The attraction of Gnosticism was very powerful, and recent studies have shown that the life and beliefs of the earliest Christian communities varied far more than had once been thought.

Christians believed that Jesus' death and resurrection from the dead freed them from the consequences of the Fall of Adam and Eve in the Garden of Eden. Commitment to this belief made the Christian, as Paul said, a *novus homo* (a new man) who literally turned his back (made a *conversio*) upon his old life and nature. Conversion stories became powerful forces in early Christian literature, those of Paul himself and Saint Augustine in the fourth century being the best known. Conversion and a new life of bearing witness to the truth of Christianity became the center of Christian conduct. Thus, Christianity tended to dismiss both the legal meticulousness of the Pharisees and the ethical and metaphysical learning of pagan philosophers.

Although Christianity seemed to many citizens of the empire merely an offshoot of Judaism or a new mystery religion—a "barbarian theosophy," as the pagan philosopher Plotinus called it—Christians considered themselves to be a "new Israel," and they reflected their sense of identity with great communal solidarity. During the intermittent persecutions of the first through the early fourth centuries, the steadfastness and brotherly love of the martyrs attracted many converts and much respect from those who remained pagans. Tending the sick, caring for their poor and orphans, visiting prisons, sharing meals, and providing burial for their fellow believers also reflected the strong Christian sense of community. Christianity also offered much more dignity to women than Roman law did. Husbands were commanded to treat their wives with respect and love and virgins and widows occupied important positions in liturgical life. In its emphasis upon individual moral responsibility, Christianity crossed sexual as well as social lines.

One sign of the attractiveness of Christianity is the nature of the hostility it generated. Not only did Roman emperors and administrators periodically persecute Christians on the legal ground that the religion was not permitted to Roman citizens, but by the second century even learned pagans deigned to take notice of its popularity. One such writer, Celsus (ca. 180), produced a long diatribe against Christianity, an indication of the growing appeal of the religion and the steps pagans were willing to take to oppose it. One of the landmarks of Christian literature is the long refutation of Celsus' work, the *Contra Celsum,* written by Origen (185–254), a priest of Alexandria and the greatest early Christian biblical scholar. Other Christian writers also defended their beliefs from what they considered unfair and misrepresentative Roman pagan hostility. By the middle of the second century some of these apologists were converts from paganism and intellectuals as well. Among the early apologists besides Origen, Justin Martyr (100–165) and Tertullian of Carthage (160–220) produced works rivaling those of their intellectual pagan opponents. The appearance by the end of the second century of Christian intellectuals who challenged the superiority of pagan opponents marks an important stage in the history of the spread of Christianity throughout the Roman world.

But Christianity did not simply denounce pagan philosophy. Slowly it absorbed some of its language and technique. Because Christianity had adopted the Greek language as it spread throughout the Roman world, it also adopted some Greek patterns of thought. The Gospel of John is generally considered one of the earliest examples of such influence. One of the greatest pagan influences upon Christianity was Neoplatonism, a philosophical movement that reached its height in the third century A.D. Its greatest pagan representatives, Plotinus (205–70), Porphyry (232–303), and Iamblichus (250–330), insisted upon a rigorous program of disciplined study throughout one's life. They also provided a philosophical approach to the relation between the invisible world of pure spiritual being and the material world. They led the philosopher to perceive the subtle and harmonious links between the spiritual and material worlds, and thus elevated the material world above the sharp condemnations of original Platonic thought, on the one hand, and Gnosticism on the other. Neoplatonism thus helped provide a conceptual vocabulary for some of the Christological controversies of Christianity, particularly in the debates over the relation between the human and divine natures of Christ. The greatest Christian representatives of Neoplatonism, Origen and Saint Augustine, shaped the philosophical terminology of Christianity.

The last assault of pagan Rome upon Christianity occurred during the persecutions of Diocletian and his associates between 298 and 312. When Constantine defeated his rivals in 312, however, he claimed that the Christian God had helped him, and he made Christianity a legal religion. The so-called Edict of Milan issued by Constantine is regarded as the first legal charter of Christianity in the Roman Empire. From the reign of Constantine until the end of the Roman Empire in the West, the emperors retained their character as supreme and awesome rulers, but they also underwent one momentous change. At the end of his life Constantine proclaimed himself a Christian and was baptized. His successors, with the exception of his grandnephew Julian (361–63), were all Christians. Thus, although the Roman emperor could no longer call himself a god, he could—and did—act as God's representative on earth. The privileges and wealth they bestowed on the Church and the extensive influence that Christian emperors exerted on the Church's structure altered the character of Christianity as well as the nature of the relation between religion and government.

CHRISTIAN EMPERORS AND RELIGIOUS DISSENT

Among the consequences of imperial participation in Christianity were the imperially funded construction of churches, the aligning of the Christian clergy with the structure of the Roman civil service, and the increasing participation of the emperors in matters of ecclesiastical government and discipline. Perhaps the most striking example of this new role—in both the empire and the Church—is the emperors' policy towards religious dissidence. The earliest Christian literature, as we have seen, reflects the existence of dissenting opinions about Christianity. Many of Paul's Epistles deal with such dissent. By the fourth century, however, dissent had grown and acquired new forms. Although Gnosticism had ceased to be a problem by the end of third century, other sets of belief had arisen to take its place, several of them not theological at all.

The first problem of dissension among Christians that came to imperial attention was that of Donatism, a sect originating in a disputed episcopal election in North Africa. Donatists claimed that Christian clergy who had submitted to imperial threats of persecution during the period 298–312 had to be rebaptized before being accepted again into the Christian community. By extension, Donatism posed the larger question of the relation between the moral character of individuals, priests, or lay persons and the indelibility of sacraments. How could a community be absolutely certain of the moral worth of its clergy and members? A secret sin by a priest might wipe away his sacramental power and plunge his entire congregation into damnation. The orthodox response to Donatism became a fundamental ecclesiological doctrine of the Christian community until the sixteenth century: the efficacy of the sacraments depends only upon the canonical ordination of a cleric, not upon his personal state of grace. With a little help from Roman law, one of the fundamental premises of ecclesiology took shape in the fourth-century Donatist experience.

The Donatist schism was resolved formally by a council of clergy that met under imperial direction at Carthage in 411. The institution of an assembly of churchmen under imperial supervision dealt with many similar crises in the ensuing two centuries, and this first great age of Church councils had a major influence upon the shape of Christian belief and life. Struggles between orthodox and heterodox beliefs, often with ''orthodoxy'' becoming sharply defined after the fact, also centered on Christology (the problem of the divine and human natures of Christ) and trinitarianism (the character of the three persons in the Trinity).

The most significant heresy in trinitarian history was that of Arius, a priest of Alexandria, who maintained that Christ had been created by God and hence was inferior to the Father, a doctrine that had wide appeal and wide consequences. Christ-founded institutions, for example, the Church and the sacraments, could be considered inferior to the power of the Father, or the emperor. The ensuing quarrels brought into Christian theology the full force of the Greek philosophical vocabulary, and the quarrel raged for more than two centuries. The Council of Nicaea in 325 laid down what ultimately became the orthodox dogma, that Christ and the Father were *homoousios,* ''of the same essence.'' Nevertheless, the divisions among the clergy, the contrary opinions of successive emperors, and the philosophical arena that had been opened by the free discussions of learned bishops heralded many of the future difficulties in the definition of theological orthodoxy. The imperial Christianity of the fourth century transformed both the empire and the Church.

Religious dissent and ecclesiastical organization were not the only areas of imperial activity to benefit the Christians. Christian emperors also drifted further away from paganism, even from the purely formal priesthoods and titles that they held as part of the imperial office. By the third quarter of the fourth century, emperors had become actively hostile to paganism. In 382 Gratian withdrew many of the funds that had supported pagan cults and priesthoods, and he removed the Altar of Victory, a venerable pagan symbol, from the Senate House. In spite of moving and articulate appeals from pagans, Saint Ambrose, bishop of Milan (339–97), convinced the emperors to keep such pagan symbols out of public places. The emperor Theodosius (379–95) outlawed all pagan practices in 392. As the aristocracy, the intellectuals, and the emperors themselves became Christians, the intellectual and social prestige they had once brought to paganism was diverted to Christianity. Only the popular culture of the urban lower classes and the rural peasantry of the empire were providing significant resistance to Christianity by the end of the fourth century. These classes provided both the last pagan resistance in the ancient world and some of the most significant new movements within Christianity itself.

HERMITS AND MONKS

About the year 269, Anthony, a young man from a prosperous peasant family in Egypt, moved by Christ's injunction to ''go, sell all you have and give to the poor and follow me,'' left his family and the narrow agricultural belt of the Nile valley and went out into the desert to live a life of devotion. From the time of earliest Egyptian civilization, the desert had symbolized the emptiness of the world and the habitation of demons. To Egyptians the desert represented the annihilation of everything remotely connected with civilization, and Anthony's self-imposed exile was a literal and figurative rejection of both the imperial church and the ancient, deep-rooted Egyptian terror of the waste. The name that Egyptians gave to Saint Anthony and those who followed him was a Greek word, *anachoresis,* which traditionally described those who had fled from the pressures of civilization into the hostile wilderness. The first anchorites were thus thought of as rejecting both the dangers of a secularized church and the social roots of civilization itself.

Saint Anthony attracted a number of followers, although he moved several times further away from civilization. His struggles with the demons of the desert, themselves a combination of Christian belief and traditional Egyptian peasant folklore, attracted much admiration, and by the mid fourth century the image of the isolated holy man had developed as a successor to the more dramatic ideal of an earlier Christian age—that of martyrdom and persecution suffered for the faith.

The *Life of Saint Anthony,* written by Saint Athanasius, the pugnacious Alexandrian defender of orthodoxy against Arianism (the heresy of Arius), was translated into Latin before 386 and started a new genre of Christian literature. The lives and passions of the early martyrs had constituted the most popular literature in the third- and early fourth-century Church. In the era of religious persecutions of 298–312 martyrdom came to be considered the highest stage of the life of the spirit, one that brought man to the very threshold of heaven. Saint Anthony and the other hermits of Egypt and Syria offered a new kind of religious ideal, the monk. Here was a "martyr" whose martyrdom consisted of making himself "dead" to the world and achieving in the desert—through rigorous self-discipline, contemplation, combats with demons, and, ultimately, mystical experience—that stage of the spiritual life that the martyrs had reached in so different a way in so different a world.

The spiritual biographies of early monks, inspired by the vast popularity of Saint Athanasius' *Life of Saint Anthony,* became the new literature of piety and the guide to the new spiritual life. Ironically, the spread of monastic popularity attracted the interest of the very world that the monks had rejected so dramatically. Lives of the "desert fathers" were widely read, and Christians thronged into the desert to consult the holy men, just as they had once made pilgrimages to the sites of earlier martyrdoms, some taking up the monastic life themselves and some returning to the corrupting world invigorated by their brief contact with the monastic ideal.

The variety of forms of monasticism was great during the fourth century. Some men retired to caves in the desert; some, especially the Syrians, took to living atop tall pillars for decades; some subjected themselves to extreme bodily tortures and privations. In the late fourth and early fifth centuries monasticism began to change. Small communities grew up around famous hermits, and these began to become organized. Under the influence of Saint Pachomius (286–346), a former soldier in the army of Constantine, an organized monastic life appeared in Egypt. Later, under the influence of Saint Basil of Caesarea (329–379), monastic organization evolved in the east as well. By constituting a model, or "perfect," Christian society, these communities offered a moral pattern whose elements might be absorbed slowly by the broader society around them. People considered the monastery, untroubled by the upheavals of the world around it, the example of ideal Christian society, a copy of heaven. By the beginning of the fifth century, monasteries were flourishing in Gaul and Italy as well as in North Africa, Egypt, Syria, and Greece. The monks, the new heroes of Christianity, represented the tradition of rejecting the secularization of Christianity, which the martyrs had originated. The appeal of the monks, like that of the martyrs, transcended the bounds of learning, philosophy, and social class. In monasticism the devotion of the humble man to God was raised to the highest level of Christian life and therefore militated against the increasing secularization of the Church.

Monasticism in a sense balanced the secular success of the Church in the fourth and fifth centuries and thus helped the Church retain its deep roots in the lower orders of society and in its concept of the relation between the individual, however lowly, and God.

Henceforth the Christian adaptations of pagan learning and Christian monasticism were to be the twin supports of the spread of Christianity, both inside Roman imperial society and in the world of the barbarians, a world ultimately more important than the demon-infested deserts or the well-stocked libraries of the urban fathers.

EMPERORS AND CHURCHMEN

The new prestige of bishops in the Christianized Roman Empire brought a new kind of adviser into the imperial court. Leaders of Christian communities were the only ones able to advise emperors about ecclesiastical matters; emperors in their turn relied more and more upon bishops as a kind of administrative class for ecclesiastical affairs and for those imperial affairs that touched ecclesiastical interests. Under Constantine the bishops Hosius of Cordoba and Eusebius of Caesarea served as theological advisers. Eusebius wrote not only Constantine's biography but also the first history of the Church, which ended with his vision of a golden age of Christianity under benevolent Roman emperors. At the same time, the Church itself was strengthened by the appearance of a new, militant type of churchman, whose career, influence, and writings helped shape an administrative kind of ecclesiastical authority that was strong enough to survive the later collapse of Roman imperial government in the West and furnish a prototype of ecclesiastical authority that later influenced medieval and modern ecclesiastical institutions.

An excellent example of this type is Saint Ambrose. He was born into the Roman aristocracy, the son of the praetorian prefect of Gaul, at Trier around 339. Ambrose entered the imperial civil service and became governor of Milan, one of the important centers of imperial administration. When the Arian bishop of Milan died in 374, the orthodox population acclaimed Ambrose as bishop, although Ambrose was only a believer and had not yet been baptized.

Ambrose at first protested his inadequacy, but he then devoted himself for more than thirty years to his flock. Throughout his episcopacy Ambrose stoutly defended orthodox beliefs, maintained the independence of the Church from the imperial government, and created in his writings what has ever since been the standard guide for a Christian bishop. In 390, after the emperor Theodosius ordered the massacre of the Christian population of Thessalonica because it had disobeyed an imperial command, Ambrose forbade Theodosius from participating in Christian liturgical ceremonies and forced the emperor to perform penance for his act. Thus, Ambrose may be regarded as one of the strongest early defenders of the superiority of the spiritual authority over the temporal power, especially in matters of belief and ecclesiastical moral discipline. Ambrose's writings not only made him the model of the ideal Christian bishop, but they also reveal in his life and thought the influence of late antique Neoplatonic philosophy and the continuing influence of traditional Roman concepts of public responsibility and civic morality that had been expressed by Cicero.

Saint Ambrose and Theodosius were not the only remarkable ecclesiastical-political figures of the late fourth century. The pontificate of Damasus (366–84) as bishop of Rome helped increase the prestige of that see by renewing the Christian history of Rome, turning the catacombs into shrines, and patronizing the cults of the martyrs in the city. Damasus also cooperated with Theodosius' ecclesiastical pronouncements on orthodoxy, and in return Theodosius recognized formally the preeminence of the bishop of Rome as successor to Peter the Apostle.

The Silver Plate of Theodosius. This plate shows a highly formalized scene of the emperor Theodosius investing an official with his rank of office, catching the extreme sense of hierarchy still present at the end of the fourth century. (Photographie Giraudon)

Damasus was one of the first of a series of dynamic popes whose efforts to elevate the see of Rome over other churches laid the foundations of the medieval and modern papacy. Angered by Theodosius' elevation of the patriarch of Constantinople, "the new Rome," to a position of personal authority second only to that of Rome, Damasus became the first pope to use the title "apostolic" in connection with his see and began addressing other bishops as "sons" instead of "brothers" in his correspondence. Damasus' fifth-century successors as bishop of Rome continued the struggle for ecclesiastical primacy. Siricius (384–99) was the first to use the title *papa,* or pope, for the bishop of Rome, and Innocent I (401–17) claimed that important cases should be judged only by the pope. By the time of Pope Leo I (440–61), the greatest of the popes who held office before the end of the sixth century, the bishop of Rome had clearly emerged as the successor of the senatorial guardians of imperial tradition and as the highest-ranking churchman in Christendom.

The prestige of individual bishops such as Saint Ambrose and the slow rise to prominence of the bishop of Rome were two of the forces that contributed to the success of Christianity between 350 and 450. The devotion of Theodosius shaped the structure of imperial Christianity, and the emergence of a series of remarkable theologians between 350 and 450 marked the Christian absorption and transformation of pagan culture. The most articulate and influential spokesman for Christianity during this period, though far from the most politically powerful, was the African Augustine, bishop of Hippo in North Africa. Augustine was one of the "new provincials" whose secular and ecclesiastical career revealed much about Christianity and about Roman society as well. The great Cappadocian Fathers of the mid and late fourth century—Saint Basil of Caesarea, Saint Gregory of Nyssa, and Saint Gregory Nazianzus—also represented the intellectual and spiritual vigor of what had hitherto been remote and backward provinces on the fringe of the empire. Their influence extended not only to monasticism and the eastern churches but to the arch-Roman, Saint Ambrose, himself. The career of Saint Augustine offers a western counter-example to those of the Cappadocian Fathers.

Born at Thagaste in North Africa in 354, the son of poor, free peasants, Augustine was baptized a Christian, but during his youth he was raised with little spiritual guidance except for the prayers of his Christian mother, Monica. Augustine's parents were unable to afford more than minimal schooling for their precocious son, but a wealthy fellow citizen undertook the expense of his continuing education at Carthage. From Carthage Augustine's success as a teacher of rhetoric brought him to Rome, and thence, in 384 under the sponsorship of the great pagan noble Symmachus, to the professorship of rhetoric at Milan, then the greatest city in Italy and an imperial capital.

Until Augustine was thirty, his career as a successful intellectual had been a classical illustration of "making it" in an open and receptive social system. From his professorship at Milan, Augustine was eligible for marriage into an aristocratic and wealthy family. With these credentials he could obtain a high administrative post in the empire, possibly a provincial governorship or the position of tutor to a future emperor. A generation earlier, the Bordeaux professor Ausonius had parlayed his own status as tutor of the emperor into a praetorian prefecture and a position of power behind the throne of Gratian. There was no reason, save one, why Augustine's career should not have followed a similar path. That reason was Augustine's restless spirit.

In the course of his education and social success, Augustine had encountered intellectually the rich spectrum of spiritual experience that the fourth-century Roman world had to offer. He had embraced Neoplatonism and the dualist Manichean heresy and flirted with mystery religions. Two hundred years before, the brilliant North African Lucius Apuleius had embraced the mystery religion of Isis and left a remarkable novel, *The Golden Ass,* which paints a vivid picture of late imperial life and the attraction of such mystery religions. But Augustine was not to be another Ausonius, or another Apuleius either. The pressures from his mother had followed him to Italy, and the emptiness in his own heart, as he was later to say, made the varieties of spiritualism he had experienced so far only dim and faulty shadows. In Milan, however, Augustine met Saint Ambrose, and the influence of the older man began to turn the professor's mind back to the Christianity that he had ignored for so long. After a moving personal religious experience, Augustine returned to Christianity in 386, renounced his professorship, and returned to Africa, there to become the bishop of the coastal city of Hippo Regius.

Augustine left one of the most remarkable documents in literary history, his *Confessions,* written in 397. This work is the first intellectual self-portrait in history; in it Augustine offered not the external events of his life but the ''history of a heart,'' the story of his own religious experience told from the viewpoint of a middle-aged bishop. In his *Confessions* Augustine transformed the traditional conversion story into the scheme of a whole life of individual struggles to come to terms with the traces of God—the *vestigia Dei*—in the human soul. For Augustine the discovery of the will of God, the conversion, was the climax of human life. But Augustine's work was not one of saccharine spiritualism; the *Confessions* read more like ''the account of a great spiritual disease and its convalescence'' than like the heroic martyr or conversion stories of old. Augustine keeps constantly before his and the reader's eyes the full complexity of human feeling and habit. Nowhere does he betray that complexity, nowhere does he offer an easy life as a result of his experience. Augustine was perhaps the first writer to reveal his own personality as the only means of describing accurately both the spiritual disorder that pervades the life of the man who ignores God and the continuing burden of the human condition after conversion, even during the episcopate. While bishop of Hippo (395–430), Augustine witnessed the great ecclesiastical reforms of Theodosius and his successors, but his role was not that of imperial adviser of Saint Ambrose. Augustine ruled his city and wrote commentaries on Scripture and treatises on dogma, sermons, and letters—270 of them—on all aspects of Christian belief and thought. More than any other Church Father, Augustine shaped the future intellectual development of Western Christianity.

Saint Augustine's vast literary output made him the foremost Latin theologian of the Christian world, a thinker whose work has influenced churchmen, lay people, and philosophers down to the present. His commentaries on Scripture formed the basis for all later medieval and Reformation biblical interpretation, and his letters and treatises laid down advice and combated heresy throughout his life.

Perhaps his most influential work was his immensely long and intricate treatise *The City of God.* The military disasters of the early fifth century had called forth from many pagans the accusation that Rome's misfortune was the result of the abandonment of her old gods and the taking up of the Christian religion. From 413 to 426 Augustine undertook to refute this argument and to lay down the principles of the ideal relations between earthly society and the spiritual community of Christian believers. His thesis was that there were two ''cities,'' the city of God and the city of the world. Insofar as Christians have to live in the world for a time, they may make use of worldly institutions in order to have peace in fallen nature. But the Christian's ultimate loyalty and concern ought to be directed to the afterlife and salvation, and no earthly society, not even a Christian Roman Empire, is anything more than the unstable creation of mortals. The duty of the rulers of any earthly society, especially Christian rulers, is to curb the baser instincts of fallen human nature and preserve that earthly peace that is necessary for the conduct of the Christian life. Such a ruler is a ''godly magistrate,'' rather than an absolute sovereign, and his duties are regulatory and punitive, rather than constructive and progressive. Augustine further denied that the pagan gods had ever helped Rome. *The City of God* became the first and in many ways still the most impressive expression of a Christian philosophy of both history and government. As such, it has remained one of the most influential works of the late antique world and a challenge to the validity of any purely secular view of history or governmental philosophy.

Saint Ambrose and Saint Augustine came to be considered the first of the Latin Fathers of the Church because of the sanctity of their lives and the subsequent influence of their thought. The third Latin Father was Saint Jerome. Born in the town of Stridon, in what is now Yugoslavia, Jerome received a good literary education, became influential in aristocratic and learned circles in Christian Rome, and was a protégé of Pope Damasus I. Upon Damasus' death Jerome was considered as his potential successor, but social and literary rivalry prevented his election. Jerome withdrew from Italy to Palestine, where he settled in Bethlehem and devoted the rest of his life to doctrinal disputes and to his great translation of and commentaries upon Scripture. Jerome's knowledge of historical Greek and Hebrew was pressed into service as he undertook this work, and he finally translated the entire Old and New testaments into Latin, a monumental work both of scholarship and of cultural achievement. The Latin Vulgate, as his translation is called, provided for the first time the entirety of Scripture in a language available to everyone in the West. Jerome's choice of a middle-style, administrative Latin instead of an elaborate literary Latin made a great impact on both Latin theology and the later development of European thought.

Under the rule of generally cooperative Christian emperors during most of the fourth and fifth centuries, not only did Christianity become the only legal religion—and the official religion—of the Roman Empire, but it developed a strong Latin character it had not originally possessed. The great works of fourth- and fifth-century Latin Christianity distinguished their own period and have exerted organizational and intellectual influences ever since. Even with the final transformation of the Roman world and the disappearance of imperial government in the West, the foundations of Latin Christian culture survived to influence the new rulers and peoples of Europe for many centuries.

FURTHER READING

See E. R. Dodds, *Pagan and Christian in an Age of Anxiety* (New York: Cambridge University Press, 1965); A. Momigliano, ed., *Paganism and Christianity in the Fourth Century* (Oxford: Oxford University Press, 1963); and Johannes Geffcken, *The Last Days of Greco-Roman Paganism* (Amsterdam: North Holland, 1978).

For Judaism and Christianity, see the general bibliography at the end of this book.

Three brilliant studies of the emergence of Christian thought are C. N. Cochrane, *Christianity and Classical Culture* (New York: Oxford University Press, 1957); Henry Chadwick, *Early Christian Thought and the Classical Tradition* (Oxford: Clarendon Press, 1966); and R. A. Markus, *Christianity in the Roman World* (London: Thames & Hudson, 1974).

On Augustine, see Peter Brown, *Augustine of Hippo* (Berkeley and Los Angeles: University of California Press, 1969); on Jerome, see J. N. D. Kelly, *Saint Jerome* (London: Duckworth, 1975).

3

The Transformation
of the Roman World

THE SECOND ROME AND THE OLD EMPIRE

Although the empire had been divided into an eastern and a western part by Diocletian and Rome remained the capital of the west, no city emerged as a suitable capital for the east until the late fourth century. Then the city of Constantinople, founded by Constantine the Great, assumed this role. Constantine founded his city on the site of the small fishing village of Byzantium, located on a triangular peninsula between the Bosporus and the Sea of Marmara (bodies of water that link the Black Sea with the Aegean) and the point at which Asia and Europe meet. Constantine gave the new city its name as well as privileges, funds, and building materials collected from other cities throughout the eastern Mediterranean. In 450 Theodosius II expanded the city walls, creating masterpieces of fortification that withstood every invader until they were shattered by Ottoman cannon in the fifteenth century.

Its easy access to the Black Sea gave Constantinople control of all trade west of the Caucasus Mountains. By the tenth century the grain, fur, gold, amber, and slaves of the Slavic lands sweeping away to the north were flowing through its port, as did later Islamic trade. Its ready access to the Aegean made communications with other Mediterranean cities easy. From Constantinople across Thrace and the Balkans ran a network of roads, defense works, and frontier forts that protected Greece and dominated the eastern

34

Adriatic Sea. Across Asia Minor ran the great road to the eastern frontier on the Tigris and Euphrates rivers. Constantinople became both a political and a commercial center, fed by the rich agricultural and fishing resources of Greece and Asia Minor, drawing on the populations of these lands for its armies and citizens. It proved a far more secure and strategic capital for the emperors of the east than did the city of Rome, the old center of the empire. From the late fourth century its strategic value was proved beyond any doubt, as wave after wave of invading peoples broke through the imperial frontiers, failed to take Constantinople, and invariably moved west to assault the weaker cities of the western part of the empire.

ENTER THE BARBARIANS

Anthropologists and archaeologists have shown that the Germanic and Iranian peoples along the edges of the Roman world were not complete strangers to that world. The presence of Rome had influenced Germanic culture, and the proximity of Germanic peoples had in turn influenced Roman culture. Indeed, the term ''Sub-Roman'' has been applied to those frontier provinces and Germanic lands outside the frontier in an attempt to clarify the character of fourth- and fifth-century Germanic society. The ''barbarians'' were not nearly as barbaric and primitive as novels and films sometimes suggest. Barbarians had served in Roman armies since the third century, often rising to positions of high leadership. Moreover, the Germanic peoples themselves were prey to other marauding groups far beyond the Roman frontiers.

Among these ''barbarians'' were Asiatic peoples, nomadic pastoralists and warriors who occasionally assembled great military empires in Central Asia, driving their immediate neighbors east and west into China and western Eurasia. These migratory empires and the peoples they drove ahead of them or absorbed lived on tribute and pillage of conquered lands. They developed new military techniques and weapons, particularly in cavalry warfare. In the late second century one of these nomadic empires, that of the Huns, began to cross western Eurasia, attacking the peoples ahead of it. By the beginning of the third century the Huns had occupied the steppe north of the Caucasus. By the end of the fourth century they had pushed farther west, where they encountered the south Russian kingdom of the Goths, a mixed Germanic and Iranian confederation. In 374 and 375 the Huns destroyed the Gothic kingdom, and many of the Goths fled west toward the frontier of Rome, seeking protection as well as pillage.

The arrival of the Visigoths, a branch of the Gothic people, at the Danube frontier in 376 constituted the first of the new invasions. Although the Romans permitted the Goths to enter the empire en masse (the first time the Romans had ever done this), Roman officers and administrators appear to have mistreated them. The Goths revolted in 378, destroyed a Roman army and killed the emperor Valens at the battle of Adrianople in 378, and began their wanderings through the Balkans, northern Greece, and northeastern Italy. Negotiations with the western imperial court proved unsuccessful, and the Visigoths marched through Italy itself, briefly capturing Rome in 410, and then moved north and west into Gaul and Spain. There they patched up a temporary alliance with Rome and settled down to establish an independent Germanic kingdom inside the western part of the Roman Empire.

Although the Visigoths' circumstances were unique, in the years 405–6 other Germanic peoples pushed across the Rhine frontier and penetrated deeply into Gaul. For

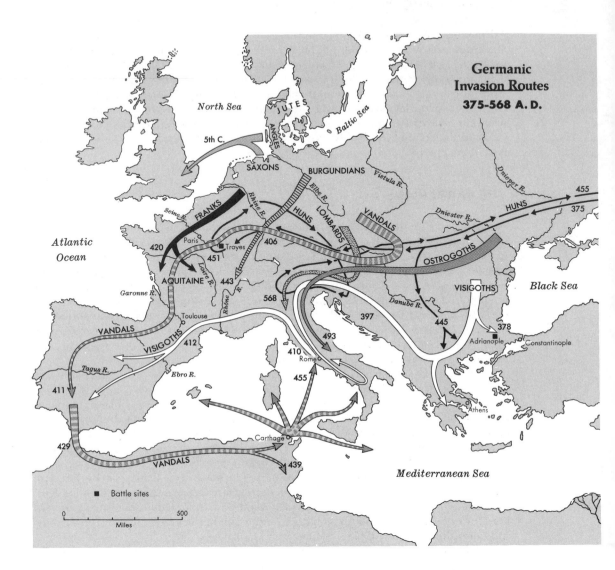

North Sea

Baltic Sea

JUTES

ANGLES

5th C.

SAXONS

BURGUNDIANS

Vistula R.

Dnieper R.

455

FRANKS

Seine R.

Rhine R.

Elbe R.

HUNS

LOMBARDS

VANDALS

Dniester R.

HUNS

375

420

Paris

451

Troyes

406

OSTROGOTHS

Atlantic
Ocean

AQUITAINE

443

Loire R.

568

Danube R.

VISIGOTHS

Black Sea

Garonne R.

Toulouse

Rhône R.

397

445

378

VANDALS

VISIGOTHS

412

493

Adrianople

Constantinople

Tagus R.

Ebro R.

410

Rome

411

455

Athens

429

Carthage

439

VANDALS

Mediterranean Sea

■ Battle sites

0   500

Miles

two years the invaders—the Vandal, Suevian, and Burgundian peoples—sacked Gaul
and settled in parts of it. The Burgundians occupied a large part of eastern Gaul, while the
Vandals and Suevians crossed the Pyrenees into Spain. Thus, when the Visigoths arrived
in Italy and Gaul in 410, they were not the first invaders to get there. One of the terms of
the alliance of the Romans and Visigoths, in fact, was the stipulation that the Visigoths
would help the Romans to control the Vandals and Suevians. For fifteen years the
Visigoths fought the Vandals, until the latter crossed the straits of Gibraltar in 428 and
began their occupation of Roman North Africa. Within the next decade, under their king
Gaiseric, the Vandals systematically removed Roman North Africa from imperial con-

trol and cut the flow of grain from Africa to Italy. The Suevians remained in central and western Spain under the domination of the Visigoths.

Rivalry among factions at the imperial courts of Rome and Constantinople prevented the formation of a unified imperial policy for dealing with the new threats posed by the invasions. Galla Placidia, the daughter of the emperor Theodosius I (379–95), was the ablest ruler of her age, but her successors as rulers of the west during this period, Honorius (395–423) and Valentinian III (425–55), proved incompetent. When the Huns, who had entered western Europe in 435, attacked a Roman army at Chalons in Gaul in 451, only the intervention of the Visigoths on the side of the Romans prevented a Roman defeat. Undaunted, the Huns, led by their able king Attila (445–53), marched against Rome itself. A deputation of Roman nobles, including the bishop of Rome, Leo I (440–61), persuaded Attila to withdraw. The Huns moved back to the Danube, where Attila died in 453. An uprising of subject peoples against the Huns resulted in the battle of Nedao in 454, when the Huns were destroyed as a people. Their survivors were either absorbed into the local Balkan population or migrated elsewhere, possibly joining the Asiatic invaders known as the Avars and Bulgars.

The invasions of the Visigoths across the Danube, the breaching of the Rhine frontier in 406, and the struggle with the Huns all affected the western Roman Empire far more than the eastern. In 446 a mixed army of Picts, Irish, and Saxons invaded the province of Roman Britain, from which the defending armies had been removed before 410 for service elsewhere. In the century following this invasion, Roman Britain slowly gave way to the Germanic kingdoms of Anglo-Saxon England. In 455 Gaiseric, the Vandal king of North Africa, sacked the city of Rome and threatened to seize all of Italy. By the second half of the fifth century other Germanic peoples had crossed the broken Rhine and Danube frontiers.

Theodosius II (408–50), *augustus* of the east, and Valentinian III (425–55), *augustus* of the west, were the last of the Theodosian dynasty to rule the empire. When Theodosius died, his sister Pulcheria raised her husband Marcian to the imperial throne without bothering, as the law required, to consult her cousin Valentinian, the senior *augustus*. This indifference to western imperial recognition suggests further the extent of the division between the eastern and western parts of the empire.

From 455 on, both eastern and western imperial courts were dominated by barbarian masters of soldiers (king-makers and king-removers), beside whom the emperors were for the most part puppets. Because of the structure and resources of the eastern part of the empire, however, the rule of the masters of soldiers was brief. Under the emperors Leo I (457–74) and Zeno (474–91), the control of barbarian generals was finally thrown off and the office of emperor restored to much of its former power. Although Leo, Zeno, and their successors had to fight off other invaders, the eastern Roman Empire proved sufficiently resilient to recover from the fifth-century threat.

In the west, however, the masters of soldiers wielded much greater power, and a series of puppet emperors sat powerless on the throne until 476. Then Odovacar, the master of soldiers in the west and effective ruler of all Italy, deposed the last western emperor, Romulus Augustulus, and sent the imperial regalia back to the emperor Zeno at Constantinople. Odovacar remarked that the empire needed only one emperor, and he appointed himself regent for Zeno in Italy. Zeno was incapable of mounting a military offensive against Odovacar, but he could—and did—use diplomacy against his western "subordinate." His diplomacy introduced the Ostrogoths into Italy.

THE AGE OF THEODERIC

The Ostrogoths were a branch of the old Gothic kingdom that had been destroyed by the Huns in 375. By the mid fifth century, however, the Ostrogoths had recovered much of their power, and under their young king Theoderic (453–526) they attacked Constantinople itself. Zeno diverted the Ostrogoths from the city by offering Theoderic a commission as master of soldiers and the charge of moving to Italy to destroy Odovacar and restore Italy to the empire. By 493 Theoderic had invaded Italy, killed Odovacar with his own hands, and established himself as ruler of Italy, combining the Roman titles of patrician and master of soldiers with his own title of king of the Ostrogothic people. But although Theoderic's titles were far more legitimate than those of Odovacar, his position was no less insecure. Theoderic's considerable talents as a ruler and his genuine ambition to rule Italy moderately always faced the problem of intrigue from Constantinople. The Age of Theoderic witnessed great possibilities of cooperative rule between Romans and Ostrogoths, but political, religious, and cultural differences between the two peoples prevented his reign from creating a new kind of Roman-Germanic state. Within a decade of Theoderic's death in 526, the armies of Constantinople and of the Ostrogoths clashed in a long series of wars that destroyed the Ostrogothic kingdom and laid waste much of Italy itself.

The Ostrogoths were Christians when they arrived in Italy, having been converted to Arian Christianity by missionaries who arrived among them to minister to Roman prisoners they held. One of these missionaries, Ulfilas, translated parts of the Bible into the Gothic language, the first written work we possess in a Germanic language. But the heterodox Christianity of the Ostrogoths was one cause of friction with the orthodox Christianity of Italians and Byzantines.

Theoderic, however, had spent part of his youth as a hostage in Constantinople and had received a Roman education. Able and intelligent, he set a goal for himself in the west that would have been impossible in the more thickly settled and more closely administered east: the peaceful establishment of his people, their culture and faith intact, in the midst of Roman Italy in a kind of economic and political symbiosis. Theoderic greatly admired many of the Roman social institutions and methods of governance. He employed high-ranking Romans in his administration. And although he was king of his own people, he never claimed a royal or imperial title over Romans. He ruled from Ravenna, not Rome, and his architectural works in Ravenna and elsewhere in Italy represent a significant effort to restore some of the material fabric of Italy.

Within Theoderic's hybrid Roman-Ostrogothic state, the Germanic warriors were the only military force in Italy and were separate from the Roman senatorial class and bureaucrats. The settlement of Goths on Roman land was conducted according to the revived principle of *hospitium,* and in affairs of law, taxes, coinage, and administrative institutions, Goths and Romans were under separate systems of rule. For the Romans, however, the old imperial institutions remained largely intact. Civil posts were restricted to Romans, the senate continued to sit at Rome, public festivals and entertainments continued, and Theoderic's official proclamations were properly called edicts—that is, administrative pronouncements issued by a Roman official subordinate to the emperor. The emperor's image continued to grace the coins struck in Ostrogothic Italy, and his foreign policy was designed to maintain different barbarian peoples in the provinces without permitting any one group to become too strong. Friction between Arian

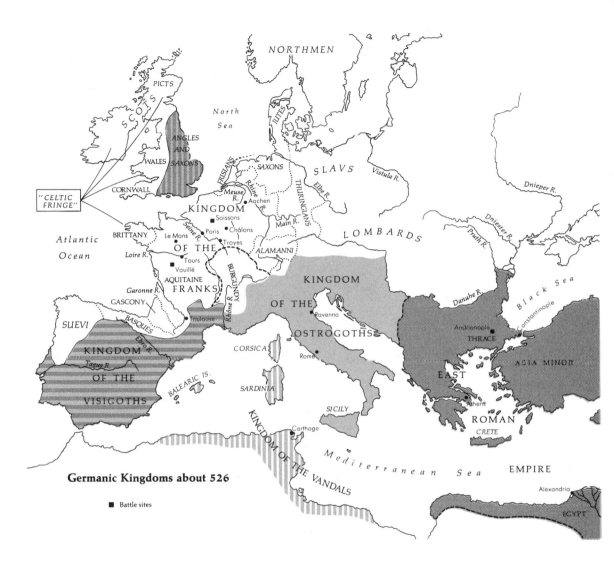

Germanic Kingdoms about 526

■ Battle sites

Ostrogoths and Romans made Theoderic's rule progressively harsher, however. In 526, the year of his death, Theoderic persecuted Pope John I (523–26) and demanded that all Christian churches be turned over to his Arian Goths. In 525 he executed his Roman master of offices, Boethius, on a charge of treason.

Theoderic was succeeded by his able daughter Amalasuntha, but Gothic internal politics resulted in her assassination. The Gothic kings who succeeded her were unable and unwilling to improve relations with Constantinople, and they ruled their Roman subjects with heavier and heavier hands. By the 530s the Ostrogothic kingdom of Italy was poised for war with the Roman Empire at Constantinople.

BOETHIUS AND CASSIODORUS

The attitude of Theoderic toward Roman culture, and the state of learning during the transformation of the Roman world in general, can best be illustrated by the careers of two remarkable men, Boethius and Cassiodorus. Both were highborn Romans, both were scholars of considerable achievement, and both were ''prime ministers'' of the Ostrogothic king in Italy.

Anicius Manlius Severinus Boethius was a descendant of the highest senatorial aristocracy. Born about 480, he was raised in the family of another representative of the oldest traditions of the senatorial order, Quintus Aurelius Symmachus. After receiving the still elaborate Roman aristocratic education, Boethius met Theoderic around 505, and from that date until his death in 525 he became an important figure in the royal court. First an adviser on what seem to have been purely technical matters—he designed, among other things, a water clock that Theoderic presented to his brother-in-law Gundobad, king of the Burgundians—Boethius soon acquired a series of public offices, which culminated in the consulship in 510 and the important post of master of offices in 523. Boethius' tasks made him the most important civil official in Italy, a constant companion of Theoderic, and, in another sense, a symbol of the extraordinary wealth of willing Roman talent available to the Ostrogothic king.

The public service of Boethius, important as it was, was not the only side of this remarkable man. Like many of the Italian and Gallic aristocracy, Boethius had considerable learning and certainly worked at scholarship during his public career. His greatest ambition was to translate both Plato and Aristotle into Latin, and with that end in view he produced several works that were to serve for the next seven centuries as the introduction to philosophical and logical thought for all Europeans. One of his first works was a translation of and commentary on Porphyry's *Introduction* to the *Categories* of Aristotle. Later, he translated some of Aristotle's other works on logic, primarily the *De Interpretatione.*

The importance of this body of work is immeasurable. By beginning with broad questions dealing with the art of classifying objects external to the mind and by classifying further all remarks that can be made on any subject, Boethius left one of the greatest legacies of late antiquity. The nature of that legacy is often difficult for modern readers to appreciate. Essentially, it involved devising in Latin a vocabulary capable of discussing the intricate mental processes that had hitherto been written about in Greek. By systematizing a Latin philosophical and logical vocabulary that could be applied effectively to the analysis of mental processes, the classification of valid arguments, the detection of logical errors, and the accurate description of the world around him, Boethius left to the European West the tools for the elaboration of theology, law, logic, and metaphysics. In this sense, Saint Thomas Aquinas and Descartes are his direct heirs, but the entire West used these works of Boethius as its own introduction to logical thought. In the great revival of the study of logic that occurred in the eleventh and twelfth centuries, the work of Boethius played the most important role. There are no more important legacies in terms of vocabulary and critical language than Saint Jerome's translation of the Bible into Latin early in the fifth century and Boethius' translation of Aristotelian logical works into Latin a century later.

Nor was formal philosophical scholarship Boethius' only other contribution to the early sixth century and to history. He never finished—indeed, he hardly began—his vast plan of translation. But he composed other works, works that differed from both public service and philosophy. He wrote a number of treatises on Christianity that constitute one of the first attempts to apply the logic of Aristotle to the theological ideas of Christianity, an attempt that played a crucial role in the shaping of later Christian thought.

Yet Boethius' most famous work really falls into none of these categories. To see it in its proper context, we must turn briefly to the problems of the last years of Theoderic's reign. Continuing eastern resentment of the Ostrogothic domination of Italy was sharpened by the renewal of the persecution of Arian heretics in the east early in the sixth century. Other eastern attempts to undermine Theoderic's rule appear to have occurred at the same time. One such attempt may well have been an appeal to Roman antiquity that was designed to break the loyalty of the Roman senatorial class to its barbarian master. In any case, secret communications between Constantinople and Rome appear to have taken place, and in 524 both Boethius and his father-in-law Symmachus were accused by Theoderic of treason and imprisoned. Boethius remained in prison for a year and was summarily executed in 525. The executions of Boethius and Symmachus (in 526) suggest how effective eastern imperial opposition to Theoderic had been.

During his year in prison Boethius wrote his most famous work, a dialogue called *On the Consolation of Philosophy*. The setting of the dialogue is Boethius' prison, where he has been seeking means to console himself for the undeserved fate that had befallen him. Philosophy enters, personified as a woman, and the remainder of the work is a dialogue between the two in prose, with moving verse interludes, written in a clear, simple Latin. In the course of the dialogue, Philosophy leads Boethius through various logical steps to a consideration of the nature of true happiness and the highest good, which Philosophy identifies with God, although not with any specifically Christian aspects of God. This apparent avoidance of Christianity has led many scholars to believe that Boethius was only a surface Christian, and that in time of trouble he reverted to an older and deeper-rooted philosophical paganism. It seems, however, that Boethius was attempting to resolve the problems of misfortune and justice, good and evil, within a philosophic framework. The dialogue culminates in a description of the philosopher's obligation to accept the essential justice of the divine plan and to interpret the fragments of experience accordingly. The work became so popular that it was translated in the ninth century by no less a person than King Alfred of England, and in the sixteenth century by no less a scholar than Queen Elizabeth I. Certainly Boethius was the most popular—along with Vergil and Ovid—of all Roman writers in the Middle Ages, even finding a local cult of sainthood and a place in Paradise in Dante's *Divine Comedy*. As late as the eighteenth century Boethius was described by Catholic hagiographers as Saint Severinus.

The destruction of Boethius and Symmachus and its implications for the stability of Ostrogothic Italy loom over the unhappy last years of Theoderic and the regime he founded. It is in the career of Boethius' successor at Theoderic's court, Cassiodorus Senator, that these implications were felt most fully. Cassiodorus did not come from the same high aristocratic circles of Symmachus and Boethius. He was a noble holding extensive lands around Squillace in Calabria. He had studied under Dionysius Exiguus, one of many Greek-speaking scholars who worked on Latin translations, and an influential figure in the later history of Western law. Cassiodorus' work for the Gothic king Theoderic was of a different kind from that of Boethius. The aristocratic philosopher left a body of work that was the legitimate occupation of a learned Roman nobleman of the sixth century—philosophy, translations, poetry, and high theology. Cassiodorus was far more concerned with the historical phenomena that he saw before him in sixth-century Italy—not philosophical verities but the day-to-day problems of explaining Roman culture to the Goths and the Gothic character to the Romans. Boethius' major works required no knowledge of the Goths in order to be understood, but Cassiodorus' major work is wholly inexplicable without an acquaintance with the Gothic kingdom.

When he succeeded Boethius as master of offices in 525 he undertook, in the official correspondence that he wrote in Theoderic's name, to rationalize the Gothic role in preserving Roman *vetustas* (tradition) and in guarding what Cassiodorus called *civilitas*—the essence of traditional Roman civic culture. These letters, the *Variae,* are an amazing wealth of information, digressions, learned ramblings about hopelessly obscure points, and learning paraded for its own sake, some of it pompous but much of it infinitely interesting. Cassiodorus also wrote several histories, and in these his concern for a proper understanding of the Goths became even more explicit. In several chronicles, most notably in the lost *Gothic History,* Cassiodorus extended the history of the Ostrogoths back in time until it became as ancient—and heroic—as Roman history. Cassiodorus made an impressive attempt to reconcile Goths and Romans by showing that each was of equal antiquity and that each had been created to collaborate with the other in preserving civilization.

The long war between the Ostrogoths and the Romans that followed the assassination of Amalasuntha, however, proved Cassiodorus' ambitions futile. In the 550s Cassiodorus retired with some friends to his estates near Squillace in south Italy. There he spent his time in devotional readings and assembled his last work, the *Divine and Human Readings,* an encyclopedic survey and analysis of spiritual and secular literature that remained for many centuries a guide for European scholars through the literature of Christian and pagan antiquity.

The *Divine and Human Readings* mark another important feature of late antique learning, the process of organizing and classifying knowledge into recognized and labeled subjects. In the first century B.C. the Roman writers Varro and Cicero had developed the idea (from Hellenistic learning) that the proper subjects of study for a free Roman citizen ought to be grouped and classified in terms of their place in the progression of learning and their relationship to one another. Although the proper number of these subjects varied between Varro's time and the fifth century, a very long, obscure, but influential literary work by the fourth-century advocate Martianus Capella numbered these subjects of study as seven and labeled the seven parts of knowledge the "liberal arts." This work, *The Marriage of Mercury and Philology,* is an allegory in verse and prose and extremely difficult to read. Boethius divided the seven liberal arts of Martianus into two groups, the *trivium* and the *quadrivium.* The *trivium* was essentially literary, containing grammar, rhetoric, and dialectic (or logic); the *quadrivium* was essentially mathematical, comprising arithmetic, geometry, astronomy, and music. In the *Divine and Human Readings* Cassiodorus repeated both Martianus Capella and Boethius, thus passing down to later European history a division of learning that remained fundamental until the seventeenth century.

The work of Boethius and Cassiodorus condensed in durable and greatly simplified form much of the intellectual legacy of the ancient world. The people who received that legacy were able, with much difficulty at first, to use it and then to expand it.

FURTHER READING

For Constantinople, see the general bibliography at the end of this book under *Byzantine History.*

On the Germanic migrations, see Lucien Musset, *The Germanic Invasions* (State College, Pa.: Pennsylvania State University Press, 1975). On the Huns, see J. Otto Maenchen-Helfen, *The World of the Huns* (Berkeley and Los Angeles: University of California Press, 1975).

For Theodosius and his dynasty, see Noel Q. King, *The Emperor Theodosius and the Establishing of Christianity* (New York: Westminster Press, 1962), and Stewart I. Oost, *Galla Placidia Augusta* (Chicago: University of Chicago Press, 1968). For Boethius and others, see the classic work of E. K. Rand, *Founders of the Middle Ages* (1928; reprint ed., New York: Dover, 1957), and for Cassiodorus, James J. O'Donnell, *Cassiodorus* (Berkeley and Los Angeles: University of California Press, 1979).

The best study of the impact of the invasions on the east is Walter Kaegi, *Byzantium and the Decline of Rome* (Princeton, N.J.: Princeton University Press, 1968). The most extensive general survey is A. H. M. Jones, *The Late Roman Empire, 284-602,* 3 vols. (Oxford: Basil Blackwell, 1964).

An excellent archaeological approach to the period in northern Europe is Philip Dixon, *Barbarian Europe* (New York: Dutton, 1976). See also Walter Goffart, *Barbarians and Romans, A.D. 418-554: The Techniques of Accommodation* (Princeton: Princeton University Press, 1980), and J. Hubert, J. Porcher, W. F. Volbach, *Europe of the Invasions* (New York, Braziller, 1969).

4

Christian Rome
and the New Europeans

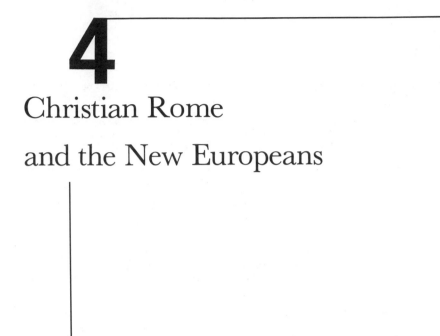

CLOVIS AND THE FRANKISH KINGDOM IN GAUL

The culture of Boethius and Cassiodorus was also that of the aristocratic Roman bishops in Gaul. Provincial aristocrats often became bishops in the late fourth and fifth centuries, and the letters of one of these, Sidonius Appolinaris (430–79), are a striking illustration of the role of churchmen in preserving late antique literary culture. The support of these Gallo-Roman bishops played an important part in the founding of the Frankish kingdom in Gaul in the beginning of the sixth century.

The Franks were a group of peoples who, after migrating southwards along the North Sea coast in the third century, had come together, settled in what are now the Netherlands and Belgium, and occasionally served the imperial armies as *federati* (allied troops). In 482 Clovis, the king of one of the Frankish peoples, set out to create a larger kingdom, married a Christian Burgundian princess, and became a Christian himself around 500. Unlike other Germanic peoples, the Franks had not been Arian Christians when they entered the empire, and Clovis's conversion directly from paganism to orthodox Christianity permitted him to emerge as the champion of Catholic Gallo-Roman Christianity against the Arianism of other Germanic rulers. The value of episcopal support for his venture is revealed in a letter sent to Clovis by Avitus, bishop of Vienne, after Clovis's baptism:

We saw (with the eyes of the spirit) that great sight, when, a crowd of bishops around you, in the ardor of their holy ministry, poured over your royal limbs the waters of life; when that head feared by the peoples bowed down before the servants of God; when your royal locks, hidden under a helmet, were steeped in holy oil; when your breast, relieved of its cuirass, shone with the same whiteness as your baptismal robes. Do not doubt, most flourishing of kings, that this soft clothing will give more force to your arms: whatever Fortune has given up to now, this Sanctity will bestow.

The transformation of Clovis's success from fortune to sanctity, indicating as much the unreserved cooperation of the episcopate as spiritual benefits, goes far to account for Clovis's image in the eyes of later generations. Of all the barbarian rulers, only he had met with absolute success. Legends circulated quickly around Clovis's baptism, the most persistent and influential being that the Holy Spirit had descended from heaven with the baptismal oil. This legend was fleshed out by later claims of French kings to be anointed at their coronations with the same oil and to possess alone the title of "Most Christian King."

In 506 Clovis led the Frankish armies against the Alamanni at Tolbiac and destroyed them, taking the defeated enemies as his subjects. In Aquitaine, the Visigoths, now intensely concerned at Clovis's success, fell before his army at the battle of Vouillé in 507. As a result of these triumphs, Clovis was able to consolidate his kingdom in northern Gaul the next year. Clovis died in 511, leaving behind him a new kind of Frankish—and Germanic—kingdom, far enough from the Mediterranean centers of political strife to retain its independence and vigor, and orthodox enough in its faith, or at least in the reputed faith of its ruler, to leave not only a memory but a legend of Clovis as the "new Constantine," a Germanic Christian king.

GOD'S CONSUL

The destruction of the Ostrogothic kingdom in Italy was accomplished by the armies of Constantinople between 532 and 554, and Italy was devastated by them. No sooner had the Ostrogoths been destroyed, however, than another Germanic people, the Lombards, invaded the peninsula in 568. Remaining hostile to imperial diplomacy and institutions, the Lombards conquered northern and much of central Italy. Arian Christians, their conversion to Catholic Christianity was slow, and their occupation of the peninsula was far harsher than that of the Ostrogoths.

Caught between an unsympathetic imperial administration and the Arian Lombards, the Church in Italy was in a precarious position. Only the advent of an extraordinarily talented pope, Gregory I (590–604), preserved its integrity. Gregory had been a wealthy Roman nobleman who had given away his vast inheritance and become a monk. But he was taken from the monastery into the service of several bishops of Rome, and was popularly acclaimed pope at the death of Pelagius I (574–90). Gregory's great achievements were his handling of Lombard–Byzantine diplomacy and his provision of food and ecclesiastical services to a desperate population.

These duties alone would have overwhelmed most men in his position, but Gregory accomplished far more than this. The register of his letters, the only collection of papal letters beside that of Pope Leo I (440–61) to have survived complete from before the end of the eleventh century, reveals a strong sense of missionary zeal and many attempts to restore communication between Rome and the bishops of western Europe. Gregory's letters contain both theological and administrative instructions, and they may justly be considered among the most important monuments in papal history. Gregory also wrote cautions, discreet letters to barbarian rulers, and to emperors at Constantinople as well. This papal diplomacy constituted the first recognition that the barbarians were here to stay; that, in effect, a new Europe had taken shape.

Gregory's register of letters depicts an ideal of clerical responsibility and conduct that had a great influence on later European civilization. The French historian Jean Gaudemet called these letters and Gregory's treatise *The Book of Pastoral Care* a "mirror for bishops." They embrace the most influential definition of episcopal office written since the work of Saint Ambrose in the fourth century, a definition reflected in later papal regulations, in church law codes, and in later biographies of saintly bishops. The straightforward and practical *Book of Pastoral Care* has as its theme Gregory's favorite maxim: "The care of souls is the art of all arts." It is largely through Gregory's work that the episcopal ideals of the Church between the fourth and the seventh centuries were transmitted to later centuries, and these ideals still define clerical conduct in most modern episcopal churches. Gregory himself, through his responsibilities for large ecclesiastical properties, knew from experience the practical requirements of ecclesiastical leadership, and, like many talented Roman administrators, he was able to apply his own experience to a treatise written for others.

Gregory also wrote a voluminous commentary on the Book of Job, the *Moralia.* In it he adapted for a far less learned and less sophisticated audience both the fourfold allegorical technique of interpreting Scripture, which had begun with Philo and Origen, and the theological works of his great predecessors Jerome and Augustine. Like *Pastoral Care,* the *Moralia* played an immensely important role in passing down to later centuries the scriptural interpretive techniques and the body of theological knowledge developed in the great age of the fourth and fifth centuries. Gregory has often been accused of thinning out the rich complexities of earlier doctrine and simplifying it, but it may also be said that he passed down these techniques and beliefs in the only form that people could use easily.

Gregory's Rome had become primarily the Rome of Peter, rather than the Rome of Augustus or Hadrian, or even the Rome of Constantine. Gregory played an important role in the devotional history of the Latin West by his cultivation of the lives and stories of saints and holy places. Gregory's approach to the saints, however, has a far larger aspect of legend and emphasis upon dramatic miracles than many earlier saints' lives. In 593–94 Gregory wrote a long work called the *Dialogues,* which, in the form of a series of saints' lives, purports to be conversations between himself and the Deacon Peter about beliefs concerning saints, relics, and miracles. The *Dialogues* too had a great influence on later thought and literature. Gregory's interest in miracle, the drama of sanctity, and the manifestations of God's power in the physical world made his stories simpler, more imaginative, and more widely appealing than many earlier lives of saints, and thus played an important—and as yet unwritten—role in the history of Christian biography.

In his instructions to bishops, his allegorical interpretation of Scripture, his miracle stories, and his letters, Gregory showed great resourcefulness. Although his work has been criticized as reflecting a decline from the theological and intellectual standards of earlier periods, it certainly reflects the concerns of Gregory's age and addresses those concerns with great care and native intelligence. For example, strong anti-Jewish attitudes appeared in the sixth century, and Visigothic kings of Spain issued the first anti-Jewish laws in European history. Gregory, however, fought powerfully against the forced conversion and oppression of Jews. In a similar vein, sixth-century Christianity demonstrated a heightened interest in demons, miracles, and legend. Although Gregory could not do away with the new fascination with demons and magicians and exotic adventures in devotional literature, his stories could at least show that such forces were always defeated by simple Christian practices. Later, in the fifteenth and sixteenth centuries, when such a simple Christianity no longer satisfied people's fears of demonic power, the new science of demonology led to the great persecutions of magicians and witches that did not end until the end of the seventeenth century. The demons and magicians were a vivid part of Gregory's universe, but they were kept firmly under control by no more than simple Christian practices and demonstrations of sanctity. When the souls of the dead or saints appeared, it was usually to inspire, not to terrify, the living.

Gregory taught by other means as well. At his urging, the visual depiction of scriptural scenes on the walls of churches (and, later, on church windows) took on a new role; they were to become "the scriptures of the unlettered," the teachers of the illiterate. The motifs of Romano-Christian visual art, like the principles of late Roman ecclesiastical administration, were transformed into instructional materials for the new European world. By his death in 604, at the end of a life wracked by physical illness and exhausting concern for the Christian world, Gregory had succeeded in beginning the reorientation of the Latin Church toward its new members. He had taken steps to define principles of missionary work and conversion, reestablished papal contact with the far-flung churches from Spain to Britain and from Italy to Alexandria, and shaped the mold of Christian devotion in forms that lasted for a thousand years. His epitaph, a long Latin tribute to his work and saintliness, calls Gregory "God's Consul." There is no more succinct expression of Gregory's Roman and Christian antecedents, nor a better description of his service to his own and future generations.

MONKS, MISSIONARIES, AND CULTURE IN THE BARBARIAN WEST

Two of Gregory the Great's major achievements were the sponsorship of monasticism in the Latin Church and—his best-known missionary achievement—the efforts to convert the pagan and Arian inhabitants of Germanic Europe. Between the sixth and the twelfth centuries, monks and missionaries not only shaped the dominant forms of Christianity and achieved the conversion of Europe, but also passed down the only legacy of the ancient world that early Europeans possessed.

As we have seen, hermits and monks became an important feature of Christianity in the third and fourth centuries, first in Egypt and then in Syria and the eastern Mediterranean. The appeal of a life of isolation and prayer spread quickly, and in the fourth century a number of individuals withdrew from the world, seeking such a life in the wilderness of Italy and Gaul. Saint Martin of Tours (ca. 335-97) was a striking and influential example of such a person. Saint Martin was a Roman soldier who converted to Christianity, left the army, wandered through Pannonia and Illyricum, and settled in Gaul, where he soon attracted followers and began to convert the rural population around Tours. He became bishop of Tours in 372 and patronized the spread of other monastic communities.

In the early years of the fifth century a Gallic Roman named John Cassian (385-440) made a journey to the monastic centers of the east and returned to Gaul with a plan for an ideal monastery and a large literature on monastic life that he had acquired in his travels. Saint John Cassian introduced ideals of monastic organization that had developed in Egypt, Syria, and Cappadocia. His own influential writings, the *Institutes,* attempted to homogenize the different rules and practices that he had found into a single ideal system. By the sixth century there was no single kind of monastic life; individuals and groups followed a wide variety of practices throughout Latin Europe.

The most substantial contribution to Latin monasticism was that of the community founded by Saint Benedict of Nursia (480–547) at Monte Cassino, south of Rome. Benedict came from a prominent Roman family, but he rejected the education and plans for a public career that his family had made and withdrew to live a hermit's life in central Italy. Benedict, like many other holy men, soon attracted followers, and early in his life he demonstrated considerable organizational ability, as well as penetrating insight into the minds of those who wished to become monks. He established a successful community on Monte Cassino, and for it he wrote his *Rule,* one of the most remarkable documents in Christian history and one of the most influential organizational programs in the history of human society.

The rule of Saint Benedict differed from earlier monastic rules in several ways. First, most eastern monastic rules were aimed at the individual monk, whereas Benedict's was directed at the monastic community. Second, many early rules were noted for their ruthless breaking of the human spirit by a rigid pattern of self-denial; Benedict's rule struck a remarkable balance between penitential discipline and human relations within the community. Third, many earlier rules reflected their regions of origin; Benedict's rule is clearly patterned on the needs of Latin Christians in general and reveals strong traditional Roman influences. Finally, many earlier rules were aimed at cultivating an exotic piety that frequently exceeded human endurance; Benedict's rule aimed at shaping the devotional life of the monk within the context of an organized community, carefully and conscientiously administered by its leader, the abbot, and intended to keep the monk from falling into vices rather than cultivating devotional excesses.

The chief emphasis in Benedict's rule is on the cornerstone of monastic life: the vows of poverty, chastity, and obedience. The individual monk owns nothing, is celibate, and gives up his individual autonomy to the community under the abbot. Thus prepared, the monk, by living a temperate life characterized by a balance of contemplation, prayer in community, and manual labor, could avoid some of the extremes of eccentric behavior that were sometimes encouraged by other rules. By setting the monk's sights lower, Benedict prevented the despair that individual hermits or extreme communities experienced when they could not live up to their often unrealistic expectations.

The *Rule* of St. Benedict is as important a document in the history of psychology as it is in the history of religion. It shows considerable concern for what today we would call the monk's personality. Its main thrust is toward a kind of psychological conditioning, dependent upon a careful balance of different kinds of activity, sensible dietary regulations, and strict but charitable discipline. Regularity, consistency, order—these are the keys of Benedictine monasticism. The earliest use of the concept of revolution in modern Western thought, in fact, comes from this monastic environment. Here it meant, not social disorder or reversal, but the repetition day after day of the same patterns of monastic devotional life. Indeed, one reason for the later success of the Benedictine rule may have been that it helped create the most stable personalities in the west between the sixth and the eighth centuries. Not until the ninth century, however, did Benedictine monasticism leave its firm imprint on the west. Between 400 and 800 a large variety of monastic rules flourished side by side in Europe. Some of them even reached out to change the ecclesiastical life of Gaul and, later, lands beyond the old imperial frontiers.

In some areas of the old western parts of the Roman Empire, monasticism played an extremely important role. Saint Martin's monastery near Tours began the conversion of the Gallic countryside, the last bastion of pagan beliefs within the old empire. Several monastic communities in the south of Gaul, notably Lérins, founded by Saint Honoratus in 410, not only influenced other communities but produced monastic bishops for churches in the vicinity, thereby maintaining the high standard of episcopal training in an age when many forces threatened it. Although the influence of the cult and rule of St. Benedict and the prestige of Gregory the Great were very strong, many independent centers of monastic life and independent movements to convert the pagan population of Europe characterize the fifth, sixth, and seventh centuries. In one spectacular case, they brought Christianity into the non-Roman, non-Germanic world of Celtic Europe.

THE CONVERSION OF IRELAND

In the fifth century A.D. Ireland remained outside the worlds of the Roman Empire and the Germanic invaders. Other Celtic Europeans had been absorbed into the empire in Italy, Gaul, Spain, and Britain. Thus, by 500 A.D. Celtic culture had been reduced to the "Celtic Fringe" of western Europe—Ireland, Scotland, Wales, Cornwall, Brittany, and Galicia—where it is ethnically traceable today.

Irish society on the eve of Christianization was very different from the societies around it. The Irish were organized in clans, which were dominated by a military aristocracy and ruled by petty kings. The aristocracy measured its status in fame and wealth, usually in land and cattle. Although the kings lived on a somewhat larger scale than the aristocracy, their authority and power were limited. Customary law and the aristocrats actually ruled the Irish people. The law was preserved in memory by a class of men known as *brehons,* who were specially trained in law schools and able to establish the procedures for adjudicating the legal relations of feuding clans and powerful aristocrats. Besides the *brehons,* noble houses also patronized the *fili,* a class of poet-historians who composed oral histories of their patrons and songs praising their bravery and generosity. This pastoral, aristocratic society of clans suggests a very old form of European culture. Irish society in the fifth century has been called "a window on the Iron Age."

The first evidence of Christianity in Ireland is the record of Palladius, a priest who appears to have gone to Ireland from Gaul in 431. But the best known figure of the fifth-century conversion is Saint Patrick. Patrick was the son of Romano-British Christians, and in his short autobiography, the *Confessions,* he states that he was kidnapped as a child and kept as a slave in Ireland for six years before escaping and returning home. In a vision, Patrick states, he heard the Irish people calling for him to return. He did this shortly after 431, and began the conversion of the island. In spite of many dangers, Patrick appears to have had great success, and by the seventh century a strong cult claimed him as the founder of Irish Christianity. His popularity has not declined since.

Although Patrick may have been trained and sent to Ireland by Saint Germanus, bishop of Auxerre in Gaul (who probably sent Palladius as well), the details of the mission and the process of conversion are obscure. It is clear that the first organization of Irish Christianity was modeled upon Continental patterns; bishops and priests led the people, and the church at Armagh emerged as a central authority. Yet Continental Christianity had been shaped by Roman society, and ecclesiastical institutions by the administrative institutions of Rome. Ireland, however, had no cities, no provinces, none of the structures that had supported the spread and established the character of Christian organiza-

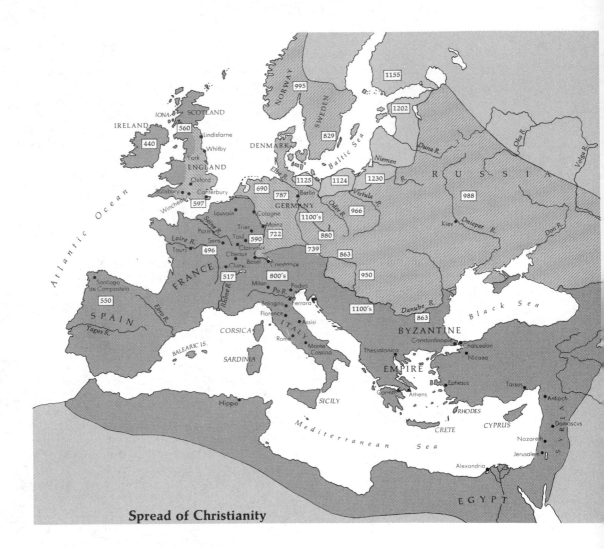

Spread of Christianity

tion elsewhere. Moreover, the culture of Ireland soon imparted distinctive characteristics to Irish Christianity. One of these characteristics was the Irish passion for asceticism—a life of austerity. A second feature was the growth of family monastic settlements, perhaps as a result of asceticism combined with the technical difficulties of Irish land law, which made monasteries easier to establish than bishoprics. These two features soon made Irish Christianity predominantly monastic, and made the abbots of family monasteries the most important ecclesiastical figures in Ireland. The bishops were relegated for the most part to subordinate sacramental roles within the monastic community.

By the middle of the sixth century large monastic foundations began to be built, and they attracted many monks. Clonmacnoise on the River Shannon was founded around 550, Bangor in the north around 560, and Clonfert around 570. By the end of the sixth century, Irish monasticism had absorbed most of Irish asceticism and had adapted one distinctive feature of Irish lay culture—the fascination with learning. Never having had to fight the battle against learned paganism that marked the Continental Church, the Irish took eagerly to Greek and Latin learning. Indeed, Irish monastic culture was the first in European history to make learning and schooling a major part of the monk's life. Learning entailed writing, and with Christianity, writing entered Irish life. The distinctive handwriting and decorated manuscripts of Irish monasteries testify to the resources, learning, time, and skill of monastic society.

Another distinctive feature of Irish monasticism was the emergence of penitential exile. Since Ireland was a society of clans, the identity of an individual was established by the place he or she held in the structure of a clan. One of the greatest punishments in Irish law was exile from the clan, for exile meant a removal of part of a person's identity, since one could never attain full membership in another clan. In monastic communities such exile was undertaken voluntarily as a sign of penitence—"exile for the love of God." Irish monastic exiles, however, did not simply go off alone into remote regions for a life of isolation.

In 565 a monk named Columcille, better known as Saint Columba, left Ireland to found a monastic settlement in exile on the island of Iona, off the coast of Scotland. From the community at Iona a missionary movement moved into northern England and began one phase of the conversion of the Angles and Saxons. Shortly after the founding of Iona, Saint Columbanus, a rigorous ascetic driven to missionary work, moved onto the Continent itself, wandering through eastern Gaul and founding monastic communities in what is now Switzerland and northern Italy. Bobbio, a community he established in the latter area, became one of the most important devotional centers of the seventh and eighth centuries. Columbanus was buried at Bobbio when he died in 615, eleven years after Gregory the Great, the other great representative of the rich and varied religious culture of the early seventh century. The distinctiveness of Irish Christianity, both in Ireland itself and on the Continent, suggests a new experience of European culture—the adaptation of monasticism and Continental forms of Christian devotion to the customs and minds of a non-Roman and non-Germanic society.

ANGLES AND ANGELS

Among the many pressing concerns of Gregory the Great was his vision of bringing to Christianity all the peoples of Europe. In 596 Gregory began his best-known attempt at conversion, the mission of Saint Augustine of Canterbury to England. Gregory may have felt particularly compelled to conversion missions because Lombard pressure on Christianity in Italy had recently increased, and in 590, the year Gregory became bishop of Rome, King Aistulf had forbidden orthodox Christians to be baptized. Gregory had already urged Italian bishops to use preaching more intensively as a means of converting the Arian Lombards. At first, Gregory was not wholly opposed to the use of coercion, especially with those who had slid from orthodoxy to heresy and those who lived under Christian rulers. During the conversion of England, however, Gregory adopted a more moderate approach and rejected the use of force as a means of conversion to Christianity.

When Gregory set about planning the mission to England, so legend has it, he was inspired by the sight of some Anglo-Saxon prisoners in Italy being sold in the slave market. Asking who these striking people were, Gregory was told that they were Angles. "Not Angles," Gregory is supposed to have replied, "but angels." Such pious fictions notwithstanding, Gregory undertook the mission to England seriously. All Gregory knew of the island, however, was what was said in late Roman geographical lore and administrative literature—and that was not much. Gregory's younger contemporary, Isidore of Seville, wrote a large encyclopedic work called *The Twenty Books of Etymologies,* in which he noted that Britannia "is an island set in the sea, wholly separated from the world." Besides such information as this, Gregory knew only of England's provincial organization under the late Roman Empire, an organization that had been totally destroyed by the end of the sixth century.

In the invasions of the 440s Roman Britain received the first challenges of Germanic invaders from the continent. Although subsequent British resistance was stiff—the great British victory at Mount Badon around the year 500 is only one indication of this—the invaders finally began to carve out small kingdoms throughout the island. Of these many kingdoms Gregory chose that of Kent, in southeastern England, as the first target for his mission.

For that mission Gregory chose Augustine, prior of the monastery of St. Andrew in Rome. Dispatched in 596, Augustine and his companions traveled through Gaul and arrived at Kent in 597. Kent was ruled by the pagan Anglo-Saxon king Ethelbert, who was married to Bertha, a Christian Frankish princess. Permitted to settle and preach, Saint Augustine and his companions soon converted the king and a large part of his following. In several letters of 601, Gregory announced that he was sending Augustine more help, wrote to Ethelbert concerning the duties of a newly converted Christian king, and described for Augustine the principles of establishing a church in newly converted lands. In these last letters Gregory abandoned force as a motif in conversion and urged Augustine instead to convert people gradually by persuasion, using their old shrines and sacred places as new Christian church sites. Gregory's close supervision of the mission to England and his urging of what seem to us to be anthropologically sound means of organizing Christianity in a pagan land suggest something of his vision of Christianizing the world.

As Roman Christianity spread from Kent northwards into other kingdoms, notably Northumbria, in the middle of the seventh century, it encountered Celtic Christianity already at work in the north of the island. The resulting form of Christianity that took shape in England drew heavily from both Celtic and Roman traditions, and marks a second distinctive example of the role played by Christianity in the transformation of the life of the new Europeans. Among the conflicting issues that divided Roman and Celtic Christianity were the Celtic concept of individual, rather than public, communal confession of sins, and penitentials—books of meticulous lists of penances to be performed for various sins. In addition, the tonsuring of Celtic monks differed in form from that used in Rome, and the Celtic churches celebrated important Church feasts, notably Easter, according to a calendar different from the one in use at Rome.

These differences led to friction between Celtic and Roman Christians, and their disagreement came to a head at the court of Oswy, king of Northumbria (641–70). Oswy, a Celtic Christian, and his wife, a Roman Christian, found themselves celebrating religious feasts at different times, and they therefore sponsored a debate between representatives of Celtic and Roman Christian practices. At the Synod of Whitby, held in Northumbria in 663, the authority of Rome was recognized by the king and by many of the Celtic clergy. The first encounter of two varieties of Christian practices outside the Roman Empire had been resolved in favor of Rome.

From 663 until the end of the eighth century, the fusion of Celtic and Roman Christianity under the guidance of Roman ecclesiastical organization produced a church that was thoroughly loyal to Rome, yet retained many of its distinctively Celtic features. Like Celtic Christianity, English Christianity developed a powerful monastic culture, although under the influence of an episcopal organization. At the head of the English church was the archbishop of Canterbury, Saint Augustine's own center. Later a second archbishop was added at York. Dioceses for bishops, which had not taken root in Ireland, did so in England, although several centers were changed or abandoned before the late eleventh century. Asceticism and learning became features of English monastic life as well. So did the ideal of exile and missionary work among pagans.

In the eighth and ninth centuries, a stream of English missionaries carried Romano-Irish learning and devotion to the Continent. The results of those missions included not only the conversion of still-pagan peoples but the beginnings of the reform of the Christian church in Gaul. The English loyalty to Rome gave the popes a new voice in northern Europe, and laid the foundations of ecclesiastical renewal among the Franks and other Germanic peoples that so marked the age of Charlemagne in the late eighth and early ninth centuries.

These developments in Ireland and England suggest the extent of the transformation of the Roman world by the middle of the seventh century. They also reflect the new organization of European life and culture that permitted the circulation of Roman influences under the direction of churchmen long after the direct rule of Rome had been forgotten.

FURTHER READING

On the early Franks, see J. M. Wallace-Hadrill, *The Long-Haired Kings* (New York: Barnes & Noble, 1962), and Peter Lasko, *The Kingdom of the Franks* (New York: McGraw-Hill, 1971).

On the early papacy, see Jeffrey Richards, *The Popes and the Papacy in the Early Middle Ages, 476–752* (Boston: Routledge & Kegan Paul, 1979), and idem, *Consul of God* (Boston: Routledge & Kegan Paul, 1980). For the Lombards, see Paul the Deacon, *History of the Lombards,* trans. William Dudley Foulke (reprint ed., Philadelphia: University of Pennsylvania Press, 1974).

On Benedict and early monastic culture, see David Knowles, *Christian Monasticism* (New York: McGraw-Hill, 1969), and J. N. Hillgrath, *The Conversion of Western Europe, 350–750* (Englewood Cliffs, N.J.: Prentice-Hall, 1969).

On the conversion of Ireland, see the general bibliography under *Political History: Regional.*

For the conversion of England, see Henry Mayr-Harting, *The Coming of Christianity to England* (New York: Schocken, 1972).

On Visigothic Spain, see E. A. Thompson, *The Goths in Spain* (Oxford: Clarendon Press, 1969), and P. D. King, *Law and Society in the Visigothic Kingdom* (Cambridge: Cambridge University Press, 1972).

On the transformations of the city of Rome, see Peter Llewellyn, *Rome in the Dark Ages* (New York: Praeger, 1971), and especially Richard Krautheimer, *Rome: Profile of a City, 312–1308* (Princeton, N.J.: Princeton University Press, 1980).

For a particularly important aspect of Christian culture, see Peter Brown, *The Cult of Saints* (Chicago: University of Chicago Press, 1981).

PART II

TWO HEIRS
OF THE ANCIENT WORLD

5

The Making of
Byzantine Civilization

THE EAST ROMAN EMPIRE, 450–527

The success of the emperors Leo I and Zeno in freeing the imperial court at Constantinople from the domination of barbarian masters of soldiers was as remarkable as the emperors' ability to head off threats of invasion into the west. When Odovacar deposed Romulus Augustulus in 476 and sent the imperial regalia back to Constantinople, Zeno was the sole emperor of Rome. No matter how little power he actually exercised in the western provinces, the East Roman emperor claimed a unique character: he was the ruler of the Christian Roman world. Since 450, emperors had been crowned by the patriarchs of Constantinople in a religious ceremony that gave them a quasi-priestly character; the emperor claimed, at least in theory, a kind of authority that no other earthly ruler could match. Moreover, imperial currency remained strong, and even imperial extravagance and high military costs did not impose in the east the crushing burdens they represented in the west. Finally, the core of an imperial civil service survived at Constantinople, and the regulation of imperial government proceeded efficiently. The late fifth century reveals the extent to which the East Roman Empire survived the crisis of the third century and the disasters of the fifth.

Although the east was prosperous and its defenses grew stronger, it faced yet another danger in the fifth and sixth centuries that the west was generally spared—religious dissension. Although the Arian heresy (except, as we have seen, among the Germanic invaders of the empire) was virtually extinct within the empire by the early fifth century, other religious disputes quickly followed it. Most of these dealt with the problem of the relationship between the divine and human natures of Christ, and few of them were restricted to clerics. In fact, the deep penetration of Christianity within the eastern Roman Empire meant that just as more of society was Christianized, so religious disputes touched wider social circles and influenced political affairs as well. One of the most significant of these movements was Nestorianism, named after Nestorius, who became patriarch of Constantinople in 428. Nestorius, and the school of Antioch from which he came, claimed that the divine and human natures of Christ were separate, and that the latter was dominant. Nestorius also denied the application of the term *Theotokos,* ''Mother of God,'' to the Virgin Mary, conceding to her only the title *Christotokos,* ''Mother of Christ.''

Among the opposition to Nestorianism was a faction led by Eutyches of Constantinople, which insisted upon the single nature (*physis*) of Christ, and claimed that the single nature was divine. Monophysitism (from *monos,* ''one'' and *physis,* ''nature''), the name given to the Eutychean doctrine, became a serious social and theological problem through the late fifth and early sixth centuries.

One response to these powerful dissensions was the calling of Church councils to debate and resolve the issues raised by the dissenters. Thus, the First Council of Ephesus in 431 condemned Nestorianism. The Council of Chalcedon in 451 condemned Monophysitism, stating what became and has since remained the orthodox dogma—that Christ had a completely human and a completely divine nature:

Following the holy Fathers, we teach with one voice that the Son of God and our Lord Jesus Christ is to be confessed as one and the same person, that He is perfect in Godhead and perfect in manhood, very God and very man, of a reasonable soul and a human body consisting, consubstantial with the Father as touching his Godhead, and consubstantial with us touching his manhood; made in all things like unto us, sin only excepted. . . . This one and the same Jesus Christ, the only-begotten son of God must be confessed to be in two natures, unconfusedly, immutably, indivisibly, inseparably united, and that without the distinction of natures being taken away by such union, but rather the peculiar property of each nature being preserved and being united in one Person and subsistence, not separated or divided into two persons, but one and the same Son and only-begotten, God the Word, our Lord Jesus Christ, as the prophets of old time have spoken concerning him, and as the Lord Jesus Christ hath taught us, and as the creed of the Fathers hath delivered to us.

This ringing definition of orthodox Christology by the Council of Chalcedon denounced a large number of rival beliefs and made clear certain implications of orthodoxy. By insisting upon the inseparability of the divine and human natures in Christ, the members of the Council of Chalcedon avoided one of the chief tendencies of early Christianity, that of rejecting the material world as represented in Christ's humanity. On the other hand, they elevated human nature itself, in the Greek philosophical tradition, so that it was deemed capable of sharing a single person and substance with the divinity.

The decision of Chalcedon did not, however, end the disputes satisfactorily. Throughout their reigns Zeno and Anastasius were forced to try to compromise with both sides, and the bishops of Rome, particularly Leo I (440–61) and Gelasius (492–96), took up strongly pro-Chalcedon and anti-Monophysite positions. Moreover, the arena of religious dispute was not confined to the sessions of ecclesiastical councils, or to the learned (and sometimes physically violent) arguments of ecclesiastical figures. Strongly held heterodox beliefs were stoutly maintained in the provinces, particularly in Syria and Egypt, and in the capital city of the empire, Constantinople itself. There, religious opinion centered in the factions formed by various groups within the city's population, and found its focus where all broad popular disputes were aired, in the games and chariot races held in the great Hippodrome.

The Christological conflicts also underlined deep regional differences within the provinces of the East Roman Empire. In the fourth century the idea had become widespread that certain cities, because of the founding of their churches directly by the Apostles, enjoyed preeminence in Church affairs; these cities were Jerusalem, Alexandria, Antioch, and Rome. Since Rome was the only city in the western part of the empire to claim apostolic foundation, the prestige of the bishop of Rome was considerable, and this apostolic status contributed to the primacy of the bishop of Rome in western ecclesiastical affairs. At the Council of Constantinople in 381, the patriarch of Constantinople was raised to a level of dignity equaling that of the leaders of the apostolic churches. Thus, a degree of rivalry became evident in the fifth century between the leaders of the other apostolic churches and the patriarch of Constantinople. As we have seen, Nestorius had come to Constantinople from the church of Antioch. One of his opponents, who veered toward heresy himself, was Cyril, patriarch of Alexandria. Alexandria became a center of Monophysite sympathies, and since Alexandria was the ecclesiastical center of Egypt, its dissent represented the alienation of the population of a large and important province from the orthodox capital of Constantinople and from the emperor who resided there. The spiritual alienation of the southeastern provinces of the empire posed a great problem for East Roman emperors until those provinces themselves were lost in the Islamic conquests of the seventh century.

Zeno's successors Anastasius (491–518) and the Illyrian soldier Justin I (518–27) managed to calm the worst of the religious quarrels, reform the imperial fiscal and administrative systems, and undertake considerable programs of public works and charity. By the accession of Justin's nephew Justinian in 527, the East Roman Empire had escaped domination by barbarian masters of soldiers, invasion by barbarian armies, the worst effects of religious dissension, and the strain on the administration and economy that the events of the fifth century had imposed.

THE EMPEROR WHO NEVER SLEEPS

Flavius Petrus Sabbatius Justinianus (or Justinian, as he is generally known) was a remarkable ruler in many ways. He was the first emperor since Theodosius II to have been trained in imperial administration. He spent his young manhood observing the machinery of imperial government, and he probably knew it better than any emperor in seventy-five years. Justinian was also well educated, and he knew law and theology with the familiarity of a professional. Moreover, he had made an extraordinary marriage with one of the ablest women ever to share a throne in the western world.

Justinian's wife, Theodora, was born, not into the aristocracy, but into the family of a bear trainer in the circus. Although the sources agree that she was strikingly beautiful and possessed a commanding presence, her role in Constantinople suggests other, more important qualities, including intelligence, great personal bravery, and a strong will. The world in which Theodora grew up was not the equivalent of a twentieth-century "cir-

Theodora and Her Attendants. This mosaic portrait of the empress Theodora and her retinue in the Church of San Vitale at Ravenna suggests the richness and majesty of the imperial court ceremonial and the deliberate invocation of these elements in churches in the far-flung corners of the empire. (Alinari/Editorial Photocolor Archives)

cus world,'' however. The entertainment industry of the sixth century was an unsettling mixture of spectacular performances, athletics, gymnastics, and pornography. It generally included prostitution and other forms of erotica. Much of our knowledge of Theodora's early life comes from *The Secret History,* a malicious portrait of Theodora and Justinian written by the court historian Procopius. Procopius, like Theodora's other enemies, made much of her past life, and the historian John Barker has called her portrayal in *The Secret History* ''probably the most infamous and scurrilous piece of sustained character assassination in all of literature.''[1] Ostensibly, marriage to Theodora might have been a great mistake on the part of the heir to the imperial throne. As things turned out, the marriage was probably the most sensible act of Justinian's very sensible life. Although Theodora held strong Monophysite sympathies, her contribution to the empire far outweighed the religious dissension she helped to perpetuate.

The importance of Theodora's presence became dramatically evident during the first great crisis of Justinian's reign, the famous Nika riot of 532. The factions supporting the Blue and the Green chariot-racing teams in the Hippodrome had waged a bitter rivalry through the early years of Justin's reign, a conflict rendered more serious because the factions had been armed and made into an urban militia some years earlier. In 532,

---

[1] John W. Barker, *Justinian and the Later Roman Empire* (Madison: University of Wisconsin Press, 1966), p. 68.

Justinian and His Attendants. This portrait, a twin of that depicting the empress Theodora, stands across the apse of the church from the empress's mosaic. (Alinari/Editorial Photocolor Archives)

for once disregarding their opposition toward each other, the Blues and Greens erupted in a riot in the Hippodrome directed against Justinian. The riot spread from the arena into the city, destroying most of the old town and killing thousands. Justinian, who fled from the Hippodrome, is said to have contemplated abdication and flight and to have been restrained only by Theodora's firmness, embodied in her alleged remark that "the [imperial] purple makes a glorious winding-sheet." The emperor regrouped his scattered forces and quelled the riot with a force and thoroughness previously unsuspected. He then unleashed reprisals against the aristocrats and their followers that may have killed as many as 30,000 people.

Immediately after the Nika riot (so called because of the rioters' cry of the Greek word for victory) Justinian began to establish firmly his own imperial authority against the powers of the aristocracy and the urban population. By the middle of his reign he had destroyed most of the traditional powers in the empire and had made himself supreme, basing his strength upon the vast fiscal resources of his predecessors and the support of the Christian provincial population of the empire. The necessity of rebuilding the shattered city of Constantinople and the need to reassert the political prestige of the emperor gave Justinian his opportunity.

In rebuilding Constantinople, Justinian gave it the shape it was to have throughout its long history. His triumph was the reconstruction of the great Church of Hagia Sophia (Holy Wisdom), in which the boundless architectural and engineering talent available in Constantinople created one of the greatest buildings in history. Justinian's architects,

Anthemius of Tralles and Isidore of Miletus, created an immense quadrilateral of four arches, on the top of which was set a vast dome that seemed to hover lightly over the heads of those far below.

Justinian's architects and engineers completed the physical form of the great city and nearly filled the space inside its eighteen kilometers of fortified wall that had been built by Theodosius II in 450. The city contained a palace complex across the square from Hagia Sophia, many other churches, a hippodrome seating 60,000, and a population of around 350,000. Wide avenues carried ceremonial and commercial traffic through the city. The water and food supplies were supervised by competent city officials, as were the markets, ports, and labor organizations. The public services of Constantinople were greater than those of any other European city before the nineteenth century. Because of its prominence as the imperial capital the city also thrived economically, becoming a great port and trading entrepôt.

Justinian's passion for thoroughness is reflected in many of his other achievements, particularly in his reform and codification of Roman law. Until the reign of the emperor Hadrian in the second century, Roman law had been the archaic Law of the Twelve Tables, the primitive law of the early Roman community. Under Hadrian's reforms, some of the changes that had developed under the pressure of new prosperity and the relations among the new classes were regularized, and the influence of legal philosophy was recognized. The flow of imperial commands increased in the third century, however, and the administration of imperial law had by then fallen into the hands of bureaucrats who appreciated little of Rome's earlier legal history. By the fourth century private collections of imperial edicts were the most commonly used legal reference books, although they varied greatly in quality and availability. In 438 the emperor Theodosius II issued *The Theodosian Code,* an official collection of imperial edicts of the fourth and fifth centuries, systematized according to topic.

In the East Roman Empire the study of law flourished, and Justinian knew it well. He commissioned the jurist Tribonian to assemble a new and systematic collection of imperial edicts. By 529 Tribonian had completed the *Codex,* the first part of what came to be known as the *Corpus Iuris Civilis,* "The Body of Civil Law." In 533 Tribonian and other jurists compiled the *Digestum,* a systematic anthology of the writings of great jurists that had the force of law. In the same year, Justinian's commission produced the *Institutes,* an introductory textbook on Roman law. Finally, throughout the rest of his reign Justinian issued new edicts, the most important of which were included in the fourth section of the *Corpus,* as the *Novellae,* or Novels. Justinian's *Corpus Iuris Civilis* formed the basis of imperial law until the end of the Byzantine Empire in 1453, even though later emperors enacted additional collections of law. Moreover, because it was written in Latin, the *Corpus* was accessible to western European societies, although its great influence dates only from the late eleventh century. By the end of the Middle Ages Roman law had influenced every legal system of Europe, and it is arguable that the *Corpus* is Justinian's greatest legacy.

Justinian had many other able servants besides the architects, lawyers, and theologians with whom he surrounded himself. In fact, Procopius remarked that these talented individuals were God's greatest gift to the ruler. Among them Justinian's generals were perhaps the most striking. Under his general Belisarius, Justinian destroyed the Vandal kingdom of Africa in 533. In 535 he began a war with the Ostrogoths of Italy that lasted twenty years and caused more damage to the old heartland of the empire than any of the disasters of the fourth or fifth centuries. Justinian's ambition to reunite all the old parts of the empire was perhaps the only area of his reign in which the usually prudent emperor finally overreached himself.

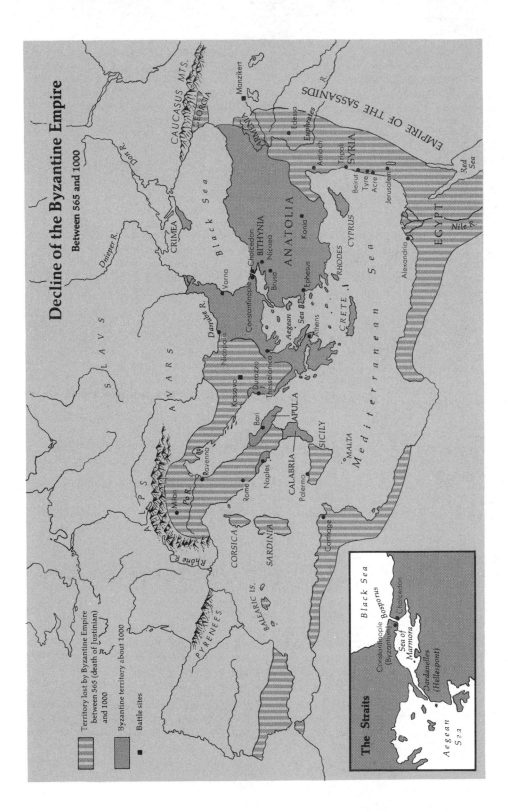

Decline of the Byzantine Empire

Between 565 and 1000

CAUCASUS MTS.

GEORGIA

Manzikert

ARMENIA

EMPIRE OF THE SASSANIDS

Don R.

CRIMEA

Black Sea

Dnieper R.

S L A V S

A V A R S

Danube R.

Nicopolis

Varna

Constantinople

Chalcedon

Nicaea

BITHYNIA

Brusa

ANATOLIA

Ephesus

Konia

Euphrates R.

Edessa

Antioch

SYRIA

Tripoli

Beirut

Tyre

Acre

Jerusalem

Red Sea

Kossovo

Durazzo

Thessalonica

Aegean Sea

Athens

CRETE I.

RHODES

CYPRUS

Mediterranean Sea

Nile R.

Alexandria

EGYPT

Bari

APULA

SICILY

MALTA

Milan

Ravenna

PO R.

Rome

Naples

Palermo

CALABRIA

ALPS

Rhône R.

CORSICA

SARDINIA

BALEARIC IS.

PYRENEES

Carthage

Territory lost by Byzantine Empire
between 565 (death of Justinian)
and 1000

Byzantine territory about 1000

Battle sites

The Straits

Black Sea

Bosporus

Chalcedon

Constantinople
(Byzantium)

Sea of
Marmora

Dardanelles
(Hellespont)

Aegean Sea

After the great triumphs of the first fifteen years of his reign, Justinian witnessed new threats and disasters and spent the last twenty-three years doggedly trying to cope with them. In 540 the king of Persia broke the long truce that Justinian had so painfully arranged, and the eastern frontier once again became a troubled land—a land, moreover, with few soldiers left to defend it. In 542 a devastating plague struck the empire, weakening the population and dealing the economy a severe blow. In the 540s also, new immigrants to the Danube and the Black Sea began probing the frontiers and making tentative raids into Thrace and the Balkans. The Bulgar, Avar, and Slavic peoples plagued the northern frontier and occupied much of the time, money, and energy of Justinian and his successors.

The emperor's efforts to stem these new disasters and yet preserve something of the triumphs of the 530s shaped the contemporary image of his last years. To the chroniclers, he became "the emperor who never sleeps"—constantly vigilant, eternally deceptive, all day and night directing the vast and intricate process of salvaging an empire. Justinian gained this reputation by cutting costs, exhausting the treasury left by his predecessors, keeping the western armies small, and experimenting constantly with new military organization and new techniques of diplomacy, restructuring the imperial civil service, and drawing the provincial cities more tightly into the imperial fiscal system. At his death in 565 Justinian saw many of his greatest achievements still intact. Constantinople remained the greatest city in the world, and from it the emperor ruled Thrace and Asia Minor, Syria, Palestine, Egypt, and North Africa. Imperial rule was restored in Italy, and from the old imperial and Ostrogothic capital of Ravenna, a window on the east and the end of the sea route from Constantinople, a restored imperial Christianity glittered in the mosaics of imperial churches.

THE CITY

Constantinople—the city that Constantine founded, Theodosius fortified, and Justinian rebuilt—remained the largest, most complex city in Europe until its fall to the Ottoman Turks in 1453. Although it was often besieged and twice captured by invaders, it repelled its enemies far more often than it succumbed. Because of the role of Christianity in the life of its founder, Constantinople claimed a novel sort of Christian legitimacy, and its advocates argued that the city was particularly favored by God because pagan rites had never polluted it. If Rome may be said to have become the city of its patron, Peter, and its bishop, the pope, Constantinople must be said to have been the city of Christian imperial rule, the city of the emperor. Thus, a look at the city as it came from the hand of its imperial restorer, Justinian, tells us more than just a piece of early European urban history. Constantinople was the center of the only Christian empire, and it generated great affection and loyalty in its citizens, as well as awe and envy in the hearts of others.

One of the results of the Nika riots of 532 was the destruction of much of the city; indeed, no building earlier than the sixth century can be identified today. One of the consequences of Justinian's success in quelling the riots was his replanning and rebuilding of much of the great city, which gave it the form it had for almost a thousand years, a form that is still detectable in modern Istanbul. Justinian refurbished the great avenues and arcades of Constantinople, and he constructed immense underground reservoirs to improve the city's water supply—several of which are still in existence. Large public buildings, including hospitals and even the great palace complex itself, were rebuilt.

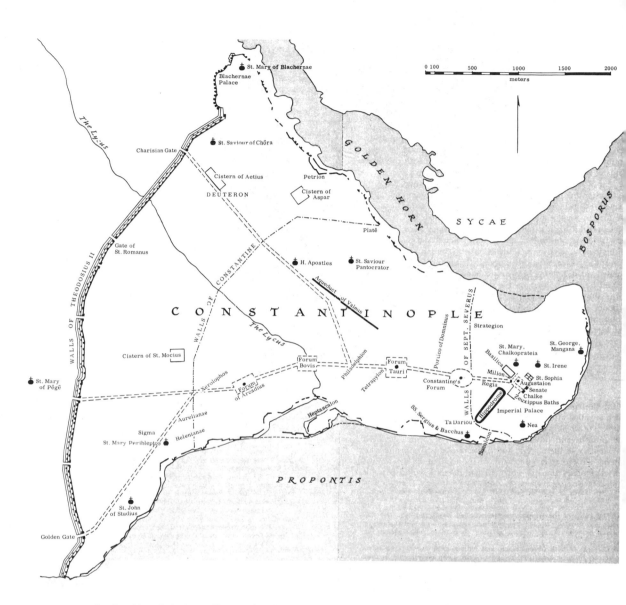

The map labels include:

St. Mary of Blachernae
Blachernae Palace

THE LYCUS

GOLDEN HORN

0 100   500   1000   1500   2000
meters

SYCAE

BOSPORUS

Charisian Gate

St. Saviour of Chôra

Cistern of Aetius

Petrion

Cistern of Aspar

DEUTERON

Platē

Gate of St. Romanus

WALLS OF THEODOSIUS II

WALLS OF CONSTANTINE

H. Apostles

St. Saviour Pantocrator

Aqueduct of Valens

C O N S T A N T I N O P L E

The Lycus

Strategion

St. George, Mangana

Cistern of St. Mocius

Portico of Domninus

St. Mary, Chalkoprateia

Basilica

St. Irene

Milion

Forum Bovis

Philadelphion

Tetrapylon

Forum Tauri

Constantine's Forum

St. Sophia
Augustaion
Regia
Chalke
Senate
Zeuxippus Baths

WALLS OF SEPT. SEVERUS

St. Mary of Pêgē

Forum of Arcadius

Xerolophos

Aurelianae

Heptascalon

SS. Sergius & Bacchus

Ta Dariou

Hippodrome

Imperial Palace

Nea

Sigma

Helenianae

St. Mary Periblepos

Bucoleon

PROPONTIS

St. John of Studius

Golden Gate

Reprinted from Cyril Mango, *The Art of the Byzantine Empire 312–1453: Sources and Documents* (Englewood Cliffs, N.J.: Prentice-Hall, 1972), pp. 8–9.

Justinian's city, as archaeologists and art historians have reconstructed it, is clearly one of the most important examples of urban design in human history (see map above).

Constantinople was a sacred city as well. Its churches and monasteries were as important as its streets, squares, and walls. Justinian shaped the spiritual city as well as the material one. His triumph was the reconstruction of the magnificent Hagia Sophia. The historian Procopius remarked of this striking building:

Hagia Sophia, Interior. The interior of Justinian's great church, shown here with later Islamic additions, gives some sense of the awe with which its congregants were struck and helps explain its reputation as the greatest church in the Christian world. (Courtesy of Dumbarton Oaks).

The great door of the new-built temple groaned on its opening hinges, inviting Emperor and people to enter; and when the inner part was seen, sorrow fled from the hearts of all, as the sun lit the glories of the temple. And when the first gleam of light, rosy-armed driving away the dark shadows, leapt from arch to arch, then all the princes and peoples with one voice hymned their songs of prayer and praise; and as they came to the sacred courts it seemed to them as if the mighty arches were set in heaven.

The sense of vast interior dimensions culminating in the great dome was heightened by intricate marble paving of a great variety of colors and designs, and completed in the great eastern and western apses and in the rows of pillars that supported the north and south galleries, which in turn led the eye upward toward the four great arches. In the pendentives, the spaces where the arches join, the figures of great angels appeared to loom over the floor far below; with the row of clear glass windows at the base of the dome, the effect created is that the great dome is not supported by the arches, but is suspended delicately from heaven. No other achievement of Justinian captured both the variety of resources and talents available to the emperor and the emperor's intelligence in using them. Procopius summed up the impression the church made upon the people of the city and the empire:

Whenever anyone enters the church to pray, he realizes at once it is not by any human power or skill, but by the influence of God that it has been built. And so his mind is lifted up to God, and he feels that He cannot be far away, but must love to dwell in this place He has chosen. And this does not happen only to one who sees the church for the first time, but the same thing occurs at each successive visit, as though the sight were each time a new one. No one has ever had enough of this spectacle, but when present in the church men rejoice in what they see, and when they are away from it they love to talk about it.

The reaction thus described was surely not unanticipated by Justinian, nor was it limited to the sixth century. When in the tenth century Vladimir of Kiev was negotiating with Constantinople for an alliance, his envoys were shown the glories of the city's ecclesiastical centers and were apparently swayed by them toward Constantinople:

The Greeks led us to the edifices where they worship their God and we knew not whether we were in heaven or on earth. For on earth there is no such splendor or such beauty, and we are at a loss how to describe it. We only know that God dwells there among men and their service is fairer than the ceremonies of other nations. For we cannot forget that beauty.

The later strength of Constantinople lay in her economy, in the new armies and military leaders of the seventh through the early eleventh centuries, and in the talents of her government administrators. But when Constantinople reached out, from the sixth century on, to Slavs, Armenians, and Bulgars, it was the spiritual grandeur of such churches as Hagia Sophia that caught and held peoples' hearts in bonds as strong and enduring as the diplomacy of rulers, the wealth of the empire, or the might of her armies.

AFTER JUSTINIAN

Against Justinian's triumphs must be set his failures. The great and expensive military campaigns in the west brought few permanent results. The Visigoths in Spain and the Lombards in Italy slowly extended their control over imperial lands. The emperor's insistence upon orthodoxy in religious belief deeply alienated several key provinces, including Egypt and Syria. Even the great fiscal legacy of Anastasius and Justin I could not support the vast plans of Justinian; by the end of the sixth century the empire was almost bankrupt. Moreover, natural disasters took their toll. As we have noted, a great plague swept the empire in 542, and throughout the rest of the sixth century and the seventh century the empire underwent a serious population decline. A smaller population meant a smaller tax base, but the need for money did not diminish. As Justinian's successors discovered, new problems on the northern and eastern frontiers—precisely those areas that Justinian had left unattended—increased the need for money and troops. Not only had Justinian neglected the northern frontiers; he had bought peace with Persia at the cost of a high tribute. The burden of that tribute grew heavier every year. When Justinian stopped paying it, the eastern frontier with Persia became another danger spot.

Justinian's successors thus faced the prospect of expensive wars on two frontiers. They also had to create a new society in the empire, one geared for continual war. The success of this society lay in drawing upon the vast reserves of manpower among the populations of Thrace and Asia Minor and maintaining close control over the armies by means of a complex bureaucracy in the capital. This program was to be financed by new forms of social organization and taxation.

Unlike the organized opposition of Persia to the east, the presence of migrating and invading peoples from the north was intermittent and has left few records. Slavic peoples had begun migrating into the empire after the mid sixth century, and the invasion of the Asiatic Avar people in the late sixth century drove the Slavs further south and westward. By the end of the sixth century the Slavic peoples were exerting steady pressure on Macedonia and Greece. Thessalonica, the second largest city in the empire, was often under Slavic and sometimes under Avar siege. In 617 a combined Slav and Avar force unsuccessfully assaulted the city of Constantinople itself. Besides Macedonia and Greece, Slavic peoples migrated into eastern Bavaria, Moravia, and Bohemia during this period. Further north, Slavic tribes extended along the shores of the Elbe River. The Avar kingdom in southeastern Europe lasted until its destruction by the armies of Charlemagne in 795.

The threats along the northern and eastern frontiers tested both the abilities and resources of Justinian's successors. The greatest of the late-sixth-century emperors was Maurice (582–602). After ten years of war he achieved a temporary peace with Persia. Facing Lombard pressure in Italy and Slav-Avar pressure south of the Danube, Maurice reorganized the western frontiers. He turned the city of Ravenna into a frontier fortification. He created the office of exarch, combining civil and military government in one official. Maurice also created an exarch at Carthage. These steps helped to turn the provinces into defensive societies protecting a frontier threatened on many sides. During the next two centuries the system developed by Maurice spread from troubled frontier provinces into most of the empire and led to the organization of different regions into *themes,* areas whose civilian population was also its defending army, whose military commanders were also its civil governors. This mobilization of social resources was one of the reasons for the survival of the East Roman Empire. But the price of survival was a different kind of empire.

Maurice was assassinated after a military revolt in 602, and a brutal and incompetent military officer, Phocas, usurped the throne. Probably the worst of the East Roman emperors, Phocas fiercely repressed political opposition at home, and his accession signaled a renewal of the Persian wars. After the first decade of the seventh century, the empire was plunged into a crisis that completed its transformation.

THE AGE OF HERACLIUS

In 610 Heraclius, the son of the exarch of Carthage, led a fleet to Constantinople, captured and killed Phocas, and made himself emperor. The renewal of Persian hostilities under Shah Khosroes II (591–628) occupied most of Heraclius' attention. In a series of quick and thorough campaigns, Khosroes conquered Antioch in 613, Jerusalem in 614, and Egypt in 619. From 620 on he assaulted Constantinople directly. In combination the problems posed by the Slav-Avar coalition and the Persians seemed insurmountable. By 618 Heraclius was seriously considering moving the imperial capital from Constantinople to Carthage.

The population of Constantinople, however, resisted. The church and the citizens submitted voluntarily to even more stringent economic measures. They raised enough money to enable Heraclius to hire a new army, which he took into Persia in a dramatic and unexpected move, leaving Constantinople's own citizens to defend their city against the last and greatest combined offensive of Slavs, Avars, and Persians in 626–27. Heraclius' "new model army" carried all before it. His victories in Persia culminated in the defeat of the last Persian army near Nineveh and the destruction of the shah's palace at Dastgerd. Khosroes II, humiliated by the unexpected reversal of his fortunes, was assassinated in 628. As Heraclius fought his way through Persia in 627, the citizens of Constantinople achieved a victory as great as their emperor's. They destroyed the barbarian fleet that lay before the city, and with it the other great threat to the empire's survival.

But victory proved to be immensely costly. It had exhausted the empire economically and militarily, and it proved that Justinian's dream of a restored Mediterranean Roman Empire was gone forever. The western frontiers proved less important than the north and east. Facing the greatest crisis in the history of the empire, Heraclius and his successors turned away from the Latin west, converting the peasantry of Thrace and Asia Minor into a citizen-army and mobilizing the empire for a different kind of life in a new world.

ARABS AND BULGARS

And they did so just in time. With the arrival of the Arabs and the Bulgars, the empire faced new enemies, who remained a threat until the fall of the Byzantine Empire in 1453.

Molded into a new kind of cultural and political force by the religion of Islam, Arab armies began to move out of Arabia proper. By 636 they had reached the ancient Mediterranean and Persian worlds. Disaffected imperial provinces in Egypt, North Africa, and Palestine put up little resistance to the conquerors, and the military resources of the emperor Heraclius were not sufficient to stem the invasions. The major Arab defeat of an East Roman army at Yarmuk in 642 cost Heraclius the provinces of Syria and Palestine, and at the same time the Arabs swept into the old Persian Empire and conquered it entire. During the next thirty years Arab commanders prepared for an assault on Constantinople itself. The first major siege came in the years 674–78, when Arab fleets blockaded the city. In 717 and 718 Arab armies and fleets assaulted the city again. Although Constantinople withstood these attacks, much of its southern Mediterranean empire vanished. Indeed, as the Arabs swept across North Africa and into Spain, which they conquered between 711 and 719, most traces of the old Roman world were swept away. From the beginning of the eighth century, Arab and Roman forces struggled along a mountainous frontier in southern Asia Minor. The eastern frontier had once again become of major importance to the East Roman Empire.

In the Balkans another Asiatic people, the Bulgars, established themselves around 680. After checking the Slavs and Avars the empire found itself unable to prevent the establishment of a Bulgarian kingdom. The defeat of the emperor Constantine IV in 679 by the forces of the Bulgar khan Asparuch guaranteed Bulgar control of the lower Danube valley. With the establishment of a Bulgar kingdom the local Slavonic peoples came under Bulgarian domination. Although the new state experienced dynastic conflicts and rivalries for the kingship in the late seventh and early eighth centuries, from the mid eighth century on a strong kingship emerged, based upon the high degree of integration of Bulgar and Slavic elements in the population. The Bulgarian kingdom, like the empire of Islam, became a permanent force in imperial foreign relations.

THE AGE OF ICONOCLASM

The crises in imperial defense of the late sixth, the seventh, and the early eighth centuries were not without their internal consequences. The horizons of the empire had shrunk to the eastern Balkans and southern Asia Minor, and the empire had exhausted the last resources of its people to defend and preserve itself. Heraclius had invoked the aid of supernatural powers to defend Constantinople against the Slavs and Avars, and the appearance of yet newer and more threatening enemies seemed to indicate God's anger at the Christian empire. The permanent war-footing of the imperial economy and the importance of orthodox religious observation helped shape the transformation of the East Roman into the Byzantine Empire, a process that was well under way by the early eighth century. An eastern Mediterranean Christian state, the Byzantine Empire depended for its survival upon stringent economy and military alertness and religious uniformity. Its horizons were limited to the Black Sea, the Balkans, northern Greece, and Asia Minor.

Under the able leadership of a Syrian general turned emperor, Leo III (717–41), the last great Arab assault on Constantinople was turned back and a temporary truce was reached with the Bulgar kingdom. But Leo faced internal problems of great importance. To understand them, we must consider the religious temper of the Byzantine world in the beginning of the eighth century.

As we have seen, the Near East was an extraordinarily fertile incubator of religious feeling and thought. The meeting place of Jewish, Christian, Oriental, Persian, and Greek thought, it is the home of most of the heresies and orthodoxies of the religions of the Western and Near Eastern worlds today. Between the fifth and the ninth centuries it gave birth to three heretical movements in particular that threatened the stability of the East Roman Empire. Arianism in the fifth century and Monophysitism in the sixth had been resolved only with great effort and with many irreversible consequences. The emergence of iconoclasm in the eighth century under Leo III and Constantine V struck the empire as forcefully as any earlier heresy. Unlike them, however, it had enduring consequences in the west.

The problem of iconoclasm centered in the increasingly widespread popularity of religious images—in mosaic, sculpture, and icons—in the Byzantine Empire during the sixth century. In the trying years of the early seventh century, the appearance of divinely created icons and images and the belief in their magical powers grew under the Heraclians. As early as the sixth century non-Christians, such as Jews and pagans, directed substantial criticism against what they considered idolatrous practices. In the seventh century even Christians began to object to the extremes of image worship. The use of images, of course, could easily border upon idolatry. Against the Oriental reluctance to depict the ineffable divine mysteries in human forms, thereby implicitly limiting them, and the Old Testament prohibition of the building and worship of graven images, there emerged a Neoplatonic doctrine justifying image veneration as a pious help to the unlettered faithful. This view was expressed most eloquently and influentially by Saint John of Damascus, a seventh-century Christian Syrian theologian who was employed by the Moslem ruler of Syria.

The origins of the iconoclastic movement are still a matter of disagreement among scholars. Explanations of its rise vary from positivistic economic ones to the purely political and extremely metaphysical. It is possible that the iconoclast movement brought to a head opposition to the cult of images that had been growing among otherwise orthodox Christians for some time. Whether the origins of the movement were ecclesiastical or not, Emperor Leo III appears at first to have proceeded cautiously; not until 730 did he issue an imperial edict abolishing icons. Under Leo's successor, Constantine V (741-75), iconoclasm became a church dogma as well. At the Synod of Hereia (754), the assembled fathers denounced icons and, backed by the experience of three centuries of complex theological debate, identified iconodules (image worshipers) with earlier forms of condemned heresy. By the 760s extensive persecution had begun, at least partly because several ecclesiastical elements, particularly the monks, had turned on the emperor and urged political resistance to the iconoclastic laws.

Part of the policy of Leo III was his determination to strengthen the authority of the patriarch of Constantinople, since 451 the preeminent ecclesiastical leader in the east and second in dignity only to the bishop of Rome. During Leo's first moves against the icons he encountered the firm resistance of Pope Gregory II (715-31), many Italian ecclesiastics, and Pope Gregory III (731-41). The intransigence of the Latin church may well have contributed to Leo's decision to drastically reorganize the ecclesiastical provinces subject to the patriarch of Constantinople. Leo first deprived the pope of the rich lands in South Italy and Sicily that had constituted such a substantial part of papal income. Leo then withdrew these two areas, as well as the whole province of Illyricum, from the pope's jurisdiction and placed them under that of the patriarch of Constantinople. At the same time, around 733, he also attached to the patriarchate several Anatolian ecclesiastical provinces hitherto under the jurisdiction of the patriarch of Antioch. At one stroke Leo had vastly increased both the jurisdiction and prestige of the patriarchate of Constantinople and lessened nearly to insignificance those of the bishop of Rome.

The reigns of Leo III and Constantine V produced significant changes in the Byzantine world, and they brought to the fore the particularly pressing question of the rivalry between Greek and Oriental cultural traditions, which focused upon, but did not restrict itself to, the question of images. The iconoclast movement under these two men placed the relations between the Latin and Greek parts of the Church under great strain and created sharp divisions in Byzantine intellectual, political, and spiritual life. The reign of Constantine V in particular, which was marked by the harsh persecutions of the iconodules, was also a period of considerable military triumph and great strengthening of the Byzantine state.

At Constantine's death in 775 his far less competent son Leo IV succeeded him. Leo died five years later, leaving his wife, the empress Irene, and an infant son, Constantine VI, to succeed him. An image worshiper herself, Irene governed in her son's name and worked to undo the results of the iconoclast movement. In 787 the Council of Nicaea reversed the anti-icon ruling of the Synod of Hereia and reopened good relations with Rome. However, Irene alienated a considerable segment of the Byzantine ruling class, particularly the Asiatic soldiery, and her ambition led her in 797 to blind her son (thereby making him ritually unfit to rule) and to reign from that date in her own name.

Irene's death in 802 brought a resurgence of iconoclasm, but the establishment of the Amorian dynasty on the imperial throne (820-67) led to the abolition of iconoclasm under Michael III (842-67) and the restoration of financial and military resources. The

Amorian dynasty and its successor, the Macedonian dynasty (867–1060), provided strong, able leadership and assured the security of the Byzantine Empire for nearly three centuries.

SAILING TO BYZANTIUM

In spite of the wars, political upheaval, and religious crises of the seventh and eighth centuries, there is striking evidence of a powerful cultural revival that reflects the transformation of the East Roman to the Byzantine Empire. Although many of the greatest cities of the empire were either lost to Islam or suffered from war, Constantinople itself thrived. A core of educated aristocratic civil servants and churchmen in the city preserved some of the traditions of older learning and generated new cultural interests. Greek became the common language of a population that was, in fact, ethnically heterogeneous—"an ethnographic zoo," as one historian of Byzantine civilization has called it. The Greek language and the orthodox Christianity that had been shaped between the sixth and the ninth centuries constituted the basis of Byzantine civilization. With the triumph over iconoclasm, Byzantine culture took on the vitality that has attracted the interest of historians of art, religion, and culture ever since. To the twentieth-century Irish poet William Butler Yeats, the culture of ninth- and tenth-century Byzantium seemed to epitomize the triumph of the human spirit in a material world. In some of his poems, notably "Sailing to Byzantium," Yeats caught the immensely creative Byzantine cultural spirit in a manner that speaks vividly to a modern student of Byzantine history and civilization.

One of the most striking features of Byzantine civilization is the character of its most representative figures. Churchmen and civil servants, they came from the same ranks of urban Constantinopolitan society, received similar educations, and often followed similar careers in the civil service until their paths divided into the church and government. Such similarity between churchmen and government officials was not to be found in the west until much later, and thus it is possible to speak of an educated class consisting of both churchmen and government officials that formed the basis of Byzantine civilization. Schools appear to have increased and improved in the late eighth century, and a new, more efficient form of handwriting appeared. The study of the Greek classics was resumed, and although Justinian had closed the academy of Plato in Athens in 529, influences of Platonic philosophy remained strong in the highly developed philosophical interests of Greek Christian theology.

A second feature of Byzantine civilization is the pouring of artistic talent and innovation into religious ceremonies and church decoration. From the sixth century on, Syrian musicians helped create liturgical services that were marvels of ritual and of aesthetic achievement. In spite of the threat of iconoclasm, the Byzantine genius for pictorial representation survived and indeed triumphed in the new programs for church decoration that were called for in the ninth and tenth centuries. Although Byzantium has sometimes been criticized for its traditionalism and lack of innovation, its culture was, in fact, more integrated into different social levels and tastes than any European culture until the nineteenth century. Imperial court ceremony, like the liturgy of churches, reflected Byzantine philosophy, and the emperors remained great patrons of the arts.

Third, the high quality of Byzantine churchmen and their similarity in origin to the governmental ruling class meant that there was no division, as there was in the west, between ecclesiastical and temporal affairs. It is in this light that Byzantine political theory ought to be understood. Although the Byzantine emperor is often accused of ''caesaropapism''—that is, imperial rule of the Church—it is important to note that the highly developed cosmological ideas of the Byzantines provided a special place in God's favor for the emperor, as ruler of the world and ''head of the family of rulers'' of all peoples. Moreover, the integration of spiritual and temporal culture meant that the emperor, churchmen, and civil leaders were close together. The genius of Byzantine culture lies precisely in the spiritual bonds that held the secular state together. Byzantines considered their state to be the ideal community, charged by divine command to preserve the true faith. This attitude produced the rich ecclesiastical culture that absorbed much of the Byzantine genius that seems so foreign to modern eyes.

The mosaics, icons, sculpture, and architecture of Byzantine civilization should be looked at with these principles in mind. Beneath the glittering, superbly arranged decorative surfaces lies a spiritual ideal, which literally charges each picture with meaning. In the sonorous, intricate liturgy of the Orthodox church is reflected a whole theology. And through ecclesiastical art and liturgy the ideals of Byzantine civilization were expressed to all classes of the empire. Indeed, it may be said that Byzantine civilization was more deeply and thoroughly rooted in its population than either the civilization of the ancient world or that of the Latin west.

FURTHER READING

In addition to the works cited at the back of the book in the general bibliography for this period, see John W. Barker, *Justinian and the Later Roman Empire* (Madison: University of Wisconsin Press, 1966), and Philip Sherrard, *Constantinople: Iconography of a Sacred City* (New York: Oxford University Press, 1965). See also Romilly Jenkins, *Byzantium: The Imperial Centuries, A.D. 610–1071* (reprint ed., New York: Random House, Vintage Books, 1969).

6

The Rise of Islam

THE ARAB PEOPLES BEFORE MUHAMMAD

Far to the east of provincial Roman Africa there lived Arab peoples, Semitic-speaking desert nomads and intermittent town-dwellers who had long played a role in Near Eastern history. In earliest Arab history the South Arabian kingdom of Saba, whose most famous ruler was said to have been Solomon's queen of Sheba, was wealthy from the trade in incense and from its place as a middle point between India and the ancient Mediterranean world. The Arab peoples are mentioned by the Greeks as early as the fifth century B.C., and they appear in the Old Testament somewhat earlier. During the rise of Rome, the southern Arabian kingdom grew poorer, and the Arabian peninsula came to be dominated by the nomadic tribes of Bedouins that had long flourished in the north of the peninsula. By the sixth century A.D., many Arabs lived in trading cities, and several Arab kingdoms, notably Nabatea and Palmyra, had risen to considerable prosperity. In addition, two of the northern Arab peoples, the Ghassanids and Lakhmids, were important allies of the Roman and Persian empires. In spite of the prosperity of some segments of northern Arab society, however, the majority of Arabs remained Bedouins, and the "Bedouinization" of Arabian society between the fourth and sixth centuries A.D. is a feature marked by all historians of the period. The nomadic tribe, the 'Umma, under the direction of its elected shaikh, became the module of Arab society. The tribe was characterized by its fierce independence, its warlike character, its devotion to tribal gods, and its contempt for the life of the urban Arabs.

In the fifth and sixth centuries A.D., however, the urban Arabs became more prominent and more wealthy. The trade routes between Yemen and Persia, made dangerous by the wars between Rome and Persia, and the trade routes between Ethiopia and Egypt, made dangerous by the attacks of nomadic tribes, declined in importance. The third route of trade between the Mediterranean and Yemen ran down the western edge of the Arabian Peninsula, and this route increased in importance as the other routes declined. Although the towns along the western Arabian route were not the equal of the earlier great cities of South Arabia, several of them grew prosperous, and one, Mecca, became a pilgrimage site as well. Growing trade and the presence of a number of important shrines made Mecca attractive to the desert peoples as well as the urban Arabs. The city's most important shrine was a black meteorite kept in a sanctuary called the *Ka'ba.* The desert tribes that came to Mecca brought their fierce independence with them, and the presence of the Bedouins along with the growing commercial wealth and the inability of traditional Arab culture to deal with such pressures made sixth- and seventh-century Mecca a boom town with a highly volatile civil life.

THE PROPHET

Around 610 a middle-aged Meccan caravan manager, Muhammad, began to receive visions and commands from heaven. In the following years Muhammad dictated to scribes "recitations" that God had commanded, his *Qu'ran.* Muhammad had been born around 570 in Mecca, the son of 'Abd Allāh, a poor member of the important Quraysh clan. An orphan by the age of six, Muhammad was brought up in the lively and turbulent world of Mecca by his grandfather and uncle. As a young man he became a successful caravan manager and later married his wealthy employer, the widow Khadija. He did not simply retire to the prosperity that his marriage offered, however. He had been a religious thinker all of his life, and his experience of Mecca made the fate of the Arabs in that violent society his chief concern.

Muhammad's revelations directly addressed that concern. He announced that the single god Allah had been his inspiration, and that the substance of his "recitations," the *Qu'ran,* was a body of instructions concerning the only acceptable life a subject of Allah was to live. Although Allah had partially revealed himself to Jews and Christians through the prophets Moses and Jesus, Muhammad received the final and ultimate revelation of divine truth. Muhammad was the "seal of the prophets." The *Qu'ran,* which was arranged in *suras* (chapters), declared Allah the only god, to whom man must subject himself. The religion Muhammad proclaimed, *Islam,* means "subjection to the will of Allah." Like Jews and Christians, Muslims were considered "People of the Book," but only they knew the final revelation of Allah's will. The injunctions contained in the *Qu'ran* attacked the ills of contemporary Arabian society and professed to forge all believers into one great *'Umma,* an expanded conception of an Arab tribe, to which all the faithful would feel primary loyalty, regardless of former ties and allegiances.

At first Muhammad gathered around him a few followers from his family and clan, but subsequently he encountered opposition from the ruling aristocracy of Mecca. Possibly fearful of the decline of the city as a pilgrimage center, and certainly disapproving of Muhammad's low social origins, the Meccan rulers were at first indifferent to the new faith and then actively hostile to it. In 622 Muhammad and his followers were invited to the city of Yathrib, where Muhammad had been designated an outside arbitrator of the city's internal difficulties. The flight from Mecca to Yathrib, which thereafter changed its name to Medina, was called the Hegira, and the official calendar of Islam is dated from its beginning, September 24, 622.

At Medina Muhammad was able to give his conception of the Islamic '*Umma* a practical form and to begin the alliances among his original followers, the population of Medina, and the neighboring Bedouin tribes. From Medina Muhammad led a triumphant military force back to Mecca in 630, where he was recognized as a religious leader to whom most of the population of the cities and many more of the desert tribes made submission. Using the ethical force of his religious visions to overcome the divisions that separated the desert Arabs from the Arabs of the cities, Muhammad began to forge a new unified Arab society.

THE FAITH

Although it responded to the cultural, social, and political needs of the Arab people, Islam was unquestionably a religious revolution. Like other religious revolutions, it established a new role for religion in the lives of its followers. The old tribal gods, whether worshiped in the desert or in such sanctuaries as the *Ka'ba* in Mecca, either disappeared or were transformed into *djinn* (spirits of the air). The varieties of religious ritual and custom were obliterated, and in their place stood a unified theological and ethical system that bound the individual soul to God and all believers to one another. Unlike Christianity, Islam offered no distracting theological problems, such as that of the Trinity or that of the relation of the two natures in Christ, that might detract from the absolute single majesty of Allah. Unlike Judaism, it possessed no complex history of theological and eschatological movements, nor was its practice limited by intolerant Christian rulers. The intensity and directness of Islamic belief gave the faith the power to appeal to peoples at all levels of social and theological development. The historian D.M. Dunlop has said:

Islam was no doubt accepted at first by the finer natures and the simple-hearted among [Muhammad's] hearers, then by a process of growth, the exact character of which remains obscure, but which was certainly not unconnected with Muhammad's growing militancy, proved irresistible, so that the most independent of the tribal chiefs and the most hard-headed of the merchants in general found it necessary to give at least a formal assent to the astonishing claims of Muhammad as Messenger of the Lord of the Worlds and accept the new rules of conduct which he enjoined.[1]

The attractiveness of Islam to the ferocious Berbers of Northwest Africa as well as to the subtle theologians and country gentlemen of Persia is eloquent testimony to the personal force of Muhammad and the eloquence of his spiritual message.

At the core of Islam is the *Qu'ran* and its great message: there is but one God and Muhammad is His prophet. Muhammad appears to have recited portions of the *Qu'ran* aloud during the years from 610 to his death in 632. These recitations were copied down by his secretaries and friends, probably with direction from the Prophet as to which part of

[1] D.M. Dunlop, *Arab Civilization to A.D. 1500* (New York: Longman, 1971), pp. 11–12.

the whole each recitation belonged to. Muhammad regarded his recitations as his own repetition of an unwritten heavenly book, uttered at the command of an angel. The entire *Qu'ran* is believed to have assumed its present shape between 651 and 656. By that time, the language of the *Qu'ran* was regarded as sacred and absolutely authoritative. The 114 *suras* in it were considered to have been dictated by God, and therefore no Muslim may read the *Qu'ran* for spiritual benefit in any language other than Arabic, nor may the text be altered in any way. The expansion of Arabic political power in the seventh and eighth centuries was accompanied by the spread of the Arabic language as new converts to Islam were made. The *Qu'ran* became a spiritual guide, a language manual, and the greatest schoolbook in the Islamic world. It was also a code of law and ethics, a book of political theory, and a guide to conduct.

At the core of Islam is the single truth that Allah is God and Muhammad is His Prophet. Radiating from that core is the dramatically simple ethical law of Islam, the *Shari'a,* a code of law and theology at the same time. The first of the demands of that law was the acknowledgment of Allah and of Muhammad's authentic prophetic role. The ritual prayer said five times a day, with the great public prayer at midday on Friday, was the second element. The third was the observation of the holy month of Ramadan by fasting from dawn to sunset. Visiting Mecca once in a lifetime, if possible, was the fourth. Alms giving was the fifth demand. These elements of Islam are the same for Muslims today as they were in the seventh century, and the moving passage in *The Autobiography of Malcolm X* describing Malcolm's pilgrimage to Mecca is in the direct tradition of the earliest recorded Arabic pilgrimages. Faithful observance of the law gave the Muslim a place in paradise.

Throughout the Middle Ages—in fact, to the present day—Islam has been much misunderstood and maligned in the West. In particular, the elements of Islamic law that reflect directly the customs of the seventh-century desert tribesmen—especially the predominance of the male, the abstention from pork and alcohol, and the surprisingly fleshly delights of the Muslim paradise—have detracted attention from other and ultimately far more influential Muslim beliefs. For the Muslim no priest intervenes between the individual and God; there is no Islamic liturgy; the visual representation of living things is forbidden; and knowledge of the *Qu'ran*—even the memorization of the entire text—is praiseworthy.

THE PROTECTORS OF THE FAITH AND THE SPREAD OF ISLAM

Muhammad died in 632, leaving no instructions concerning a successor. Since many of the tribes that had submitted to him considered his death the severance of their bond, the problem of a successor became extremely important. Such a leader could not be called Prophet, for that title always designated Muhammad alone. Nor could he be a *shaikh,* which was a tribal title. Ultimately, one of Muhammad's followers, Abu Bakr, was elected by the others as Muhammad's "representative" and given the title *khalifa* (protector of the faith). Islamic historians recognize three groups of *khalifas* between 632 and 1258: the "rightly guided" caliphs, from Abu Bakr (632–34) to Muhammad's son-in-law Ali (656–61); the Umayyad dynasty, from Muawiyah (661–80) to Marwan II (744–50); and the Abbasid dynasty, from Abu-l-Abbas (750–54) to the end of the caliphate in 1258.

The "rightly guided" caliphs faced the problems of organizing the Muslim peoples

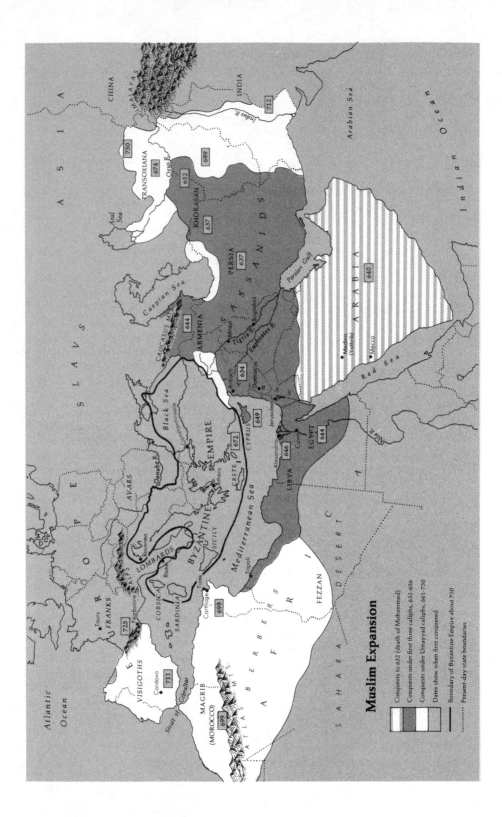

Muslim Expansion

Conquests to 632 (death of Mohammed)

Conquests under first three caliphs, 632–656

Conquests under Umayyad caliphs, 661–750

Dates show when first conquered

Boundary of Byzantine Empire about 750

Present-day state boundaries

in the absence of Muhammad. The Umayyad dynasty directed the great eastward expansion from their capital at Damascus. The Abbasid dynasty represented the culmination of Muslim expansion and the rise to prominence of non-ethnic Arabs in the Islamic world, symbolized by their move of the capital to Baghdad. There occasionally arose rival caliphates (by the tenth century there were two others, in Spain and Egypt) and sectarian leaders who denounced the caliphs. Nevertheless, the caliph, first at Damascus and then at Baghdad, was the official orthodox protector of the faith, interpreter of the *Qu'ran,* and temporal and spiritual leader of Islamic society.

Muhammad's small community of original followers at Medina bitterly resented their exile from Mecca, and they adopted the old tribal custom of the *razzia* (raid or expedition) against those who had scorned them and driven them out. The *Qu'ran* calls these activities "striving in the way of the Lord," or *jihad fi sabil Allah.* The *jihad,* misleadingly called the "Holy War" by Westerners, was a Muslim adaptation of the tribal *razzia.* Used against persecutors of Muslims, and later against pagans, the *jihad* became one focus of Muslim society under the first caliphs. Raiding against infidels was permitted, then encouraged so that the energies of the warlike desert tribes could be channeled. The purpose of the raids was not to convert the victims, however, but to make them submit to Muslim rule and pay taxes. The plunder of the old *razzia* became the territorial conquests of the new *jihad.* Only Christians, Jews, and Zoroastrians were entitled to the status of protected minorities if they surrendered to Islamic armies; they were called *dhimmis,* and had to pay a smaller tax. For Muhammad and his successors, the conversion of the Arabs to Islam was the primary goal. Others were to be plundered and governed, but they were never faced with the choice of Islam or the sword, as historians once believed. Although many non-Arabs became Muslims, they did not do so because they were forced.

Under Abu Bakr Islam was consolidated among the Arabs, and tribes that had broken off from Islam at the death of Muhammad were brought back into the Islamic federation. Under Abu Bakr's successor Umar (634–44) and the great general Khalid, Arabic armies raided outside the peninsula into the Byzantine and Persian worlds. Exhausted border provinces and disaffected provincials of Palestine, Syria, Egypt, Africa, and Persia passed quickly under Muslim rule. Even the armies of the Byzantine and Persian empires, worn out after the long Byzantine–Persian war, fell before the skillful generalship and superior tactics of the Arabs. The battle of the Yarmuk (Jordan) in 636 destroyed Byzantine resistance, and the battle of al-Mada'in in Persia in 638 virtually wiped out Persian resistance. By 642 Byzantine Africa and Egypt had fallen to Islamic armies.

The direction of the Arab armies was in the hands of able caliphs and their talented generals, supported by an Arab military aristocracy comprising male Arabs who were given a stipend by the caliph if they fought or performed other work for the state. Relieving the Arab military forces of the need for other work and promising a place in paradise to anyone who died a warrior's death, the caliphs and their generals soon created a large, able, and dedicated army. Nothing in the Mediterranean or Persian worlds could match it. Further, the army was kept intact as it cut its way through the south and east of the ancient world. It was contained in separate camps when it conquered territory, isolated from the life of the cities it conquered. The cities of Basra, Kufa, and al-Fustat (the earliest settlement of Cairo) began as such military camps.

Under Abu Bakr and Umar, Arab armies were usually irresistible. Military success was followed by political success, as the Arabs organized their newly won states into wealthy, tribute-paying provinces ruled by the caliphs at Medina. With the reign of

Uthman (644–56), however, the problem of succession to the caliphate once more came to the fore. Uthman's successor was Ali, son-in-law and cousin of Muhammad. Ali's rule (656–61) encountered opposition from among Muhammad's old followers and from the great general Muawiyah, who eventually succeeded Ali in the caliphate (661–80).

The second half of the seventh century was a period of great instability in the central provinces of the Empire. Civil wars and revolts finally drove Ali's dynasty from the throne and replaced it with that of Muawiyah, the Umayyad dynasty, which ruled Islam until 750. The devastation of central Arabia inspired Muawiyah to move the capital of the empire to Damascus, and the displacement of Ali's dynasty contributed to the formation of Shi'ism, the belief that recognizes only Ali's descendants as true caliphs. The victors in the struggle called themselves Sunnites, claiming that they alone followed the orally transmitted commands of Muhammad and were therefore orthodox. From the end of the seventh century to the present, Shi'ite Muslims have been rivals of Sunnite orthodoxy. Politically, Shi'ites recognized lines of successors descended from different wives of Ali. They called the representatives of these lines *Imams,* and they believed that the last *Imam* would appear at some future time as the *Mahdi,* the savior of Shi'ite Islam. Different Shi'ite groups recognized different *Imams* as the future *Mahdi,* and one of these groups established a separate caliphate at Cairo in 973, ruled by the Fatimid dynasty.

The internal crises that established the Umayyad dynasty at Damascus and sowed the seeds of Shi'ite–Sunnite dissension in the Muslim world did not, however, slow the process of conquest for long. As early as 647 Muawiyah had begun raids into Asia Minor, and at the same time he began to build an Arab fleet so that Constantinople itself might be assaulted by sea and land. As we have seen, in 678 and again in 717–18 massive Muslim forces assaulted the great city. The frontier between the Byzantine Empire and the Caliphate at Damascus slowly stabilized in southern Asia Minor. At the other end of the Mediterranean, Arab armies swept across North Africa. In the first years of the eighth century one military leader, Tarik, crossed the Strait of Gibraltar into Visigothic Spain, and between 711 and 720 Arab armies destroyed the Visigothic kingdom. Tarik's route has been memorialized in the name Gibraltar, for the Arabic *Gebel-al-Tarik* means "the hill of Tarik." The rapid Muslim conquest of Spain drove the last Visigothic rulers north, where the tiny kingdom of Asturias and the independent Christian Basques maintained their precarious independence.

From Spain Arab raiding armies pushed into southern Gaul, and only the exhaustion caused by the long drive across North Africa and the conquest and settlement of Spain prevented a permanent Arab settlement there. Arab armies regularly raided Gaul until the tenth century, but resistance proved to be stiffer there than elsewhere. After several governors of Muslim Spain had lost their lives in raiding parties, Abd-ar-Rahman, the governor of northern Spain, made an initially successful campaign around Poitiers and then marched on the old city of Tours. Near that city, in 733, he encountered an army of Franks led by Charles Martel, the mayor of the palace of Austrasia. Charles's forces defeated the Muslim army, killing Abd-ar-Rahman and forcing the Muslims to withdraw to Spain for a time. Although Charles Martel's victory has long occupied a prominent place in Western history, it was far more significant in increasing his personal power than in preventing the Arabs from conquering Gaul. In the latter respect, the successful defenses of Constantinople in 678 and 717–18 were far more important in the long run for Christian Europe. As later history shows, the area from the head of the Aegean Sea to the Caspian Sea was the real gateway to Europe, and the centuries-long resistance of Constantinople played a very important part in controlling the northward expansion of Islam.

THE UMAYYAD DYNASTY AT DAMASCUS

Damascus, the new capital of the Muslim Empire, quickly fell under the influence of Byzantine civilization. Greek scientific learning, Syrian art, and the vibrant commercial and social life of Egypt, Palestine, and Syria attracted the conquerors, and until 750 Syria was the first province of the empire. The culture of the conquerors was developed by prolonged contact with that of the old Hellenistic world. Greek and Syrian Christian administrators ruled in the service of the caliph, and subject peoples supported the regime with their taxes. The court of the Umayyad caliphs appears to have been modeled upon the imperial court at Constantinople.

The prosperity of the Umayyad caliphate was also reflected in the building and decorative programs undertaken in Damascus itself, as the tribute of a conquered world flowed into the hands of the Arab ruling elite. Although two wars with the Khazars, a Turkic people settled north of the Caucasus, in 642–52 and 722–37, stopped the Muslim advance to the north, Islam moved far to the east with the conquest of Iraq and Persia and victories in Turkestan and Sind. An Arab army even defeated a Chinese army north of the Jaxartes River in 751, but the conquest of China was beyond Muslim resources. From their capital at Damascus the Umayyad caliphs ruled an enormous empire, and they prospered from the material and the cultural gains that empire gave them. Tolerant of other cultures and religions, the Umayyads profited from them too.

The conquests of the late sixth and seventh centuries brought great power and wealth, and also a great stimulus for cultural development, to the Arabs. The rude warriors of the first conquests educated and acculturated their children in the complex and fascinating ways of the world they had conquered. In addition to this slow change in Arabic culture was a change of even greater importance. Although the Muslims did not proselytize among the conquered peoples, many of them converted to Islam nonetheless—so many, in fact, that by the early eighth century the ethnic Arabic element among the Muslims had begun to decline sharply.

THE ABBASID DYNASTY IN BAGHDAD

In 747 a revolt broke out in Iraq against Umayyad rule, and by 750 Abu al-Abbas had defeated and killed the last Umayyad caliph and exterminated the rest of the family, except for one prince, Abd-ar-Rahman I, who escaped to Spain and founded an emirate (a local principality) and later an independent Umayyad caliphate at Córdoba. The Abbasid dynasty founded by Abu al-Abbas represented not only a political revolution but also a cultural change in Islam of great importance. The Abbasid caliphs greatly emphasized their religious orthodoxy and criticized the earlier secularizing tendencies of the Umayyads. In addition, they viewed Arab and non-Arab Muslims as equal, regarded the merchant, the judge, and the administrator as ideal citizens, rather than the soldier, and fell under the progressively greater influence of the old Sasanian Persian culture. In 762 the Abbasids built a new city, Baghdad, on the Tigris River, far to the Persian east of Damascus. From the foundation of Baghdad dates the decline of Syria into a second-class province and the rise of Persia as the center of the Islamic Empire. During the first century of the Abbasid reign, large numbers of scientific, philosophical, and theoretical works were translated into Arabic from Greek, Syriac, Persian, and Hindi, and extensive building programs began to create the new face of the Near Eastern world.

The period 750–833 marked the highest achievements of the Abbasid caliphs.

Several of them, notably Harun-al-Rashid (786–809) and Al-Mamun (813–33) have become legendary figures even in the West, the former through the *Arabian Nights* and the legends of his wealth and personal style of rule, and the latter from his patronage of learning. But from the late ninth century, the Abbasid caliphs were gradually overshadowed by their powerful advisers and administrators, and local princes often proclaimed their independence of Baghdad. By 1055 a new official called the sultan had become the effective head of the Abbasid state. From the very beginning of the dynasty, Spain had broken away and later proclaimed its own Umayyad caliph. Other princely dynasties in North Africa proclaimed their independence. As we have seen, a Shi'ite caliphate of the Fatimid dynasty was proclaimed in Egypt in 973, and it lasted until 1171.

Political fragmentation of the Islamic world was thus a marked feature of the ninth, tenth, and eleventh centuries. The Abbasid caliphate survived, much weakened, until 1258, when the Mongols captured the city and killed the last caliph, Al-Mustasim. What survived the Abbasid power was not the political unity of an empire, then, but a politically divided world bound by a common religion, language, and culture. Islamic civilization replaced Islamic political unity.

THE CIVILIZATION OF ISLAM

The desert Arabs who had struck out at the Greco-Roman and Persian worlds in the middle of the seventh century became, by conquest and by choice, the cultural heirs of these worlds. Possibly as early as 700, the intellectual and artistic legacy of the ancient world began to influence Arabic culture. By the tenth century Muslims had absorbed and put to their own uses the cultures of the Byzantine and Persian worlds. As some indication of the rapidity and completeness of this cultural revolution, one need only glance at western Europe in the eighth, ninth, and tenth centuries, where the cultural legacy of ancient Greece and Rome took far longer to be assimilated than it did among the Muslims.

In terms of material culture, the Muslims created a physical "look" to their world that is readily identifiable even today. They were great city-builders, and two of their early triumphs, Baghdad and Cairo, are still great cities. Even in modern Spain, the Islamic architectural influences are readily visible. The mosques (houses for prayer), with their distinctive courtyards and minarets, the *madrasas* (schools for the study of law), the baths, bazaars, and markets reflect a flowering of urban culture. The life of the cities was supported by a rich agriculture, scientific and innovative, which made material life for the better-off Muslims as comfortable as anywhere in the world. The Islamic development of such architectural features as the pointed arch, traceried windows, and decorative script, as well as fountains, gardens, and secluded courtyards, not only shaped the physical appearance of the Islamic world, but may very well have contributed to important aspects of western European architecture.

Islamic architecture and its highly developed material culture should also be regarded in the light of the Islamic interest in mathematics and the natural sciences, in which Muslims did some of the greatest work the world had ever seen. They studied the logical and scientific works of Aristotle and even surpassed the Greek philosopher in mathematics and astronomy. They adopted and perfected a new system of numeration (the Arabic numerals used today throughout the world), and they invented the concept of zero. They developed a means of solving mathematical problems by transposing part of the problem to the "zero" side of an equation, calling the process *al-jebr,* or algebra.

Muslim scholars discussed the possibility of the earth's rotating on its axis, and they mapped the skies, giving many stars and constellations the names they bear today. From their work in mathematics and astronomy Muslim thinkers went on to new studies and discoveries in optics and experimental chemistry. In the latter field they were the first people to perfect the processes of distillation and sublimation.

The remarkable skill that the Muslims displayed in the physical sciences carried into medicine as well. Avicenna (Ibn Sina, 922–1037) produced a medical encyclopedia that outlined the contagious character of tuberculosis and proposed a theory of the etiology of disease based upon the contamination of water supplies. His work was translated into Latin and European vernacular languages and became, along with several other Arabic medical studies, a major medical reference work in the west. Arabic medicine was especially successful in treating eye diseases and plague. In addition the Arab world saw the earliest development of the modern hospital.

In philosophy too, Muslim thinkers absorbed and transformed the work not only of Aristotle but of Plato and Neoplatonists as well. The greatest of all medieval commentators on Aristotle was Ibn Rushd (Averroës, d. 1199), many of whose commentaries were made known to the west in Latin translations at the beginning of the thirteenth century.

On less formal levels of culture too, the Islamic conquests produced a thoroughgoing cultural revolution. The *Qu'ran* was the basic textbook, as we have seen, for learning the Arabic language. The *shari'a,* the ethical law of the *Qu'ran,* shaped legal decisions and individual conduct, down to matters of personal hygiene and proper social behavior and responsibility. Thus, in spite of political divisions, the daily life and thought of most of the Muslim world centered on the *Qu'ran;* it played an immensely important social and philosophical role as well as a major religious role. As a body of commentary and interpretation grew up around the text of the *Qu'ran* and other religious literature that was regarded as pious (such as the *hadith,* stories of Muhammad's life), schools of formal theology and law created new intellectual elites who played prominent roles in the Islamic world. Independent devotional movements, such as Sufism, drew their inspiration from the *Qu'ran* and created a mystical movement in Islam that proved immensely attractive to many people who had no part in the more formalized intellectual circles of their world.

The economic, intellectual, and spiritual vitality of the Muslim world, particularly between the seventh and the twelfth centuries, is a remarkable part of the rise of Islam. To some extent it is just as remarkable as the appearance of the faith itself, the achievements of Muhammad, and the great early conquests. A religion of desert Arabs created armies, generals, and caliphs, plus a genuine cultural revolution that transformed, once and for all, not only the southern and eastern parts of the old Roman Empire, but the ancient Persian world as well, and extended beyond to the Caucasus, India, and even southeast Asia. Where conquest went and religion followed, language went too. The Arabic-speaking world is the world of Islamic belief, and beneath that belief lies a formidable culture. That culture shaped the golden age of Islam and later provided for western Europeans many of the scientific and philosophical tools and economic institutions that contributed to the numerous changes in European society in the twelfth and thirteenth centuries.

FURTHER READING

See the general bibliography at the end of the book.

PART

THE EARLY MIDDLE AGES, 650–950

7

The Environment
of North Temperate Europe

THE PHYSICAL GEOGRAPHY OF TRANSALPINE EUROPE

The geographical focus of this book so far—and of the history of the ancient world generally—has been the Mediterranean basin, the societies around it, and the frontiers drawn by Romans to defend it. By the beginning of the eighth century the Mediterranean basin no longer housed a universal society, but rather three contending societies, those of Islam, Byzantium, and the Latin west. Thus, its role in medieval and modern history is different from its centrality in the history of the ancient world. In addition to the transformation of the Mediterranean, northern Europe for the first time ceased to be either a frontier province of a Mediterranean empire or the setting of an Iron-Age, preliterate Germanic culture. The growth of settled societies that began to increase the agricultural production of northern Europe was well under way by the eighth century. It is therefore necessary to survey the land of the new Europeans in order to understand something of the nature of their achievements. Whatever else the history of medieval Europe may be, it is certainly the story of the opening of north temperate Europe to extensive agricultural production by peoples whose descendants still inhabit it.

On the physical map of Europe, unencumbered by familiar but often misleading political, cultural, and linguistic boundaries, three broad areas, each with distinctive characteristics, are prominent: (1) the Mediterranean basin, (2) the mountains and plains of central and eastern Europe, and (3) the western parts of transalpine Europe.

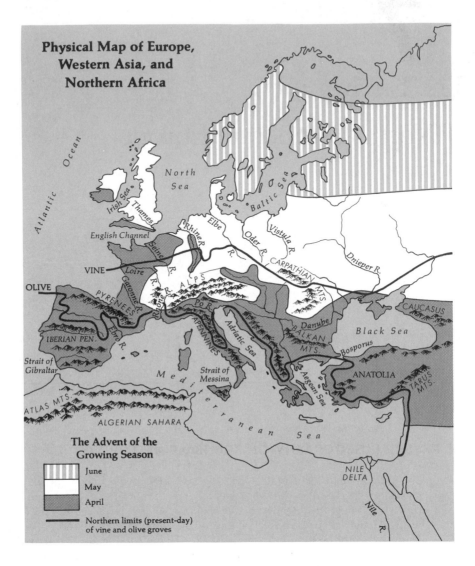

Physical Map of Europe, Western Asia, and Northern Africa

Atlantic Ocean

North Sea

Baltic Sea

Irish Sea

Thames

English Channel

Seine R.

Rhine R.

Elbe R.

Oder R.

Vistula R.

CARPATHIAN MTS.

Dnieper R.

VINE

Loire R.

Garonne R.

PYRENEES

Ebro R.

IBERIAN PEN.

OLIVE

Rhône R.

Po R.

ALPS

APENNINES

Adriatic Sea

Danube

BALKAN MTS.

Black Sea

Bosporus

CAUCASUS

Strait of Gibraltar

Strait of Messina

Aegean Sea

ANATOLIA

TARUS MTS.

ATLAS MTS.

ALGERIAN SAHARA

Mediterranean Sea

NILE DELTA

Nile R.

The Advent of the Growing Season

	June
	May
	April
——	Northern limits (present-day) of vine and olive groves

These areas constitute the three great geographical and climatic zones of the European world. Considered together, they remind us of the proximity of Europe and the western part of Eurasia generally to the great sweep of the Baltic and North seas, the Atlantic Ocean, the Mediterranean Sea, and the Black Sea. Few places in Europe are far from one of these bodies of water, and the remarkable systems of navigable rivers that reach out from the deepest parts of the land mass bring much of European society even closer to the sea. Coasts and rivers, valleys, mountains, forests, and plains offer different physical landscapes in each of our three major areas, but the elements they have in common must be kept in mind as we consider their distinctive features.

Among the movements of peoples that can be detected from prehistory and recorded in history, that from western Asia to transalpine Europe is one of the best known.

The route from western Asia led through the narrow gate between the northern edge of the Caspian Sea and the southern tip of the Ural Mountains. From South Russia a few routes led southward toward the Mediterranean, around or over the Balkans. Due west of this area the protective ring of the Carpathian Mountains offered settlement areas for a number of different peoples, notably the Avars. Beyond the Carpathians the upper Danube Valley carries a Mediterranean-type climatic area into what is now Czechoslovakia and Austria.

For the most part, however, western Europe consists of a vast plain slowly rising from west to east, its southern border lying along the great chains of mountains that begin with the Pyrenees in northern Spain, continue east and south along the Alps and the Dinaric Alps, and end with the Balkans and the Black Sea. North of these mountain ranges Europe consists generally of a great fan-shaped plain that begins in southern France and opens out north and east all the way to Russia. This great plain is crossed by many navigable rivers and by low mountain ranges rich in minerals. South of the plain the long ridges of the Pyrenees, Alps, and Balkans lie in an east–west axis that separates western and central Europe from the Mediterranean. The maritime and riverine character of western Europe gave access to the sea and, for sea people ranging from Bronze Age migrants to the Vikings, access to the land. Surrounded by the sea, the fan-shaped plain of western and northern Europe extends east to Russia and includes southern England and southern Sweden in its sweep. The rivers that cross it are evenly flowing and suitable for navigation. From the Atlantic coast of France to western Russia, the Garonne, Loire, Seine, Meuse, Thames, Rhine, Weser, Elbe, Oder, Vistula, and Duna systems offer both transportation and agricultural possibilities perhaps unequaled anywhere else in the world. Some of these systems extend even beyond the western European geographical region. The Rhine-Danube corridor offers virtually unimpeded routes from the North Sea to the Black Sea, and the Duna-Dnieper system nearly constitutes a water route from the Baltic to the Black Sea.

In western Europe rainfall is plentiful and generally even. This area does not experience the sharp differences of hot dry summers and cold wet winters of the Mediterranean. European soil, which is heavy and wet, can produce two crops per year instead of the Mediterranean one. The heavy soils of western Europe tend to leach out mineral content and retain excessive moisture unless they are plowed deeply and turned so as to afford good drainage for fields. Drainage and fertilization are thus two essential elements in maintaining the soil of western Europe. Forests grow thick and usually consist of hardwoods. Although much of the economic history of early Europe is the history of agricultural development, the presence of these great, thick forests is a constant in European history until the modern age, and the forest economy played an important role in the early Middle Ages.

Of all the physical features of Europe, the last to be adapted to the will and needs of humans was the ocean. Atlantic civilization did not begin to replace Mediterranean civilization until after the sixteenth century. Yet even the Atlantic and the North Sea, far more stormy and capricious bodies of water than the Mediterranean, Black, and Baltic seas, offered Europeans advantages that they were quick to accept. The North and Baltic seas (like the Grand Banks off Newfoundland) teem with fish, and the European Atlantic coast is not so difficult to sail that maritime cultures from as early as the Bronze Age could not exploit the ocean itself as a means of transportation. The Gulf Stream (which Europeans call the North Atlantic Drift) warms the Atlantic very far north in Europe; even the winter water temperatures off the North Cape of Norway are no lower than those off

Boston, Massachusetts (35°F). The Gulf Stream contributes to the cool summers and rarely bitter winters of Europe. When Europeans began to cross the Atlantic they had two easy corridors. In the tenth century the warmer North Atlantic and the reduced drift ice allowed Scandinavian sailors to reach and colonize Iceland and Greenland and to touch North America. In the late fifteenth century Columbus and his successors had only to sail south to meet the easterly trade winds that blow steadily across the Atlantic. But for even the best-rigged and manned sailing ships, travel to the east is far more difficult.

ENVIRONMENT AND SOCIETY

Ancient and medieval sources and modern scientific techniques, such as the study of glacier movement, pollen analysis, and the examination of tree rings, have contributed to our knowledge of climatic history in the ancient and medieval periods. From 100 B.C. to A.D. 400 the climate of Europe seems to have slowly become warmer and dryer. From A.D. 400 to around 1250, the Atlantic Ocean was relatively free of drift ice and great storms. Mediterranean writers noted that it was possible to cultivate the vine and the olive, the characteristic Mediterranean crops, much farther north than they are found today. A mean summer temperature several degrees higher than at present reduced the dangers of May frosts and produced milder Septembers, the two crucial periods of the agricultural year. Between 1200 and 1400, however, mean temperatures dropped and rainfall increased considerably. The Northern Hemisphere as a whole appears to have grown colder, and records indicate erratic seasons of drought and flood, abundance and famine. During the crucial period of the opening of transalpine Europe to agricultural activities, however, the climate was ideal.

The fragile balance between population levels and agricultural production in the Mediterranean region was upset by disease, war, and social turmoil, but the world of northern Europe was little better off. In that world of heavy forest and rivers, in which less than 10 percent of the land was under cultivation, societies remained small and lived precariously. Both Romans and Germans suffered high infant- and maternal-mortality

England: Population in Millions, 100–1650

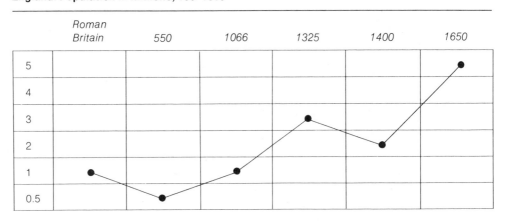

rates and very low life expectancy. Both societies produced many children, most of whom died very young. The survivors were exposed to high mortality risks throughout their youth, as well as the general shortcomings of medical science and the risks of the warrior's or farmer's life.

Much of transalpine Europe was thinly settled, with small, densely populated communities of farmers and warriors widely separated from each other by thick forest, swamp, and ridge. Until after the eleventh century, the hardships of the transalpine environment set firm limits to population growth and increased agricultural productivity. A glance at the population trends in England from the Roman period to the seventeenth century suggests the difficulty of sustaining population growth and the vulnerability of population to natural disasters, such as the invasions of the fifth century and the wave of plague in the fourteenth century. Although England is not typical of the European demographic experience in all its details, it does reflect some common elements. The population remained small, averaging no more than two to ten persons per square kilometer. Small villages, tiny markets and fairs, small areas of rational, careful cultivation, and large areas of wasteful, unproductive cultivation constituted the physical profile of transalpine Europe between the sixth and tenth centuries.

The small societies of early medieval Europe sustained themselves by cultivating at first a very small portion of the land available to them. Their productivity was low, and their resources—from tools to theory—were few. For most people the village or the isolated farmstead constituted the social horizon, and growing and finding food the principal occupation. Economic historians have suggested that in the early Middle Ages not enough land was in cultivation to feed even the small population of Europe, and that hunting and fishing played an essential part in forming the European diet. The bulk of that diet was cereal-grain products. Meat and fish were not as common. Studies of skeletons reveal considerable dietary deficiency, and the diet appears to have been relatively uniform throughout most social ranks. One difference between rich and poor was that the rich ate more, but not necessarily better or different food.

Because of the difficulties of plowing the heavy soil of northern Europe, cultivated acreage remained small. Because there was generally no fertilizer, fallowing (letting a field lie idle for a season) was the chief way of restoring at least some of the land's fertility. These limitations point to the very low ratio of yield to seed, the standard index of agricultural productivity. Throughout the Middle Ages one measure of seed yielded about three measures of grain, a ratio that rarely changed. Twentieth-century farmers are accustomed to getting twenty measures of grain for one measure of seed. In addition, agricultural tools were few and generally of poor quality. They usually had to be made locally. Although the eleventh and twelfth centuries saw the development of the water mill and windmill on a relatively large scale, the period before the eleventh century knew only animal power as a supplement to human effort.

The rhythm of the agricultural calendar is the oldest and most wide-ranging of Europe's social rhythms. The agricultural calendar dominated individual and social life, but local agricultural and landholding customs varied considerably from place to place. Thus, there was not only great seasonal variation in Europe but considerable regional variation as well. The need of small communities for the cooperation of all their members at critical times during the agricultural year imposed great solidarity, but at the price of restricting personal choice.

Above all, these societies were prone to a wide scale of natural disasters. A bad harvest brought the threat of starvation for many. A series of bad harvests brought the threat of famine. Dietary deficiencies made early Europeans more vulnerable to many more diseases than later Europeans. Too much rain drowned fields and vineyards; too little brought drought. Because early Europeans depended for most of their life support upon field and forest, they tended to overuse the land they had. Indeed, inefficient early medieval agriculture required large areas of land to support relatively few persons. The land also had to produce trees for building and tool making, hay and oats for animal feed (there were no fodder crops), and grazing land for sheep and areas for flax growing—the latter two needed for the production of wool and linen clothing.

Although the agricultural riches of northern Europe were beginning to increase by the eighth century, they did not yield much, and they did not yield it easily. The archaeology of population and settlement in this area reveals a small world living precariously on a limited agricultural economy, subject to the ravages of disease and the blows of natural disaster. That world was hard, and making it marginally less hard took centuries of labor.

FAMILIES, *GENTES*, AND KINGDOMS

The material limitations upon early medieval transalpine society contributed to the shape and structure of that society. So too did the historical experience of migration and settlement and the emergence of new political structures as a result of these. The old "tribal" societies were greatly transformed by the migrations across Europe, into and out of the Roman Empire, and by the pressure of other peoples who were also migrating. Contact with the empire itself offered new models of social organization. Not only were the political structures of the empire, the Roman armies, and the Roman provincial governments available for imitation, but the pattern of life suggested by Roman fields, communities, and cities offered prospects unthinkable in the world beyond the imperial frontiers. The decay of Roman institutions and the formation of a sub-Roman culture among the Germanic immigrants meant that both societies were becoming more like each other. And just as the late Roman Empire barely resembled the empire of the first and second centuries, so the Germanic peoples of the fifth, sixth, and seventh centuries bore little resemblance to their ancestors, whose life had been described so extensively by the Roman writer Tacitus at the end of the first century.

For most of the Germanic inhabitants of seventh-century Europe the most important social bond was that of the family, the unit that worked the land together, owned or held its own land, and passed land down to succeeding generations. Whether grouped in villages or isolated in farmsteads, those who worked the land thought in terms of family. So did societies as a whole, as a study of Germanic legal codes reveals. Much of the terminology that describes military service or tax assessment measures society in terms of households. In several early law codes the *hide,* or possessions of a single household, and the *mansus,* meaning the land and possessions required to support a household, are terms used frequently. These may be considered the elemental social forms of early medieval society.

In these legal codes the family and household are generally assumed to consist of free individuals—that is, fully fledged members of "the people," the largest group to which any individual professed loyalty. Freedom entailed the right to carry weapons in the wars of the people, the right to participate in the settlement of legal cases and disputes, and the right to participate in community decisions. In other words, freedom meant full membership in a group larger than the family. In day-to-day experience the free peasant was a fully privileged member of an agricultural community. Membership in the village community also meant full membership in the larger people, which was signaled by the right to be judged by the law of the people, whether Visigothic, Frankish, Burgundian, or Lombard. It also meant the obligation to fight—either in the expeditions of occasional war-leaders or in the wars of the king. Throughout the Middle Ages one sure sign of personal freedom was the right to carry weapons.

The settlement of Roman provincial Europe and non-Roman Europe contributed also to various social orders that conspicuously lacked freedom. Both the ancient Mediterranean world and the early Germanic world knew the institution of slavery, the possession of one human being by another as a form of chattel property. Roman slaves and even Roman freemen who had taken on servile status constituted part of the slave population, as did Germans captured in war or purchased. The early Middle Ages also knew several statuses that are generally described as "half-free." Lombard law, for example, recognized the *aldius,* a person who did not have the full legal status of a freeman and was tied to the land he worked, rather than regarded as the personal property of someone else.

One way to recognize these different statuses below the nobility is to look at the institution of *wergild* in the early law codes. *Wergild* (literally, "the money for a man") was the assessed value of individuals of different social status. Since most Germanic law was personal (the members of a people could be judged only according to the law of that people), and since most legal disputes were treated as matters involving personal injury (or *tort,* in modern legal terminology), the focus of Germanic law was compensation rather than punishment. Thus, the way by which compensation was determined reveals the "worth" of different members of society. The slave (or rather the slave's owner) received the lowest amount of *wergild,* the *aldius* somewhat more, the freeman much more, and the noble most of all. Formally, at least, the law codes give us an approximate profile of social status and offer rudimentary terminology for distinguishing among members of society.

The society of the codes, however, was not fixed forever. As the conquests slowed down and stopped, as society was transformed by settlement, and as individual circumstances changed, the fixed categories of law had to be adapted to new circumstances. One general trend after the seventh century was the gradual emergence of the institution of lordship and the "dependence" of different kinds of individuals upon a lord. A second trend was the general lessening of formal slavery and the general depression of many peasants of technically free status. Thus, at the beginning of this period the "half-free" group became a more common social status than either freemen or outright slaves. With this general leveling at the bottom of society the dependent agricultural worker, tied to the land and under the protection of a lord, became a characteristic social type. The institution of serfdom was in the process of formation.

The *gens* (plural *gentes*), or "people," was the aggregate of all free individuals who lived under the same law and fought in the same armies. Roman writers had used the term *gens* to describe either a family clan or, more frequently, a people organized on a level just below that which the Romans considered civilized. *Natio* (plural *nationes*) was a Roman category whose status in Roman eyes was well below that of *gens.* Roman writers and Germanic writers using Latin referred to the Germanic peoples of Europe as *gentes.* Thus, one could speak of the *gens Merovingorum* for the dynasty of Clovis, or the *gens Francorum* for the Frankish people as a whole; *gens Langobardorum* was the proper term for the Lombards.

The term *gens* meant something more than a "tribe" and something less than a state. It reminds us that the focus of Germanic culture was the individual and his membership in a larger group, reflected in personal law, rights within that group, and recognition of a common king. The *gentes* were loosely structured, however, and membership in them was not the same as either citizenship or subjecthood in a later form of kingdom. In general, public organized life existed on a small scale.

As the body of free peasants shrank into half-free status, the idea of freedom came to be restricted to powerful men who dominated others—the first European nobility. Originally, the Germanic nobility consisted of the most successful warriors, the richest men, and relatives and favorites of the kings of the *gentes*. If families managed to retain their wealth, connections, and prominence over several generations, they were considered *nobilis,* or noble. The *wergild* of their members was far higher than that of other persons. One means of maintaining their status was marriage to members of other powerful families. Another was the benefits derived from royal favor and service. Powerful men who served the king and acted as his representatives could easily dominate others and pass to their heirs the rewards he gave. Although the seventh and eighth centuries witnessed family fortunes rising and falling, the most powerful, wealthy, and fortunate great families of the Germanic kingdoms came slowly to constitute a generally recognized social rank having special *wergild* and privileges, a special name, and an increasing consciousness of their superior status.

At the head of these societies stood the king, but the office of king had also changed from its tribal status. It too had been subjected to the cultural pressures of migration, war-leadership, models of Roman office, and the demands of ruling a newly settled society. Thus, by the eighth century kings were no longer priests and symbolic tribal chiefs, nor were they simply successful war-leaders who had managed to conquer a territory and hold on to it for a sufficient length of time. One justification for kingship was descent from a single family from which the kings were always chosen. Dynastic right, rather than individual right, was one of the most important bases of early medieval kingship. Second, kingship was regarded as distinguishing a people, a *gens,* from other societies who did not have kings. The Merovingian kings of the Franks wore their hair long and flowing as a visible sign of their royal rank. They and other kings were expected to give gifts to their loyal followers, an echo of the division of booty in the war band. The kings, and their guardianship of the law of the *gens,* were living embodiments of the common origin and history of their peoples, and they were rulers of peoples, not of land. Early medieval monarchy was generally not based upon territory, as in the modern state. Although the king could and sometimes did make new laws for the *gens,* he was regarded far more as the protector of the people's law. This law, as we have seen, remained essentially private, settling disputes between equally free litigants.

With the Christianization of the Germanic peoples, kingship began to be regarded partly in terms of Old Testament institutions and partly in terms of the late imperial concept of the Christian emperor. The figures of David and Solomon frequently appear in the sources as bases for comparison with sixth- and seventh-century Germanic kings, and such Old Testament practices as anointing the king at his accession slowly appeared in the ceremonies of early medieval kingship. The new, larger territories of the kings of the Franks and Visigoths in the sixth, seventh, and eighth centuries strengthened the concept of kingship, and the use of Latin in royal documents and in the writing of law codes suggests the Roman influence upon Germanic institutions in a changing social and political world. The two influences of Christianity and decayed imperial ideas and institutions worked upon the kings of the seventh and eighth centuries in their new circumstances in settled kingdoms far larger than ancient Germanic tribal societies.

The role of king also came to include the protection and patronage of the Church, and the royal office appeared in liturgical prayers. Sometimes kings themselves or members of their families were venerated as saints, and Christian chroniclers held before contemporary kings examples of good and bad royal behavior. In Bede's *Ecclesiastical History of the English People,* finished in 731, the figure of King Oswald of Northumbria is held up as that of an ideal monarch, whereas other kings are held up as examples of evil rule. Although one cannot say that the chroniclers' world views directly influenced royal conduct, through them we may observe the formation of new kinds of political communities in seventh- and eighth-century western Europe. Superimposed upon the social realities of family and *gens,* the idea of a Christian people ruled by a Christian king came to be a commonplace by the eighth century.

RELIGION AND CULTURE

The emergence of a concept of Christian kingship among the Germanic peoples of sixth- and seventh-century western Europe is one striking sign of the fusion of Christian-Roman and Germanic cultures that marks these centuries. When Clovis, king of the victorious Franks, called a meeting of the Gallic clergy in Orleans in 507, he began a tradition of royal patronage of the Church—and royal interest in seeing that the Church was properly organized—that ran through the Middle Ages and early-modern European history. But regular meetings of Church councils were not a sustained feature of seventh-century life, either among the Franks or among any other Germanic people, except the Visigoths in Spain, where frequent councils met at Toledo until the extinction of the kingdom in 711. Although kings and their clerical advisers might preserve the ideal of a well-organized church, the actual state of Christianity and paganism in the sixth and seventh centuries was far from ideal.

The battle with paganism was not yet won, especially in the countryside and in the lands not conquered by Christian rulers. Many sermons of the sixth and especially the seventh centuries were based no longer on the Bible, with which most Christians were generally unfamiliar, but on proverbs, moral stories, and the histories of saints and martyrs. They were also directed against surviving pagan beliefs and practices. Much of the tone of Christian culture in this period is combative—designed to prove the superiority of Christianity over pagan beliefs or to Christianize pagan practices. Thus, as we noted above, much pagan practice was simply redesignated as worship of demons, although the muscular Christianity of the seventh century always showed the demons defeated by Christian holiness. Lists of "superstitions" forbidden to Christians appeared regularly down to the twelfth century. Among the most original legislation of Germanic kings was that dealing with violations of Christian beliefs on the part of their people. One result of such legislation was the imposition of Christian values upon older non-Christian customs. Thus, the legal procedure of the ordeal, according to which an individual was subjected to physical injury and later examined to see if the injury had miraculously disappeared, slowly acquired Christian patronage. Since the outcome of the ordeal "proved" guilt or innocence of a criminal charge, and since Christians, like pagans, believed in "immanent justice"—that is, in the direct intervention of God in human life—a Christian liturgy for preparation, execution, and interpretation of ordeals slowly developed in the early Middle Ages.

The hierarchy of the clergy, developed in late Rome and based upon an urbanized empire, was originally ill suited for the Germanic kingdoms. Too often archbishops and bishops were ill trained, not entirely separated from the noble classes from which they came, and out of contact with Rome. The canons of Frankish church councils always represent an ideal state of the Christian community, but rarely do they describe actual practice. The purest forms of devotion were to be found in monasteries, which survived less touched by the world than did the higher clergy who were still in it. But even monasticism was fragmented by a multiplicity of rules and by the problem of monastic subjection to the local bishop. The creation of rural parishes brought religion to some of the population, but it fragmented the unity of the diocese. Bishops on the whole were inconsistent in their devotion and inept in their administration. Therefore, the chief concern of the clergy was to impose uniform religious practices upon the people. By substituting orthopraxy (correct religious practice) for the ceremonial aspects of paganism, seventh-century churchmen could influence conduct, even if they were generally unable to exert as much influence over popular beliefs.

It is in the realm of popular belief that early medieval Christian culture is most striking. Christians, like pagans, wanted above all security in this world and salvation in the next. Security in this world was a matter of appeasing the proper god, and much of the tenor of missionary Christianity in this period was to prove the superiority of the Christian God in providing help in *this* life in terms of more abundant harvests, fewer natural disasters, and protection from the forces of the other world. Such fears were overcome by changes in practice, not changes in belief. Even the saints came to acquire specialized functions and to be localized; each region venerated its own proven saintly patrons, and those patrons in turn protected those who venerated them. Just as certain kinds of conduct distinguished a member of a *gens* from members of other *gentes,* so certain kinds of conduct marked off a Christian from non-Christians. Early medieval Christianity is characterized by behavior rather than by belief, and the king's insistence upon proper behavior in the Church was the sole guarantee of preserving divine favor in a turbulent world.

The image of God in the early Middle Ages was that of a remote and terrible judge, always ready to strike down humans for their sinful lives, yet willing to show mercy if attempts at reform were made. By extension, the theory of immanent justice applied to divine wrath as well, and the causation of events was seen as a manifestation either of divine favor or of divine anger. God was a power to be appeased rather than loved, for only by faithful observance of His commands could a society expect earthly peace and some assurance of heaven, however slight. In a world characterized by the worst effects of fallen human nature, plagued by demons, full of uncertainty and insecurity, the Christian first wanted help and protection. In their search for help and protection for everyday cares, men and women turned to the local saints, through prayers and liturgies, and then to God, remote and barely approachable. Saints' and holy men's triumph over demons, illustrated in sermons and stories and art, was the visible proof of God's mercy in a world that regarded itself as existing precariously under the dominion of Satan.

FURTHER READING

Besides the works listed in the general bibliography under the headings *Economic History, Social History,* and *Church History,* two works of anthropology may be helpful, both by Robert Redfield: *The Primitive World and Its Transformations* (Ithaca, N.Y.: Cornell University Press, 1953) and *Peasant Society and Culture* (Chicago: University of Chicago Press, 1956). For agrarian history, see B. H. Slicher Van Bath, *The Agrarian History of Western Europe, A.D. 500–1850* (London: Edward Arnold, 1963).

8

The Book
and the Sword

AN ISLAND SET BEYOND THE WORLD

The link that Gregory the Great forged between Rome and England with the mission of Saint Augustine in 596 resulted in the conversion of the Angles and Saxons to Christianity and was strengthened by the victory of Roman customs at the Synod of Whitby in 663. The English church was the first northern European community to have been shaped by both Roman and non-Roman Celtic influences. As such, it exerted great influence upon the communities near it, particularly the still-pagan Germanic peoples and the Frankish kingdom. The influence of English churchmen upon the Frankish kingdom in the first half of the eighth century set the stage for the later reforms of Pepin III and the later triumphs of Charlemagne.

In 668, five years after Whitby, Pope Vitalian consecrated Theodore, a native of Tarsus in Asia Minor, as archbishop of Canterbury. Theodore traveled to England with Hadrian, a north African monk, and together they completed the organization of the English church and gave great impetus to monastic development. Learned men both, Theodore and Hadrian brought what was left of classical learning with them, and they established a series of monastic schools that became the best in western Europe. Theodore ruled the English church for twenty-one years, and his influence was felt in diocesan organization and was reflected in the greatly heightened intellectual level of monasticism.

Saint Hilda, a contemporary of Theodore and Hadrian and the founder of the abbey of Whitby in 657, raised learning and study to a major role in the monastery at Whitby and in other ecclesiastical centers where her influence reached. By the end of the seventh century the English clergy was probably the most learned and best trained in western Europe. Study of the Scriptures was, of course, the focus of monastic and cathedral schools, but in addition it constituted a framework for the preservation of the liberal arts. It also influenced the devotional lives of those who knew no Latin. Saint Hilda patronized the first known poet in vernacular English, Caedmon. Under her patronage Caedmon produced Old English poems on religious topics, thereby bridging one of the gaps between the literary Latin culture of ecclesiastics and the oral, vernacular culture of Christian lay people.

The influence of these individuals is seen in the next generation of ecclesiastical leaders, particularly in the careers of Benedict Biscop and Wilfrid of Ripon. Benedict Biscop was born around 628 and spent his youth in the service of King Oswy of Northumbria. About the time he turned twenty-five Benedict left royal service, distributed his goods, and undertook a pilgrimage to Rome. He traveled with Wilfrid of Ripon, another wealthy young noble who became a controversial and influential churchman. Benedict made five pilgrimages to Rome during his life, and he traveled to monastic communities on the Continent, where he observed different customs and took monastic vows himself. He was in Rome when Theodore was made archbishop of Canterbury, and he accompanied Theodore back to England. Benedict founded a monastery at Wearmouth in 673 and a second monastery at nearby Jarrow a few years later. Under the abbacy of Ceolfrid, another Northumbrian nobleman who had left secular life to become a monk, the two monasteries founded by Benedict Biscop exerted spiritual and intellectual influences as far away as Ireland and the Continent.

The extraordinary intellectual and spiritual vitality of late-seventh-century England is exemplified by the careers of Aldhelm and Bede. Aldhelm was born around 640 and studied with Celtic Christian teachers until he was about thirty. He then went to Canterbury and studied under Abbot Hadrian, acquiring great learning and proficiency in Greek and some Hebrew. Late in life Aldhelm became abbot of Malmesbury, an important monastic community, and throughout his life he produced literary works of considerable learning in an extremely ornate and difficult Latin style. Poems, letters, and theological treatises flowed from his pen, and his career suggests the high level of ecclesiastical culture that characterized England in the late 600s.

Bede (ca. 672–735) was born a few miles from Benedict Biscop's monasteries of Wearmouth and Jarrow, which he entered as a small boy around 679. He spent his entire life at Jarrow, chiefly as a teacher of young monks, and most of his literary works were pedagogical. He wrote, around 701 or 702, an essay on versification, as well as other works introducing students to the technical problems of the primarily literary subjects that they studied. Bede later wrote two longer works on chronology, as well as many biblical commentaries and lives of saints. His greatest work, however, and one of the greatest histories ever written, was his *Ecclesiastical History of the English People,* which he completed in 731. The culture that produced Bede and his *History* is clearly remarkable. In it, the reform of monasticism, including the introduction of Benedictine influences by Benedict Biscop and Wilfrid, the diocesan organization, and the high level of learning mark an important moment in European history and constituted a threshold for the reforms of Charlemagne later in the eighth century.

Bede's *History* is in many ways the climax of that movement in learning, devotion, and the arts that distinguishes late-seventh- and early-eighth-century England. Bede consciously shaped a unified history of his England within the framework of England's conversion to Christianity. But Bede's England is also Roman, and the figure of Gregory the Great, whom Bede calls the "apostle" of the English, clearly dominates the early part of the history, which preserves many of Gregory's original letters to the English mission. From the early martyrdoms, through Saint Augustine's mission, to the portrait of Oswald of Northumbria as the ideal Christian king, Bede's *History* is a remarkable intellectual document. At Bede's death in 735, the scholar-monk was still working on the biblical literature that had occupied most of his life. The level of learning achieved by Bede in a life spent at a small monastery in a remote part of "an island set beyond the world" was equaled elsewhere in England during his lifetime—at Hexham, Ripon, Malmesbury, Canterbury, and York. This cultural revolution marked English society for centuries and greatly influenced the Continent as well. Indeed, it may be considered the first European culture. It is reflected in the epithet that Saint Boniface applied to Bede later in the eighth century—*candela ecclesiae,* "the light within the Church." The culture of Bede and of eighth-century England in general may also be regarded as the "light within Europe."

THE LONG-HAIRED KINGS AND A REVOLUTION

The distinctive religious and political culture of late-seventh- and early-eighth-century England contrasted sharply with that of the rest of northern Europe. In 711, as we have seen, the Visigothic kingdom in Spain was swept away by Muslim invaders. The slow conversion of the Lombards in Italy from Arianism to Catholicism prevented the growth of a strong Lombard Catholic Christian culture. The travails of the Byzantine Empire during the attacks of Bulgars and Muslims and during the ensuing iconoclastic controversy played havoc with the Byzantine enclaves in Italy and weakened the position of the popes. Only the Frankish church and society appeared to resemble the great success of England, but the great resources of the Frankish kingdom required a political and cultural revolution in order to be mobilized in the direction of social change. The English developments of the late seventh and early eighth centuries constitute one essential part of the background for this revolution. The history of the Frankish kingdom constitutes the other.

The kingdom created by Clovis before his death in 511 was a wholly new entity in the experience of the Franks, and the problem of succession was a new problem. Although Frankish law stated that privately owned land had to be divided equally among the surviving sons of a deceased father, there is no indication that the Franks considered the kingdom as property in quite this way. It is likely that contemporary political and dynastic considerations dictated the solution—a division of Clovis's kingdom into four parts, each ruled by one of his four sons as king. Except for brief periods between 558 and 561 and between 613 and 639, when a single ruler governed the whole kingdom of the Franks, the realm was usually divided among three or four rival, and usually hostile, kings.

During the sixth and seventh centuries some of the divided kingdoms acquired a sense of regional continuity and identity. Gradually three divisions became customarily recognized. The territory known as Neustria, with its capital at Soissons, emerged out of the Romanized western Frankish lands. The kingdom of Austrasia took shape out of the more Germanic eastern Frankish lands; its capital was at Metz. The third kingdom, Burgundy, was generally dominated by one or the other of the remaining two kingdoms. Although all three kingdoms were ruled by descendants of Clovis—the Merovingian dynasty, marked by their long hair and their royal wealth—no individual ruler was entirely secure, either in inheriting a kingdom or in holding on to one once he acquired it. A combination of membership in the ruling dynasty and approval by the powerful clergy and magnates of the realm assured succession, but civil war, rebellion, or assassination might as quickly remove a ruler. When heirs were minor children, Merovingian queens played prominent political roles in the succession. And the powerful individuals surrounding the ruler and the court, members of wealthy families, always played a role in distributing the royal power as well.

Royal favorites were appointed king's representative—whether count, duke, or patrician—to look after royal interests in different parts of the kingdom. Command of the king's army was usually in the hands of one of the Merovingian dukes. Beneath the military and supervisory ranks of dukes and patricians, counts carried out most of the daily responsibilities of the rudimentary administration of the kingdom. Although the titles of the nobility appear to have derived from royal service, most of the great families found it to their advantage to attempt to consolidate their royal delegated powers with their own lands, wealth, and rights and in this way weaken the wealth of the monarchy and enhance their own status. In at least one area they were successful: as royal service became regionalized in the seventh century, families were able to consolidate their own lands with the lands they administered for the king.

Even in the royal household the position of *major domus,* "mayor of the palace," began to overshadow that of the king. But the process by which the Merovingian aristocracy increased its wealth made it generally independent of the mayor of the palace, as well as the king. Especially in the lands on the edges of the kingdoms, virtually independent noble families came to dominate both their regions and the rival families. During the late seventh and early eighth centuries, both the mayor of the palace and the regional nobility began to increase their wealth and power at the expense of the kings. A succession of minor children to the thrones of Neustria and Austrasia in this period helped both these new forces to assert increased power.

Of the two main Frankish kingdoms, Neustria remained the more powerful, particularly under Ebroin (657–83), the mayor of the palace, or chief adviser of the kings. Ebroin's power depended upon the loyalty to him, rather than to the king, of the prosperous and increasingly powerful and self-conscious regional aristocracy. In Austrasia too a regional aristocracy was forming. The most prominent of its families was the Arnulfings, whose leader, Pepin II of Heristal, asserted his military supremacy over Neustria at the Battle of Tertry in 687. Pepin's son, Charles Martel, who succeeded him as mayor of the palace of Austrasia in 714, greatly strengthened that office and began to impose his own rule over many provinces that had slipped out of the hands of the weak Merovingian kings. In addition, Charles led a successful attack on an invading Muslim army at Poitiers in 733. At his death in 741 Charles Martel was virtually the undisputed ruler of the Franks in Austrasia, Neustria, and Burgundy. He had assembled and enriched his supporters by confiscating church lands and ignoring the rights of the legitimate king. He left his office and his power to two sons, Carloman and Pepin III.

The rise of the aristocracy and the family of Charles Martel in the kingdoms of the Franks coincided with a vigorous missionary movement launched by English churchmen. Their primary purpose was to convert the still-pagan Germanic peoples in Frisia, Saxony, and Thuringia.

In 718 a monk from Wessex, Winfrid, also undertook a mission to convert the Germanic pagans. In 719 he went to Rome to receive official sanction from the pope, and at that time he changed his name to Boniface. Between 719 and 722 Boniface worked in Frisia, Bavaria, and Saxony. In 722 he went once more to Rome, where he was made bishop, and in 739 he became an archbishop. At the pope's recommendation, he received the protection of Charles Martel. During the next twenty years, Boniface's independence and the hostility of the Frankish clergy often blocked his attempts to further his missionary work and reform the Frankish higher clergy. Nevertheless, under Charles Martel's sons, Pepin III and Carloman, an alliance between the English missionaries and the Frankish mayors of the palace was forged. In 742 Boniface presided over the first of the reform councils of the Frankish church. In 746, with Pepin's blessing, the Frankish bishops sent a series of ecclesiastical questions to Rome, and in 747 Pepin and the Frankish aristocracy sent a declaration of faith to Rome. Through the work of the English missionaries a new contact between the Franks and Rome was slowly being forged.

During the 740s and early 750s, Boniface was the most prominent churchman on the Continent. He laid the missionary groundwork for the Frankish expansion to the east, as well as leading the reform movement inside the Frankish church. Focusing upon his Frisian mission once more, Boniface was killed by the pagans in 753. After his death he was revered as the apostle to the Germans. He had called himself *exul Germanicus*—"the exile in Germany." In him we see the full power of recent English tradition carried to the Continent, not only to the still-pagan Frisians and other Germanic peoples but to the decayed Frankish church. Missionary and reformer, Boniface brought to the Continent a sense of proper ecclesiastical order and secular religious responsibility, as well as the link to Rome that contributed to the shaping of the kingdom of the Franks after Pepin's revolution and throughout the life and reign of Charlemagne.

In 751 Pepin III, son of Charles Martel and mayor of the palace of both Neustria and Austrasia, deposed the last Merovingian king of the Franks and ascended the Frankish throne in his place. To effect his revolution, which had immense consequences in Western political history, Pepin used his own power, an alliance with some of the Frankish aristocracy, and his relationship with Saint Boniface. The association between the new Frankish rulers, Pepin III and Carloman, and the English missionaries—brief as it had been, and intermittent as well—contributed several important elements to the new conception of kingship. A chronicle entry gives what must have become the "official" version of Pepin's revolutionary act:

Burghard, bishop of Wurzburg, and the chaplain Fulrad [of St. Denis] were sent [by Pepin] to Pope Zachary to ask him about the kings in Frankland, who at that time had no royal power. Was this right or not? Pope Zachary replied to Pepin that it was better for the man who had power to be called king rather than one who remained without royal power, and, to avoid a disturbance of the right ordering of things, he commanded by apostolic authority that Pepin should become king.

The seeming naturalness of this text must not cloud its genuinely revolutionary character. Pepin invoked ecclesiastical support to overturn the Merovingian claims to kingship by blood right. His supporters devised a new kind of liturgical ceremony to make him king. In short, Pepin transformed the character of Frankish kingship. A near-contemporary account suggests the diverse elements he and his supporters combined to create the new model monarchy of the Franks: "Pepin was a pious king . . . raised to the throne by the *authority* and *order* of Pope Zacharias, . . . by *anointing* with the holy chrism at the hands of the blessed bishops [and] by the *choice* of the Franks." No longer did simple blood right make a Frankish king, but energy and zeal for the welfare of his people and his church. If he is indifferent to power, dissipates wealth, and neglects his people's spiritual welfare, he loses his title to legitimacy. Pepin's revolution was not merely a *coup d'état* among the Franks, but the creation of a new theory of society and power entailing new standards for rulership. According to those new standards, the Merovingian long-haired kings were anachronisms, and a new line of Frankish kings ascended the throne.

THE EXPANSION OF FRANKISH POWER

From the reign of Pepin (751–68) to that of Charles the Bald (848–77), the Carolingian kings of the Franks stabilized the monarchy's resources within the kingdom of the Franks and expanded Frankish power throughout Europe on a scale not seen since the days of Roman expansion. Within half a century the Franks controlled all of western Europe except for the British Isles, most of the Iberian peninsula, and southern Italy. Their frontiers marched against those of the pagan Danes, Balts, northern and southern Slavic peoples, Christian Greece, and Muslim Spain. The immediate driving force behind this expansion was the Frankish army, but the organization of the kingdom by Pepin and his son Charlemagne (768–814) played an equally important role. From their reorganization of the royal household, which they grandly called the "royal palace," to their institution of counts and dukes as royal representatives throughout the kingdom, and their patronage and support of the Frankish church, the kings reshaped the political order of Frankish society.

Among the royal resources available to govern the kingdom, the greatest was land. The income, often in food and goods, that the land produced supported the king, his household, and his officials. In order to obtain the regular services of the nobility, the king granted lifetime tenure of part of the royal lands to those who served him. When the person so rewarded was a bishop, the lands and income he received were called the *episcopatus.* When the servant was a count, the total was called the *comitatus.*

The count (*comes,* or *grafio*) was the essential unit of royal administration outside the household itself. Counts had existed under the Merovingians, and in old Roman territories they had come to control the former public services and sources of income that had become the property of the Frankish king. They combined the functions of judge, provincial governor, military commander, court clerk, and royal representative. Under the later Merovingians many counts had assimilated their royal duties and resources to their own personal and family property, thus alienating much of the royal wealth. Under Pepin and Charlemagne the counts were controlled more effectively. They were made to serve in areas where they had no personal connections, their offices ceased to be heritable by their children, and their duties were spelled out in directive after directive issued by the royal court. Traveling circuit inspectors called the *missi dominici* ("those sent by the king") reviewed the counts' activities and corrected them when necessary. Charlemagne also made the counts work harder, especially in administering the law courts and assembling their local contingents of soldiers and supplies for the army campaigns of the summer. The counts had small staffs of assistants, including the *vicecomes,* or viscount, and the *scabini,* or *judices,* men learned in the law. But the count, like the king, worked out of a household rather than an office.

Although the system of administering the kingdom by counts (and in particularly troublesome places by margraves and dukes, counts with increased powers and resources) is clear enough in theory, it had many shortcomings, even under Charlemagne. Ideally the system would have required around 2,500 officials to operate efficiently, but it is doubtful that Charlemagne ever assembled that many. Many of the ills that had plagued Merovingian governance could only be checked, not overcome. Long distances, the tendency of counts to localize themselves, the inefficiency of supervision and communications—all worked to reduce efficiency, and the kings often reiterated their demands that loyalty be the count's primary virtue.

Fidelity—and its opposite, betrayal—dominate the literature of the ninth century. The limitations of the ethical world of these royal servants are shown nowhere more clearly than in the constant emphasis upon personal loyalty to the king. As late as the thirteenth century, treason was understood chiefly in terms of personal disloyalty to a lord to whom one had taken an oath of allegiance.

Out of these limited resources and on the tenuous foundations of personal oaths of loyalty, the Carolingian rulers of the Franks built their extensive kingdom. Its fabric consisted of the church and the palace household, the local courts, the *scabini,* the vicars, and the counts. The great frontier lords were conceived as a kind of supercount, and the seven marches that they ruled—Spain, Brittany, Bavaria, Pannonia, Friuli, Nordgau, and Swabia—guarded the edges of the expanding but always threatened kingdom. Through these territories traveled the king's *missi,* his household servants, ecclesiastical officials going back and forth to Rome, pilgrims, and strangers.

The new and insistent tone of the Frankish king's ecclesiastical mission makes the ecclesiastical reforms under Pepin and Charlemagne an illuminating aspect of the character of Carolingian kingship. The divisions of ecclesiastical administration created in the last years of imperial rule in the Roman west had virtually disappeared by the late seventh century. Episcopal offices were left vacant for long periods or given to royal relatives and favorites without consideration of personal qualifications or the ecclesiastical legality of elections to ecclesiastical offices. The ecclesiastical reforms urged by Saint Boniface changed the course of the Frankish church in the late eighth century, but the power of Pepin and Charlemagne prevented the church's establishment of an autonomous hierarchy. Part of the royal mission was the assumption of responsibility for a Christian people, and the Carolingians retained considerable power in the matter of ecclesiastical appointments. The reorganization of the church, however, was now sponsored powerfully by the kings themselves, and the restoration of the old archbishoprics, the subordination of bishops to their metropolitans and of local clergy to bishops, and the frequency of ecclesiastical synods and councils contributed to the restoration of administrative order within the Frankish church and constituted simultaneously a new kind of organized support for the king. Not only were older sees reconstituted, but new ones were founded and some, such as Salzburg in 798, were raised to metropolitan status. This vigorous, newly organized episcopate, many of whose members were drawn from the greatest families of the kingdom, became one of the strongest supports of the monarchy and eventually a nearly independent group in the complex ecclesiastical and political atmosphere of Charlemagne's son and successor, Louis.

Besides the bishoprics, Pepin and Charlemagne restored and enriched the monasteries of Gaul and founded new ones in other parts of their territory. The monasteries, whose reform was continued brilliantly through the reign of Louis, provided the norms of religious life in the rough Frankish kingdom, personnel for royal service, scribes, advisers, and allies to the ruling dynasty. Such monasteries as St. Denis, near Paris, Corbie and its daughter house to the east, Corvey, St. Gall in Switzerland, and especially St. Martin at Tours are the best-known of Charlemagne's day. Under Louis's ecclesiastical adviser, Saint Benedict of Aniane, the influence of the Benedictine rule grew much greater in the Frankish kingdom.

The internal stability created by the king's use of counts and dukes, bishops and abbots, enabled Pepin, and still more Charlemagne, to turn to the expansion of the kingdom. The frontiers moved slowly outward toward Spain, Italy, Germany, the Slavic lands, and the Netherlands. Territories that had been in the kingdom but had continually proved restive whenever a crisis troubled the royal authority—areas such as Aquitaine, Bavaria, and Brittany—received particular royal attention, and the commanders of the marches were in a state of almost continuous military preparedness. The Carolingian kings also developed the ability to conduct different military operations on different fronts at the same time. During the period 752–59, Pepin fought both the Lombards in Italy and the Arabs in Septimania in northeastern Spain. Later, kings were often recalled from one area of military activity in order to quell a local rebellion or defend another frontier from invaders.

The driving mechanism of Frankish expansion was the 8,000-man military force that the Frankish kings could assemble every spring, after a winter's military planning. The army consisted primarily of infantry, well armed and highly disciplined, and some cavalry, wearing mailed coats and helmets and armed with sword and spear. Depending upon the area of campaigning, some parts of the kingdom contributed more fighting men, some less, from year to year.

After putting down local revolts in Aquitaine, Brittany, and Bavaria, Pepin and then Charlemagne directed Frankish power primarily toward Spain, Germany, and Italy. In 778 Charlemagne entered Spain. His failure to take Saragossa became the kernel for the epic poem *The Song of Roland,* but he captured Gerona in 785 and Barcelona in 801–3. In addition, he established the Spanish March, a durable enclave of Frankish power south of the Pyrenees that protected the frontier against the Muslim forces to the south.

The conquest of the Saxons proved to be Charlemagne's longest and most costly campaign. The nobles from the eastern parts of the kingdom and the missionary churches along the eastern border had long faced the power of this Germanic people settled between the Elbe and the North Sea. Charlemagne directed a substantial campaign into Saxony virtually every year between 772 and 785. Frankish victories were followed by Saxon rebellions, and Charlemagne's early policy of forcing Saxons to convert to Christianity helped to maintain their resistance. By 804, however, Charlemagne was able to add the vast territories of Saxony to his domain. The fall of Saxony made it easier for Charlemagne's armies to overcome Frisian resistance in the Netherlands, and the conquest of these two areas brought Charlemagne's borders to the base of the Jutland peninsula and face to face with the Danes.

To the southeast, Charlemagne defeated Tassilo, duke of the Bavarians, in 787 and incorporated his realm into the Carolingian kingdom. The conquest of Bavaria led Charlemagne to Carinthia, and thereby into the affairs of the southern Slavs and the Avars. The Avars, as we have seen, entered the Danube valley in the sixth century, divided the Slavs and incorporated many of them into their kingdom, and participated in the great assault upon Constantinople in 626. Their military capabilities had been considerably reduced by the late eighth century, however. Charlemagne's armies destroyed their capital in 796, removing the great Avar treasure to Aachen and causing the Avars to disappear from history.

The military reforms of Charles Martel, the political revolution of Pepin, and

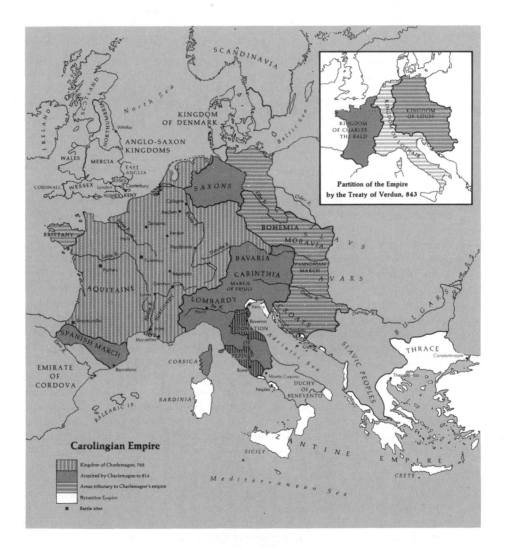

Partition of the Empire
by the Treaty of Verdun, 843

Carolingian Empire

Kingdom of Charlemagne, 768
Acquired by Charlemagne to 814
Areas tributary to Charlemagne's empire
Byzantine Empire
Battle sites

Charlemagne's single rule for forty-three years after 771 contributed to the development of a new type of power under Charlemagne. The weaknesses of surrounding peoples, the remarkably wide base of support that Charlemagne received from the church and the laity, and the effectiveness of the Carolingian army all contributed to the expansion of the kingdom. The kingdom was held together by the only successful means known—loyalty to a single ruler who was sufficiently powerful to enforce loyalty or submission when they were not voluntarily forthcoming. The kingdom itself, particularly in the newly conquered lands, underwent no governmental revolution, and the common Christianity of the whole kingdom cannot have been expected to constitute the bond that it became only much later. The kingdom of the Franks was still the kingdom of the Franks. But it was also the kingdom of Charlemagne, and it could only have been ruled, its particular loyalties and local and regional senses of independence only overcome, by a ruler as able, vigorous, and fortunate as Charlemagne. But no other such king of the Franks was forthcoming. Even in Charlemagne's old age, the kingdom began to come apart.

THE CAROLINGIAN RENAISSANCE

Charlemagne accompanied his successes as a king and a warrior by a heightened conception of himself as having a divinely ordained mission that included responsibility for the quality of spiritual as well as temporal life. The quality of spiritual life turned upon the quality of the clergy, and Charlemagne's clerical reforms gave rise to a vigorous Latin literary and artistic culture often called the Carolingian renaissance. Charlemagne's first steps were to continue his family's patronage of Frankish church reform and to secure accurate texts of essential items of Christian literature—the Bible, canon law, a reliable sacramentary, and the Benedictine rule. From this essentially practical emphasis on proper learning there quickly grew up active book-producing centers that copied the works of classical writers as well as those of church fathers, borrowing books to copy from Spain, Italy, Ireland, and England and in turn circulating copies to other monastic and episcopal centers. If not the intellectual profundity or originality, then certainly the sheer volume of book production in the late eighth and early ninth centuries characterizes the reigns of Charlemagne and Louis as critical in the intellectual history of Europe.

The Carolingian literary renaissance was marked not only by the increasing circulation and standardization of basic Christian literature, but also by striking changes in the techniques of book production, particularly decoration and handwriting. Book covers of jewels and precious metals adorned the most important sacred writings. A new and much clearer form of handwriting, the Carolingian minuscule, replaced the irregular and difficult-to-read Merovingian script, and durable vellum and parchment replaced papyrus. The organization of the *scriptoria* (writing rooms) of the monasteries included the selection of works to be copied, the assignment of works to copyists, and the training and supervision of new scribes. The head of the monastic *scriptorium* became an important figure in the monastery and not uncommonly, when the abbot himself happened to be a learned man, produced literary works whose importance cannot be overestimated. The Carolingian bishops constituted administrative and disciplinary support for the new Frankish monarchy, and the monasteries constituted its intellectual and literary complement. In order to promote these intellectual reforms, Charlemagne developed the palace school, transforming an older institution for the training of young boys into an academy where literary learning and other forms of training were combined under the watchful care of the king himself and the scholars he brought to court.

Carolingian scholars' search for authentic texts of fundamental documents had important consequences. The *Dionysio-Hadriana,* the collection of ecclesiastical law sent to Charlemagne by Pope Hadrian I in 774, became the foundation for later collections of canon law. The copy of the Roman Sacramentary that the king received in 786 became the foundation for Continental liturgical practice. The copy of the rule of Saint Benedict that Charlemagne ordered from Monte Cassino in 787 became the basis for the monastic reforms of the next several centuries.

Charlemagne sought out scholars from the far reaches of his empire and beyond. Peter of Pisa and Paulinus of Aquileia, both grammarians, and Paul the Deacon, the historian of the Lombards and of the church of Metz, all came from Lombard Italy in the 770s and 780s. Theodulf of Orléans was a Visigoth. Dicuil the geographer and Dungal the astronomer came from Ireland.

The man associated most closely with the Carolingian renaissance, Alcuin of York, also came from a great distance. Alcuin was intellectually a product of the great growth of learning in England in the late seventh and eighth centuries. On a trip to Rome he met Charlemagne at Parma in 781 and was invited to the king's court. From 782 to 796 Alcuin was Charlemagne's major ecclesiastical adviser and perhaps the greatest scholar in the kingdom. His influence can be seen in the intellectual tradition of the great ninth-century monastic schools and their teachers. For twenty years the most powerful ruler in the west and this individual who, probably more than anyone else, was his guide and consultant on the most important intellectual issues of his day shared an extraordinarily close relationship.

In 793 Einhard, a young layman from the Main valley, came to Charlemagne's court, participated in its intellectual and administrative life, and much later, after Charlemagne's death, paid the king the tribute of writing his biography, the first biography of a layman in many centuries. Although much of Einhard's style and approach derived from Roman and later Latin sources, his portrait of Charlemagne is invaluable. In it one can see a semiliterate barbarian prince, a second-generation king who rose from a *coup d'état* of doubtful legitimacy, dressing and acting much like those around him, fond of hunting and baths and fighting. One can see something more, too. Something in Charlemagne's imagination made him view his conquests and power as more than private acquisitions. With his conquests there grew in him a mighty sense of personal responsibility for the lives and the souls of his subjects. The legacy of this vision influenced the thought of Europe for centuries to come. Warrior and king, Charlemagne was also Christian Europe's first great lay patron of religion and the arts, and perhaps its first political idealist.

Some of Charlemagne's intellectual legacy is tangible. Around 8,000 manuscripts survive from the late eighth and ninth centuries, and many more are known to have been produced. These books are usually clearly written—many of them in the new style of handwriting called the Carolingian minuscule, which spread throughout Europe in the ninth century—usually well edited, and sturdily made. They consist not only of the expected ecclesiastical treatises, saints' lives, and chronicles, but also of the work of earlier Latin writers, many from the classical period.

Two examples may suggest the range of the revival of learning under Charlemagne. In the first half of the ninth century, several collections of Church law appeared that are known to have been forgeries. The most famous of these is the collection attributed to Pseudo-Isidore. Many of them purported to contain documents as old as the second and third centuries. Although they were forgeries, the skill of those who made them, the wide range of ideas they contain, and their sheer bulk testify to the technical and intellectual abilities even of the forgers, themselves a product of the Carolingian renaissance. Many of the documents they fabricated played a prominent part for centuries in European intellectual history.

A second indicator of the renewal of learning is the degree of sophistication found in the theological disputes of the ninth century. One of the most prominent participants was the Irish scholar John Scotus Erigena, who taught at the court of Charlemagne's grandson, Charles the Bald, learned Greek, and translated the important sixth-century treatise *On the Celestial Hierarchies,* by Pseudo-Dionysius, into Latin. The disputes ranged from the nature of sacraments to predestination, reflecting the continuing influence of Carolingian educational reforms in the monastic and court schools through most of the ninth century.

The Carolingian intellectual and artistic renaissance played as important a role in European history as the political and military achievements of the eighth-century Franks.

THE "KINGDOM OF EUROPE" AND THE EMPIRE OF THE ROMANS

Around 776 the Anglo-Saxon monk Cathwulf referred to Charlemagne's kingdom as the *Regnum Europae,* the kingdom of Europe, reviving the obscure Roman geographical designation *Europa* to indicate the breadth of his new power. In the last decades of the century Charlemagne's relations with the kings of Northumbria and Mercia indicated their sense of inferiority to him, as did the tribute from the increasingly powerful King Alfonso II of Asturias in northern Spain. Shortly after 780, Empress Irene of Constantinople negotiated with Charlemagne concerning a marriage between his daughter Rotrud and her son Constantine VI. This recognition, along with the embassies from Harun al-Rashid, the caliph of Baghdad, and the overtures from the Christian inhabitants of Jerusalem that reached Charlemagne in 800, indicates one level of his position. The prestige of the king of the Franks was greater than that of any other Christian ruler.

Charlemagne's immense prestige and power in northern Europe were also well known to the popes, and during his reign the link between the Franks and the popes grew considerably stronger. To understand Charlemagne's unique position in papal eyes, we must consider some important crises in papal history during the second half of the eighth century. Of these, the most important were generated by the Lombards and the iconoclastic controversy in Byzantium. From the early eighth century a restored, ambitious Lombard monarchy, first under Liutprand (712–44) and then under his more ruthless successors Ratchis (744–49) and Aistulf (749–56), moved against the powerful and largely independent Lombard duchies of Spoleto and Benevento, to the east and south of Rome. The tactical importance of the position of Rome and the weakness of the unsupported Byzantine garrisons in central Italy made the independence of Rome precarious, and when in 751 Aistulf finally captured Ravenna, which had been for two centuries the chief seat of Byzantine imperial power in Italy, he placed Rome under his own authority.

The popes, who were unable and perhaps unwilling to treat with the Lombards, sought allies beyond the Alps. As we have seen, the middle of the eighth century was a period of crisis and instability in many parts of Europe, and the papal approval of Pepin's revolution in 751 drew the bishop of Rome and the king of the Franks closer together. In 754, when the Synod of Heireia pronounced firmly against the cult of images, when only Byzantine emissaries, not troops, were forthcoming from Constantinople, and when Aistulf's forces were threatening Rome more ominously, Pope Stephen II (752–57) made his way to the kingdom of the Franks. There he anointed Pepin again and implored his aid, which he obtained in spite of considerable resistance among the Frankish magnates and Pepin's doubtful security so soon after his revolution. Stephen had also crowned Pepin's sons Carloman and Charles kings in perpetuity, making Pepin *patricius Romanorum,* a title implying the status of special protector of Rome. The relationship between the pope and the king of the Franks—tentatively begun earlier in the century, established firmly by the approval of Pepin's revolution in 751, and cemented by the meeting between Pepin and Stephen II in 754—had enduring consequences, both for the future history of Italy and the papacy and for the concept of Frankish protection of the Latin church.

The lands that Pepin guaranteed to the pope comprised large parts of the old Exarchate of Ravenna. Pepin's donation of these lands, confirmed by Charlemagne, created the Papal States, a block of territory in central Italy under the direct rule of the bishop of Rome. They played an important part in medieval history and survived until the invasion of Rome in 1870. Not until the papal concordat with Mussolini in 1929 did the popes formally acknowledge the loss of these territories.

Around the middle of the eighth century, perhaps as late as 778, a document began to be cited by papal scribes that had a great bearing on the constitutional history of European Christian society. This document, the *Donation of Constantine,* professed to be a deed issued in the year 313 in which the Emperor Constantine extended many privileges to the pope and clergy, chiefly in the matter of rank, possessions, and privileges. The most important statement in the document, however, was a passage that could be interpreted as granting rule over the entire western part of the Roman Empire to the bishop of Rome. The document probably was intended to provide independent legitimacy for the Papal States and to shore up the position of the bishop of Rome in the face of Byzantine, Lombard, and Carolingian pressures. Although little used in the eighth and ninth centuries, the *Donation* became a key document in twelfth-century collections of Church law and a foundation for later papal claims to control of the rulers of Europe. Its authenticity was not formally disproved until the critical work of the scholar Lorenzo Valla in the fifteenth century. The donation of Pepin and the *Donation of Constantine* both contributed to the strengthened relations between pope and ruler of the Franks in the later eighth century.

Between 754 and 790 the popes ceased sending notification of their election to the emperors at Constantinople and sent it instead to the kings of the Franks. Imperial portraits disappeared from Roman coinage and were replaced with portraits of the issuing popes; popes ceased dating their official documents in terms of imperial reigns, doing so instead in terms of their own. In spite of continuing Byzantine difficulties and Lombard resistance, the papacy in the second half of the eighth century reconstituted itself as a distinctly Latin power and slowly removed the lingering traces of imperial authority from central Italy.

By 780 new negotiations appear to have temporarily restored good relations among the pope, Charlemagne, and Byzantium. The Papal States had come into being, and the extension of Charlemagne's power had brought him not only the iron crown of the Lombards but a newer and closer relationship with the pope and a renewed official status in the eyes of Rome and the Roman church. This aspect of the expansion of the Frankish kingdom opened the way not only to a double royal title, ''King of the Franks and the Lombards'' and the Roman title *patricius Romanorum,* but also to the idea of a new title appropriate for all of the lands Charlemagne ruled, a renewed imperial title in the west.

We have already seen how Charlemagne's concern with ecclesiastical questions began early in his reign and, if anything, increased markedly toward the end of the century. The 780s witnessed extensive ecclesiastical reforms in the capitularies (ordinances issued by Charlemagne). The first suppression of iconoclasm in Byzantium had taken place in the Council of Nicaea of 787, whose canons, agreed upon by Pope Hadrian II but badly translated into Latin, reached the Frankish kingdom and elicited a complex response written principally by Theodulf of Orleans but signed by Charlemagne. This response, the *Libri Carolini,* strongly criticized the iconodule position, challenged the right of Irene, as a woman, to rule the empire, and undercut the claims to universality of imperially sponsored church councils in Constantinople. At the same time, it reiterated the traditional orthodoxy of the Franks, Charlemagne's conversion of infidels, and the traditional ties between the Franks and the pope, the true authority for the determination of orthodox beliefs.

At the Council of Frankfurt in 794 the Carolingian king and high churchmen dealt with the heresy of Adoptionism, a dispute concerning the natures of Christ that reflected a rivalry between the Christian churchmen of Muslim Spain and those in the Christian kingdom to the north. Throughout the 790s the correspondence of Alcuin, Charlemagne's closest adviser during these years, reflected a great concern for the survival of orthodoxy and the dangers to orthodox belief posed by various movements in Spain and Italy. In 797 Charlemagne issued the *Capitulare Saxonicum,* a broadly conceived and diplomatic approach to a program for the peaceful introduction of Christianity among the Saxons and Slavs, a program very different from the earlier, more brutal policies of Christianization that the king had insisted upon.

From 795 on, another ecclesiastical crisis confronted the king. Pope Leo III, Hadrian's successor, encountered formidable opposition in Rome, was accused of crimes, and was ultimately kidnaped. Both Alcuin and Charlemagne were particularly concerned about the situation of the pope and the consequent welfare of the Church. These ecclesiastical concerns, which show a steady sharpening of Charlemagne's concept of his own role, as well as the influence of articulate advisers, occurred at the same time as the first successes of Carolingian educational reforms and the building of the palace at Aachen, which had been under way since 794 and reflected a new concept of a palace-capital for the king. Echoes of the difficulties of both Byzantium and Rome resound in a remarkable letter written by Alcuin to Charlemagne in 799, at the height of the crisis:

Until now, there have been three men of highest rank in the world. The first is the apostolic sublimity, governing from the throne of the blessed Peter, prince of the apostles, as his vicar. . . . The second is the imperial dignity and power of the other Rome [Constantinople]. . . . The third is the royal dignity which by the dispensation of our Lord Jesus Christ is conferred upon you as the governor of the Christian people.

After remarking upon the present weakness of the papacy and the crimes of the empress Irene, he concludes:

Charlemagne's Palace Chapel at Aachen. Borrowed from Roman imperial buildings at Ravenna, the design for this chapel (now a part of Aachen cathedral) suggests visually Charlemagne's heightened sense of Christian rulership. (Ann Münchow, Aachen)

The royal dignity is more excellent than the other dignities in power, more shining in wisdom, more sublime in rank. Now on you alone rests the tottering safety of the churches of Christ. It is for you to avenge crimes, to guide the erring, to console the sorrowing, and to raise up the good.

In Alcuin's view at least, Charlemagne, the just king, must now act alone and imperially.

Pope Leo was kidnaped in April of 799, but he escaped and made his way to Charlemagne at Paderborn. In November 800 Charlemagne arrived outside Rome and was greeted by the pope with the ceremonial procedures appropriate for an imperial entrance into the city. Early in December Leo cleared himself of all charges by an oath of purgation, and the ensuing synod that he held probably decided to crown Charlemagne emperor, possibly at the urging of Frankish clerics then present. On the evening of December 25, 800, following the third mass of Christmas, Pope Leo placed a crown on Charlemagne's head and declared him emperor of the Romans. The imperial *laudes* were chanted, and the pope prostrated himself in the *proskynesis* (ritual bow) before the emperor.

FURTHER READING

On England in the late seventh and eighth centuries, see S. J. Crawford, *Anglo-Saxon Influence on Western Christendom, 600–800* (reprint ed., Cambridge: Cambridge University Press, 1966); Wilhelm Levison, *England and the Continent in the Eighth Century* (Oxford: Clarendon Press, 1946); Peter Hunter Blair, *The World of Bede* (London: Secker & Warburg, 1970); and Paul Meyvaert, *Benedict, Gregory, Bede and Others* (London: Variorum, 1977).

On Carolingian Europe, see Donald Bullough, *The Age of Charlemagne* (New York: Putnam's, 1966); Jacques Boussard, *The Civilization of Charlemagne* (New York: McGraw-Hill, 1971); Heinrich Fichtenau, *The Carolingian Empire* (reprint ed., Toronto: University of Toronto Press, 1978); Pierre Riché, *Daily Life in the World of Charlemagne* (Philadelphia: University of Pennsylvania Press, 1978); H. R. Loyn and John Percival, *The Reign of Charlemagne* (New York: St. Martin's, 1976); F. L. Ganshof, *The Carolingians and the Frankish Monarchy* (Ithaca, N.Y.: Cornell University Press, 1971); Louis Halphen, *Charlemagne and the Carolingian Empire* (Amsterdam: North Holland Publishing Co., 1977).

9
Europe Emerges

THE FRAGMENTS OF EMPIRE AND THE NEW INVADERS

Charlemagne's triumphs did not guarantee political or military stability to the Franks and the other subject peoples of his empire, nor was Charlemagne under any delusion that they would. Toward the end of his life he is said to have asked ''whether we are truly Christians.'' Throughout his last years he faced the reality that the imperial title (and the imperial idea he shared with Alcuin) was the concept of a small aristocratic and ecclesiastical elite close to Charlemagne personally. Most of Charlemagne's other subjects, including the rest of the aristocracy and clergy, expected a more traditional Frankish monarchy and society. Louis the Pious (814–40), Charlemagne's son and successor, faced this difficulty, plus the new invasions that the Frankish armies were less able to resist.

Charlemagne handed the imperial crown personally to Louis, and not until a few years later did Louis permit Pope Gregory IV to anoint him as Leo III had anointed Charlemagne. But Louis's independence, native intelligence, and unquestioned devotion to the responsibilities of being a Christian emperor were offset by problems his father had never had to face. The costs of war rose, and there were fewer clear-cut victories. The Frankish armies were far better on offense, when they could plan long campaigns, than on defense, when they might be called unpredictably to different parts of the empire.

113

Finally, Louis faced the problem of dividing his empire among several sons. Civil wars clouded the last years of Louis's reign. After his death in 840 further fighting among his sons, Louis, Lothair, and Charles, led to the Treaty of Verdun of 843, when three kingdoms were cut from the old Frankish kingdom. These divisions began the fragmentation of the empire. Of Louis's three sons, Charles the Bald (d. 877) received the western part of Louis's territories, which became the kingdom of West Francia. Louis the German (d. 876) received the eastern portion, the kingdom of East Francia. Lothair (d. 855) received the central portion, the "Middle Kingdom," extending from Rome to the North Sea, as well as the imperial title. But the division of the empire according to the laws of inheritance meant that these kingdoms too could be subdivided among the surviving sons of their own rulers.

In the years that followed the Treaty of Verdun a strong new sense of regional loyalties displaced the idea of central royal authority. The grandsons and great-grandsons of Charlemagne surrounded themselves with local nobles in their little kingdoms. Sometimes, as in Aquitaine and Bavaria, old ethnic memories contributed to this sense of localism. Because the new kings were dependent upon their local nobility, noble families increased their power, often by combining lands received from the kings with lands they owned privately, as had the wealthy Merovingian families two centuries before. In this way they laid the base for large territorial principalities. The title "Emperor of the Romans" usually went to the strongest of these kings or, failing strength, to the one who seemed most likely to protect central Italy.

With the deposition and death of Charles the Fat in 888, the disintegration of the late Carolingian kingdoms proceeded swiftly. Non-Carolingians assumed crowns in West Francia and Provence. The imperial title itself was assumed by non-Carolingian warlords in Italy. In 911 the last Carolingian king of East Francia died, and the local dukes elected one of their own number, Conrad of Franconia, as king. In 987 the last Carolingian king of West Francia was deposed, and a non-Carolingian, Hugh Capet, was elected ruler of the shrunken kingdom in his place. Although the later kingdoms of Germany and France did not yet exist, their origins lie in the disintegration of the Carolingian monarchy in the late ninth and tenth centuries.

The disintegration of the empire and the little kingdoms of East and West Francia meant that the local nobility grew stronger at the expense of the king. During the ninth and tenth centuries the nobility grew stronger still, as a new wave of invasions pierced the once secure Carolingian world. During the late eighth and ninth centuries Muslim sea power had grown considerably stronger, and from bases in North Africa, Spain, and southern Gaul Muslim raiders penetrated most of the southern coasts of Europe, reaching even the passes of the Alps. By 900 Sicily had fallen to the raiders and most of the Carolingian defenses in northern Spain were in ruins.

In eastern Europe another people, the Magyars, proved more deadly than even the Muslim raiders of the Mediterranean. The Magyars were a Finno-Ugrian people from western Asia (their later name, Hungarians, derived from the name of one group of them, the Onogurs). In 896 the Byzantine Empire urged the Magyars to attack the Bulgars. But the Bulgars invited another Asiatic people, the Pechenegs, to attack the Magyars, and the latter fled west into central Europe, established themselves in the Carpathian basin, and launched lightning cavalry raids into Germany, France, and Italy. Between 898 and 920 Magyar war bands descended into Italy, Burgundy, eastern France, and especially Germany. Magyar warlords dominated their people until the end of the tenth century, when the Arpad dynasty began to establish its own superiority, con-

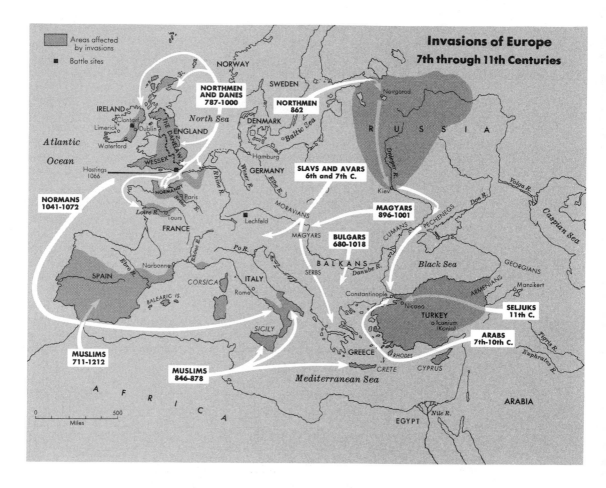

verted to Christianity, and began to stabilize the kingdom of Hungary. The raids of Muslims and Magyars hastened the political disintegration of ninth- and tenth-century western Europe. The raids of the Vikings nearly completed the process.

THE VIKINGS

The third and ultimately the most influential group of invaders were the Vikings, bands of Scandinavian warriors who sailed south in their long wooden ships in the summer, looted and pillaged freely along the coasts and river valleys of western Europe, and sailed home in the autumn. Scandinavian traders and fighters had been known in eighth-century Europe and Asia, but in the ninth century their raids became more frequent. Their superbly built ships were not only the finest oceangoing vessels of the age, but their shallow draft allowed them to sail far up the western European rivers, attacking Rouen and Paris on the Seine and Trier on the Rhine, as well as the Frisian ports of Quentovic and Duurstede. The Viking dragon ships, carrying 50 to 100 men and propelled by a single great sail and banks of oars, devastated the European seaboard. They ravaged undefended ecclesiastical lands, defeated the small armies that local lords and kings sent against them, and sacked the little towns that lay in their path.

The weakness of kings' resistance to these raids gave plenty of opportunities to powerful local lords to protect weaker people from the Vikings and, in return, take over several of the functions of governance that had once been only the king's to give. In many cases, what the Vikings left, or never even touched, also fell into the hands of powerful warlords, including ecclesiastical property. This secondary effect of the Viking, Magyar, and Arab raids should not be overlooked. Carolingian Europe was defenseless, but this situation did not exclude opportunities for strong and ruthless warriors to increase their own power at the expense of both the victims of the Viking raids and their own neighbors.

The paths of Scandinavian expansion were many. Norwegians moved chiefly into Ireland and western England. Swedes moved into the eastern Baltic and across northwestern Russia to Lake Ladoga, then down the great north–south river systems of Russia to Novgorod and Kiev, trading and raiding alike, until they came into contact not only with Byzantium across the Black Sea but with Arab merchants on the Volga and the Sea of Azov. The Danes attacked eastern England, Frisia, and the Rhineland and then penetrated upriver into the heart of the old kingdom of Francia itself.

By the middle of the ninth century, the patterns of raiding had changed. Groups of Scandinavians established winter quarters in Europe, and the raiding parties grew larger. They turned, in fact, into expeditionary armies seeking land to take and settle. By the 850s there were Norse settlements in Ireland, and in 865 the famous Great Army landed in England and stayed. By 878 a substantial part of northeastern England had fallen under Danish rule; it was known for centuries afterward as the Danelaw. English kings raised large sums of money by taxation to offer to the Danes as tribute. The Danegeld, as this money was called, played an important role in later English royal finances.

The Vikings clearly knew something about the lands they raided and captured. There is strong evidence that they had advance intelligence on defenses and military preparations and raided accordingly. By the tenth century they had begun to settle on the Continent as well as in the British Isles. In 911 the king of West Francia, Charles the Simple, formally ceded to one Viking leader, Rolf, some land at the mouth of the Seine. Under Rolf and his successors, this territory was greatly expanded to become the eleventh-century Duchy of Normandy. The Vikings did not confine themselves to Britain and the Continent, however. Between 860 and 865 they sailed westward across the North Atlantic, and in 874 they settled Iceland. Not only did the strong egalitarian sensibility of the Icelandic settlers survive the settlement, but their privately owned farms, their great seamanship, and their public assembly laid the foundations for the oldest democratic community in western Europe. In 984 Erik, an exile from Iceland, discovered the island of Greenland, and small settlements sprang up there as well. In 1000 Erik's son Leif sailed even farther west and made a landfall at a place he called Vinland, which is certainly none other than North America. By the end of the tenth century, western Europe had been subjected not only to the ravages of Viking raids but also to the pressure of Viking settlements. It had received a new maritime vocabulary and been drawn closer to the Atlantic than ever before, and it had been expanded enormously by the wide-ranging voyages of the Vikings.

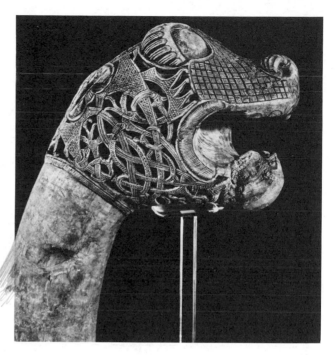

The Oseberg Dragon Head. Viking artistic skills are strikingly evident in this dragon's head on a cart found in the Oseberg ship burial. (Copyright University Museum of National Antiquities, Oslo, Norway)

From the mid ninth century on, royal dynasties in Denmark, Norway, and Sweden began to increase the authority and control of the king over the marauding bands of pirates and raiders. Some Viking leaders fled to England, the Continent, or Iceland rather than live under royal rule. With the expansion of royal authority and the Christianizing of the Scandinavian kings in the late tenth century, the great age of Viking expansion came to an end. By the twelfth and thirteenth centuries the early tales of the Viking period, particularly of Iceland, had begun to be worked into heroic tales called sagas, the last genuine European epics. Preserving their rough history in this form, the Scandinavians joined the Magyars as the newest peoples on the edge of Christian Europe.

KINGS AND WARLORDS

The most successful defenders of western Europe in the tenth century were the kings of England and Germany on the one hand, and the tough warlords of West Francia who protected their little territories with ruthlessness and skill on the other. Late Carolingian-style monarchs and illiterate warriors, kings, and lords survived with the help of churchmen and the labor of peasants, and in their age the history of Europe dissolves into the histories of two successful monarchies and several hundred territorial principalities. In these territories were the beginnings of recovery. Old landholding systems, archaic social forms, and much custom had been swept away by the shock of the invasions. The land was fertile, however, and the little populations of warriors and peasants, tied to the land more closely than ever but secure once more, began to increase. Lords, once the greatest military threats to their rule had been removed, began to explore ways to legitimize their titles and powers. Churchmen sought ways of insuring peace in a society that had become more warlike than ever before.

The tenth century has long rivaled the seventh for the title of the "darkest" of the "Dark Ages," but recently historians working with very different kinds of sources have changed the conventional picture of this period. The economic historian Robert Lopez, basing his case upon the signs of steady population growth and new economic developments, even postulated a tenth-century renaissance. In a book dealing chiefly with political culture, Geoffrey Barraclough noted:

The ninth and tenth centuries were a formative period in European history, every bit as much as the better known periods which preceded and succeeded them, and it was out of the anarchy and tribulation which men and women of that generation suffered that a new Europe took shape.[1]

The tide of invasion began to turn in Anglo-Saxon England with the victory of Alfred the Great (871–99) over a large Danish army in 879. Alfred, originally the king of Wessex only, proceeded to consolidate his authority in other English kingdoms, and his tenth-century descendants proved to be strong, able monarchs. By the reign of Edgar (959–75) the English monarchy was the most highly developed in Europe. The kings and the nobility cooperated, and the old units of local government, the hundreds and shires, provided a broad base of support. The English church, under the leadership of a remarkable group of prelates, notably Saint Dunstan of Canterbury (909–88) and Aethelwold of Winchester (963–84), patronized learning and the arts and placed their skills at the service of the monarchy. During the tenth century the Old English language, the most precocious vernacular language in Europe, experienced its greatest age. Epic and lyric poems, sermons and scriptural commentaries, and the first vernacular national history—the *Anglo-Saxon Chronicle*—were produced, as were compilations of royal laws and even translations from such Latin writers as Gregory the Great and Boethius.

But the strength of England depended upon the cooperation of the kings and the nobility, and continuing Scandinavian threats weakened that cooperation at the end of the tenth century. Ethelred II, the "Ill-Counseled" (987–1016), lost his nobles' loyalty when he proved incapable of resisting the renewed Danish threat. He was succeeded by Cnut, king of Denmark. Cnut, however, was not a Viking: he continued the English-style monarchy and preserved English laws, language, and other institutions. When Cnut's line died out in 1042, Edward the Confessor (1042–66), the last surviving son of Ethelred II, became king. But Edward's reign did not stabilize the relations between king and nobles, and it attracted the attention of still other peoples to the English scene.

The old kingdom of East Francia faced similar problems in the early tenth century. This part of the Frankish empire had been conquered most recently, and its native peoples had been placed under Carolingian officials called dukes. As we have seen, with the death of the last Carolingian ruler in 911 the surviving dukes—of the Saxons, Bavarians, Lotharingians, Thuringians, Franconians, and Swabians—elected one of their own number, Conrad of Franconia, as king in 911. Conrad's short reign was unsuccessful, however, and in 918 Henry the Fowler, duke of Saxony (918–36), was elected to

---

[1] Geoffrey Barraclough, *The Crucible of Europe* (Berkeley and Los Angeles: The University of California Press, 1976), p. 7.

succeed him. The Saxon dynasty, which lasted from Henry I to Otto III (983–1002) achieved considerable success, but it never molded Germany into the compact kingdom that England became.

The Saxon kings had to defend a very large kingdom against both outside invaders and local rebellions, and they had to create a new kind of legitimacy, since they were not Carolingians. The Saxon kings faced other problems: they could not, unlike the Carolingians, reward their local followers with lands and titles throughout a large kingdom, as Charlemagne had; they were not individually wealthy enough to be able to partition the kingdom among their sons; much of the Saxon nobility that might have aided the kings in other parts of Germany could not be spared from the wars with the Slavic peoples on the eastern border of Saxony. Moreover, people did not forget that the Saxon kings had once been dukes themselves. Their only resources for ruling all of East Francia were lands and incomes they owned personally as dukes. Lacking regular sources of men and money, the Saxon kings turned to the church of East Francia, and that institution became one of their most important sources of support. To maintain themselves, therefore, the Saxon dynasty had to either acquire other duchies or control appointments to high church offices. Usually they tried to do both. The vast size of their kingdom, and their widely scattered possessions throughout it, meant that they spent most of their lives in the saddle. Their only means of imposing their rulership was to travel constantly throughout East Francia, being seen by their subjects, giving judgments, bestowing rewards and punishments as best they could, and trying to stem the strong sense of independence, particularism, local rivalries, and resistance to their rule.

The most successful Saxon king was Otto I (936–73). In 955 on the River Lech Otto led an army that annihilated a large force of Magyar invaders, thus turning the tide in favor of East Francia. In later successful campaigns against pagan Slavic peoples Otto founded a chain of missionary bishoprics that played an important role in Christianizing the pagan Slavic and Scandinavian peoples. Otto I also intervened in Italy, and his immense personal prestige led to his coronation as emperor of the Romans in 962 by Pope John XII. For the remainder of his own reign and those of his son Otto II (973–83) and grandson Otto III (983–1002), the Saxon kings faced the difficulties of managing the large and difficult-to-control kingdom of Germany as well as the smaller but historically very different kingdom of Italy.

Unlike the kings of England and East Francia, the kingdom of West Francia had shrunk considerably by the late tenth century. The early Capetian kings of West Francia directly ruled only a small territory surrounding Paris. Although their titles made them the nominal lords of the powerful territorial princes whose lands surrounded theirs (and in some cases were far larger), they possessed no effective control over the warlords of their kingdom. These men were the real powers in West Francia. The nature of their lordship reached back into the Roman and Germanic past, but it took on new significance in the ninth and tenth centuries. Many powerful Roman landowners had controlled large armed followings dependent upon them. In early Germanic society powerful and popular war leaders were surrounded by their *comitatus*—a group of young fighting men who had taken an oath to follow them into battle, share the spoils of victory, and share death, too, if they lost. To return from a battle in which the lord of the *comitatus* was slain shamed the warrior forever. The rise of royal power among the Franks in the eighth and early ninth centuries had prevented the independent survival of such private followings. But the emergencies of the late ninth and tenth centuries offered a new opportunity for the warlord to surround himself with military followers and acquire new independence, borrow the legitimacy of a royal title such as count, and make service to him attractive by virtue of the prestige of his noble blood.

Although the idea of dependence and service had originally been repugnant to free Germanic warriors, the wealth, glory, and prestige derived from serving a Carolingian king or other powerful lord slowly overcame such cultural reluctance. The very terms that came to designate the institutions of lordship—*dominus* (lord) and *vassus* (vassal)—reflect the humble roots of the bond between fighting men. The English word "lord," for example, derives from the Old English term *hlaford*, "the giver of the loaf," or provider of food. *Vassus* is a Latinization of an old Celtic word meaning "boy" or "menial servant." One psychological root of lordship and vassalage, then, is reflected in the acceptance by members of relatively high social status of a terminology that once designated functions of a very low social standing. Even in Carolingian royal household service, performed by men of very high social status indeed, such terms as constable, marshal, and seneschal all derived from older Latin and Germanic words designating menial domestic service. The language of lordship described an old domestic relationship between superiors and inferiors that rose in social esteem and increased in acceptability as it became a specialized description of relationships among powerful persons.

The strongest and sometimes the only bond between lord and follower was the oath of loyalty. The vassal commended himself to the lord by offering acts of homage (becoming the *homme,* or man, of the lord) and later fealty (from the Latin *fides,* meaning faith or loyalty). Upon receiving homage the lord swore to protect the vassal and be loyal to him in turn. The lord might signal his favor by conferring a conditional gift of land, money, or rights upon the vassal. Such a gift was called a *beneficium* ("good deed" or "benefice") or a *fief.* In theory, this mutual assertion of personal loyalty could be breached by either party, if either thought that the other did not fulfill his promises.

Upon the vassal's death or breaking of faith, his benefice returned to the lord, who might grant it to another vassal. On the lord's death, the vassal had to become the vassal of the lord's successor. Increasingly, pressure from vassals led to the possibility of the vassal's son (or, in some cases, daughter) succeeding the vassal in the benefice. The complex bonds of these personal relationships were often confusing, especially when land received as benefice was confused with land held privately, or when lands held from two different lords became the object of mixed loyalties.

Originally, the chief value of a vassal was his military ability. As vassal of a lord (and perhaps as the domestic lord of a large household himself), he was able to maintain the expensive equipment and specialized training of a mounted warrior and to take the time to fight in his lord's wars. Socially, lords and vassals constituted the class of fighting men that came to dominate the composition of the European nobility in the eleventh and twelfth centuries. The turbulent character of these warlords led churchmen to try to impose the sanctions of morality upon their relationships with each other, and the oath of lord and vassal was surrounded by liturgical rites.

The growth of the ninth- and tenth-century nobility and of territorial principalities is as much a chapter in the history of European communities as a segment of the history of European invasions and post-Carolingian "anarchy." In imposing their own rule the small and great lords, who controlled lands ranging from tiny single castles in Castile to the great Duchy of Saxony, made themselves responsible for the keeping of the peace, the privileges of diverse communities, and the safety of the Church. In return they received, sometimes grudgingly, loyalty and prestige. They ruled the most manageable territories that the tenth and early eleventh centuries could create. They also patronized the beginnings of the agricultural revolution and the eleventh- and twelfth-century spiritual revolutions as well. Often enough, they were brutal, suspicious, abrupt, and ferocious. Yet they were also devout after their own fashion, efficient, and ambitious for their dynasty and their territories. Often possessing no family history, they had histories made up; lacking traditional legitimacy, they cultivated and patronized the monasteries and the holy men of the tenth century. Unlike the newly Christianized kings of Norway, Poland, and Hungary, they did not become saints. But they cultivated those saints they could find, and they did become pilgrims. William the Bastard succeeded to the dukedom of Normandy in 1035 because his father, Robert, had died on a pilgrimage to Jerusalem. Some lords went two or three times, and to Compostela and Rome as well as to Jerusalem. They ransacked land and labor alike for their fortresses, but they also gave away favorite hunting lodges to monks, allowed exceptional privileges to colonizing peasants, and sometimes entered the religious life themselves after a lifetime of looting and fighting. In practice they became successful warlords; in theory they retained spiritual horizons and ideas of loyalty to higher powers that held the germ of wider social bonds.

THE FLOWERING OF BYZANTINE CIVILIZATION

The Byzantine Empire was also troubled by invasions and internal revolts in the ninth century, as well as divided by the iconoclastic controversy. But it survived these threats and reached its greatest development from 843 to 1025, the golden age of Byzantine civilization. The reign of the emperor Theophilus (829–42) witnessed the beginnings of Byzantine recovery. But the iconoclastic controversy and the Photian Schism later in the ninth century also revealed how deep the divisions were between Greek and Latin Christendom. The revival of Byzantium did not herald a restoration of harmonious relations between Greek east and Latin west. Indeed, the problem of Christianizing the still pagan Slavic and Balkan peoples of eastern Europe made the question of Greek and Latin spheres of religious influence even stronger than it had been in the days of Charlemagne.

Under Theophilus's son and successor, Michael III (842–67), iconoclasm was abolished and Michael's great minister Bardas succeeded in mobilizing the resources of the empire and introducing remarkable reforms in secular education, ecclesiastical life, the military, and the peasant economy. The university at Constantinople came under the direction of Bardas himself, and under his great contemporary, Patriarch Photios (858–67, 877–85), a new energy was given to religious studies as well. Such men as Bardas, Photios, Leo the Mathematician, and the linguist and missionary Saint Constantine (Cyril) led an intellectual renaissance easily comparable in importance and influence to the military and social reforms of the imperial administration.

The Byzantine revival of the 860s was not, however, without its darker side. From the reign of Irene to that of Basil I (867–86) ecclesiastical problems became hopelessly intermingled with politics. The end of the iconoclast controversy in 843 did not end the difficulties within the Greek church nor did it lead to improved relations with the Latin church. Internal struggles over the office of patriarch of Constantinople at the accession of Photios in 858 led to a Byzantine faction of the clergy appealing to Pope Nicholas I (858–67), a brilliant and ambitious man. The problem of Photios and a letter from the khan of the Bulgars, Boris, in 864, asking the pope about Rome's view of certain liturgical and theological problems, led to a clash between pope and patriarch. In the course of the dispute Photios accused the pope of heresy, on the ground that the Latin church had erred in making the Nicene Creed state that the Holy Spirit proceeded from the Father *and the Son* rather than from God the Father alone—an issue that still divides Greek Orthodox and Roman communions. The Photian Schism, as the division between pope and patriarch is known, shows the strains in the relationship between the eastern and western branches of the Church and the increasing tendency of both pope and patriarch to make claims that were very close to universal authority.

The ecclesiastical difficulties of the 860s were rivaled by new military crises. In 860 a fleet from Kiev attacked Constantinople but was repulsed—the first hostile contact between Byzantium and the society out of which the first Russian principality grew. Under the powerful khan Symeon (893–927) a new Bulgar attack on the empire was launched, and between 911 and 925 the Bulgar threat loomed very large on the Byzantine horizon. The Arab domination of the eastern Mediterranean, their occupation of Sicily, their landholds in south Italy, and their control of the island of Crete also posed a threat to Byzantium. In 895 Byzantine diplomacy introduced the Magyars to the west, inviting them to attack the Bulgars from the rear. As we have seen, however, Symeon of Bulgaria induced the Pechenegs to attack the Magyars, and in their flight the Magyars drove not south toward Bulgaria but west toward Moravia. Between 896 and 909 the Magyar hordes destroyed the Great Moravian Empire and settled on the plains of Transylvania, from which they proceeded to raid Germany, Italy, and Poland. The Pechenegs moved west to take the place that the Magyars had vacated. In 904 Arab raiders sacked Thessalonica, the second city of the empire, and as the tenth century opened, Byzantium appeared to be threatened by overwhelming external enemies and severe internal religious and social dissent.

Byzantine civilization, however, proved extraordinarily resilient. The new Macedonian imperial dynasty, led by Leo VI (886–912), Constantine VII Porphyrogenitus (913–59), and Basil II (976–1025), succeeded in reducing the power of the empire's external enemies and restoring internal stability to the troubled cities and provinces.

The foundation of new *themes,* the expansion of missionary activity and diplomacy, the collaboration of the patriarchs of Constantinople with the emperors, and the great patrician civil servants of the ninth and tenth centuries constituted the foundations of Byzantine survival and triumph. Palace revolutions, usurpations of the throne, and military blunders in the face of new enemies failed to undo the work begun in the mid ninth century. The administrative and legal genius of Leo VI and Constantine VII was augmented by skillful generals, several of whom even usurped imperial rank temporarily yet at the same time strengthened the defenses of the empire. Under the first of these, Romanus I Lecapenus (920–44), the threat of the Bulgarian ruler Symeon was finally turned back. In 911 and 945 trading treaties were signed with the rulers of Kiev. During the last years of Romanus's reign Byzantine forces defeated the Bulgars, the Muslim forces from Syria, and the attacks of the Kievans and participated in operations in South Italy and even in southern France against the Arab raiders there. Romanus also resisted the growing powers of the landed aristocracy and legislated in favor of the farmer-soldiers, the settlers of the *themes,* on whom most of the Byzantine military success had long rested. Under Basil II the final period of Byzantine triumph was ushered in with the conversion to Christianity of Vladimir, prince of Kiev, in 989, and the final war to suppress Bulgaria, which took place between 986 and 1019.

The successful defense of the empire and, after the first quarter of the tenth century, the rapid and virtually unopposed expansion of its power to the Euphrates, Crete, South

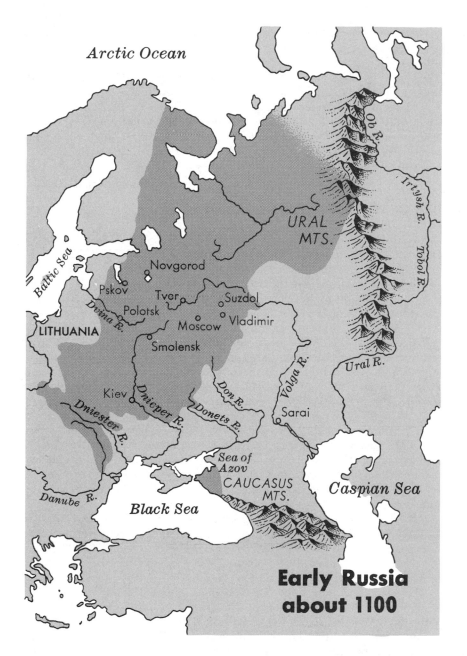

Arctic Ocean

URAL MTS.

Ob R.

Irtysh R.

Tobol R.

Novgorod

Pskov

Tver

Polotsk

Suzdol

Vladimir

Baltic Sea

Dvina R.

LITHUANIA

Moscow

Smolensk

Volga R.

Ural R.

Kiev

Dnieper R.

Don R.

Donets R.

Sarai

Dniester R.

Danube R.

Sea of Azov

CAUCASUS MTS.

Caspian Sea

Black Sea

Early Russia about 1100

Italy, Hungary, and Russia reveals both the great strength and the wisdom of its ninth- and tenth-century rulers. A series of successful, learned, and able emperors, generals, churchmen, and scholars, an ecclesiastical administration that skillfully included missionary activity alongside diplomatic negotiations, and a talented civil service of urban aristocrats constituted the resources of imperial policy. The basis of that strength consisted of the farmer-soldiers of the *themes,* the busy commercial activities in the cities, and the most successful mobilization of state resources since the fourth-century Roman Empire in the west.

Besides its military, political, and economic survival Byzantium continued its renaissance of scholarship and literary activity, its remarkable innovations in the liturgy and in religious art and music, and its creation of a style of urban life that astonished ally and enemy alike. From Hagia Sophia and the imperial palace, the influence of Constantinople extended throughout the empire and into the lands beyond it. The city became as much a legend to the traders and warriors of northern Russia as to those of eastern Persia and North Africa.

THE GARDEN OF ISLAM AND THE WORLD OF WAR

The revolution that overthrew the Umayyad dynasty and brought the Abbasids to the caliphate in 751 resulted in the increasingly autocratic character of the caliphate, a greater degree of parity between Arabs and non-Arab Muslims, and a period of considerable social and economic growth in the Islamic world. The eighth, ninth, and tenth centuries were a period of cultural development as well. Although during this period the single caliphate broke up into separate kingdoms, a distinctive Islamic civilization emerged to influence the lives of all who lived under it. The *Qu'ran* recognized two kinds of world: *Dar-al-Islam,* the world of Islam, and *Dar-al-harb,* the non-Islamic world, the world of war. Muslims referred to Persia as "a garden protected by our spears." The important changes within the Muslim world in the ninth, tenth, and eleventh centuries and the relations between the garden of Islam and the world of war outside it suggest that the changes in western Europe and the Byzantine Empire in the tenth century were not the only important changes in the lands around the old Mediterranean world.

The immense wealth controlled by the Abbasids at first transformed the Islamic world. The rich agricultural areas of North Africa, Spain, and the Tigris and Euphrates valleys produced food supplies in abundance, and speculation in foodstuffs was forbidden. The conquests brought under Islamic control rich resources in precious metals and jewels, as well as productive copper and iron mines. Damascus steel remained prized for weapon making for centuries. The public works of the Abbasids produced irrigation projects and the draining of swamps. Domestically produced textiles, particularly linen and cotton, contributed to trade, and the acquisition of papermaking skills from captured Chinese papermakers around 751 led to the extensive use of paper throughout the Islamic world; by 900 it had reached even Spain. Paper provided material not only for government use but for commercial and literary purposes as well.

Baghdad grew more important as both an imperial capital and a center of a vast trading network. It controlled not only local imports but a growing reexport trade connecting the edges of the Islamic world with each other and with the most remote corners of Asia and Europe. Muslim ships plied the Indian Ocean regularly and even entered the China Sea, and developed lucrative trading relationships with the Khazars and Bulgars. Muslim coins have been found along the shores of the Baltic, and northern trade goods, particularly furs and amber, moved south to the Muslim world. Muslim traders reached sub-Saharan Africa.

The scale of trade and the high degree of government interest in it, the wide variety of rates of exchange and prices of precious metals, and the problems of commercial relations throughout a vast community accelerated the development of commercial institutions such as banking and the branching out of trading families to different parts of the Islamic world. It has often been noted that by the ninth century a check drawn on a bank in Baghdad could be cashed in Morocco. The double revolution of paper record-keeping and long-range commercial and financial transactions had a great impact upon the upper levels of Islamic society. Above even the traders and bankers, however, was the aristocratic group of families close to the caliphs. These families combined personal wealth and official government appointments to make themselves the most affluent and powerful ruling class in the world.

The growth of wealth and governmental activity, coupled with the immense size and resources of the markets inside and outside the Islamic world, made the civilization of Islam more cosmopolitan and diverse than it had ever been. Arabic-speaking Muslims were generally accepted everywhere, whether they were ethnically Arab or not. The *Qu'ran* and the Islamic law, the *Shari'a,* contributed further to the homogeneity of Islamic society from India to Spain.

The economic, political, and social changes in the eighth and ninth centuries were accompanied by important intellectual changes. The Arabic language was slowly expanded and adapted to the rich intellectual and religious legacies of Persia, the eastern Roman Empire, Egypt, Palestine, and Spain. Arabic, originally the language of an ethnic conquering elite and of a religious faith, slowly became the chief cultural medium of expression of the southern Mediterranean and Near Eastern worlds. Even such non-Semitic languages as Persian and Turkish came to be written in Arabic script and to borrow many Arabic terms.

Although the *Qu'ran* condemned the art of poetry, pre-Islamic Arabian poetry survived and a rich rhetorical and poetic culture grew up, not only among the ethnic Arabs but in Persia and elsewhere in the Islamic world. The study of the *Qu'ran* became a starting point for the study of law, history, and theology. Translations from Greek and Syriac of older scientific and philosophical works also contributed to the vigor of Islamic thought. The precocious development of Islamic scientific and philosophical literature was one of the most striking intellectual achievements in the world in the ninth and tenth centuries. The Latin west had begun to draw heavily from it by the twelfth century. Under the caliph Ma'mun (813–33) a school of translators was formally established, and later in the century the works of Aristotle were translated into Arabic. The result was several centuries of brilliant and original commentary, one of the greatest philosophical legacies of all time.

The rich and varied culture of the Muslim world was not, however, exempt from the stresses of rapid expansion and dramatic social and cultural change. The increasingly autocratic character of the caliphate and the increasing luxury of the caliph's court generated hostility on the edges of the Muslim world and financial weakness at the center. In the ninth century the caliphs took to awarding anticipated revenues to favorites and making the favorites governors general of provinces. In this way the power of the caliphs slowly dissipated and the actual rule of territories fell under powerful local families. The military commanders also increased their power at the expense of the caliphs. In 945 one such military dynasty assumed control of the caliph. After that date the caliph became a figurehead while the real power in the Islamic world was localized.

The weakening of the caliphs was not the only important political problem the Muslims faced. The social and economic changes generated a number of revolutionary movements throughout the eighth and ninth centuries. All of these were primarily religious in character, since the *Qu'ran* was a code of public and private conduct as well as of religious belief. Indeed, the *Qu'ran* has been appealed to by Muslim revolutionary movements from the eighth century to the present day. Not only did slave and peasant revolts plague the Islamic world, but sectarianism also became a problem in the ninth century, especially in the rise of the radical and esoteric Ismaili movement. Such movements formed the background for the separatist states that appeared to challenge the unique authority of the caliph in the tenth century. By the end of that century the Muslim world and civilization had developed on a vast scale, and the faith of Islam and the homogeneous Arabic culture it carried with it became the unifying forces in a world that was in the process of political and economic fragmentation.

FURTHER READING

For the late ninth and tenth centuries, see Geoffrey Barraclough, *The Crucible of Europe* (Berkeley and Los Angeles: University of California Press, 1976); Eleanor Shipley Duckett, *Death and Life in the Tenth Century* (Ann Arbor: University of Michigan Press, 1971); and David C. Douglas, *The Norman Achievement, 1050–1100* (Berkeley and Los Angeles: University of California Press, 1970).

PART

IV

CHRISTENDOM:
AUTHORITY AND ENTERPRISE,
950–1150

10
Material Civilization

THE POPULATION GROWTH OF MEDIEVAL EUROPE

Between Scandinavia and Spain, Ireland and Kiev, late-tenth-century Europe probably numbered around 38 million people, most of them living in irregularly spaced, isolated, densely populated rural communities. Most of these communities lacked the resources to make their agriculture more efficient, and they required extensive cultivated land to feed a very small number of people. By the mid fourteenth century the population of Europe stood at around 75 million, before it was decimated by the wave of drought, famine, and plague from which it did not fully recover until the seventeenth century. The population of mid-fourteenth-century Europe cultivated far more land than that of tenth-century Europe, and it did so far more efficiently. The food surplus helped the population to grow, to break the old Carolingian patterns of settlement, to undertake the cultivation of new lands, and to build much larger cities. Thus, the population growth between the tenth and the fourteenth centuries transformed the way of life of late Carolingian Europe and rearranged the demographic and economic map of western Europe.

The population growth after the tenth century did not occur at the same rate all over Europe. A glance at an approximate population table for different areas of Europe in the years 1000, 1300, and 1500 reveals two striking features of this population growth: first, the population grew most rapidly between 1000 and 1300; Second, the repopulation after the disasters of the mid to late fourteenth century occurred even more rapidly.

Approximate Population of European Regions in Millions, 1000–1500

	1000	1300	1500
Balkans	5	6	6.5
Low Countries	1	5	2
British Isles	2	5	5
Danube Region	—	—	6
France	5	15	15
Germany	3	11	13
Italy	5	10	11
Poland	2	3	3
Russia	6	8	18
Scandinavia	1	2	2.5
Spain/Portugal	7	9	7
Switzerland	—	0.8	0.8

Source: Adapted from J.C. Russell, *Late Ancient and Medieval Population* (Philadelphia: Transactions of the American Philosophical Society, 1958), p. 36.

These figures alone do not suggest the full importance of European population growth from 1000 to 1500. The leading demographic historian of the Middle Ages, J. C. Russell, notes that while the population of Europe was increasing from around 25 million in the sixth century to 38 million in the year 1000 the Islamic world was falling from about 22.5 million to approximately 12.5 million. This kind of contrast sets off Europe's population growth even more dramatically.

In traditional societies population growth may begin because fertility rates increase, mortality rates decrease, or both. But in order for a growth rate to continue, the amount of food available per person must remain the same or increase. For social diversification, significant numbers of people must be freed from the necessity of producing their own food. All three of these elements played a part in European population growth after the tenth century.

Although medieval people were fertile and prolific, infant mortality was high and many women died in childbirth or succumbed to related diseases shortly thereafter. In addition, mortality rates remained high for both sexes through early adolescence. Cemetery evidence indicates that in the age group 14–19 there were 114 females for every 100 males, a relatively small ratio. But whereas male mortality was greatest in the age group 40–59, female mortality was greatest between the ages of 20 and 39—the childbearing years. Realizing that statements of average life expectancy can be misleading, especially when they include the risks of infancy and early childhood, we can nevertheless note that the life expectancy of males in England around 1300 was about 39 years. There were people who lived much longer; we know by name a great many individuals who lived into their eighties and nineties and a few who reached 100.

There are other aspects of the demographic profile of medieval Europe. First, the clergy, a significant proportion of the population, was celibate and did not reproduce. Second, Europeans tended to marry later than other peoples, which reduced the childbearing years of a couple. Third, religious and social customs in marriage reduced the absolute childbearing period even further. In general, the population of Europe remained far younger in the aggregate than that of the modern world. In 1980 about 25 percent of the population was under 14 years of age. In the thirteenth century this figure was as much as 40 percent. In short, Europe between 1000 and 1300 still faced considerable obstacles to economic development based on population growth.

The high proportion of the young meant that a smaller percentage of the population was economically productive. On the other hand, it meant that the young had to be included in the work force early. The birthrate tended to stay just slightly ahead of the mortality rate, and people tended to remain in the work force late in life. If too many people in a society grew too old to work, the burden on the work force increased because it had to support both youth and age.

The second element in medieval population growth, the availability of food per capita, will be discussed in the next section of this chapter. Here it may be noted that food production did, in fact, increase considerably, that new lands were brought under cultivation, and that the generally mild European climate during the period 1000–1300 may well have improved agricultural conditions. So too did the ending of the tenth-century invasions and the return of security, perhaps the essential requirement of a peasant society.

The final element, the freeing of part of the enlarged population from the necessity of producing its own food, led to the possibility of social diversification, to the growth of the nobility and clerical orders, and to the expanding population of towns. It also permitted new settlements to grow up within the vast, largely empty lands of western and central Europe. Forests could be cut down, swamps drained, lands reclaimed even from the ocean (as occurred in the Netherlands). Scholars have estimated that by the end of the thirteenth century more land in Europe was under cultivation than at any time before or since. Specialized crops began to be grown, because people could depend upon markets to provide them with the food they did not grow themselves. The population expansion between the tenth and the fourteenth centuries is the basis for the development and articulation of medieval European civilization, from the specialization of agriculture to the diversification of the nobility, clergy, and urban centers and crafts.

THE AGRICULTURAL REVOLUTION

Agricultural communities were the basis of European society and the original centers of population growth. Essential to survival, trampled over by invaders and defenders, worked by serfs and free peasants, they altered the rhythm of county and kingdom alike by their success and failure. Their essential product was grain, which in the forms of bread, porridge, and ale constituted the primary diet of Europeans. The more land that was cleared and the better the cleared land was worked, the more grain was grown. The increased availability of grain sustained population growth, and slowly vegetable proteins, meat, and fish supplemented the grain diet. Improved methods of planting led to the introduction of vegetable proteins and soil-renewing crops at the spring planting. Markets traded in food as well as craft and luxury goods. Dairy and stock herds were sustained by increased grain production, and some regions were able to cultivate single crops, such as grapes, because other elements in their diet could be provided from elsewhere.

There was much work to be done, but from the tenth century on there was also a new kind of help. From this century date the earliest references to the new sources of nonhuman power and the new labor-saving devices that constitute such a distinctive feature of western European history from the seventh to the nineteenth century. By the sixth century there is evidence of the increased use of waterpower. At first used chiefly to turn mills, by the twelfth century it was employed in a remarkable variety of ways. The sixth-century volume of saints' lives by Gregory of Tours mentions one of the earliest examples of its use:

The Abbot Ursus [d.ca. 500] . . . had the idea of [diminishing] the labor [of his brethren] by establishing a mill in the bed of the river Indre. Fixing rows of stakes in the river, with heaps of great stones to make dams, he collected the water in a channel and used the current to make the wheel of the machine turn with great speed. By this means he diminished the monks' work and one brother could be delegated to this task.

The water mill had been used sparingly by the Romans. In the tenth century it began to be used more regularly for a variety of tasks.

As important as the wider use of the water mill was the revolution in the use of animal power for plowing. The development of the stirrup and the breeding of the great and expensive war-horses that appeared in Europe early in the eighth century represent another new power source. Less spectacular but ultimately more important were two further ways in which the horse was employed in society. Widespread use of the faster and more versatile horse in agriculture had been hampered under the Romans and in the early Middle Ages by the limitations on the weight a horse could pull, limitations imposed by the traditional system of harnessing. A tight collar around the horse's neck choked off the animal's air supply if too great a weight were attached to it. The great French historian Richard LeFebvre des Noettes discovered that a new system of harnessing horses had appeared during the tenth century. The new horse collar allowed the pressure points of the load to be placed on the horse's shoulders instead of the throat, which increased the pulling power of the animal. The horseshoe, too, appeared around this time. It complemented the increased pulling power of the horse by improving both footing and traction and by protecting the hooves against the damp, heavy clay soils of northern Europe. Thus, an animal of hitherto limited military and domestic use suddenly became the second great nonhuman power source available to Europeans. The third source of power was wind. By the end of the twelfth century windmills had appeared. The power revolution of the tenth through the twelfth centuries was the first major development of nonhuman sources of power since the domestication of oxen and the invention of the ship, and the most important before the discovery of steam power in the eighteenth century.

These new sources of power were soon put to work. By the twelfth century water mills and windmills were used in different phases of the process of cloth manufacture, and soon after they were turning saws and releasing triphammers. The horse and the ox were used in front of an equally important machine, the heavy plow. The plow of the Mediterranean and the Near East had been developed for the soils of that world—light, sandy soils that were easily broken and pulverized. The agricultural engineering of the ancient world was not concerned with plowing techniques, but with water engineering—the complicated business of keeping the dry soils moist, either through irrigation or planned flooding—and with terracing and supporting fragile hillside fields. But the Mediterranean scratch plow proved barely effective against the heavy, poorly draining clay soils north of the Alps. Although literary references suggest that the sixth century witnessed the appearance of a new kind of heavy plow, archaeological research indicates that it may have been invented even earlier. This new plow, called *carruca* by the sources (as opposed to the Mediterranean *aratrum*), appears to have begun to circulate widely after the ninth century.

Several features of the new plow bear closer examination, because they helped transform social as well as mechanical relationships. The new plow consisted of three parts: the coulter cut the sod, the plowshare lifted and turned the earth to a considerable depth, and the mouldboard shaped the turned earth into a furrow. These three parts, in other words, cut the earth, raised important soil elements to the surface, and provided for essential drainage. In order to operate efficiently, the new plow required considerably greater power than the older plow; not one or two oxen or horses but six or eight were needed to pull its load. The thinness of early medieval population and the unlikelihood that a single peasant would possess eight oxen suggest that a pooling of plow teams was necessary. Second, the ideal way to plow a field was to move in a straight line as far as the pitch of the field would permit. The long narrow fields of the world of the heavy plow contrasted sharply with the square fields cultivated by the cross-plowing techniques utilized with the older scratch plow. Thus, the heavy plow introduced a degree of peasant cooperation, a redesigning of fields, and an increase in labor productivity that made faster headway in lands hitherto unsettled or vacated rather than in lands crowded with peasants who had divided their fields in traditional ways. The new plow required a long field (measures of field lengths varied greatly), a headland at the end to permit the plow to make its great turn, and a layout of fields that saved time for peasants going to and from work.

The old and new systems of plowing operated on land whose use had been developed over centuries. Because animals were few and were often turned out to graze when not working, much animal manure was lost. The necessity of fertilizing the heavy soils of Europe or letting them rest fallow in order to restore their fertility directed that early plow lands generally be divided into two parts. One field was planted in the fall and the other left fallow, the process being reversed every year. Thus, half of all the arable land lay fallow at any one time. The fallow field was restored in part by animals grazing over it, leaving their manure to restore its soil. Around the eighth century, however, possibly earlier, another system appeared. Instead of two fields, one of which lay fallow, the new system provided for three. One field was planted in the fall with grain, one was planted in the spring with spring grain and peas, beans, and vetches, and the third lay fallow. Both winter and spring plantings were harvested in the summer, at which point the cycle altered: the fallow field became the winter field, the winter field became the spring field, and the spring field turned to fallow.

The advantages of the three-field system are obvious: the amount of land that was out of use was reduced from one half to one third; the varieties of vegetable protein from the spring planting improved and varied the diet; the beans yielded by the same spring planting returned valuable nitrogen to the soil; and the rotation of crops made less likely the exhaustion of the land by exclusive grain growing. The two- and three-field systems were not, of course, separate in time. Both coexisted with other kinds of agricultural practices. Land might be cleared, sown for a few seasons, and then left fallow indefinitely; some land might be cultivated intensively and continuously while most of the rest was cultivated and left fallow in alternate years, or planted one year and left fallow for two or three. To impose uniformity upon medieval agricultural practices, whether in the form of an ''ideal'' manor or a single system of cultivation, is to distort seriously the variety reflected in, and the chronology of, agricultural history.

VILLAGE, TOWN, AND CITY

The agricultural economy of medieval Europe bound lords and peasants alike into communities of enterprise and management. The term *manor* describes the holding of a single lord and the laboring community of serfs and free peasants who worked his land. A manor might be so small as to be part of a village, or so large as to include several villages. The manor and village were also legal communities, and the customs of the manor, ruled upon in the lord's manor court, constituted the only law that most rural people knew. The village church also constituted a community. It compelled the parish community's attendance at religious feasts, baptisms, marriages, and funerals. After the Fourth Lateran Council in 1215, the parish also compelled yearly confession and communion. The patron saint of the church was also the patron of the village community. Most villages also possessed at least one rural confraternity—a religious organization whose members banded together to care for their sick, bury and pray for the dead, and celebrate its annual feast together, distributing food and clothing to their members once a year. Manor, village, and parish thus overlapped and together constituted the social framework for almost every person's life and death.

The lands of the manor, of course, stretched beyond the village center, extending out into, and including, the woodland, forest, and meadow that surrounded rural villages. These lands were usually linked by a path or rough track, rarely by roads. In theory, each manor consisted of enough land to support a lord's household and peasant tenant farmers; in fact, many lords had several manors, and traveled from one to another throughout the year. The manor required not only a house for the lord and houses and barns for the lord's tenants, but cultivated land, pasture, meadow, and woodland as well. The outer woodland provided kindling, rooting ground for the village pigs, berries, timber, and hunting—the last a privilege usually reserved for the lord alone. The lord commonly controlled the appointment of the village parish priest. This person was obliged to cultivate his own plot of ground, which was given him by the lord in return for his services. On most manors the lord took a percentage of the harvest, since his own land was scattered throughout the manor fields. Villagers took their own percentages, based upon the number of pieces of land they held.

Although manor and village can often be discussed as if they were ideal types, it is inaccurate to consider rural society as static and uniform. The character of European agriculture and the historical development of rural society made for much diversity in village economic, legal, and spiritual institutions and hence in village life.

In spite of the rough similarity of manors and villages the European landscape was socially diverse. Several features of eleventh- and twelfth-century life contributed to this variety. First, large areas beyond the local village woodland began to be opened up for greater agricultural production. Second, lords' new interest in exploiting the economy of their property often led to changes in peasant status and obligations. Third, the settlement of hitherto sparsely populated lands along the edges of Europe offered new opportunities for lords and peasants alike. The eleventh and twelfth centuries saw both the internal and the external colonization of western Europe.

As new regions in settled areas were opened up for cultivation, and as unsettled areas attracted settlers, the shape and structure of manor and village slowly changed to accommodate the new character of agricultural enterprise. Such changes often benefited both lords and peasants. When lords with uninhabited lands supervised their colonization, as they did in northern Germany, Ireland, and northern France, the patterns of set-

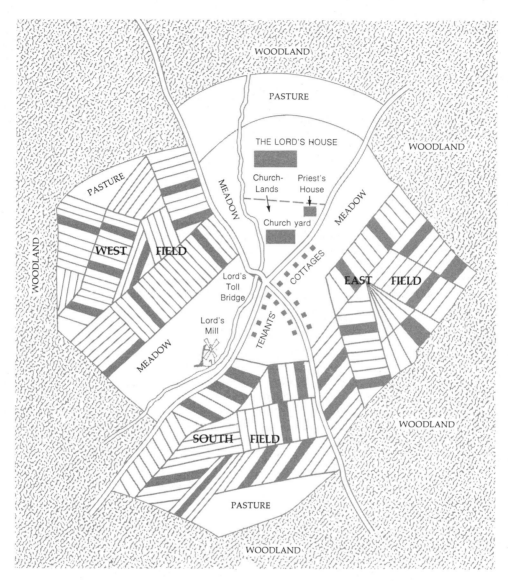

An Idealized Manor

tlement in the new lands resembled those of the old and involved similar conditions of service and social status. When lands were let by remote lords and ecclesiastical establishments, individual entrepreneurs would be empowered to offer attractive terms to the colonists, acquire such concessions as milling and baking rights for themselves, and guide the new inhabitants to their new land, rather like the wagon masters in the nineteenth-century United States. Cities, too, required a steady increase of settlers from the countryside. Traditionally, cities do not replace their own populations; steady immigration is required if urban populations are to sustain their numbers or grow. Migration to the cities—indeed, the entire urbanization of early Europe—took place between 900 and 1300.

The small rural village and the slightly larger country market-town were the largest societies in which most medieval people lived. But in the eleventh and twelfth centuries the differences between villages and towns on the one hand, and cities on the other, began to stand out more sharply as the latter began to grow larger and form different kinds of societies from those in the village and town. The most striking feature of the early medieval landscape was probably the ruins of old Roman cities. Even they housed only very small populations, but they made useful fortifications in time of invasion. In the eighth and ninth centuries these fortified towns grew more attractive to merchants, and many a *portus,* the center of transportation and market facilities, grew up at their edges. Especially along the great rivers of France and Germany trade, communications, and fortifications all contributed to the continuation of some forms, at least, of urban life.

Outside of northern Europe, however, city life survived in more clearly marked ways. The Islamic cities of Spain and most cities of the East Roman Empire thrived at the two ends of the Mediterranean. In South Italy, particularly after the Byzantine reconquest of the ninth century, such towns as Bari, Amalfi, Salerno, and Naples remained in contact with northern Italy and Byzantium. In northern Italy Rome remained a shell of the old imperial city, although the papacy and the ecclesiastical affairs of the city sustained its concentration of population. Such port towns as Genoa and Pisa recovered slowly from the Lombard and Arab domination, but by the end of the tenth and the beginning of the eleventh centuries the small fleets of both cities had begun to regain some maritime success.

One extraordinary example of urban growth took place in the west. A region of lagoons, islands, and marshes at the head of the Adriatic Sea had long sheltered a population of fishermen and small marine towns. The invasion of the Lombards late in the sixth century drove many wealthy Italians into these regions, and by the end of the eighth century the town of Venice had emerged. Under Byzantine control (except for its capture by Charlemagne's forces in 809), and always maintaining its close maritime and commercial ties with the Byzantine Empire, Venice developed a mercantile fleet. Throughout the ninth century it engaged in trade with Byzantium and the Islamic world and with the hinterland of the Po Valley. Salt and slaves constituted the earliest bases of Venetian prosperity, and by the tenth century Venice was the central trading depot in the west for Byzantine and Islamic commerce. The remarkable growth of Venice was unique, however; few cities of the west could compare to it in wealth and power before the thirteenth century.

Venice was unique in yet another sense; she possessed very little territory on the Italian mainland, depending upon a far-flung seaborne trading empire throughout the eastern Mediterranean and the Levant. Other medieval cities, however, were much more a part of the economic and political life of their surrounding regions. They drew upon the rural areas close by for population, food, and labor. Towns also existed as parts of larger territorial lordships, and many lords failed to treat the cities any differently from the way they dealt with their other lands. However, the lords quickly found that cities desired greater autonomy and different treatment from other forms of society. From the eleventh century on, associations of nobles and urban patricians, sometimes helped by rebellious clergy, often wrested administrative and legal control of their cities from the counts or bishops.

The new comunes, which were often bitterly and savagely resisted, regulated town law and institutions, appointed their own town officials from among an urban aristocracy, and distributed their new authority across a system of offices and powers that aimed to increase the prosperity of at least that part of the population that counted as citizens. By the twelfth century, comunes had begun to acquire charters from royal and episcopal authorities that specified their newly won rights and powers. Within the cities there was an increasing regulation of both economic and political affairs, as well as the beginnings of a new kind of social mobility.

Some lords, however, saw an advantage in granting to cities those rights and privileges that the citizens wanted. London, for example, was an old Roman city that had fallen on hard times after the fifth century, being displaced as the capital of Britain by Winchester in the Anglo-Saxon period. By the end of the eleventh century, however, London had begun to grow, both as a commercial center and as the center of royal government in the kingdom. At the death of Henry I in 1135, Londoners proudly proclaimed that it was they alone who determined who would be king of England. More important (and less exaggerated), Henry I issued a charter of privileges to London's citizens during his lifetime. This charter freed the city from the jurisdiction of Middlesex County and permitted its leading citizens, as a municipal corporation, to be solely responsible for paying all fees and taxes owed by the city to the king. In the twelfth century London won the privileges of burgage tenure (the right to transfer ownership of land, usually as collateral for credit) and the farm of the town (to arrange internally the collection of all dues owed by the city), and the right to administer its own law courts.

The kings of England, however, like many other lay and clerical lords in the twelfth century, were never quite comfortable with town liberties. William the Conqueror (1066–87) built the Tower of London to assure that he could control the city when he needed to. But English and French kings also found it to be to their advantage to increase the liberties and privileges of townspeople, especially since grants of liberties increased their own revenues and offered allies in the king's dealings with the landed nobility. By the end of the twelfth century London had a population of 30,000, a charter, a corporate seal, a mayor, more than 130 churches, and a growing collection of neighborhoods, trades, and crafts. It was the greatest city in England.

The movement for town independence in Europe was greatest where the rule of lords was weakest—in northern Italy, southern France, and the Iberian peninsula. The hardy frontier society of Castile and Aragon needed settlers and fighters more than it needed traditional forms of lordship, and the towns of the Iberian peninsula won considerable rights and privileges as a result. The urban Spanish *fueros* (municipal codes of local law) and the powers of municipal representatives in the *cortes* (representative institutions of the kingdoms of Castile and Aragon) made Spanish towns precocious examples of virtually independent municipal corporations. In southern France, where traditional territorial lordship was difficult to establish because of the large number of small, ferociously independent lordships and because of the survival of Roman cities, towns also showed a remarkable degree of independence. The city of Narbonne, for example, was governed by its own consuls as early as 1056.

The most striking examples of the movement toward urban independence are to be found in the cities of northern Italy, in Lombardy and Tuscany. The northern Italian cities were generally ruled by a count, a bishop, or both. The cities' resistance to the invasions of the ninth and tenth centuries often permitted urban groups to bypass the powers of count and bishop and undertake corporately the defense of the city. In the eleventh century the citizens of the northern cities played prominent roles in instituting ecclesiastical reforms, and this experience permitted the citizens to reduce the authority of the local bishop. In general, the lords of the northern Italian cities were not as powerful as the kings of England and France or the counts of Flanders or Champagne. During the eleventh and twelfth centuries municipal corporations took over more and more rights of governance, usually with a charter from their bishop or the emperor authorizing them to do so.

The new municipal corporations, with their roots in recent military, political, and religious change, invented new political offices through which to rule themselves. The office of consul, for example, appears in many northern Italian towns from the late eleventh century: in Pisa around 1085, in Asti in 1095, in Milan in 1097, in Arezzo in 1098, and in Genoa in 1099. The consuls ruled what came to be called the comune. They were elected by those citizens possessing the franchise (members of the municipal corporation) and served as rulers of the cities for a specific period. Votes on important matters were often presented to the citizens at larger assemblies, and the consuls were frequently more like city managers than city rulers. The need for the municipal corporation to delegate authority to consuls, or to representatives of the city in its dealings with other cities, the pope, or the emperor, created a precocious constitutional climate in which corporate authority, delegated power, representative government, and other aspects of a new political order became highly developed. Although none of the comunes was democratic and all continued to be ruled by a corporate patrician elite, the nature of political authority in them was novel in the eleventh and twelfth centuries.

By the end of the twelfth century urban corporate lordship was far advanced in northern Italy, and its experience widened the political horizons of Europeans for centuries to come. Not yet democratic, barely republican in a classical sense, the northern Italian cities nevertheless were genuinely new and disturbing political communities. Even though they were closely governed, their political power was distributed more widely and used more versatilely than anywhere else in Europe. With the new political order came increased population growth, a commercial revolution, and even new forms of urban spirituality and lay culture. In the fourteenth century the Italian jurist Bartolus of Sassoferrato coined a formula that seemed to a world of kings, lords, and princes the troubling embodiment of urban freedom: *civitas sibi princeps*—"the city is a prince unto itself." The new reality of independent city-republics was thus cast in the constitutional language of medieval Roman law.

THE ADVENTURE OF TRADE

In the Byzantine and Islamic worlds, trade played an important and recognized role in social, legal, and economic life. Merchants' journals, their correspondence, and descriptions of trade and travel conditions from North Africa across the Middle East as far as the Baltic Sea illuminate whole regions and classes of people about whom no western source speaks until the late tenth century. In the matter of trade, as in many other areas, eleventh-century western Europe was far less developed than Byzantium and Islam.

The strangers who came to trade in the small western European markets and fairs were sometimes pirates and thieves (as were the Vikings), more often hard-working, small-scale traders in wool, foodstuffs, and craft goods. *Homines duri* ("hard men") they were called, and their lives involved far more risks than pleasures. Like all strangers in the early Middle Ages, they possessed no legal identity and at first received little protection from local authorities. They had to overcome the infinite variety of weights and measures, which differed from region to region and were an important sign of the particularism of eleventh-century Europe. Their activities were confined to specific places; they might sell their goods only for the duration of a fair; they had to deal fairly, pay their bills, and leave when their work was done. Before the eleventh century European communities had no place for people who possessed no local identity, who had no status (in the anthropologist's sense of the word), who were not part of the local community.

By the end of the eleventh century, trading conditions had improved. Some lay and clerical authorities worked out the rudimentary structure of markets and fairs and began to create a protected identity for merchants. The *homines duri* became a more common sight, and the image began to change from that of a "hard" man to that of a "sly" man. Ecclesiastics worried more about the moral consequences of the merchant and his money than about his sword and his wrath. The changing adventure of trade in the period between the tenth and the twelfth centuries reflects not only economic growth and diversity, but also the alteration of a warrior and peasant society into a society with room for merchants, administrators, and townspeople.

Lords and communities that did not accommodate merchants soon found themselves at a disadvantage compared with those who did. The most striking example of aristocratic patronage of trade is the series of great fairs held annually in Champagne, where the trade of southern Europe could meet that of northern Europe. The counts of Champagne, ambitious territorial princes, offered protection to visiting merchants, having devised novel legal procedures for this purpose, and regulated the practice of commerce carefully. In the twelfth and thirteenth centuries Champagne developed a cycle of six fairs a year, from the fair at Lagny in early January through fairs at Provins and Bar-sur-Aube to the "cold fair" at Troyes in December. These fairs represent the first regular large-scale commercial enterprise in European history.

With the development of the Champagne fairs, luxury goods and exotic items became part of a large-scale trading network that included raw and finished wool, furs, crafted goods, grain, and wine. The variety of regions represented at the fairs helped begin the long process of standardizing weights, measures, and coinage. Mercantile law spread from developed fairs to places just beginning to establish their own markets. Like the travels of pilgrims, those of merchants opened up new routes of communication and exchange throughout most of western Europe. In fact, the fairs held by the monks of the monastery of Saint Denis, near Paris, combined the pilgrimage to the shrine of the saint with the sale of the wine produced on the monastery's lands.

European agricultural conditions and the European climate both created demands that could be satisfied only by manufactured goods. Iron tools, wine, building materials, and wool for clothing were not usually produced locally; they had to be bought from their manufacturers or traders. More than the expensive consumption of luxury goods by aristocrats and high clergy, this necessary domestic trade marks a distinctive change in European life. Sometimes the two kinds of trade were combined. Venice began its great commercial career by trading salt from its own region, then by shipping grain and timber to Constantinople, and then by bringing back luxury goods from the east.

In many areas of Europe the towns signaled the new importance of trade. In Flanders, northern Italy, and southern France, urban centers became centers of economic exchange. The rich wool of England and Flanders was processed in the Flemish cities and sold at fairs. It even passed through northern Italy, whose merchants then transported it to the Near East and traded it with Muslim merchants. Both the urbanization of trade and the kinds of goods being manufactured at this time help explain another feature of European economic development—technological innovation and its rapid influence on all forms of life.

The early history of the water mill reflects this characteristic of European culture. By the eleventh century, not only had this method of grinding grain spread more widely than ever before but new applications of its physical principles were continually appearing. The principle of water-powered rotary motion was adapted to the creation of reciprocal motion from the same power source. Thus, by the twelfth century water mills were being used for the fulling of cloth and the powering of sawmills. The extent of the use of these new devices suggests a propensity for the application of technological developments to industrial use very quickly, more so than in earlier periods and in other civilizations. The organization of new monasteries and settlements in former wasteland, the increase in the demand for such products as cloth, iron, and spices, and the existence of a complex market system all contributed to the spread of technological developments and their application across a broad band of the labor spectrum. Although the scale of such development was very small by modern standards, its mere existence is significant. Agriculture on a very large scale and small local centers of industrial enterprise were the driving forces of the medieval economy.

FURTHER REFERENCES

Besides the works listed in the general bibliography under *Social History and Economic History* and the references at the end of Chapter 7, see Norman J. G. Pounds, *An Economic History of Medieval Europe* (New York: Longmans, 1974); Robert L. Reynolds, *Europe Emerges* (Madison: University of Wisconsin Press, 1961); and C. N. L. Brooke, *Europe in the Central Middle Ages, 962–1154* (New York: Longmans, 1975).

On urban history, see Edith Ennen, *The Medieval Town* (Amsterdam: North Holland Publishing Co., 1978); Susan Reynolds, *An Introduction to the History of English Medieval Towns* (New York: Oxford University Press, 1977); and Harry A. Miskimin, David Herlihy, and A. L. Udovich, eds., *The Medieval City* (New Haven: Yale University Press, 1977).

A brilliant survey of eleventh-century culture is R. W. Southern, *The Making of the Middle Ages* (New Haven: Yale University Press, 1953).

11
Power and Society

LORDSHIP AND KINGSHIP

The most common formula that medieval people used to describe the structure of their society was that of the three orders. These orders first appeared in King Alfred's translation of Boethius's *Consolation of Philosophy:* ''A king's raw materials and instruments of rule are a well-peopled land, and he must have *men of prayer, men of war,* and *men of work.* '' This idea of a tripartite society reflected both an idealized conception and a descriptive norm.

The prayers of the clergy, in an age when most lay people were considered too sinful and inarticulate to pray for themselves, were essential for the spiritual well-being of the men of war and the men of work. In turn, the kings and lords fought to protect the men of prayer and the men of work. Finally, the men of work labored to feed the men of prayer and the men of war. About a century after Alfred, Abbo of Fleury took up the theme again:

Concerning the first order of men, that is laymen, it must be said that some of them are farmers, others warriors. Farmers sweat at agriculture and other crafts in a rustic manner, whereby they sustain the multitude of the whole Church. The warriors, supported by the dues of military service, ought not contend with each other in the womb of their mother [the Church], but by their military skills contend against the enemies of the holy Church of God.

141

For Abbo, the men of war and the men of work were two subdivisions of the laity in "the Church," parallel to the other caste, the clergy.

In spite of its conventional popularity, however, the image of the tripartite society concealed great differences among men of war. It is true that bearing arms was common to kings and great lords as well as to poor knights. Not only the expense and character of military expertise, but also the institution of knighthood bound the men of war together and contrasted them with the men of work. But in order to understand the character of eleventh- and early-twelfth-century political power, it is essential to understand the social divisions among the men of war.

In the preceding chapters we saw a new nobility take shape in the late ninth and tenth centuries. These individuals combined the social status of high birth with old royal titles of service (count, duke, viscount) and landed wealth that enabled them to bind subordinates to them by oaths of vassalage. The creation of this new lordship transformed older social relations and made the bond between lord and vassal more important than that between king and subject. In order to rule effectively, kings had to control lords, who in turn controlled their vassals. One way for kings to do this was to make themselves the lords of the lords. But to do this was to transform the older Carolingian and Anglo-Saxon ideas of kingship. Such a step required assistance—from the clergy, who emphasized the sacred character of kingship, and from the nobles themselves, who had to recognize the king's superiority over them. Kings first had to become effective lords in the lands they ruled personally—their royal domain—before they could hold sway over distant and independent lords who preferred to exercise their inherited or usurped authority untroubled by royal interference.

This authority of the eleventh- and twelfth-century nobles derived from the older private and public wealth and offices that they had accumulated from the wreckage of Carolingian kingship. In addition to consolidating and perpetuating land and income, they assumed control of older public financial obligations that had once belonged to the king and his servants. Such rights, from the collection of fines in courts that they ruled to the collection of old and sometimes forgotten taxes, made the aristocracy of the eleventh and twelfth centuries a mixture of private lords and "public" authorities.

In order to break down the somewhat simplistic notion of "public authority in private hands" as a criterion for *feudalism,* some historians have distinguished the *kinds* of lordship that were exercised. Three in particular are worth noting. Domestic lordship was a relationship between a lord and individuals who were directly attached but infinitely subordinate to him, generally serfs. A second type, landlordship, was based upon control of land rather than individuals. Tenants of a lord's land owed him services and rents because they held land that owed these things, not because they were personally bound to him. A third type was banal lordship. Here, the rights of lordship that had been usurped from older public authority were wielded by individual lords for their own benefit. When differentiated in this manner, lordship is seen as the essential basis of the different kinds of power that the "men of war" had come to exercise by the eleventh and twelfth centuries.

Although warfare had been one of the phenomena that created the noble class, the changing character of warfare helped give that class shape. The legitimacy of private warfare was challenged after the tenth century. From that time on, in a number of different places, movements of clergy and laymen had sprung up with the intention of curbing the violence of private warfare. It was not for nothing that warlords gave lands and income to the church, undertook penitential pilgrimages, and sometimes became members of monastic communities at the end of their lives. The nobility that saved Europe from the invasions of the late ninth and tenth centuries was hardly better than the invaders at enforcing its own rights and wants, whether real or imagined.

The idea of peace had been surrounded with spiritual legitimacy in the Gospels and the writings of the church fathers, and it echoed in the canons of ecclesiastical councils down to the tenth century. At a council at Charroux, near Poitiers, in 989, an assembly of bishops pronounced a solemn condemnation, over relics, of anyone who attacked a cleric or robbed the poor. From this date on, longer and longer lists of specific prohibitions against attacking certain classes of people were issued by ecclesiastical assemblies, frequently with local laymen joining in the pronouncements. By the mid eleventh century the Peace of God had become formalized; it designated protected classes of persons and regulated the character of violence. The Truce of God, which soon followed, protected certain times. At first the periods of Easter, Lent, and Advent and later the period every week from sundown Wednesday to sunrise Monday were declared to be free of violence.

These movements did not consist simply of pious pronouncements by ecclesiastics. Laymen joined in the acts of proclamation, and by the end of the eleventh century the peace associations had emerged as powerful local groups, joined by a common oath and secured by a willing armed force. In some areas these groups grew powerful enough to be considered local governments in themselves, and in strong local principalities such as Normandy the Peace of God became the Peace of the Duke, a new means of expanding the local ruler's power over independent nobles. The emperor Henry III publicly preached a peace sermon in Cologne cathedral in 1043. As the end of the century approached, peace movements, peace associations, and the concept of the Peace and the Truce of God themselves acquired great emotional and institutional strength. The lords against whom many of these movements were directed often found themselves either facing strong resistance or being invited to participate in the movements themselves. In the latter instance, lords could further legitimate their military prowess by casting an air of sanctity over themselves as warriors and over their particular warlike functions.

Although the peace movements reduced one early prerogative of the nobles, they did so by justifying the use of limited violence against breakers of the peace and large-scale warfare against infidels. Along with the private and banal rights of the aristocracy there emerged a new form of legitimizing noble status—that of protector of the peace of the Church. It is in the light of such movements and the nobility's efforts to justify its social superiority that the institution of knighthood ought to be understood. Once the skills of the fighting man were dedicated to a set of values approved by the clergy, one obstacle to the elevation of his status was removed—the traditional Christian ban on violence. From the tenth century on, in art, saints' lives, chronicles, and cult, the figure of the warrior dedicated to God became very prominent. The act of receiving arms was ritualized into a religious ceremony, and weapons and other accoutrements of war were blessed and dedicated to Christian service. Thus, the men of war—whether wealthy hereditary rulers or simple knights—constituted something more than a functional ''order'' within a tripartite society. They created social and economic divisions among themselves but at the same time linked the highest and wealthiest group with the lowest and poorest. They transformed the character of political power within society, and they posed to kings the problem of transforming lordship over territorial principalities into territorial monarchy.

The achievements of eleventh- and twelfth-century kings should be regarded in terms of that challenge.

ANGLO-NORMAN ENGLAND

The last Anglo-Saxon king of England, Edward the Confessor (1042–66), succeeded to the throne after the extinction of the Danish dynasty of Cnut. Edward had spent much of his life outside of England, a good deal of it at the court of the duke of Normandy, with whom he maintained generally good relations. Edward was not able to hold the loyalty of the greatest magnates of England, and some of the most powerful English families increased their independence during his reign. Harold Godwinson, a member of the greatest of these families, claimed the kingship of England for himself upon Edward's death without heirs in 1066. Across the English Channel, William, duke of Normandy, claimed to have been designated Edward's legal heir and prepared to back his claim by force.

In September 1066 William of Normandy assembled a fleet and a large army, crossed the Channel, and challenged Harold for the crown. Harold, who had just routed a Scandinavian invasion in the north of England, hurried south, gave William battle at Hastings, and fell under the swords and spears of the Norman invaders. At Christmas William was crowned king of England in London, and a new era of English history began.

The reign of William the Conqueror (1066–87) began as a continuation of the reign of Edward, but William soon imposed a different style of kingship. His need for resources, his obligations in Normandy, and the turbulence of his subordinates forced him to impose a stronger personal rule than that of the last Anglo-Saxon kings. In doing so, William created a stronger English monarchy. Not only had he inherited the lands formerly owned by Anglo-Saxon kings and the lands confiscated from rebellious nobles, but he had conquered the island and became lord of England in a novel way. Keeping about one fifth of England under his personal rule, William gave the rest to his nobles and churches, thus ensuring that every piece of land in England was held as a fief, directly or indirectly, from the king. The Anglo-Norman aristocracy stood in a different relation to the Norman kings of England than had the Anglo-Saxon aristocracy to the Anglo-Saxon kings. About 180 great lords held land directly from the king, and several hundred lesser nobles held land from the king's tenants in chief. The massive transfer of nearly all the land of England from Anglo-Saxon kings with limited territory and great independent landed families to a hierarchy of nobles holding ultimately from the king himself transformed the nature of English kingship and nobility. Because William did not give large blocks of land in one location to a single person, but scattered a person's holdings throughout England, the English baronage developed a perspective more "national" in character than that of the Norman or French aristocracy. In addition, William's decision permitted earlier English units of local government, such as the shire and hundred, to survive and become integral parts of the Anglo-Norman state.

Although much of the old Anglo-Saxon culture was preserved in local administration and law, much was swept away in the twenty years following the Conquest. The genius of the Old English vernacular literary language slowly withered in the face of the conquering aristocracy's Norman French; the unique calendar of Anglo-Saxon saints and liturgy gave way to the reform ecclesiology of the Norman churchmen. The tough and troublesome Old English aristocracy slowly disappeared before the numerous and powerful Normans. Nor was the kingship of England the only concern of William and his successors. Normandy and the Continent occupied them routinely. Not until the thirteenth century did England by itself become the primary concern of its kings.

Upon William's death in 1087, his possessions were divided among his sons, in keeping with the Norman law of inheritance. William II Rufus (1087–1100) inherited England, Robert inherited Normandy, and Henry received some land and money. At William Rufus's death in 1100, Henry inherited England and made a strong bid for the control of Normandy as well, which he achieved by 1106. The reign of Henry I (1100–1135), the last of the Conqueror's children, witnessed the strengthening of royal lordship in England and the shaping of a system of governance that later came to characterize English monarchy and the role of kingship in English society. Faced with pressing financial needs for his defense of Normandy, Henry I raised a group of men from the lower nobility—or sometimes from no nobility at all—to serve his interests in England. These royal servants, dependent solely upon the king's favor and backed solely by his power, turned their attention and energies not to traditional structures of privilege and the acquisition of great landed fortunes, but to the institutions of uniquely royal governance—the courts, tax systems, wardship, and administrative privilege—in order to funnel as much money as possible to the king. As a result, they strengthened these institutions and made the royal court focus on governance and administration as well as power and prestige. By making the royal law courts recognized centers of recourse for injuries, the servants of Henry I offered wider opportunities to those who resorted to law and created a structure that was easily supervised by the king and his chief servants. With few exceptions, the strength of the English monarchy was built up by royal servants working for hard taskmasters.

The energy and skill of William the Conqueror and Henry I managed both to preserve Anglo-Saxon monarchy and to impose a Continental-style lordship upon England. By the middle of the twelfth century a native English culture had begun to revive, a culture that lacked the earlier brilliance of Anglo-Saxon culture but was distinctive in its own right and drew more heavily upon French and Mediterranean influences. Moreover, in the late eleventh and twelfth centuries the Continental concerns of England's kings drew the country more and more into Continental affairs and created for it the role of treasury for Continental enterprises. Not until the thirteenth century did England's role among its king's possessions change significantly.

Henry I, who had lost his one legitimate son in a shipwreck in 1120, entrusted his kingdom and duchy and their cares to his daughter Matilda, who had been successively the wife of the Roman emperor Henry V and of Geoffrey Plantagenet, count of Anjou. At Henry's death in 1135, however, his nephew Stephen of Blois (the son of William the Conqueror's daughter Adela and Stephen, count of Blois) assumed royal authority and kept it for the rest of his life. The nobles who had chafed under Henry's strong rule took the opportunity offered by Stephen's easygoing disposition and his need for support to rebel against him and encourage his rivalry with Matilda. A final compromise established Matilda's son Henry Plantagenet Fitzempress as the successor to Stephen. Upon Stephen's death, Henry II Plantagenet (1154–89) became king of England. Far more than his grandfather Henry I, Henry II had extensive possessions on the Continent. He was count of Anjou, duke of Normandy, king of the English, lord of Ireland, and, through his marriage to Eleanor of Aquitaine, duke of Aquitaine. The history of England in the later twelfth century is inextricably bound up with the Continental empire of the Plantagenet house.

FROM WEST FRANCIA TO FRANCE

The king of West Francia whose vassal William of Normandy conquered England in 1066 was Philip I (1060–1108), son of Henry I (1031–60) and Anna of Kiev. Philip I and his successors, down to his great-grandson Philip II Augustus (1180–1223), had to tolerate the independent empire-building of many of their powerful vassals, although none of the others were quite as successful as the dukes of Normandy and Aquitaine who added the royal title of England to their Continental titles.

Hugh Capet (987–96), his son Robert II (996–1031), and his grandson Henry I had to fight hard to preserve the shrunken monarchical possessions of West Francia. Chronicles and official documents suggest strongly that the kings were surrounded by local subjects only, with few distant lords appearing at their courts. Ties of vassalage to the king weakened among higher clergy as well during the first half of the eleventh century.

During this period the kings of Francia were effective kings only where they were effective lords, and this meant strictly the royal demesne lands around Paris. The counts or dukes of Champagne, Blois, Chartres, Anjou, Maine, Normandy, and Flanders were far more powerful than the kings of Francia but they were also rivals for greater territories, and they never collaborated against the weaker kings. Even this nominal recognition of the distinctiveness of the royal title helped preserve the kingship of Francia, however. In theory at least, some of the traits of late Carolingian theocratic kingship differentiated the kings from the other great lords. During the reign of Robert II, for example, the legends of the king's power to cure certain diseases by his touch began to circulate, and the ecclesiastical literary patronage of Robert managed to preserve some of these important traditional attributes even in the most difficult days of the kings, when they were hard put to establish their lordship even in the heart of their own demesne.

Hugh Capet and Robert II spent their reigns trying without marked success to enforce their lordship over their own territories and to expand their dominion over neighboring lands. Elected to the kingship, the early Capetians strengthened their hand by associating their sons (and later their wives as well) in their rule. Thus, although the monarchy of France was not formally declared hereditary until 1223, the Capetian dynasty was strengthened by the continuity provided by the genetic good fortune of eleven monarchs having sons usually old enough to share power from the beginning of a reign. Indeed, much of the legitimacy of the Capetians was acquired through sheer endurance.

The reign of Philip I marked the beginning of effective royal attempts to establish lordship securely in the region of Ile de France, to establish royal justice against arbitrary local lords, and to establish royal authority within the royal demesne. This process of creating a strong lordship within the compact territory ruled by the king was the real beginning of the French monarchy. Exploiting both ecclesiastical and temporal resources, Philip paid little attention to the wider movements for ecclesiastical reform that stirred Europe within his lifetime. Unlike William the Conqueror, he had little to gain by supporting the reformers, and like his other contemporary, Emperor Henry IV, he had much to lose. Excommunicated from 1092 to 1108, Philip went on no crusade and kept his political horizons narrow. He made himself lord in his small domain, and his descendants built upon that lordship in expanding the horizons of French kingship.

The struggles between popes and emperors in the last quarter of the eleventh century and the first half of the twelfth made the kingdom of France an attractive ally for the papacy. Philip's son Louis VI the Fat (1108–37) and his grandson Louis VII (1137–80) developed this relationship. The close connection between France and the papacy lasted until the end of the thirteenth century. It increased greatly the strength of the royal dynasty while affording the popes sure allies in their imperial struggles. During this period the Capetian dynasty also profited from the dynastic crises among the neighboring nobility. England, Flanders, and Normandy were all affected by French royal interference in their dynastic affairs. Such accidental opportunities, the consolidation of power within the royal demesne, the connection with the papacy, and the stubborn retention of the trappings of monarchical authority—often without the power to make them effective—constitute in large part the first century and a half of Capetian lordship and the slow creation of the kingdom of France.

THE *RECONQUISTA*

The Muslim conquest of the Iberian peninsula between 711 and 720 had destroyed the kingdom of the Visigoths and brought most of Iberia into the orbit of the prosperous southern Mediterranean and Iranian empire of Islam. To the small Christian communities surviving independently in the northern part of the peninsula, as well as to some of the Christians living under Muslim rule, Iberia was still Hispania, as it was called by Christians elsewhere in Europe. To its Muslim conquerors and settlers, however, Iberia was *al-Andalus,* "the land of the Vandals." The Muslim term *al-Andalus* later became used to designate only southern Spain, the last Muslim stronghold after the Christian "reconquest," the *Reconquista.*

After a period of Muslim territorial division Abd-ar-Rahman I (756–88), an exiled Umayyad prince, established a single emirate in Spain with its capital at Córdoba. Muslim expansion was checked several times in the far north of the peninsula and across the Pyrenees in southwestern Gaul. In 721 Eudes, duke of Aquitaine, repelled a large Muslim raid. In 733 Charles Martel, mayor of the palace of the Frankish kingdom, defeated a Muslim expeditionary force near Poitiers. In the late eighth century Charlemagne established a buffer zone, the Spanish March, north of Barcelona.

Under the vigorous rulership of Abd-ar-Rahman II (912–61), the emirate of Córdoba became a full-fledged caliphate, rivaling Baghdad in its claims to legitimacy. After Abd-ar-Rahman, and into the reign of the caliph al-Mansur (977–1002), *al-Andalus* reached the height of its prosperity and power. Neither Muslim nor Christian enemies could gain advantage over it, and the prosperity of Muslim towns and agricultural regions increased considerably. The cities of Córdoba, Valencia, and Seville boasted great wealth and large populations. Córdoba appears to have approached Constantinople in population, somewhat over 300,000 people. The city contained many mosques, schools, public baths, libraries, bazaars, and lavish private homes. The productivity of Muslim agriculture elsewhere was legendary, and *al-Andalus* too began to grow rice, melons, oranges, lemons, and other crops in abundance. Leather, steel, and other manufactured goods became known as the best of their kind in the Muslim or Christian worlds. Wool, cotton, and silk came from Andalusian looms, and papermaking was introduced to Europe in *al-Andalus.*

Muslim Spanish devotion and learning were well known in the Islamic world. Extensive libraries and large schools preserved in Spain the Muslim versions of Greek philosophy and scientific thought. Ibn-Rushd (Averroës to the Latins), the greatest of all commentators on the works of Aristotle, lived in *al-Andalus*. With devotion and learning and prosperity went art and architecture, particularly the latter. Such buildings as the Alhambra at Granada and the Great Mosque at Córdoba, with their delicate structural elements, brilliantly colored and arranged tiles and mosaics, and exquisite ivory and rare wood inlays, have survived to the present and give even modern Spain its characteristic Muslim architectural flavor. In spite of the political rivalry between *al-Andalus* and Baghdad, Muslim Spain continued to be nourished by contact with the rest of the Islamic world.

Although Muslims in Spain, as elsewhere, were generally tolerant of Jews and Christians, not many conversions appear to have taken place. Thus, substantial populations of Jews and Christians survived in *al-Andalus* and shared some of its material prosperity and rich cultural life. Some Christians adopted Muslim culture, if not Islam itself, and spoke Arabic. These individuals were called Mozarabs. Although they developed their own unique liturgy and Christian culture, they were regarded with suspicion by the Christians in the north of the peninsula and by Christians elsewhere.

Growing population pressures, especially in the north, brought Muslims and Christians into frequent military contact during the late ninth and tenth centuries. The northern Christian kingdoms, particularly Castile, began to press south against the frontiers of the Muslim caliphate. The rule of al-Mansur proved to be the last of the great Muslim reigns in the peninsula. In the eleventh century the Muslims lost about a third of their territory in northern Spain, and the young Christian kingdoms of Castile, Aragon, León, and Navarre emerged as substantial Christian powers, calling their expansion a *Reconquista,* a "reconquest" of Hispania from the Muslims. Under the patronage of the apostle Saint James (Santiago Matamoros), whose cult was centered in the northwestern town of Compostela, they appealed for aid from Christians across the Pyrenees and mobilized their own forces for expansion to the south.

The *Reconquista* provided a focus for the expansion of these northern Iberian kingdoms, and its publicizing north of the Pyrenees appealed to fighting men and

Christian Reconquest of Spain

910

1491

pilgrims who were beginning to see, in war against the infidels, a means of legitimating their own warlike inclinations. During the tenth century legends of "Saint James the Killer of Moors," of Pelayo, the legendary successor of Roderigo, the last Visigothic king, and of Fernán González, a great warrior of Castile, helped develop the Iberian consciousness of the sacred character of the *Reconquista*.

Navarre, under Sancho I (1000–1035), achieved considerable success and preeminence in the north. The division of Sancho's lands at his death made kings of his sons, and the three kingdoms they created, Navarre, Aragon, and Castile, constituted a growing Christian power, as we have seen. The earlier kingdoms of Asturias and Galicia united to form León, and the old Spanish March became the County of Barcelona. The combination and separation of these small kingdoms and principalities continued into the later eleventh century. Under King Ferdinand I of Castile (1035–65), León and Castile were united into a single kingdom. Although the two parts divided briefly, they later reunited to form the great Castilian kingdom in the center of northern Spain.

The reign of Alfonso VI of Castile (1065–1109) proved Castile's endurance and ability. The Muslim south paid tribute and yielded booty to Alfonso's warriors. Alfonso also opened communications across the Pyrenees; French aid, warriors, monastic foundations, and clergy assisted his efforts in the south. In 1085 Alfonso captured the city of Toledo, the old Visigothic capital and ecclesiastical center of Spain, a triumph that increased his reputation at home and in the north.

Alfonso's greatest servant, Rodrigo Díaz de Vivar, who was called El Cid (from the Arabic word *siddi,* meaning "chief"), led his master's armies heroically, but other aspects of El Cid's career suggest the kind of life northern Spain offered in this period of turbulence. El Cid fell out with Alfonso in 1081, entered the service of some Muslim princes, was briefly reconciled with the king, and then undertook to conquer Valencia for himself. The independence and occasional indifference of El Cid to Alfonso's political difficulties, his willingness to serve under Muslim leaders, and his political adventurousness in Valencia suggest that the ideal of a Christian warrior fighting God's war was not his unvarying self-image. The epic poem in the Castilian vernacular produced in the late twelfth century, however, *El Cantar del Mio Cid,* tried to mold the frontier adventurer and local warlord into a model Christian warrior.

The enemies against whom Alfonso VI and El Cid fought were no longer the great caliphs of *al-Andalus.* With the collapse of the caliphate in the first half of the eleventh century, about the same time as the Abbasid caliphate collapsed in Baghdad, petty rulers of small regions and individual cities, the *reyes taifas* ("kings of parts") now constituted the political and military strength of *al-Andalus.* Strong at home, they were nevertheless vulnerable to the forces of Christian expansion, and with the fall of Toledo several of these kings invited the puritanical warrior sect of the Almoravides into Spain from North Africa. The victory of the Almoravides over Alfonso VI at Zalaca in 1086 temporarily halted the *Reconquista* and briefly unified *al-Andalus* under Almoravid rulers, but they did not win back much territory from the Christians.

Even this temporary unification of *al-Andalus* could not prevent the kings of Castile, Navarre, and Aragon from consolidating their earlier gains and even expanding more slowly. In 1139 a noble adventurer named Afonso Henriques established Portugal as an independent lordship and began to build it into a monarchy with himself as king. With the slowing of the *Reconquista* after 1086, the rulers of the Christian kingdoms consolidated their newly expanded realms and laid the foundations for the next phase of expansion.

Muslim *al-Andalus* was slowly giving way to *Hispania Christiana*—Roman, Christian Spain.

FROM LORDSHIP TO KINGSHIP IN SOUTH ITALY AND SICILY

One of the most spectacular instances of the shaping of royal lordship was the creation of the Norman kingdom of Sicily and South Italy, not out of older Visigothic, Anglo-Saxon, or Frankish traditions, but out of fragments of Byzantine and Lombard institutions through the dynamism and ruthlessness of an able Norman dynasty. "The Other Norman Conquest," as historians sometimes call it, created a state where none existed before, a state whose wealth, character, and power made it the most powerful kingdom in Europe by the end of the twelfth century and a major point of contact among Christian, Jewish, and Muslim cultures.

In the tenth century Byzantium had regained control over much of South Italy, including its restive Lombard principalities and its largely Greek population. The eleventh-century crisis in the Byzantine Empire (see Chapter 12), however, weakened Byzantine control and sparked a Lombard revolt. The Lombard rebels hired a number of Norman pilgrims as mercenary warriors, and between 1017 and 1029 Norman military power led the Lombard resistance to Byzantine authority. In 1029 Rainulf, a Norman leader, won for himself the countship of Aversa, and in the following two decades other Norman leaders also carved out territories for themselves.

In 1053 Pope Leo IX sent a military force into South Italy, intending to displace the Normans and reassert papal claims to the territory south of Rome. The papal force was soundly beaten by the Normans at Benevento in that year, however, and the pope himself was taken prisoner. In the negotiations that followed, Leo recognized certain Norman rights in South Italy, and in 1059 Robert Guiscard, the Norman count of Apulia, formally became the vassal of Pope Nicholas II. In turn the pope recognized Robert's title as duke of Apulia and Calabria. From 1059 until his death in 1085, Robert Guiscard continually enlarged his territory and consolidated his control in South Italy. Robert's younger brother, Roger, "the Great Count" wrested Sicily from its Muslim overlords between 1061 and 1068. In 1071 Bari, the last Byzantine stronghold in South Italy, fell into Robert's hands. In 1081 Robert Guiscard launched an attack against the western coast of Greece itself, but the campaign had to be interrupted when Guiscard was called back to Italy to rescue Pope Gregory VII in his struggle with the Emperor Henry IV (See Chapter 12). Robert Guiscard died shortly after his rescue of the pope, and his lands went to his son, Roger Borsa.

At his own death in 1101, the Great Count left his widow Adelaide and a young son, Roger II (1095–1154). Adelaide, one of the most remarkable noblewomen of the late eleventh century, maintained a successful regency for her young son until he legally came of age and was knighted in Palermo cathedral in 1112. During the first years of the rule of Roger II Sicily was welded into a territorial principality. In 1129 Roger II succeeded Roger Borsa, thus uniting all of Sicily and South Italy under a single ruler. In 1130 the antipope Anacletus II pronounced Roger king of Sicily, Apulia, and Calabria, and on Christmas day 1130 Roger was crowned in Palermo. More effectively and dramatically than any other twelfth-century ruler, Roger II had transformed lordship into kingship.

FURTHER READING

Besides the references listed in the general bibliography under *Political History: General* and *Political History: Regional,* see David C. Douglas, *The Norman Achievement* and *The Norman Fate* (Berkeley and Los Angeles: University of California Press, 1969, 1977), and John Le Patourel, *The Norman Empire* (Oxford: Clarendon Press, 1976).

Specialized studies include Frank Barlow, *The Feudal Kingdom of England, 1042–1216,* 3rd ed. (New York: Longmans, 1972), and Charles Petit-Dutaillis, *The Feudal Monarchy in France and England From the Tenth to the Thirteenth Century* (reprint ed., New York: Harper & Row, 1964).

12

Christendom East and West

THE IDEA OF REFORM

From the fifth to the eleventh century in western Europe lords and churchmen recognized two main goals: the conversion of pagans to Christianity and the establishment of proper order within the Christian community. The expansion of Frankish power and Christianity under Charlemagne, and Charlemagne's insistence upon clerical reform and education, illustrate both goals at a moment in early medieval history when they seemed closest to achievement. In spite of the disasters of the late ninth and tenth centuries, the process of conversion went on, including that of the Viking and Hungarian invaders. By the end of the eleventh century, most western European pagans had become converted to Christianity and one of the religious aims of the early Middle Ages had been accomplished. One sign of this change is the decreasing frequency with which ecclesiastical writers described forbidden pagan customs and superstitions in their works on penance in the twelfth century; they concentrated instead upon the proper attitudes of Christians within Christian society.

The period between the tenth and the late twelfth centuries, designated Romanesque by historians of art, witnessed a new stage of European religious consciousness, one that reflects a heightened awareness of the proper ordering of Christian society. At the end of the long duel with paganism, Romanesque religion faced the problem of order inside the Christian world. Among the main aspects of this problem were the monastic life, the perception of abuses within the Church, the relation between lay and clerical authority, and lay piety.

The first signs of the new temper are to be found in the strongest centers of early medieval Christianity, the monasteries. Perhaps the most influential and best-known center of monastic reform was the monastery of Cluny in Burgundy. Established in 910 by Duke William the Good of Aquitaine, Cluny was exceptional from its very origins, for the duke gave the monastery not to an individual abbot or lay protector but directly to Saint Peter. The monastery was therefore independent of all local ecclesiastical and lay authority and directly subordinate only to the pope. The power of the spiritual attraction of Rome was considerable even in the dark days of the tenth century, and some of Cluny's early prestige may have derived from its particular connection with Rome.

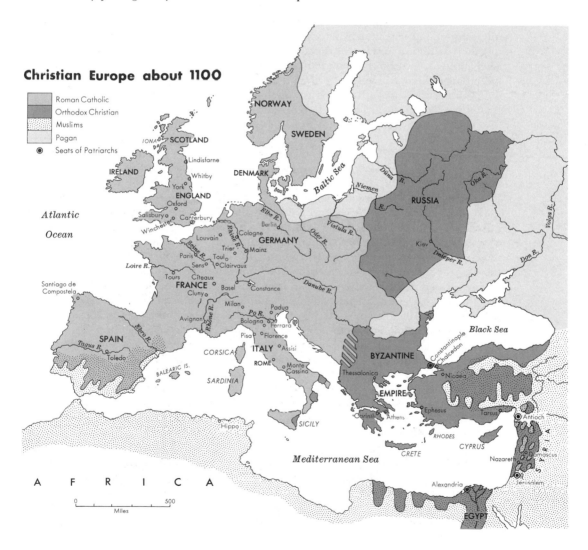

Christian Europe about 1100

Roman Catholic
Orthodox Christian
Muslims
Pagan
Seats of Patriarchs

A series of extraordinarily distinguished abbots—Berno (910–27), Odo (927–42), Aymard (942–54), Mayeul (954–93), Odilo (993–1048), and Hugh (1048–1109)—supervised the development of Cluny into a reformed and remarkably influential monastery. The closely supervised life of the monks at Cluny made them models of monastic devotion. The monastery greatly emphasized liturgical reforms, and its liturgy became a model for monastic liturgies throughout western Europe. Local and distant nobles came under the influence of this dynamic institution, and asked for instructions about reforming their own monasteries along Cluniac lines. Many other monasteries were slowly put under the direct control of Cluny, and the Cluniac influence began to reach out into corners of Europe where there had been little previous hope of ecclesiastical reform.

The abbot of Cluny was the only abbot in the order; all other monasteries controlled by Cluny were governed by subordinate officials called priors. The fact that the abbot could select his own successor and that he was the single abbot among the 1,500 or so monasteries that were attached to Cluny enabled the houses of the Cluniac system to work together for reform and to coordinate their activities closely. The abbots traveled extensively, and they were as familiar in Rome and northern Italy as they were in France. The kidnaping of Saint Mayeul by Arab raiders in the Alps appears to have been the rallying point for the final southern French assault that destroyed the powerful Arab stronghold of La Garde Freinet toward the end of the tenth century.

There is no greater monument to the synthesis of aristocratic reform monasticism represented by Cluny than the great monastic church, now destroyed, called Cluny III. Begun in 1088 and financed largely by gifts from King Alfonso VI of Castile, the building was completed, after many delays, in 1130. Until the rebuilding of St. Peter's Church in Rome in the sixteenth century, Cluny III was the largest church in Latin Christendom. Its ambitious architecture and its glorious decoration represented the greatest achievement of aristocratic monasticism. Like Hagia Sophia in Constantinople, Cluny III was not only the monks' church but a church to which others, clergy and laity alike, could come and see God worshiped with a devotion, elegance, and purity that were achieved nowhere else in western Europe. In a culture that valued the purity of ritual and knew all too well the distractions of secular life, the impression that Cluny III made upon those who witnessed its services was lifelong. It may be seen as the fulfillment of the old Carolingian monastic ideal; lay patronage and enlightened protection created the setting and the security that enabled men of religion to raise the value of human life and perfect the act of prayer, to struggle against the forces of darkness by their unceasing liturgies, and to accept the bodies of their patrons and pray for their souls forever after their death. Such a religious culture was not concerned primarily with spiritual development or the interior spiritual life, but it disciplined the attention and energies of those it attracted. Moreover, it played a key role in circulating a new religious spirit among the warlords of western Europe and among the other pilgrims who had laid aside their tedious labors to find, in a physical pilgrimage to a perfect religious community, an authentic echo of the spiritual pilgrimage of which they, as Christians, were always a part.

By creating a highly organized and disciplined association of monasteries, the abbots of Cluny and other reform monasteries brought monasticism into its greatest age, when it reached out to shape and inform the lay world and train future bishops and other high churchmen. But even the most extensive monastic reforms could not change the lives of the secular clergy (the clergy who were not members of a religious order), and these were the clergy with whom most lay people had the most extensive contact. Among reform churchmen and lay people the ideals of reform often outran the actual process of reform, and the heightened spiritual consciousness of eleventh-century Europeans made them sharply aware of the shortcomings of many of the clergy. Among the abuses in the clerical life that were criticized especially sharply were two practices that became the central points of debate: clerical marriage and clerical dependence upon lay power.

Although the Church had forbidden clerical marriage previously, the circumstances of clerical life between the fifth and the eleventh centuries made the prohibition relatively a dead letter outside of monasteries. With the demand for a purer and more authentic clergy that emerged in the eleventh century, however, and with the increased influence of monastic standards on reformers' thought, there rose the question of clerical marriage and concubinage. The charge of "Nicolaitism," the technical term for clergymen who were married or kept mistresses, was hurled with increasing vigor at clergy throughout the eleventh and twelfth centuries. Popes legislated against it, councils forbade it, and individual bishops were urged to combat it. In many cases clerical marriage became a weapon with which lay people attacked nonreformed clergy, and the problem generated a large literature in the twelfth century. Behind the growing distaste for clerical marriage was the ideal of a pure clergy, separated sexually as well as sacramentally from the laity.

Of greater importance was the second great abuse of the century, the problem of the dependence of the clergy upon the laity. Several elements had contributed to the lay domination of the clergy. One of them, obviously, was the clergy's need for defense and protection against rapacious neighboring lords or invaders. A second was the influence of Old Testament thought upon early medieval political theory and the resemblance of early medieval kings—at least in their own and the clergy's minds—to David and Solomon, the great kings of Israel. Other elements were technical and legal. Germanic law had permitted privately owned churches, called *Eigenkirchen* (literally, "churches of one's own"), whose owners appointed clergy, often in return for a gratuity or fee. In the larger world, kings and emperors often appointed bishops and abbots, either as their vassals or because of customary right. The altar, according to this view, was the province of grace, but the church building, property, and income were the province of the patron. As we have seen in the case of Cluny and elsewhere, the power of a reform-minded lay patron could be the easiest path toward reform; on the other hand, an indifferent or wicked lay patron could cripple the devotional life of many people. In the eleventh century the general practice of laity dominating clergy came to be called simony, after the figure of Simon Magus, the charlatan who allegedly attempted to buy religious power from Peter.

By the second half of the eleventh century two distinct attitudes toward reform had become predominant. The first, traditionally Carolingian, left it to the emperor and his clergy to rectify abuses, even, if necessary, to the point of removing from office canonically consecrated prelates, from abbots to popes. This great responsibility was considered to be justified by the emperor's priestly status. The second view, which necessarily possessed political as well as spiritual dimensions, attacked the whole concept of lay authority of any kind over clergy, whether that of a local lord or that of the emperor himself. This view was maintained by radical reformers in the name of *libertas,* the freedom from interference of any sort that was guaranteed by God to the Church so that it might carry out its sacred mission. In the first half of the eleventh century the two views did not necessarily find themselves in conflict, for the agenda of reform was vast, and imperial and other lay help was badly needed. From the middle of the century, however, their ways divided, and the one view opposed the other with increasing sharpness. The polarizing of views on Church reform, and the great conflict between spiritual and temporal authority that they generated toward the end of the eleventh century, constituted a major departure from the spiritual ideals of Carolingian Europe and opened new horizons for both government of Christian society and the character of religious sensibility.

ROMANESQUE ART AND ARCHITECTURE

The spiritual concerns of reformers and new forms of devotion were not the only signs of a revived religious culture in the eleventh and early twelfth centuries. Writing in the early eleventh century, the chronicler Radulphus Glaber noted that around the year 1000 Europe began to be covered with "a white robe of churches." A new wave of church building and a new consciousness of the meaning of the church building and the priestly order accompanied the spiritual concerns of the eleventh and twelfth centuries and gave them a visual dimension that is important to note.

The Church of St. Philibert, Tournus: Interior. This is a good example of Romanesque church architecture. Note particularly the rounded vaults and small windows, as well as the ambitious formality of the design. (Archives photographiques, Paris)

The new and larger churches that appeared in eleventh-century Europe were based upon several tenth-century architectural innovations and a new awareness of late imperial Roman architectural technique. Among the former influences is the appearance in several tenth-century churches of stone vaulting, the construction of a church ceiling completely out of stone arches instead of the timber that had characterized Carolingian architecture, especially in northern Europe. Among the latter influences are the size of late Roman buildings, particularly the basilicas, the use of the round arch, and the dignity and solemnity of late antique architecture. The early eleventh century also reveals the earliest sources for ceremonies surrounding the dedication of a church, as well as depictions of the role of the priest in art that suggest a new respect for the mystical sacramental powers the clergy claimed. This enhanced sense of the dignity of the church building and the person of the priest helps to explain the enthusiasm with which church builders constructed their new churches in the eleventh and early twelfth centuries.

Late-tenth- and eleventh-century builders also considered church building a penitential act, as did William the Conqueror when he built Battle Abbey at the site of his

Church of Ste. Foy, Conques: Interior. An important pilgrimage church, the Church of Ste. Foy suggests the increased architectural solemnity of Romanesque church architecture and an impressive command of building techniques. (Marburg Art Reference Bureau)

victory over the forces of King Harold at Hastings in 1066. In thanks to God the monks who had escaped from the Vikings and settled at Tournus built the church of St. Philibert shortly after 950. The patronage of the German emperors and the ambitions of imperial German churchmen accounted for a wave of large, new churches appearing in Germany throughout the eleventh century. These churches were deliberately modeled upon late Roman basilicas, and their large naves, high, rounded stone arches, and generous interior spaces were livened by a lavish use of color in their interior decoration. One of the most striking of these is the Church of St. Michael at Hildesheim, which was begun in 1010.

Still other churches were the result of rebuilding programs. That of the monastery of St. Savin-sur-Gartempe, rebuilt in 1021, had its ceiling covered with remarkable frescoes depicting scenes from the Old Testament. Such churches as these, first in Germany, then in France, Spain, and Italy, and finally in England, reflect not only the development of tenth-century techniques and an imitation of Roman monuments and

Monastery of St. Martin, Canigou. Perched high in the Pyrenees, this monastery and others like it witnessed the monastic reforms of the tenth and eleventh centuries. It was founded by a layman, Wifred of Cerdaña. (Photo Reportage)

ruins but also internal influence within western Europe and architectural influences from the Byzantine and Muslim worlds.

The new churches of Romanesque Europe are testimony to the new ease of communications and the popularity of pilgrimage during the period in which they were built. As the pilgrimage to the shrine of St. James at Compostela in northwestern Spain became more and more popular, many towns along the routes to Compostela built, or rebuilt, churches to accommodate the large numbers of pilgrims who wished to visit as many holy places and venerate as many relics of saints as possible on the long and dusty road to their destination. A fine example of one such church is that of St. Sernin in Toulouse, begun in 1060 and consecrated in 1096. Churches of this type were constructed in the form of a cross, with a nave large enough to hold a considerable crowd. The high side aisles of the nave continue around the north–south arms of the cross and meet in the apse at the east end of the building. This route inside the church is called an ambulatory, and it was a prominent feature of Romanesque church architecture. Its purpose was to offer a path for pilgrims walking around inside the church that would take them as close as possible to the relics they had come to venerate. The new appearance of churches, their size, and the increased degree of veneration people felt for them contributed an important visual dimension to an age of spiritual unrest and reform.

POPES, EMPERORS, AND CHRISTIAN SOCIETY

The first centers of religious reform had been the monasteries of France, Germany, and northern Italy. The high standards of some imperial German churchmen and emperors and the popular religious sentiment in Flemish and Italian towns contributed other elements to the reform movement. But the papacy had been slow to change. From the reign of Otto III, however, emperors had attempted to install reform-minded churchmen in the throne of Peter. In 1046, when a particularly offensive scandal produced three claimants for the papal title, the emperor Henry III (1039–56) called the Synod of Sutri, at which he and a group of sympathetic higher clergy declared all three claimants deposed from the papacy and installed the first of a series of German reformers as pope. Although the first two reform popes after Sutri died soon after their election, in 1049 Henry III's cousin, Bruno of Toul, was elected and took the papal name of Leo IX (1049–54). Leo brought with him to Rome representatives of the reform movement in Lorraine and Burgundy, traveled back across the Alps to hold reform councils and synods in France, and by his own reputation for holiness greatly increased the prestige and presence of the papacy in the reform movement of the late eleventh century.

Among the reformers who rose to prominence under Leo IX and his successors was Humbert, Cardinal of Silva Candida, the most articulate and radical proponent of reform. Humbert's treatise *Against Simoniacs* argued not only that bishops who had purchased their ecclesiastical offices be deposed, but that ordinations to the priesthood that they had performed not be recognized as valid. Other reformers, such as Saint Peter Damian (1007–72), argued a more charitable position. Nevertheless, on a mission for Leo IX to Constantinople, Cardinal Humbert excommunicated the patriarch of Constantinople, Michael Kerularios, and abruptly launched one of the many schisms that further separated Latin and Greek Christendom.

The sense of mission on the part of the reform papacy is illustrated by Alexander II (1061–73), who sent a papal banner to William of Normandy as he was departing to conquer England, urging him to reform the English church and thereby link Normandy and England with Rome. The church of Aragon adopted the Roman liturgy instead of the older local Mozarabic liturgy, thereby forging another kind of link with Rome. Nor did the reform papacy neglect the workings of the church in Rome. During the vigorous pontificate of Nicholas II (1059–61) a new rule for electing popes was adopted. Henceforth only the cardinal clergy and the people of Rome itself were to have the right of designating and electing the pope, although the "due honor and reverence" owed to the emperor were to be respected. The decree of 1059 also forbade for the first time a cleric's acceptance of a church from the hands of a lay person.

The most active and controversial of the reform popes was Gregory VII (1073–85). Unlike some of his predecessors, Gregory saw the causes of abuses in the Church not in specific faults that might be corrected one by one, but in the defective ordering of the Christian world. Gregory's pontificate launched a great debate about the nature of Christendom, *Christianitas,* between the two great powers that claimed responsibility for the ordering of spiritual and temporal life, the pope and the emperor. Against the old Carolingian idea of the emperor's ultimate responsibility for Christian society, Gregory set an alternative vision of two contending societies on earth—Christian society and the city of Satan—thus echoing one aspect of Saint Augustine's fifth-century work *The City of God.* According to Gregory and his supporters, only the pope at the head of Christian society, strengthened by the authority and merits of Peter, could fulfill God's plan for the world. Any challenge to such a plan was a threat from the forces of Satan and had to be countered by whatever force was required.

Thus, a large part of Gregory's pontificate was devoted to outlining systematically the nature and history of papal authority. To this end he had some of his subordinates, including the aged Peter Damian, now Cardinal Bishop of Ostia, search out old collections of laws and treatises to substantiate his case. The work of earlier eleventh-century reformers in building a doctrinal basis for the attack on clerical marriage and simony had already produced a significant body of research on doctrinal and papal history, and some of it had begun to be organized in the form of legal texts. *The Collection in 74 Titles,* compiled in Rome, possibly under the direction of Cardinal Humbert, first established papal authority over the whole Church in the form of a legal code. Earlier searches, various collections, and the renewed efforts of Gregory VII turned up a vast amount of literary material, and much of the late eleventh and twelfth centuries was spent in shaping it into a constitutional theory of Latin Christendom, largely through the increasingly important profession of canon law. Some of this material came from the great ninth-century collections of forged material, particularly that of Pseudo-Isidore, which, as we have seen, contained the text of the Donation of Constantine. The *Dictatus Papae,* a list of papal privileges and powers intended to serve as an index of the diverse aspects of papal authority, was produced by Gregory VII and included in the official register of his correspondence, the first full surviving register of papal correspondence since that of Pope Gregory I, who died in 604.

In the process of organizing the theory of papal authority, describing it in collections of canon law, and building an administrative system through which it might be distributed and applied regularly and effectively everywhere, Gregory VII contributed substantially to the foundations of papal power in the twelfth and thirteenth centuries. Not only did he increase the workload of the staff of the papacy in Rome, but he dispatched papal legates, representatives for special occasions, throughout Europe; in some places he established permanent legates. The clergy of the city of Rome, hitherto important chiefly for its role in assisting the popes in their many liturgical functions throughout the city, grew into an administrative body. The cardinals, titled priests, deacons, and bishops of key Roman churches slowly grew into an administrative body that directly handled papal affairs. In both the realm of ideas and the translation of those ideas into institutions and programs of action, Gregory VII transformed the papacy and made himself the spokesman for a new vision of the ordering of Christian society.

Although Gregory VII began his pontificate on good terms with the emperor Henry III's successor, Henry IV (1056-1105), the pope's vision of the respective places of pope and emperor soon led to direct conflict. Gregory, for example, supported the reform-minded citizens of Milan who rejected Henry IV's candidate for archbishop, although the position of archbishop of Milan was an important imperial office in northern Italy. Moreover, resistance to Henry's methods of governance in Germany had grown stronger, and Gregory found allies among the German nobility when he pressed further with new regulations against lay investiture of clergy. In 1076 Gregory declared Henry excommunicated and deposed, after Henry and a synod of imperial bishops at Worms had announced Gregory himself deposed from the papacy. In the winter of 1077, in one of the wisest and most dramatic moves of the conflict, Henry IV suddenly crossed the Alps and presented himself as a penitent at the Tuscan castle of Canossa, where Gregory VII was staying, asking forgiveness from the cleric who had excommunicated him. Gregory agreed to absolve Henry, thus weakening the opposition to Henry in Germany, which nevertheless proceeded to elect an antiking on its own and wage civil war against the emperor for the next three years.

Relations between Gregory and Henry quickly broke down again, but Gregory's censures had far less effect the second time they were used, and by 1080 Henry had overcome his opponents in Germany and turned his full wrath on Rome. The synods of Bamberg and Mainz in 1080 renounced obedience to Gregory and elected an antipope, the archbishop of Ravenna, in his place. With the antipope in his train Henry IV invaded Italy in 1084, and forced Gregory to flee Rome and go to Salerno, where he was protected by the Norman dukes of Apulia. Gregory died in Salerno in May 1085.

The greatest of Gregory's successors was Urban II (1088-99). Urban, unlike Gregory, was a nobleman and had been prior of the monastery of Cluny. By compromise, diplomacy, and a reorganization of the administration of the papacy, Urban II undercut much of the support of Henry IV and greatly strengthened the prestige of his own office. The intransigence of Henry IV, who died in 1106, and of his son and successor Henry V (1106-25), dragged out the formalities of the conflict between pope and emperor. Not until the pontificate of Calixtus II (1119-24) was the formal aspect of the conflict finally resolved. In 1122 pope and emperor agreed to a treaty, the Concordat of Worms, according to which the emperor retained the right to oversee the election of high churchmen, to decide between disputed candidacies, and to confer the temporal privileges of ecclesiastical office by means of the scepter. He gave up the right to invest prelates with the ring and the crozier, precisely those ceremonial rights that had appeared to confer spiritual as well as temporal authority upon a churchman.

The Concordat of Worms formally ended the Investiture Conflict, but it did not conceal the real triumph of Gregorian ideals that the papacy and its supporters had achieved. Never again could an emperor successfully invoke the old Carolingian idea of the emperor as God's vicar on earth, responsible for laity and clergy alike. Only the popes could now make such a claim. The image of a tripartite society comprising men of prayer, men of war, and men of work became less important than that of a bipartite society.

"There are two kinds of Christians," said a popular text often quoted by churchmen in the twelfth century—"laity and clergy." Of the two, the clergy now claimed the ultimate responsibility for the spiritual welfare of humanity. This legacy of Gregory VII led to a widening of the idea of reform, new monastic and clerical movements, and a new search for lay piety.

NEW MONKS IN A NEW DESERT

By the late eleventh century a new ascetic spirit was inspiring a number of monastic leaders to try once more to remove monks from close contact with the world and restore the rule of Saint Benedict to its place of supremacy over local privileges, customs, and diverse practices. The most successful of these movements was that begun at Cîteaux in Burgundy. Founded in 1098 by a group of monks who sought a stricter application of the monastic rule than existed at their old monastery of Molesmes, Cîteaux (*Cistercium* in Latin, whence the common name for the order—Cistercians) prospered under the directorship of Stephen Harding (1070–1134) and the immense prestige of Saint Bernard of Clairvaux (1090–1153). By the late twelfth century there were nearly three hundred Cistercian religious houses, as well as several hundred more that followed one variation or another of the Cistercian rule. That rule, drawn up by Stephen Harding in 1114 and called *Carta Caritatis (The Charter of Love),* was a modification of the rule of Saint Benedict. It organized and regularized the liturgical life of Cistercian houses, their relationships with one another, and the relations between the order and the world outside, and it emphasized the development of the spiritual discipline of the monks.

Principles of monastic organization were not, however, the greatest legacy of the Cistercians. The order offered not merely a rigid austerity and a puritanical view of the dangers of worldly temptation, but the prospect of a new interior spirituality, a wholly new relationship between humanity and God. In their scriptural commentaries and devotional writings, the Cistercians opened new avenues of spiritual awareness that exerted profound and enduring influences upon the world around them. Both in organization and spirituality, the Cistercians illustrate the role of monasticism in the age of Gregorian reform.

One of the most striking features of the *Carta Caritatis* was the constitutional principle of Cistercian organization that it laid out. The abbot of Cîteaux was, as was the abbot of Cluny, the head of his order, but there were far more checks upon the former than upon the latter. First, Cîteaux developed a strong sense of the relationship between motherhouse and daughterhouses. The abbot of any Cistercian monastery that had directly sent out monks to found other monasteries had to inspect those monasteries and in turn be inspected by their abbots at the motherhouse. The abbot of Cîteaux, for example, had the right to inspect the four daughterhouses of La Ferté, Pontigny, Clairvaux, and Morimond, and the abbots of those four houses had the right to inspect Cîteaux. In addition, all Cistercian abbots were to convene annually at Cîteaux to make collective decisions about the order, a reflection of a considerable corporate awareness in the governance of the order.

Cistercian recruitment was also versatile. Those who seemed less suitable than others for participation in the full austerity of the monastic program were enrolled as *conversi,* or lay brothers. They came to operate the farms and granges of the order and to live a regulated life separate from that of the monks. For the Cistercian monks themselves, life

Church of St. Peter, Moissac: Tympanum. The tympanum is the part of the church façade just above the doors. Romanesque tympanum imagery is particularly striking. In this tympanum Christ in Majesty is represented as in the Apocalypse with the symbols of a widely understood pictorial religion. (H. Roger-Viollet)

was strict. Only the most severe decorations were permitted in Cistercian churches. Clear glass alone filled the windows. Bright colors, intricate sculpture, bell towers, metal crucifixes—all these were banned from Cistercian churches. The cloisters too were stripped of their architectural ornament. A ''typical'' Cistercian style of church architecture carried the aesthetic and devotional principles of the order into the farthest corners of Europe as the order itself spread south to Italy and Spain, northwest to England, and northeast to Germany and Poland.

The greatest attraction of the Cistercian movement, however, was its creative role in developing the new spiritual outlook of twelfth-century Europe. Traditionally, monasticism was a defensive institution, consciously isolating its members from the temptations of a fallen world by placing them, through self-discipline and community life, in a tiny earthly duplication of heaven. In Cistercian spiritual writings there appears less emphasis upon the defensive character of monastic life and much more on its role of developing the inner spirit of the monk, enabling him to reach out and grasp God's love for humanity. This new spirituality is also reflected in the way artists from the tenth century on depicted the crucifixion of Jesus. Instead of a remote, majestic being superim-

*Cathedral of Autun, Tympanum:
The Torment of Souls.* The great
tympanum of Autun depicts salvation and damnation. In this detail,
the signed work of the sculptor
Gislebertus, demons are torment-
ing the souls of the damned.
(Photographie Bulloz)

posed upon a cross, they depicted a suffering figure who aroused the viewer's sympathy
and affection, not merely their awe and dread. Depictions of the Virgin and the Child
Jesus became more popular at the same time. No longer in art and spirituality was all of
humanity depicted as fighting a hopeless rearguard action against the inevitable triumph
of the devil. Rather, people followed a path, conducted a quest, or climbed a ladder—all
these images appear frequently in the twelfth century—toward inner spiritual growth.
This new sense of God's affection for humanity and the obligation of interior spiritual
development was largely an invention of twelfth-century Cistercian writers.

The most prominent individual in the Cistercian movement—indeed in the
religious life of all western Europe—in the twelfth century was Saint Bernard
(1090–1153), abbot of Clairvaux. Part of the importance of Saint Bernard lies in the extent of his personal influence outside as well as inside the cloister. Bernard was born to a
noble family near Dijon. In 1112, with his brothers and a large group of other young
noblemen, Bernard suddenly left the lay life and joined the still young community of
Citeaux. Bernard's arrival traditionally marks the surge of the order; indeed, it greatly
increased the attractiveness of the order throughout France. In 1115 Bernard was sent out
to found the third daughterhouse of Citeaux, at Clairvaux. Throughout his life he remained devoted to the ascetic ideals of the Cistercian program. In spite of continually
debilitating illness, his physical austerities became well known throughout Europe. His
flawlessly ascetic character, the burning lyricism of his devotional works, his concept of

human dignity, and his explorations in the psychology of devotion establish him securely in the great exemplary tradition of Benedictine monasticism. Yet Bernard was also the most widely respected holy man of the twelfth century, and it is as one of the last and most outstanding examples of the holy man, a type that developed in antiquity, that Bernard is perhaps best understood.

Bernard played a role outside the cloister as extensive as his role in it. In 1128, for example, he was the secretary for the Synod of Troyes, where he composed a work in praise of the new orders of monk knights in Jerusalem (see p. 168). In 1130 his prestige alone determined the outcome of a disputed papal election. In 1140 he attacked the new theology of Peter Abelard at the Council of Soissons. In 1144 he preached the Second Crusade and even traveled to Germany to put a stop to the persecutions of Jews and to persuade the emperor Conrad III to join the crusading expedition. In the last decade of his life he wrote an influential handbook for his protégé, the Cistercian pontiff Eurenius III (1145–53), on how to be a pope. In 1145 Bernard traveled to southern France to preach against heresy. In addition to these personal journeys, Bernard poured forth a stream of correspondence, treatises on devotion, prayers, and meditations, and instructions to diverse groups and individuals in European society. It might almost be said that Saint Bernard single-handedly designed the devotional character of western Europe in the twelfth century.

The world of Saint Bernard, the world both inside and outside the cloister, is reflected in his wide and passionate concerns. The life of the militant church in synod and council and papacy, the Crusade, the relations among Christians, Jews, and heretics, the new military orders, and lay society itself—in channeling the new intensity of their devotion, individuals in all of these contexts came increasingly to look for spiritual guidance to the last great representative of the monastic tradition and of monastic supremacy in the Latin church.

The success of the Cistercians, the Carthusians, and similar monastic movements inspired other clerics to reform their lives outside of strict monasticism. Since individual clerics often found it impossible to live reformed lives without the support of a religious community, groups of pastoral clergy (those actually serving the spiritual needs of lay people) began to organize themselves in communities. There they lived according to a rule, as monks, but served the laity as priests. One such group, the Augustinian Canons, took their rule of communal life from the rule for religious that Saint Augustine had produced in the fifth century. As Canons Regular (pastoral clergy who lived like monks), they became a very effective branch of the clergy. The Premonstratensian Canons, founded by Saint Norbert at Laon in 1120, were a second important group of Canons Regular. The form of life of both groups of canons greatly improved the quality of the ministry in areas where they worked, and they began the long labor of improving the quality of the secular parish clergy. They thereby made themselves a bridge between the new monasticism and the ill-educated and poorly trained parish clergy that ministered to lay people.

THE EXPEDITION TO JERUSALEM

Throughout the early years of his pontificate, Urban II (1088–99) made extensive reforms in the operation of papal government and continued the diplomatic struggle with the excommunicated emperor Henry IV. He also entered into favorable relations with the emperor at Constantinople, Alexius I Comnenus, attempting to heal the breach caused by the mutual excommunications of pope and patriarch that had taken place in 1054. In 1095 Alexius sent legates to the Council of Piacenza in northern Italy, requesting papal aid in enlisting mercenary soldiers for the defense of the Byzantine Empire. As Urban moved across southern France during the summer of 1095 he decided upon his response to Alexius. At the Council of Clermont in November 1095 Urban made no call for mercenary recruits. Instead, he appealed to a large assembly of laity and clergy to impose peace everywhere in Christian Europe and to turn Christian weapons only against infidels. Urban proposed a large armed pilgrimage to Jerusalem, offering forgiveness of sins to those who undertook the journey from pure motives. In proposing the armed pilgrimage (which he and his successors always called a "journey," "expedition," or "pilgrimage"), Urban II created the ideal vehicle for the expression of the growing piety of the lay warrior class. Indeed, the First Crusade, which Urban's plea created, was first and foremost a vehicle for lay warriors to participate in a renewed Christian society in the one capacity for which they were ideally suited—controlled violence in God's service against non-Christians.

By the late eleventh century the Byzantine Empire had been wracked by political rivalry between the imperial civil servants and the landowning rural aristocracy. The extinction of the Macedonian dynasty in 1056 had given rise to a series of civil wars, which only the accession of Alexius I (1081–1118) had been able to stop. Byzantine economic and military power had declined, moreover, at the moment when new invasions threatened the empire again. The greatest threat had come from the Seljuk Turks, an Asiatic people who had converted to Islam and risen to control Iran. In 1055 a Turkish leader even entered Baghdad, proclaiming himself a "deliverer" of the caliph, and assumed effective control of the Abbasid Empire. Turkish leaders called themselves sultans, and two of them, Alp Arslan (1063–72) and Malik Shah (1072–92), threatened even the Byzantine Empire and the Fatimid caliphate of Egypt. In 1071 the armies of Alp Arslan destroyed a Byzantine army at Manzikert, and for the next two decades Byzantine foreign policy was dominated by the twin threats of the Normans in South Italy and the Seljuk Turks in Baghdad. With the death of Malik Shah in 1092, however, Seljuk power became briefly decentralized, and Alexius I's request for western mercenaries was made with a view to exploiting the breathing space that Islamic disunity had given him.

The response to Pope Urban's proclamation of the "expedition to Jerusalem," however, was not that of a mercenary army. The very first groups to march east were not even knights, but an ill-assorted assembly of fighting men, townspeople, and peasants led by the independent preacher Peter the Hermit. The "Crusade of the Poor," as Peter the Hermit's expedition is often called, suggests the depth of response stirred by Pope Urban's call for a campaign in the Holy Land. Peter's army terrorized the Rhineland and Hungary as they passed through, massacring Jewish communities and looting their way east until they passed through Constantinople and met their deaths in Turkish Anatolia.

In 1096 four well-organized armies of western fighting men set out for Constantinople. They were led by great nobles and directed by Adhemar, bishop of Le Puy, Pope Urban's legate, or representative, on the expedition. Alexius I Comnenus, a skillful diplomat, worked out treaties of agreement with each leader, forcing some of them to swear allegiance to him personally. He then escorted the huge army across the Bosporus, where it captured the city of Nicaea. After marching south through Anatolia the westerners encountered and defeated a Turkish army at Dorylaeum and marched east to

Antioch. The siege and subsequent defense of Antioch lasted from late 1097 to the end of 1098. Not until January 1099 did the final march to Jerusalem begin. Led by Raymond of St. Gilles, count of Toulouse, who was clad as a penitent and a pilgrim, the armies first sighted Jerusalem on June 7. After a fearful five-week siege the city fell on July 15.

Two principalities had already yielded to the Crusaders before the siege of Jerusalem began. Antioch had fallen into the hands of Bohemund, son of Robert Guiscard of Sicily. Edessa, an Armenian principality to the east of Antioch, had fallen to Baldwin, brother of Godfrey of Bouillon, one of the expedition's leaders. The capture of Jerusalem and the existence of two other independent principalities immediately raised the question of the organization of the captured territories. Many members of the expeditionary army left Palestine and Syria to return to Europe, their mission completed. The occupying forces remaining in the Holy Land shrank dangerously. Byzantium made several claims concerning its own rights to captured territories, especially Antioch. In 1099 Godfrey of Bouillon was elected advocate of the Holy Sepulcher, but that title could not be made to work effectively as a force of governance. When Godfrey died in 1100 his brother Baldwin of Edessa formally became king of Jerusalem. By 1111 most of the important coastal cities had been taken by the Crusaders; the last, Ascalon, fell to them in 1153. During the reign of Baldwin I (1100–1118), four principal Crusader states took shape: the principality of Antioch; the county of Edessa; the county of Tripolis in the center of the Holy Land; and the kingdom of Jerusalem in the south.

The turbulent Crusader states rarely agreed on a single policy, and Muslim resistance grew measurably after 1125. In 1127 a talented Seljuk prince named Zangi established a strong Muslim principality in the city of Mosul and expanded his territory at the expense of Muslim and then Christian leaders. In 1138 Zangi captured Damascus, and in 1144 he assaulted and captured Edessa, the first Christian principality to fall back into Muslim hands. The capture of Edessa stimulated the pope to call another armed pilgrimage and to send out preachers and promise spiritual benefits on a large scale. As we have noted, among the preachers of the Second Crusade was Saint Bernard, whose fiery eloquence stimulated many, including the emperor Conrad III, to go to the east.

The Second Crusade of 1147 was very different from the First. Led by the emperor and King Louis VII of France, the two main armies were virtually uncoordinated and far worse organized than the noble armies of the First Crusade. In addition, dissension in the lands that the Europeans had begun to call simply Outremer (''Overseas'') prevented any significant action except a futile assault on Damascus. Both king and emperor headed home without any of the glory that had covered the leaders of the First Crusade half a century before. Human sinfulness, said Saint Bernard, had lost the Crusaders God's favor. Human wickedness and cunning, said apologists for the king of France, had betrayed the Crusaders. Louis was particularly enraged at the Byzantine emperor Manuel I, whom he believed had betrayed him in alliance with Conrad III. This attitude sharpened the Latin dislike of Greek Christians and contributed to the deteriorating relations between Byzantium and the west, already aggravated by the frictions caused by the First Crusade and the rise of Venice.

Of all the effort expended in the Second Crusade, only two elements are worth noting. First, some forces from eastern Germany were permitted to fight against the still pagan eastern European Baltic and Slavic peoples. Thus was crusading legitimacy added to the old conflict between expansionist Christian states and non-Christians in northeast Europe. Second, the city of Lisbon was captured by a mixed army of English, Flemish,

French, and Portuguese soldiers in 1147—an important step in the history of the *Reconquista*.

The four Crusader states in Palestine, Lebanon, Syria, and Armenia were Christian principalities situated precariously in a turbulent and disunified but still powerful Muslim world. Since relations between the Crusaders and Byzantium had begun to deteriorate quickly, the new lands were especially dependent upon the Italian maritime cities for their lifeline to western Europe. Genoa, Pisa, Lucca, and Venice grew wealthy from the concessions they won in Palestine and Syria, and their new wealth played an important role in their drives toward independence from domestic powers. The prominence of Venice in both the Crusading and Byzantine worlds grew particularly quickly in the twelfth century, and Venice, like the Crusader states, experienced a deterioration of relations with Byzantium, although Venetian importance in Byzantine commerce grew during the same period.

One result of the new energies of the Italian cities and the Crusader states was the economic undercutting of Byzantium. The loss of lands and manpower, the continuing high expenses of Byzantine imperial government, heavier taxes drawn from a diminishing tax base, and a debasement of Byzantine coinage weakened Byzantium considerably during the twelfth century. Besides threats from Norman Sicily and South Italy, Byzantium faced the economic ambition of Venice and the sullen distrust of the Crusader states. Although the twelfth-century Byzantine Empire profited from the abilities and good sense of the Comnenian imperial dynasty from Alexius I to Manuel I (1143–80), it failed to recover fully from the crises of the eleventh century and the shift in wealth and power to the Latin west.

Although Zangi was assassinated in 1146, his son and successor Nur-ad-Din (1146–74) assisted in the defense of Damascus against the armies of the Second Crusade, and by 1154 he had acquired Damascus for himself. For the next twenty years Nur-ad-Din strengthened his state and profited from the dissensions and political crises in Outremer, which put the Christian states at a distinct disadvantage. Disputes over the succession to the kingship of Jerusalem, conflict between the noble families and the kings, and the important role played by the Military Orders (communities of knights who took monastic vows and lived a life of war and prayer) all weakened the stability and strength of the Crusader states in the face of growing Muslim resistance.

Although some collaboration between the kingdom of Jerusalem and the Byzantine Empire held off Muslim forces in the 1150s and 1160s, their combined efforts were achieved only at great expense. In 1176 the Byzantine army under the emperor Manuel was crushed at Myriocephalum by the Seljuk Turks, a defeat that lost the whole of Anatolia and exposed the Crusader states to a powerful Muslim enemy. In addition, the forces of Nur-ad-Din grew stronger elsewhere in the Muslim world. Under the vigorous leadership of one of Nur-ad-Din's officers, Saladin (1169–93), a Muslim army conquered Egypt. After Nur-ad-Din's death in 1174 Saladin succeeded him and directed his combined forces at the Crusader states. In 1187 at the Battle of Hattin Saladin routed the Crusader forces, and shortly afterward he captured the city of Jerusalem. The Christians were left with a few coastal cities and the island of Cyprus, to which the kings of Jerusalem moved.

The triumph of Saladin ended the century of the Crusader states, but it did not stop the Crusade movement. The vigor of the early Crusades had created an image in European minds that the disasters of the twelfth century did little to diminish.

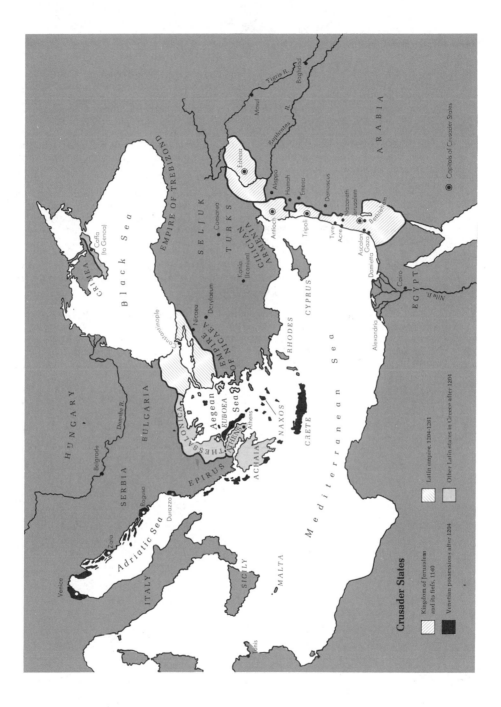

Crusader States

Kingdom of Jerusalem and its fiefs, 1140

Venetian possessions after 1204

Latin empire, 1204-1261

Other Latin states in Greece after 1204

⊙ Capitals of Crusader States

HUNGARY

SERBIA

Belgrade

Ragusa

Zara

Venice

ITALY

Adriatic Sea

Durazzo

EPIRUS

BULGARIA

Danube R.

THESSALONICA

Aegean Sea

ATHENS

Athens

EUBOEA

ACHAIA

SICILY

MALTA

CRETE

NAXOS

RHODES

Mediterranean Sea

Kotis

CRIMEA

Caffa (to Genoa)

Black Sea

EMPIRE OF TREBIZOND

SELJUK TURKS

Constantinople

Nicaea

EMPIRE OF NICAEA

Dorylaeum

Konia (Iconium)

Caesarea

CILICIAN ARMENIA

CYPRUS

Edessa

Mosul

Tigris R.

Baghdad

Euphrates R.

ARABIA

Aleppo

Hamah

Emesa

Damascus

Antioch

Tripoli

Tyre

Acre

Nazareth

Jerusalem

Bethlehem

Ascalon

Gaza

Damietta

Cairo

EGYPT

Nile R.

Alexandria

FURTHER READING

On the idea of reform, see Gerhart Ladner, *The Idea of Reform* (Cambridge, Mass.: Harvard University Press, 1959). On Cluny, see H. E. J. Cowdrey, *The Cluniacs and the Gregorian Reform* (Oxford: Clarendon Press, 1970); Robert G. Heath, *Crux imperatorum philosophia: Imperial Horizons of the Cluniac Confraternitas, 964–1109* (Pittsburgh: Pickwick Press, 1976); and Joan Evans, *Monastic Life at Cluny, 910–1157* (Oxford: Humphrey Milford, 1931).

A good brief introduction to Romanesque style is Gustav Künstler, *Romanesque Art in Europe* (New York: Norton, 1973), as is Kenneth John Conant, *Carolingian and Romanesque Architecture* (Baltimore: Penguin, 1974).

A classic on the Gregorian reforms is Gerd Tellenbach, *Church, State and Christian Society at the Time of the Investiture Contest* (Oxford: Basil Blackwell, 1948). See also Karl F. Morrison, *Tradition and Authority in the Early Church, 300–1140* (Princeton, N.J.: Princeton University Press, 1969), and Walter Ullmann, *The Growth of Papal Government in the Middle Ages,* 3rd ed. (London: Methuen, 1970).

On the Cistercians, see Wolfgang Braunfels, *Monasteries of Western Europe* (Princeton, N.J.: Princeton University Press, 1972), and Jean Leclerq, *The Love of Learning and the Desire for God* (New York: New American Library, 1962).

On the rise of the Crusade movement, see Vera and Helmut Hell, *The Great Pilgrimage of the Middle Ages* (New York: Clarkson N. Potter, 1967); Carl Erdmann, *The Origins of the Idea of Crusade* (Princeton, N.J.: Princeton University Press, 1977); Hans Eberhard Mayer, *The Crusades* (New York: Oxford University Press, 1972); and T. A. P. Murphy, ed., *The Holy War* (Columbus: Ohio State University Press, 1976).

PART V

CULTURE AND SOCIETY
IN THE HIGH MIDDLE AGES

13
The New Learning

SCHOOLS AND SCHOLARS

The intellectual history of medieval Europe is closely bound up with the character of medieval schools. From the monastic schools of the tenth century to the great universities of the thirteenth, institutions of learning and their curricula constituted a setting for intellectual development of far greater influence than any comparable process in the ancient world and different from the circulation of ideas in other civilizations. One reason for this aspect of medieval thought was the important role that monastic schools, libraries, and *scriptoria* had played in Charlemagne's revival of ancient Christian learning. In Carolingian monasteries the old curriculum of the *trivium* and *quadrivium* governed the primarily literary education that monasteries provided. From the tenth century on, changes in thought took place in the context of monastic literary education.

The first change was the increasing sophistication of grammatical and rhetorical education. The high literary quality of eleventh- and twelfth-century monastic literature is eloquent testimony to the improved status of these traditional subjects. The second change was the growing interest in the study of dialectic, or logic. An example of both changes may be found in the monastery of St. Emmeram at Regensburg, which boasted in the eleventh century of being a "second Athens" because of the reputation of its schoolmaster, Otloh. A passage in Otloh's autobiography suggests how early and in what manner logic had begun to challenge grammar and rhetoric for primacy:

[Dialecticians are] simple enough to hold that Scripture should be construed according to the authority of dialectic, and to believe in many passages in Boethius, rather than Scripture. Following Boethius, they reproach me for ascribing the name of ''person'' to anything but rational substance.

Otloh was a great teacher and a sensitive and troubled spirit. He was also a good prophet, for the formal study of logic challenged traditional ways of understanding Scripture. It also offered critical means of comparing apparently conflicting statements in Scripture and the writings of the church fathers. Throughout the eleventh and twelfth centuries considerable tension existed between the logical and literary analysis of key texts, especially in the monastic world.

Outside that world, in the schools attached to cathedrals and in the schools founded by private individual teachers in the eleventh century, the study of logic moved faster, partly because it could be applied in areas of study and thought that were not always prominent in monastic curricula. These schools became more and more popular in the late eleventh and twelfth centuries, and represent a second stage of the transformation of the setting for European learning. Under talented and dedicated bishops and individual teachers, such cathedral schools as those at Reims and Chartres, Laon and Paris, took advantage of their urban setting and their wide appeal to build an educational tradition that did not always rival but certainly complemented that of the monastic schools.

In the absence of widespread lay literacy and with limited means of communicating ideas, the schools of the eleventh, twelfth, and thirteenth centuries played a more prominent role in the history of thought and literature than modern schools usually do. As the relationships between literary and oral culture became more complex, the schools influenced wider areas of society and even lay thought. This influence may be seen in the thought of prominent theologians at monastic schools, the private schools of the twelfth century, the appearance of new subjects, and the universities.

SAINT ANSELM

The career of Saint Anselm (1033–1109) reflects many facets of the learning of the eleventh century. Born in Aosta in northern Italy, Anselm withdrew from the world and sought the contemplative life in the monastery of Bec in Normandy, then newly patronized by the rulers of Normandy. He eventually became schoolmaster and abbot of Bec, and then archbishop of Canterbury. Anselm was primarily a monastic theologian, and his literary works focused on the monastic life and monastic devotion. But in some of those works Anselm gave considerably more importance to the use of reason in devotion than had earlier monastic theologians. His best-known expression of this use of reason is the phrase *fides quaerens intellectum,* ''faith seeking understanding.'' Anselm proposed logic not as a road to faith or as an alternative to it, but rather as an important dimension of human nature that could be used only in conjunction with faith: ''I do not seek to understand in order that I may believe,'' he once wrote, ''but I believe in order to understand, for I also know that if I did not have faith, I would not be able to understand anything.'' Or, as he wrote elsewhere, ''I want my understanding to comprehend in a certain way that same truth that my heart believes and loves.''

Although he subordinated reason to faith, as all medieval thinkers did, Anselm greatly opened the role of reason in theological discourse. In a work called the *Proslogion* Anselm demonstrated that the truths of faith were not incompatible with reason. In his

The Faces of God: Christ in Majesty. The image of Christ in majesty, triumphant and serene, was a popular theme in early medieval art. It is shown here on the ninth-century Lorsch Gospels.

famous "ontological argument" about the proofs of the existence of God, he claimed to discover a proof of God's existence that needed no further proof outside itself. Here again reason reaches the same conclusion as faith and revelation.

PETER ABELARD

Peter Abelard (1079–1142) was the son of a knight in the service of the count of Brittany. Instead of taking up his father's profession of arms, he left the little town of Le Pallet and traveled through northern Francia studying under private teachers, including Anselm of Laon, a student of Saint Anselm and a prominent logician. Having a quick mind and a striking personality, Abelard claimed to have surpassed his own teachers. He became a professional teacher himself and moved to Paris. Although Abelard belonged to no monastery and had no formal right to teach theological matters, he began to lecture on precisely that subject. He soon became the most popular teacher in Francia, attracting students from England, Germany, and Italy as well as from the provinces of Francia itself.

But Abelard made enemies as well as friends and admirers, as much because of his sometimes abrasive personality as because of the novelty of his thought and teaching. Fulbert, a canon of the Cathedral of Notre Dame in Paris, invited Abelard to tutor his niece, Heloise, a brilliant student and later an eloquent and touching writer. Heloise and Abelard fell in love and married. Fulbert, outraged at the secrecy of the marriage and Heloise's pregnancy, hired a gang of thugs, who broke into Abelard's living quarters and beat and castrated him. Both Heloise and Abelard withdrew from the world and took religious orders, Heloise at the convent of Argenteuil and Abelard at the monastery of St. Denis. After a brief retirement, however, Abelard resumed teaching and again students flocked to hear him. Although some of his theological ideas were condemned at the Council of Soissons in 1121, he became once more the most popular thinker in Europe. Condemned again at the Council of Sens in 1140, Abelard made plans to go to Rome and plead his case directly before the pope, but he died before he could do this. He recounted his earlier career in his autobiographical *History of My Troubles.*

Individual teachers of logic had stepped into theological speculation before Abelard, but none had acquired his reputation—or encountered as violent an opposition. During Abelard's own lifetime such theological doctrines as the Eucharist (the presence of Christ in the consecrated bread and wine of the Mass), the reasons for Christ's Incarnation and Crucifixion, and the nature of conscience all attracted much discussion, some of it traditional but some of it extremely novel. The most important novelty in the new theological literature was the question of realism and nominalism, or the problem of universals. Late antique Neoplatonic thought had speculated upon whether individual things, species, and genera exist as substances or as mental abstractions. In one influential work, the sixth-century thinker Boethius had followed Aristotle and stated that existence can be predicated only of real things; mental categories were mere abstractions, convenient cognitive devices and nothing more. In another work, however, Boethius followed Plato, arguing that such categories as species and genera were real things that existed in the mind of God, and that this existence was superior to the material imperfection of earthly things. Some twelfth-century thinkers argued for the Aristotelian approach: only individual things have reality; the groups into which we classify them are simply *nomina* (names) and possess only a cognitive reality. Others argued for universalism, the Platonic notion that only the ideas in the mind of God were real, that individual things possessed only an inferior reality. Nominalism in its broadest sense argued that truth could be discovered only by the study of individual things and material creation; realism argued that truth could be discovered only by the contemplation of universals. Abelard himself adopted a modified nominalist position. Begun in the late eleventh century, this debate continued throughout the Middle Ages. It was one of the most significant frameworks for theological and philosophical discourse down to the seventeenth century.

Abelard's most important works were the *Ethics* and the *Sic et Non.* The former is subtitled *Know Thyself,* and it was this knowledge that Abelard regarded as the cornerstone of good and evil actions. Echoing the current theological emphasis upon the love of God for humanity and the necessity for humans to participate actively in achieving their own salvation—the latter a topic in Saint Anselm's writings—Abelard stressed the importance of human intention in any estimate of the gravity of a sin or the virtue of a good act. He thereby contributed to the psychology of the twelfth century a view of human motivation that greatly widened the concept of the human personality. In addition to his emphasis upon intention and consent, Abelard stated that internal sorrow for sin was the essential stage of penance.

The *Sic et Non* ("Yes and No") is a teaching manual in which apparently contradictory passages from Scripture and the writings of the church fathers are placed side by side. Thus was revealed the problem of reconciling the diverse texts upon which Christianity based its beliefs. In his preface to *Sic et Non*, Abelard laid down the criteria for systematically reconciling the apparent contradictions and, as in many of his other works, insisted that the application of logical method was the key to understanding the self, the self's relation to God, and the complexities of revelation. Aside from the colorfulness of his career, it is in this insistence on the supremacy of logical method that Abelard's originality lies and his influence is seen most clearly. Indeed, in his logic, his moral theology, and his autobiography we see one of the most remarkable and original thinkers in European history.

FROM CUSTOM TO LAW

Just as the increased study of logic led to its application to theological problems, it also aided the development of a critical method in the study of law. The great rational legal work of the sixth century, Justinian's *Corpus Iuris Civilis,* appears not to have been known in western Europe, except at second hand and through early Germanic law codes that it influenced, until the early twelfth century. The renewed interest in logic and rhetoric during this century led the rhetorician Irnerius (1088–1125) of northern Italy to begin studying a text of this work. Irnerius and his successors in the twelfth century first faced the task of explaining the literal meaning of the words of the Roman law to their students. Then, as legal study became more sophisticated, teachers and students began to appreciate the stupendous intellectual achievement that Roman law represented.

By the mid twelfth century the "Four Doctors," Martinus, Bulgarus, Rogerius, and Hugo, had developed the techniques of explaining the texts of the law by writing marginal glosses, composing short treatises on legal reasoning, and writing summaries of individual titles in Justinian's collection. Medieval teachers of Roman law believed that the law was binding throughout Italy and the Holy Roman Empire, and the cities of Pavia and Bologna became especially well known as centers of Roman legal study. After more than a century of scholarship on Roman law, the jurist Francis Accursius (d. 1260) arranged the long tradition of commentary on the law into a single systematic commentary that became known as the *glossa ordinaria,* the ordinary gloss, of Roman law. In time the *glossa ordinaria* was routinely taught in schools of Roman law along with the text of the law itself.

Of course, the development of early European legal institutions had produced a body of law very different in complexity and purpose from Roman law. From the earliest Germanic law codes to the customary legal arrangements of individual manors, villages, and towns, early European law possessed little of the philosophical and professional attraction of Roman law. In addition, the fragmenting of political authority in the ninth and tenth centuries had tended to turn legal institutions into the private property of lords who controlled law courts, pocketed the fines they awarded, and administered a heavy-handed and primitive kind of local justice. Some legal systems, such as that of Anglo-

Christ Pantocrator. The image of Christ Pantocrator, "the Judge of all," was of Byzantine origin. This dome mosaic from the church at Daphni, near Athens, influenced the West at a time when church decoration was being developed in order to overawe the spectator. (J. Powell, Rome)

Saxon England, were relatively highly developed, but Anglo-Saxon law was subsumed under the oppressive legal practices of William the Conqueror's Norman aristocrats. In most of the principalities that made up eleventh- and twelfth-century France, regional customs determined legal practice. Moreover, much law operated under heavy procedural limitations and according to the theory of immanent justice—the belief that in certain cases divine intervention is required to indicate the guilt or innocence of the accused. Thus, various forms of the ordeal and trial by combat were practiced because it was believed that in them the will of God was revealed.

Much eleventh-century law resembled the older Germanic laws of the migration period; it was part of a system of undifferentiated social control by religion, ethical custom, and kin discipline. Law, as much else of life, was a kind of contest in which an accuser and an accused engaged not so much in a legal dispute but in a confrontation to determine whose interests the majority of the community favored. Unless the accused had been caught in the act, the court could do little to convict him if he denied the accusation. And unless the court could set a number of compurgators—persons whom the accused would assemble and have swear to his reputation (they did not produce evidence)—agreeable to both accuser and accused, the judgment of the case had to be handed over to God. The infinite classification of status in the early European world meant that in law courts, as elsewhere, each individual had a certain legal identity. This identity reflected in the law court what the individual and his community knew already—that status determined both the extent of the court's control over individuals and the character of that control. The great emphasis in early European law on procedure, status, immanent justice, and the sanctity of custom provided a viable means of social control, one that accommodated to the requirements of eleventh-century society, but it did not constitute a very good system of law.

The rediscovery of Roman law threw traditional practices into sharp relief. Twelfth-century teachers of Roman law tried to fit it into the law of the towns of northern Italy, southern France, and parts of the empire. Naturally, they encountered a great many difficulties, but their efforts tended to make law more rational and systematic. In Ranulf de Glanvill's treatise *On the Laws and Customs of England* (1188), it was suggested for the first time that English law was susceptible to explanation in an orderly and logical manner, just as Roman law was. At the same time, King Henry II of England was engaged in sweeping away the variety of jurisdictions and practices in English law and imposing instead the law practiced in the royal courts, which later came to be called the common law of England. In the thirteenth century a royal justice named Henry De Bracton wrote the most sophisticated and rational analysis of a national legal system in European history, *On the Laws and Customs of England.* Between 1279 and 1283 Philippe de Beaumanoir wrote a treatise *On the Customs of the Beauvaisis* (the region around the city of Beauvais in northern France) that showed mastery of the principles of Roman law and applied them to a body of regional law totally different in origin and development.

The revival of Roman law coincided with a growing distaste for the confusion and archaism that many thinkers found in eleventh- and twelfth-century European law. Even in those legal systems that formally remained outside the orbit of Roman law, such as the common law of England, the rationality, systematization, and regularity of Roman law made a great impact. Twelfth-century theologians protested against the use of the ordeal and the trial by battle, on the grounds that they tempted God and were a kind of blasphemy. When the Fourth Lateran Council in 1215 forbade clerics to participate in the administration of the ordeal, the older legal procedure was well on its way to becoming a dead letter. In its place theologians approved the collection of evidence, its analysis, and a decision based upon rational process. So did the teachers and students of Roman law, who also worked as scribes, agents, judges, lawyers, and consultants for the towns, principalities, and monarchies of western Europe. Even those students who did not intend to become lawyers often studied Roman law for a time in order to acquire the intellectual training and discipline that the study of Roman law offered. The recovery of Roman law in the late eleventh and early twelfth centuries was one of the most important changes in the schools and the judicial systems of Europe. It touched abstract legal learning, helped rationalize the practice of law throughout Europe, and habituated many to solving disputes by rational procedures.

CANON LAW AND THEOLOGY

The revival of Roman law and the slow spread of its influence to the customary laws of different regions in Europe illustrate the appeal that systematic, consistent thought exerted upon a society that had suddenly become aware of its own lack of system and the inconsistencies of its own law. The growth of theology and canon law in the twelfth century also reflect that perception.

With the spread of learning and the production of more manuscripts, thinkers became aware of the inconsistencies that also existed in the vast body of religious literature that the eleventh and twelfth centuries had inherited from the past. Peter

Abelard's *Sic et Non* was an ambitious attempt to illustrate the conflicts in interpretation in the sources and to devise a reliable method for resolving them. In spite of opposition to Abelard's theology, his method attracted more and more followers, for it offered an irresistible tool for solving the problems that thinkers had become more acutely aware of. In addition to Abelard's logical study there was, as we have seen, a transformation of the substance and temper of theology, illustrated in Saint Anselm's linking of reason and faith and in Abelard's sophisticated psychological analysis of intention and consent. Moreover, such theologians as Saint Bernard paved new ways in devotional literature, sharing with Saint Anselm and even with Abelard a new sense of the love between God and humankind, a fascination with the human Jesus, and a new emotional dimension to theological thought. It is in the light of these three developments that the rise of the study of theology and canon law ought to be considered.

In 1140 Gratian, a monk at Bologna, compiled a collection of apparently conflicting statements dealing with the laws of the Church. He arranged these conflicting texts in a logical sequence in order to solve a systematic set of problems of ecclesiastical law, and he called his book *The Concordance of Discordant Canons*. Far more than Abelard's work, Gratian's *Concordance* was informed by a mind both legally acute and devout. From the beginning to the end of his work, Gratian imposed order, principle, and coherence upon the previously undigestible materials of ecclesiastical law. He marshaled over four thousand different texts from dozens of authors, sometimes using as many as seventy to clarify and illuminate the diverse sides of a single topic. Between the texts, introducing them and bringing each topic to a conclusion, is Gratian's own commentary, a model of lucidity and economy. Although it always remained unofficial, the *Concordance* became the model for later official collections of canon law and for the system, used in subsequent theological works, of grouping thematically related texts and analyzing them.

Around 1150, and probably under Gratian's influence, Peter the Lombard, a master in the Paris schools and later bishop of Paris, produced his book of *Sentences,* a systematic collection of scriptural texts and writings of church fathers and masters that dealt topically with theological problems. The works of Gratian and Peter Lombard became the schoolbooks for the study of law and theology, and in some cases they were used until the beginning of the twentieth century. Arising in the schools and from masters such as Abelard, Gratian, and Peter Lombard, the principles of selecting, ordering, and typologizing diverse texts were now applied to the disciplines of law and theology.

Thus, the masters of theology in the schools moved further and further away from traditional methods of explaining Scripture. The language of theological definition and explanation became more and more that of the schools of logic and the philosophers, and less that of the meditative and literary traditions of the past. Not only did the new language and the new systematizing of thought and exposition explore further dimensions of the relationship between God and creation, it opened vistas in the definition of the human personality.

As the tools of logic and philosophy became the tools of theology, specialization, training, and formal expression became necessary for theological study. In the course of this process, the number of the sacraments was finally set at seven and their nature was defined; the complex questions touching definitions of nature, grace, sin, and salvation now received firm answers. In teaching theology the master now proceeded to treat texts, no matter how traditionally authoritative, in terms of the questions they illuminated, and the choice of these questions and their complexity directed the thrust of study. In time, such questions became the principal form of theological exposition.

The creation of canon law was as significant as the development of the new theology. From Gratian's *Decretum,* as *The Concordance of Discordant Canons* was informally known, through the unofficial and later official collections of papal legal decisions that appeared in 1234, 1298, and 1314, scholars and popes shaped a body of law that laid down a new, juridical view of the relationship between the individual Christian and the Church. This body of law remained valid and in use throughout Christian Europe until the Reformation of the sixteenth century and in the Roman Catholic Church until 1918. Part of its influence lay doubtless in Gratian's organizing principles, which displayed clearly where the greatest legal problems lay, and in the fact that the lack of a fundamental organization comparable to that of the *Corpus Iuris Civilis* left teachers and students much room to add their own thought to the body of scholarship on the law or to criticize Gratian's. From a course in the liberal arts, including dialectic, students moved on to read Roman law. They might then proceed to canon law, their minds sharpened by logicians, Romanists, and their own teacher of canon law. The first commentaries upon Gratian's collection are hesitant and elementary. Longer commentaries quickly appeared, however, modeled upon those produced by teachers of Roman law—*summae,* questions, and rules. Several of the early canonists, or decretists, greatly influenced later approaches to the teaching and the creation of church law. Such twelfth-century figures as Rufinus, Stephen of Tournai, and, the greatest of all, Huguccio of Pisa, were followed in the early thirteenth century by Richard of England, Alan of England, Tancred, and Johannes Teutonicus, who composed the *glossa ordinaria* to the *Decretum* around 1215.

THE UNIVERSITIES

The schools of Paris in the days of Peter Abelard and for decades afterward consisted of assemblies of students grouped around individual masters, the students paying the masters individually. These assemblies came under the ecclesiastical jurisdiction of the bishop of Paris and his chancellor. In Paris and Bologna the experience of individuals coming together to study in a strange city far from their homes was a social and legal novelty, and the very presence of the schools and their lack of legal status rendered the students vulnerable to much of the hostility generated by the inveterate localism of the twelfth century. Unprotected by citizenship, status, or privilege, students were subject to price and rent gouging, a lack of legal protection, and the perennial distresses of under-financed strangers.

In 1158 the emperor Frederick I Barbarossa, whom we will meet again in Chapter 15, issued the *Authenticum Habita,* in which he extended his protection to students in imperial territories. In particular the document granted students free travel and legal immunities, and recognized that their study profited the emperor and his subjects. As a professional social consciousness grew among teachers and students, so did formal recognition of the status that successful study conferred. In the late twelfth century there appeared the ceremonial inception, a public defense of one's learning that has parallels in the formal rites of initiation into the order of knighthood, the oath of citizenship in the corporation of citizens of a town, and the ritual recognition of the status of master in a craft guild.

Thus, students and teachers slowly created a collective place for themselves in a society that jealously guarded its status ranks and left unprotected the stranger without status. They formed corporate bodies called guilds, which were similar to religious fellowships and craft associations. These defensive measures taken by the late-twelfth-century schools consisted of creating for scholars a recognized corporate status. *Universitas,* the Latin term used to designate the schools, was a common word indicating any collectivity, from craft guild to confraternity to body of citizens, and the formal designation of the universities was *Universitas societas magistrorum discipulorumque,* "the university, or society, of masters and students."

Schola, from later Roman imperial and Byzantine tradition, meant many different groups regarded simply as groups. *Schola* in academic terms remained the designation of a master and his students together. A group of *scholae* working in close proximity and having a similar character was called a *studium,* and certain *studia* were given the exalted status of *studium generale.* These terms possessed no collective legal status, however, and privileges such as the *Authenticum Habita* applied to scholars individually, giving them no collective rights and recognizing no collective legal existence. The key events in the history of the universities occurred between 1200 and 1220, when the issuance of papal, imperial, and royal privileges entitled the scholars to act as a legal corporation, an *universitas.* They thereby had the right to be represented legally as a corporation, to possess a seal, to collect and administer common funds, and to sue and be sued collectively in courts of law. In some places as in Paris, the *universitas* was one of the masters alone; in others, such as Bologna, the students constituted an *universitas.* Through such societal and juridical changes, the universities came into legal as well as social existence by the middle of the thirteenth century.

In 1200 King Philip II Augustus of France provided an extensive charter of privileges to the *universitas* at Paris, a document generally regarded as the foundation charter of the present university. In 1231 Pope Gregory IX issued the decree known as *Parens scientiarum,* "the mother of knowledge," which afforded ecclesiastical privileges to the University of Paris. The universities of the thirteenth century, possessing legal existence, often suffered from the organizational problems that other "universities" suffered from: disputes between masters and students, among masters, students, and the officials of the diocese, and between scholars and townsmen. Possessing legal identity, universities could leave a city, negotiate with another city for accommodations and move there, supervise lower schools in the vicinity, issue collective pronouncements on public questions, and regulate areas as diverse as the book trade and the rate of rents charged to students and teachers. For the universities existed only legally, and not physically, except for their members. There were no university campuses, no libraries, no buildings that were distinctly and exclusively a university's. Lecture rooms were rented in private buildings. Masters took students into their homes for residence and instruction; students who did not live in a master's house had to find private lodging. Only slowly, through gifts, did individual buildings become university property. Even the earliest colleges consisted simply of endowed funds that paid for the housing, feeding, and instruction of poor students under masters' supervision; they were more charitable trusts than physical places. For example, the Sorbonne, the popular designation of the University of Paris, derived from the gift by Robert de Sorbonne in the thirteenth century of a charitable endowment for the support of poor scholars. The first buildings belonging to Oxford, Merton College, were left by Robert Merton. He had acquired them from the Oxford Jews, who had renovated them and thus helped originate what is commonly called the Gothic style of college architecture.

Within these legal and physical circumstances the schools developed their curricula and played out their role in terms of the new and the old learning. The triumph of logic, the subordination of the subjects of the *trivium* to the increasingly professional disciplines of theology and law, and the creation of the degree, the *licentia ubique docendi*—"the license to teach anywhere"—shaped their internal intellectual processes, just as their privileges, legal status, and endowments shaped their physical and social character.

The universities prospered because society needed them. The Church, faced with increasing business at Rome and in the great dioceses after the Investiture Conflict, felt an increasing need for capable, loyal, trained assistants, and it had the great power to attract the men it needed. The twelfth century was probably no more fond of legal disputes than the eleventh, but the new law courts of the towns and the courts of kings and princes and prelates had to be staffed. Moreover, lesser princes and prelates began to find that when their clerical business was not kept up, their revenues and status declined perceptibly. All of these potential patrons helped generate a new demand for learning and letters.

When Abelard returned to Paris in 1136, one of his students was a young man who had been born about 1115, raised in the old episcopal town of Salisbury, and then sent to Paris to study. In 1147, after completing his studies, John of Salisbury joined the papal court. He remained there until 1153, when he became the secretary of Theobald, archbishop of Canterbury. Europe in the 1140s and 1150s was full of opportunities even for men from places as remote as England. The chancellor of the papacy in 1146 was Robert Pullen, the English theologian, and from 1154 to 1159 the pope himself was the Englishman Nicholas Breakspear (Hadrian IV), who had previously spent many years in papal service. John worked closely with Theobald and his successor, Thomas Becket. Exiled in the 1160s, John was present at the murder of Becket in 1170. In 1176 he was elected bishop of Chartres, a post he held until his death in 1180. Becket, a friend and patron of John, was descended from a prosperous Norman citizen of London, was sent abroad to Paris to study, was also a clerk of Theobald's, and became chancellor of England and then archbishop of Canterbury under Henry II.

Such careers as these—and there were many more as striking—illuminate the changing conditions in the world of governance and power. Learning now meant success, although many students failed to achieve the careers they sought and hurled bitter charges against those they thought prevented it. Even successful men such as John of Salisbury condemned the intellectual extravagance and bombast that sometimes passed for learning; they and others complained that true learning was bypassed and that flashy superficial talents seemed to make all the headway. These criticisms have much substance, but they also remind us of the extent of the new learning and what it might have offered to ambitious, brilliant, or merely glib, aspiring officials.

Nor were the rising scholars only those whose social origins made them more mobile and adventurous than the rest. John of Salisbury and Heloise had come from ecclesiastical surroundings, Abelard from the backwoods of Brittany, Becket from the streets of London. One of Becket's contemporaries at Paris may have been Reginald von Dassel, not one of the greatest students there but a person of noble birth who later became provost of the cathedrals at Hildesheim and Münster and, after 1156, the chancellor of the Roman emperor Frederick Barbarossa (whose uncle and biographer, Otto of Freising, had also studied at Paris). Such opportunities afforded ambitious students considerable incentive to seek out the best (or the most popular) schools and teachers and to cultivate among their contemporaries those who gave promise of one day being able to dispense patronage. Such a network of schools, scholars, career aspirants, and patrons contributed much both to the patronage of learning and the spread of the schools and to the institutions of administration and governance. They imparted a new style to the centers of power, and they patronized others like themselves. In short, in a world of established ranks and orders they created the professional career. In doing so they also shaped the intellectual circumstances in which administration, communication, and educational institutions dealt with day-to-day problems, formed theories of law and governance, and contributed a new intellectual dimension to the old problems of society and its organization. The promotion of scholars also transformed the character of the offices they filled. As students moved into ecclesiastical or lay aristocratic households and took over the administration or the legal affairs of a complicated domestic establishment, they introduced management principles based upon their own experience in the schools. They approached the traditional duties of bishop, legate, and pope more and more from the point of view bred in them during their studies.

FURTHER READING

Besides the works listed in the General Bibliography under the heading *Thought and Learning,* see E. Gilson, *A History of Christian Philosophy in the Middle Ages* (New York: Random House, 1955), and Margaret Gibson, *Lanfranc of Bec* (Oxford: Clarendon Press, 1978). The best study of Anselm is R. W. Southern, *St. Anselm and His Biographer* (Cambridge: Cambridge University Press, 1963). See also Jasper Hopkins, *A Companion to the Study of St. Anselm* (Minneapolis: University of Minnesota Press, 1972).

On Abelard, see J. G. Sikes, *Peter Abelard* (Cambridge: Cambridge University Press, 1932), and Leif Grane, *Peter Abelard* (New York: Harcourt, Brace, Jovanovich, 1970). See also D. Luscombe, *The School of Peter Abelard* (Cambridge: Cambridge University Press, 1969).

No one should miss Beryl Smalley, *The Study of the Bible in the Middle Ages* (Notre Dame: Ind.: Notre Dame University Press, 1964), or M.-D. Chenu, *Nature, Man and Society in the Twelfth Century* (Chicago: University of Chicago Press, 1968). A classic work is Charles Homer Haskins, *The Renaissance of the Twelfth Century* (reprint ed., Cleveland: Meridian, 1957).

For Glanvill, see G. Hall, *Glanvill's Treatise on the Laws and Customs of England* (London: Nelson, 1966), and Michael Clanchy, *From Memory to Written Record* (Cambridge, Mass.: Harvard University Press, 1979).

On canon law, see Stephan Kuttner, *Harmony From Dissonance* (Latrobe, Pa.: St. Vincent's Abbey, 1960).

The great works on universities are Hastings Rashdall, *The Universities of Europe in the Middle Ages,* 3 vols, ed. F. Powicke and A. B. Emden (Oxford: Clarendon Press, 1936), and Lynn Thorndike, *University Records and Life in the Middle Ages* (reprint ed., New York: Norton, 1975). On one interesting case, see Beryl Smalley, *The Becket Conflict and the Schools* (Oxford: Basil Blackwell, 1973).

14

Religion and Society

DISSENT AND HERESY

The religious movements of the eleventh and twelfth centuries reflect the deepest strata of European language, consciousness, and culture. The successful struggle against paganism was virtually over by 1100. Monastic reforms, reform of the clergy, and the new prominence of the popes in European ecclesiastical and lay life all marked a new stage in the development of Christian society. But churchmen were not the only ones whose lives were touched by change. The transformation of lay piety was as important a phenomenon, and it was more complex. But for some clergy and laity even the reforms of the eleventh and twelfth centuries were not sufficient. These centuries witnessed the first recorded surge of popular religious dissent since the later Roman Empire. Religious dissent among the laity and clergy that reveals some evidence of popular interest and support appears in a few sources between 1000 and 1050, in virtually none between 1050 and 1100, and then in a great number and variety of manifestations from 1100 on.

Not only does religious dissent occur more frequently in the sources, but it occurs against a background of heightened religious sensibilities, new forms of devotion, the popularity of pilgrimage, the construction of new churches designed for large crowds, and the formalizing of beliefs and conduct by the emergence of theology and canon law. The theology of Saint Anselm, Abelard, and Saint Bernard, the elevation of marriage to sacramental status, the new prominence of the virtuous warrior on Crusade or in the service of the Church, and the expansion of such doctrines as that of purgatory (which held out the hope of salvation even after a sinful life) combined to offer both clergy and laity more hope of eventual salvation and more aids to devotional life than had been offered in the preceding five hundred years.

Much of the dissent, as we have seen, was directed at unreformed clergy, particularly during the Investiture Conflict, and was concerned with one form or another of clerical purity. Married or concubinary clergy and clergy who had polluted themselves by paying for their offices were the main targets. In the twelfth century a broader and deeper heretical movement swept through Christian Europe. Not surprisingly, its roots have been the subject of much scholarly and confessional controversy. The term *haeresis* came into Latin from Greek, where it had originally designated the general concept of choice; later it referred specifically to the different beliefs of the philosophical schools. In Christian Latin usage it gradually acquired the meaning of doctrines held contrary to the teaching of the Church. The thirteenth-century definition of Robert Grosseteste conveys both the contemporary and the original meanings of the term: "Heresy is an opinion chosen by *human* faculties . . . *contrary* to sacred scripture . . . *openly* taught . . . *pertinaciously* defended. *Heresy* in Greek, *choice* in Latin." These meanings are important to remember in considering the development, content, and spread of heretical beliefs and the Church's response to them. The individual whose opinions ran counter to those officially proclaimed by the Church was not immediately guilty of heresy. He might be instructed, cautioned, asked to change his mind, or, in the manner used by Saint Bernard, publicly denounced. For heresy to exist, it had to be openly maintained and taught; the concealed heretic did not emerge as a problem until later. Finally, the true heretic was one who, admonished and corrected, openly maintained and defended his opinion against all opposition.

The use of the word *heresy* was extremely loose in the early twelfth century. Abelard applied it to persons who held incorrect theories of grammar, and much of the conflict between him and Saint Bernard leading to the condemnation of some of Abelard's doctrines at the Council of Sens in 1140 used the term in a way more reminiscent of the correction of an erring monk than of its later twelfth-century meaning. But the worlds of the cloister and the Paris schools were slowly drawing apart, and such conflicts grew sharper in the late twelfth and early thirteenth centuries.

As far apart as they were drawing, however, the worlds of Abelard and Bernard were still closer to each other than either of them was to the popular world of devotion, which was becoming more intense day by day. Indeed, "learned heresies" were rarely attacked as bitterly as the spreading popular heresies, and scholars retained a considerably greater latitude in their teachings than did popular preachers or heretical societies. One of the strongest condemnations made by the early Church, for example, was directed at astrologers. This hostility, which is reflected in the writings of the influential twelfth-century thinker Hugh of St. Victor, did not prevent astrology from becoming a popular learned pastime. Receiving the imprint of the Islamic thinkers whose popularity grew as the twelfth century wore on, astrology slipped in the door of orthodoxy, as it were, just before that door slammed shut against heresy and other forms of the occult.

The roots of popular heresies, however, were more complex than scholars' disputes or monastic unorthodoxy. Just as the tenth century had witnessed a turn to the more human aspects of the crucified Christ and the depictions of the Mother and Child, so the

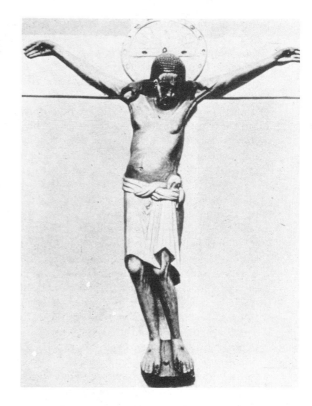

The Faces of God: The Suffering Christ. One way to trace the changing forms of Christian piety is to study the depictions of Christ and the different moods they invoke. One of the most moving and revolutionary images is that of the suffering Christ crucified, an image that gained popularity after the tenth century. This is one of the earliest of such images known, the crucifix of Archbishop Gero of Cologne, from around 975. (University of Pennsylvania)

tenth, eleventh, and twelfth centuries saw increased veneration of the Virgin. Yet side by side with this new sensibility and the new devotion it inspired, another set of attitudes appears to have evolved, attitudes that savagely attacked what was considered to be the confining of divine power in earthly material symbols. In the eleventh and twelfth centuries groups led by preachers attacked churches, overturned altars, burned crosses, and bitterly denounced the clergy. The general crisis concerning the extent of the reform movement, which worked itself out in the twelfth-century decrees of popes and councils, engendered uncertainty in the believing public. Moreover, both progressive reformers and hostile, traditionalist critics heaped scorn on the burgeoning legal business of the papal chancery and the administration of the Church. Saint Bernard's attacks upon the extravagance and materialistic Christianity of Cluny and the diversion of the papacy into the law courts found many ears and were echoed and distorted by many minds. Some scholars have drawn the distinction between movements of reform and movements of heretical unorthodoxy. Reform and dissent that became heretical were defined as sharply by the definitions of orthodoxy with which churchmen met their challenges as they were by their own internal development.

Throughout the first half of the twelfth century, the sources describing heresy and dissent tend to reflect certain traditional views of their subject. First, they tend to assume that twelfth-century movements were simply revivals of what Saint Bernard called "the heresies of old," that is, the movements of dissent and heresy that marked the first six centuries of the Church. Thus, most groups who believed in two supernatural powers, one good and one evil, were labeled Manichees. By the middle of the twelfth century, however, writers appear to have known much about the new movements and to have regarded them more as "novelties," than as older heresies revived. In addition, historians have long debated the influence of heretical movements from outside of Europe. The most controversial of these was Bogomilism. Apparently emerging as a heresy in the Byzantine Empire, Bogomilism found a home in Bulgaria and moved west on trade routes and Crusade routes in the early twelfth century. The Bogomils attacked much of the fabric of Christian orthodox belief. They echoed Manicheism by denouncing material creation and the creator as evil gods and in emphasizing the exclusive goodness of spiritual beings. Bogomil influence has generally been rejected by recent scholars, however, and the roots of all Latin heretical movements have been located in the religious excitement of the twelfth-century conscience.

The two best-known types of heresy in the twelfth and thirteenth cen-turies—Waldensianism and Catharism—flourished primarily in Provence and Languedoc in the south of France. Waldensianism, named for the merchant Valdes of Lyons, held the doctrine of the corruption of the Church, the priesthood of all believers, the necessity of preaching and reading Scripture in the vernacular, and apostolic poverty. This group, which resembled in many aspects other voluntary groups later accepted by the Church, differed from similar sects in its intransigence rather than in doctrine. Ad-monished, they would not accept ecclesiastical conditions; they were, in Grosseteste's term, pertinacious. Catharism, whose name derives from the Greek word meaning "pure," was more complex. Sharing the Bogomil concept of a material universe created by an evil spirit, Cathar doctrine may also have shared the antimaterialistic revulsion that we have noted accompanying the growth of a "humanized" relationship between God and man. The Cathars held that human spirits were imprisoned in flesh, and for them the greatest sin was procreation, imprisoning another spirit in the material world. God sent Jesus, who only appeared to take on the characteristics of a human being, to show humans the way out of the trap of material creation. None of the "human" aspects of Jesus—not the cross, not the passion, not the Church that was built on those symbols—had anything to do with God. The Church was a creation of Satan, and hell was earth, imprisonment in the material world.

One of the bitterest charges leveled alike by reformers, dissenters, heretics, and even high churchmen was at the ineptitude and immorality of the clergy. Such charges had lain behind the success of the reform movement of the late eleventh century and the church councils and local prelates of the twelfth. To a large extent, many of these charges were true. Yet it is difficult to know where to lay blame for what is, after all, an anachronistic charge. There were no training schools for clergy; bishoprics often were awarded for petty temporal reasons and with ecclesiastical connivance or the clergy's sub-mission to temporal power. The lowest clergy came untrained from the same class of peo-ple whom they served. Moreover, the rapid growth of towns and the settlement of new lands tended to make for a shortage of clergy, especially at the parish level. The growth of dissent and heresy posed acute problems to the Church and, because the Church touched the lives of all, to European society as a whole. Besides the problem of ongoing Church reform and that of the relation between spiritual and temporal powers, the problem of ordering the Christian life loomed large as the twelfth century came to an end.

THE RISE OF PAPAL AUTHORITY

From the first movement to reform the papacy, in 1046, until the end of the twelfth century, the popes exerted an increasingly active and successful headship in Christian society. Depending originally on the support of the emperor Henry III, and then, during the Investiture Conflict, upon that of prominent lay nobles and kings, the papacy slowly transformed its administration and strengthened its claims to supremacy in Christian society. By the second half of the twelfth century it was the real leader of the Church.

Among the most important stages of this process were the reform of the papal curia (the immediate servants of the pope in Rome) by Pope Urban II, the growth of papal prestige through the Crusade movement, the establishment of papal legates (officials sent by the popes to different parts of Europe with special legal and political authority), and the frequent holding of church councils to publicize and legislate the ideals of reform. In addition, the appearance of such works as Gratian's *Decretum* and later canon-law scholarship strongly emphasized the constitutional and legal authority of the popes. The papacy also gained in its ongoing struggles with kings and emperors, for in the twelfth century neither of these powers could marshal arguments as sophisticated and persuasive as those of papal lawyers. Finally, the areas from which popes were recruited also changed. The interpretation of episcopal status in the early Church was that a bishop had to remain in the diocese in which he became a bishop—he was ''married'' to his see. Early medieval popes therefore tended to come from diverse backgrounds in clerical life and not frequently from the ranks of the bishops. From the mid twelfth century on, however, this older view was relaxed (in part because of the work of canon lawyers) and more popes came from the ranks of bishops and servants of the papal curia. Many of these men also had experience and training as lawyers, and thus their early lives prepared them very differently from their predecessors for taking an active role as pope.

Among the popes of the twelfth century who helped transform the papacy into a great power were Alexander III (1159–81) and Lucius III (1181–85). Significantly both had spent long periods in papal service: Alexander III had been in charge of the papal chancery (the office for writing documents) and Lucius III had been a cardinal whose name appeared frequently on documents from the mid twelfth century on. This experience was important for men who came to occupy an office that grew more complex every year. Not only did the popes have to communicate actively with churchmen and lay people throughout Europe, they had to govern the city of Rome and the papal states in central Italy as well.

The furtherance of reform on the one hand and the eradication of heresy on the other became the twin goals of the papacy at the end of the twelfth and beginning of the thirteenth century. One means of achieving these ends was the frequent holding of church councils, both on a European scale and regionally when necessary. In 1123, for example, the year after the Investiture Conflict was ended by the Concordat of Worms, Pope Calixtus II called the First Lateran Council in Rome. There were many other councils during this century, among them the Second Lateran Council of 1139, the Council of Rheims in 1148, the Council of Tours in 1163, the Third Lateran Council in 1179, and the Fourth Lateran Council of 1215. These councils put the full force of the papacy and the rest of the Church hierarchy behind the reform movement, the organization of the Church, and the new developments in theology and canon law. The canons passed by the councils were copied by the attending prelates and taken back to their own dioceses, where they were translated into legislation tailored for each diocese. Thus was the work of the universal Church brought down to the level of the parish and individual monastery.

Not every churchman was pleased at the new influx of business that occupied the time and the minds of the twelfth-century popes. Saint Bernard bitterly denounced the volume of legal business handled by the chancery, the legates, and the popes. The legal dimension of papal activity increased throughout the late twelfth and early thirteenth centuries and imprinted itself upon the concept of the community of the Church. Popes of the late twelfth century, in fact, may be seen to alternate between men who desired to maintain papal authority to the letter of the law (and sometimes beyond it) and men who were willing to compromise with opponents, to check some of the consequences of an excessively legalistic conception of papal authority, and to cultivate devotion and piety rather than administration.

This dichotomy was perhaps more complex than it at first appears. The career of perhaps the greatest of the popes, Innocent III (1198–1216), reflects both of these aspects of the papacy. In decretal after decretal Innocent laid down with striking precision supported by juridical reasoning the principles of papal authority, assembling throughout his pontificate a formidable body of legislation that gave concrete legal shape to papal authority. Yet Innocent possessed a second side. His biographer devotes considerable attention to Innocent's care for the well-being of the Church—and of individual churches, on the restoration and decoration of which Innocent spent much money and time. He responded with surprising swiftness to the new devotional movements of the early thirteenth century, and should not be viewed solely as a lawyer and administrator acting within a narrow, legalistic tradition. Innocent's sharp sense of the different spheres of his authority may be seen in the case of the imperial election of 1198. In that disputed election Innocent favored Otto of Brunswick over the rival candidate, Frederick Barbarossa's son Philip of Swabia. The nobles who favored Philip accused Innocent of intervening improperly in favor of Otto. But his letters to them on this subject established very clearly his conception of his own power. He did not, Innocent wrote, have any intention of interfering with the princes' right to elect the king of Germany. The king, however, was only an emperor-elect; he had to be examined by the pope for his suitability as a defender of the Church, and rejected if found wanting. This literature represents a careful distinction among princely rights, explicit papal rights, and universal papal responsibility for the whole Church, and the balance among them is very carefully maintained.

The pontificate of Innocent III witnessed the most extensive application of the constitutional theories of the papacy developed in the twelfth century. In a dramatic series of councils, exchanges of letters, and diplomatic agreements with a wide spectrum of temporal powers, Innocent gave substance to the legal authority of the pope and sharpened the concept of papal authority over heretics.

Between 1198 and 1209 there was no emperor in Italy, and Innocent's control of the Papal States and his guardianship of Frederick II in Sicily gave him more practical authority than many of his predecessors had had. In 1201 Otto IV acknowledged the remarkably sweeping claims made on behalf of papal authority, as did Walter of Brienne, a candidate for the crown of Sicily. In the decretal *Sollitae* to the Byzantine emperor (1201) Innocent made vague but serious claims to universal authority. In two decretals of 1202, *Venerabilem* and *Per venerabilem,* Innocent further defined his authority in cases subject to temporal jurisdiction. At the same time, and for a while after, Innocent negotiated with

the excommunicated king of England, John. The pontificate of Innocent III, the busiest
if not the greatest of medieval popes, revealed the broad spectrum of jurisdictional areas
across which the theories of papal authority could be spread and the extraordinary ability
of the pope and his curia to make such theories the basis for practical decisions in hundreds of particular cases.

THE ATHLETES OF GOD

Part of the Church's response to dissent and heresy was to develop new approaches to
pastoral theology—the care of souls. A group of moral theologians at Paris under the
leadership of Peter the Chanter adapted twelfth-century theology to specific cases and
social needs, thereby bridging the philosophical theology of the schools and the problems
of daily living. By 1200 there were handbooks for helping preachers and confessors perform similar functions. The papacy also turned to traditional institutions within the
Church, particularly to the Cistercian monks. But in spite of the occasional successes of a
Saint Bernard, monks proved unable to win a hearing from the busy lay and clerical
world. Some laymen and clerics, however, began a new kind of pastoral movement.
Realizing that the heretics had adopted preaching in the vernacular languages, they too
began to preach. In 1206 one of the canons regular of the Spanish diocese of Osma, Domingo de Guzmán (1170–1221), having witnessed the ineffectiveness of Cistercians attempting to refute heretics in Montpellier, decided to organize a group of clerics who
would be trained to preach and to live in strict poverty. For ten years Domingo—or
Dominic—worked with a small group of trained preachers, and between 1215 and 1217
the group dispersed to carry out its mission in different parts of Europe.

Dominic himself went to Rome, where he encountered two remarkable individuals: Pope Innocent III and Saint Francis of Assisi (1182–1226). Born to a wealthy
merchant family in central Italy, Francis spent his youth and young manhood in the
military and literary secular pastimes of his society. Suddenly, at the age of about twenty,
he began to reject his own background and to circulate more and more freely with poor
priests, lepers, and beggars. In 1206 he received his mission in a vision and began to
preach. Francis and his first companions preached as laymen, rejected the ownership of
property for themselves, and drew up a simple rule that attempted to translate the gospel
into a program of action. Pope Innocent III, who was, as we have seen, both a capable and
ambitious administrator and a man of great vision, accepted Francis's rule, and became a
particular patron of the new group.

Both Saint Dominic and Saint Francis discovered in preaching and poverty two of
the most effective keys to the pastoral needs of their age. Because of their poverty, the
orders each man founded reached out to those who criticized the wealth of the established
Church. By bringing the license to preach, hitherto a prerogative of bishops alone, to
priests who were specially trained for the task, they finally began to equal the appeal of the
heretical preachers. In addition to the rights to preach of Saint Dominic's Order of
Preachers (popularly, the Dominicans) and Saint Francis's Order of Friars Minor (the
Franciscans), other individuals, even some lay people, were enabled to preach, although
in doing so they were limited to exhortation rather than the exposition of dogma. The
wave of preachers over the thirteenth and fourteenth centuries had an incalculable im-

pact, and the literature of preaching influenced thought and secular literature for several centuries.

HERESY, CRUSADE, AND INQUISITION

The new orders of Franciscans and Dominicans captured the essence of the Church's new spirituality and employed it in a pastoral context. There was another side to the thirteenth-century church, a juristic one, and it was also called into play, particularly when the orders seemed less than successful. As we have seen, the work of episcopal and papal courts had grown in the twelfth century. The procedure they used borrowed more from earlier ecclesiastical procedure and Roman law than from the kinds of law used in the lay courts of the twelfth century. Early European law, both temporal and ecclesiastical, was based upon the accusatorial process, in which a private accuser made charges before a judge and the accused party responded. This was the format of all trials, criminal and civil, including those decided by ordeal, by judicial duel, or by compurgation. Another process was sometimes used, however, one that allowed the judge to act independently of an accuser when the accused was guilty of public notoriety. Episcopal visitations—a bishop's formal visits to subordinate churches—throughout a diocese used this procedure. In the twelfth century those newly familiar with Roman law discovered the complexity of the inquisitorial procedure, in which, unlike the accusatorial procedure, the judicial authority itself might begin a case and inquire into its facts. The decretal *Ad abolendam,* issued by Pope Lucius III (1181–85) in 1184, ordered all bishops to inquire after heretics within their jurisdictions—to conduct, in effect, an inquest. Early legislation against heresy aided the spread of the inquisitorial process, but that process was still used loosely, and the chief punishment was anathema or excommunication.

In 1199, however, Innocent III published the decretal *Vergentis,* in which he increased the punishment of heretics to include the confiscation of goods and property. The chief importance of this text lies in its specific application of the old Roman legal concept of treason to heresy. In this decretal heresy became treason to God, and the forefeiture of worldly possessions and excommunication were consistent with the penalties prescribed for treason in Roman law, though they did not yet lead to the death penalty. In 1208, however, the papal legate Pierre de Castelnau was murdered in Toulouse, and Innocent decided to launch an all-out attack upon the center of Catharism. Thus began the Albigensian Crusade against the heretics and their indifferent rulers, the counts of Toulouse. Later, Innocent's successors would launch the Inquisition.

The Albigensian Crusade lasted from 1209 to 1229; it destroyed the heretical culture of Occitania (the lands of southern France) and marked the turning of the Crusade against Christians. Innocent recruited an army from the north of France. For two decades of intense military conflict, acts of brutality on both sides, and the slaughter of heretics and orthodox Christians alike, the knights of the north battered and ultimately destroyed the rich and varied civilization of the south.

But the military campaigns did not wipe out centers of heresy, and Innocent's successors, particularly Gregory IX (1227–41), doubled their efforts to urge bishops and councils to use inquisitorial techniques to discover hidden heretics. By 1233 Gregory had begun using the Dominicans and Franciscans as inquisitors, granting them powers that traditionally belonged to the bishops, particularly in those districts in which bishops seemed ineffective. By entrusting inquisitorial powers to the orders, Gregory moved a long way toward establishing a permanent tribunal directly under papal authority for discovering heresy by means of the inquisitorial process.

The continuous role of the Dominicans and Franciscans as inquisitors developed the inquisitorial process quickly. Although most of their earlier coercive power had been psychological, financial, and sacramental, the inquisitors discovered the technique of "relaxing" or "releasing" recalcitrant defendants to "the secular arm," the lay magistrates who could use physical force without violating their canonical status. In the hands of the members of the Holy Office—the official title of the Inquisition—the inquisitorial procedure developed its first oppressive features: the concealment of the identity of witnesses and the specifics of evidence, the refusal of counsel, the obligation to identify accomplices as a sign of repentance, the admission of evidence from hitherto unacceptable witnesses, and, in Innocent IV's decretal *Ad extirpanda* in 1252, the admission of torture.

Judicial torture made its first reappearance in Europe since the Roman Empire early in the thirteenth century in the city-states of northern Italy, where it probably derived both from new kinds of crime and law enforcement and from the revival of Roman law. By 1252 it had become an instrument of the Inquisition, and from that date until the nineteenth century judicial torture spread from the town courts of Italy and the Inquisition's chambers into most of the criminal courts of the Christian world. Within a century, the newly armed Inquisition had crippled heresy in Occitania, and the Church had acquired a formidable and terrifying instrument for detecting and rooting out heresy. The new coercive powers of the Church were felt by others besides heretics, particularly by the Jews of Christian Europe.

CHRISTIAN ATTITUDES TOWARD NON-CHRISTIANS

Most medieval Christians shared the ignorance of the wider world beyond Europe and the Mediterranean that characterized late Roman geography and anthropology. They generally believed that the equatorial zone was so hot that humans could not pass through it into the Southern Hemisphere; also, since Jesus had come to save all people, there could not be people in that hemisphere, which was sometimes called the Antipodes. Within the inhabitable Northern Hemisphere, however, there were many wonders and monsters, many of them drawn from the literary tradition of Pliny, Strabo, and other Roman geographers. These images of monstrous humans and humanoids survived into the Renaissance, and even Shakespeare's audience recognized the tradition when Othello told of

> my travels' history;
> Wherein of antres vast and deserts idle,
> Rough quarries, rocks, and hills whose heads touch heaven,
> It was my hint to speak—such was the process;
> And of the Cannibals, that each other eat,
> The Anthropophagi, and men whose heads
> Do grow beneath their shoulders.

Such creatures survived in literature, particularly travel accounts, long after the Middle Ages, but speculation on distant and unknowable humans was not a major concern of medieval thinkers.

More important were those yet to be converted to Christianity, such as the pagan Baltic and Slavic peoples, who were not converted until the fourteenth century, or pagans who might be converted by Muslims or Jews, as Christians feared the Mongols would be in the thirteenth and fourteenth centuries (see Chapter 18). Most important were those peoples—Muslims and Jews—who were neither pagans nor Christians and who lived both inside and outside of Christian Europe. Christian attitudes toward non-Christians were shaped primarily with Muslims and Jews in mind. Because Christian relations with Muslims took place generally in the areas of trade and crusading warfare, Christian official attitudes are best discovered in the writings of canon lawyers. By the twelfth century these legal comments had replaced the earlier literary and purely theological ideas and put Christian–Muslim relations on a new footing.

The late eleventh and early twelfth centuries witnessed distinctly new forms of anti-Muslim and anti-Jewish expression. Christian attitudes toward the Muslims were a mixture of curiosity and persistent misinformation. To Bede, the eighth-century English chronicler, the Muslims were the descendants of Hagar and Ishmael, the Old Testament outcasts. To others they were a schismatic Christian sect whose doctrines were a perversion of Christian doctrines (some even constructed an imaginary Muslim "Trinity" consisting of Muhammad, Apollo, and Termagant). For those in Spain, Sicily, and Byzantium who dealt with Islam on a day-to-day basis, however, there was much mutual understanding and even cultural sympathy; Carolingian attitudes toward Islam had been marked, one historian has observed, by "caution and sobriety." El Cid, as we have seen, could casually feud with Alfonso VI of Castile and enter the employment of Muslim leaders without apparent pangs of conscience, and so could many others. Away from the frontiers, however, the new Christian self-consciousness generated strong anti-Muslim attitudes.

By the thirteenth century, popes and canon lawyers had laid down a theory justifying Christian invasion of Muslim lands in Syria and Palestine and used that justification as an approach to the question of whether Muslims could exercise any kind of just dominion over humans. That is, could a non-Christian polity be considered a legitimate polity? Such questions as these greatly widened Christian legal and political thought, although they would not have provided much comfort to a Muslim who read them. By forcing questions of international relations into a religious framework, Christian attitudes toward Muslims greatly influenced the later development of Christian European attitudes toward non-Christians generally. The attitudes of Christians toward Muslims developed largely in the atmosphere of Crusade propaganda and legal discussions. Most Muslims lived out of the reach of Christian authorities—except for those in conquered parts of Spain and south Italy and in the Crusader states—and the problems of dealing with them were similar to those of dealing with foreigners generally.

With the Jews, however, the situation was different. The Jewish population of northern Europe appears to have increased in the ninth and tenth centuries, and as we have seen, Jewish communities in northern France and the Rhineland were the first to suffer from the first crusading forces. There is considerable scholarly disagreement on the subject of the relative status of Jews before and after 1100. Certainly, taxes imposed upon Jews date as early as 1051 at Macon in southeastern France. On the other hand, the earlier Gallo-Roman status of the Jews, as well as Carolingian protective legislation, appears to have survived into the twelfth century. Some scholars, in fact, have gone so far as to regard many Jewish communities and individuals as wholly indistinguishable from their Christian contemporaries in the eleventh and early twelfth centuries. In a relatively

Strassbourg Cathedral: Ecclesia and Synagoga. (left) The figure of *Ecclesia* (Church), suggests the power of personified images and the techniques of Gothic sculpture. The female figure symbolizing the Church stands crowned, with cross and cup. (right) The figure of *Synagoga* (Synagogue), a personification of the Jews, holds a broken spear and disused book, items that correspond in symbolic value to the cross and cup of *Ecclesia.* Such visual juxtaposition of images reflects the antisemitism of thirteenth-century Europe, suggesting the paradox of art conveying social assumptions. (Marburg Art Reference Bureau)

economically undifferentiated society in which such overemphasized Jewish activities as slave trading, moneylending, and commerce can have occupied only a small part of the Jewish population, this view has much to recommend it. Certainly it helps correct the false image of the very wealthy Jews who bought their privileges and lived in great pomp, an image that runs from twelfth-century monastic writers to the pages of Sir Walter Scott's *Ivanhoe.*

Two clear ideas appear to date from the early twelfth century: the principle that the Jews had no legal rights except those granted them by the king, first outlined in England after 1135, and the necessity for firm pronouncements guaranteeing the safety of Jews from high ecclesiastical authorities. In 1120 Pope Calixtus II issued a decretal, *Sicut Judaeis,* reminding all Christians of this responsibility, and Saint Bernard had to hurry to Germany in 1144 to stop the new persecutions of Jews that attended the preaching of the Second Crusade.

By the second quarter of the twelfth century the danger to the Jews appears to have distinctly increased. The new self-consciousness of Christendom, described in earlier chapters, may well have played a role in this new hostility. Certainly the anti-Muslim attitudes developed in the eleventh century came in part from the new Christian self-confidence. The new humanizing of the figures of Christ and the Virgin may also have contributed to the hostility to Jews, whose imaginary atrocities in twelfth-century literature surely derive from this new devotional sentimentality. Finally, the treatment of Jews in the twelfth and thirteenth centuries must be considered in terms of the broader religious and social turbulence of the period. Ruling and governed elements in a society and culture develop their own distinctive insecurities, which produce fear and hatred, and this fear is projected onto whatever groups are the aliens of the moment. However deeply rooted and however indistinguishable from Christians the Jews were, in law, religion, and culture they were the most visibly alien group, more alien than the heretics.

Those who had long been acknowledged to have an obligation to protect Jews—the emperors, kings, and popes—began in the late twelfth century to issue formal statements of protection, but also to exact from the Jews what the letter of the law (most of which dated from the fifth and sixth centuries) permitted. The need for money on the part of thirteenth-century monarchies, the popes' furious attack on heretics and dissenters, and such legislation as the requirement that Jews wear identifying marks on their clothing, which dates from the Fourth Lateran Council of 1215, made these ''protectors'' less useful than a reading of the law and the theory about the protection of the Jews might lead one to expect. Kings and popes, as it turned out, were very dubious protectors at best. What Gavin Langmuir has called ''the balance of contempt and toleration laid down in the Church's doctrines'' was impossible to maintain. And when it was overthrown it was always on the side of contempt, brutality, and sacrilege. The twelfth and thirteenth centuries marked not only a new hostility toward individual Jews and Jewish communities, but the development of anti-Semitism in its most manifold and wide-ranging aspects.

A large part of the Christian public failed to recognize its debts to Jewish culture. There was, for example, the liveliness of the tradition of rabbinic *responsa,* which revealed much of the social life in Jewish communities. The great traditions of Talmudic and biblical scholarship culminated in the work of Rashi of Troyes (1040–1105) and—through Rashi's successor, Joseph Bekhor Shor—influenced the Christian biblical studies of Andrew of St. Victor in the twelfth century, Hugh of St. Cher in the thirteenth, and Nicholas of Lyra in the fourteenth. The role that Talmudic scholarship and philosophers such as Moses Maimonides (1135–1204) played in shaping thirteenth-century scholastic philosophy was especially significant. By the mid thirteenth century the image of the hated Jew had become a commonplace of general Christian culture, a commonplace that is still invoked by many non-Jews in the twentieth century.

A higher degree of literacy, contacts with Jewish societies in non-Christian lands, the rich Jewish philosophical and medical culture in the Mediterranean, the flourishing of Hebrew literature, even translations of Christian Latin works into Hebrew—all characterized medieval European Jewish society. Yet the European Jews, lacking rights, were exploited by ambitious and greedy rulers much as other classes of servants were. They experienced the formal protection and the pragmatic powerlessness of the higher reaches of the Church, and were exposed to the unremitting and savage hostility of the lower classes. Threatened with the destruction of the Talmud, exiled from England in 1290 and from France in 1306, the Jews of Europe were attacked, herded, and forced into the role of a despised minority, in which they remained by and large until the end of the seventeenth century.

As more Christians discovered the full range of their own religious beliefs between the eleventh and the thirteenth centuries, they perceived more sharply the differences between their creeds and those of the Jews. These discoveries, the exploitation of the Jews by their rulers, and the rising sentimentality whose ominous reverse side perpetuated legends of Jewish atrocities—all contributed first to the segregation of the Jews, then to their expulsion from kingdom after kingdom between 1290 and 1492, and last to the brutal caricature of their beliefs and humanity in the earliest anti-Semitic literature and propaganda.

FURTHER READING

On the rise of heresies and the general transformations of spirituality, see Malcolm Lambert, *Medieval Heresy* (New York: Holmes & Meier, 1977), and R. I. Moore, *The Origins of European Dissent* (New York: St. Martin's, 1977) and *The Birth of Popular Heresy* (New York: St. Martin's, 1975). See also Rosalind B. Brooke, *The Coming of the Friars* (New York: Barnes & Noble, 1975); Walter L. Wakefield, *Heresy, Crusade and Inquisition in Southern France, 1100–1250* (Berkeley and Los Angeles: University of California Press, 1974); Jonathan Sumption, *The Albigensian Crusade* (London and Boston: Faber & Faber, 1978); Edward Peters, ed., *Heresy and Authority in Medieval Europe* (Philadelphia: University of Pennsylvania Press, 1980); and Bernard Hamilton, *The Medieval Inquisition* (New York: Holmes & Meier, 1981).

On Innocent III, see Helene Tillmann, *Innocent III* (Amsterdam: North Holland Publishing Co., 1980). Besides the titles listed in the general bibliography under *Church History,* see Geoffrey Barraclough, *The Medieval Papacy* (New York: Harcourt Brace Jovanovich, 1968), and Peter Partner, *The Lands of St. Peter* (Berkeley and Los Angeles: University of California Press, 1972). On the popes and non-Christians, see James M. Muldoon, *Popes, Lawyers and Infidels* (Philadelphia: University of Pennsylvania Press, 1979).

15

The Political Culture
of Medieval Europe

THE OLD ORDER: PAPACY AND EMPIRE

The Concordat of Worms of 1122, the First Lateran Council of 1123, the death of Pope Calixtus II in 1124, and the death of the emperor Henry V in 1125 brought to a close several aspects of the Investiture Conflict and inaugurated a new stage in the relationship between popes and emperors. The Investiture Conflict had generated a large literature of political theory and propaganda, most of it supporting or attacking the claims of popes or emperors to supremacy within Christendom. In the course of the conflict the old Carolingian-Ottonian imperial ideal was defeated. Theorists of papal authority transformed the figure of the pope from the chief liturgical officer of the holy city of Rome to a legitimate constitutional authority supreme in many respects over all other Christian powers. Although new claims for and against papal or imperial authority were made for the next century, the rivalry between the two became a less significant focus of political theory and discussion. After the mid thirteenth century the old polarity between papacy and empire gave way to a consideration of the rights and powers of princes, city-republics, and territorial monarchies, even against the rights of popes and emperors themselves. By the late thirteenth century a new political order, one that considered the respective spheres of authority of popes and territorial monarchies and republics, had become the framework of European political culture.

We have already traced some of the routes by which the papacy of the period 1000–1300 was transformed from an institution of the early Middle Ages into a juridical and constitutional authority. Supported by canon law and the formal study of theology, this new papacy extended its claims to legitimacy throughout Christendom. It controlled a vast system of ecclesiastical provinces and institutions, was increasingly well financed, and balanced its legal supremacy with its liturgical powers. At the highest levels of Christian society, no imperial claims could match the combination of articulate claims made on behalf of the pope as the leader and in some ways the personal embodiment of the Christian church and society. But the redefinition of the legal and constitutional authority of the papacy, as well as its new style of administration, governance, and diplomacy, cost it much of its popular appeal. Earlier popes had been numbered among the fathers of the church. They were widely revered, chiefly on the grounds that they were holy men and teachers of their people, guardians of the tombs and relics of Peter and Paul, high priests of the holy city of Rome, and mediators between God and the Christian people. By the mid twelfth century, though, supporters of the papacy were complaining about the pressing routine of legal and financial business that took up the popes' time and attention. Even Saint Bernard complained to his protégé, Pope Eugenius III (1145–53), that papal piety seemed to be giving way to papal administration. Dissident movements also complained about the new institutional character of the Church, as did literary satirists, whose stinging verses accused the popes of venality, hunger for power, and neglect of their holy office. Few popes between the mid eleventh and late thirteenth centuries were regarded as saints after their death.

Although the popes of this period were no less devout and no less concerned about the spiritual welfare of Christian society than their predecessors had been, the demands made upon them were very different from those of an earlier period. As the social and political structures of European society had changed, so too had the concept of the Church and the expectations people had of its leaders. Many of those who complained the loudest about the "new Pharisees" of Rome also flooded the Roman curia with legal appeals, petitioned it for office and placement, and became its official theologians, lawyers, tax collectors, and administrators. The last major phase of the conflict between empire and papacy, then, saw a different kind of papal office on one side of the polarity.

The imperial office also changed during the later part of the struggle. The emperors of the Romans were also the kings of Germany, and the Investiture Conflict had revealed that the two offices were not as separate in fact as they might be in theory. The needs of the kingdom of Germany colored both the functions of the imperial office in the later twelfth and thirteenth centuries and the policy of the kings of Germany, emperors of the Romans. Although much of the earlier prestige and memory of the emperors from Charlemagne to Henry V survived in imperial policy and propaganda, the actual facts of imperial rule changed nearly as much as the actual problems of papal governance.

Let us recall some characteristics of the German monarchy and the imperial office in order to clarify the changes in both during the twelfth century. In an age when the physical presence of the king counted for much, the very size of Germany, five or six times that of England, meant that the king of Germany had to be constantly on the move. Tracing the itineraries of these rulers is an important part of the historian's work, not only because the itineraries reveal how often and how extensively the kings traveled, but where they *could* travel—where they had enough personal property or loyal subjects to afford them hospitality. The kings of Germany relied on their personal wealth to pay the costs of governing the kingdom, and this wealth, usually in land, was not distributed evenly throughout the kingdom. In some areas, notably the eastern borders of Saxony, nobles had opened up extensive lands in which the kings had never possessed any property or claims at all, and thus were virtually excluded from visiting. The limits upon royal resources left the German kings two sources of support: the royal *ministeriales* and the local church and aristocracy.

The *ministeriales* were unfree knights who administered royal property. Like the lowborn royal servants of the kings of England and France, they tended to dissolve into the local nobility as time went on. In order to control them efficiently, the German kings would have had to possess a sophisticated system of supervision, but they were never able to develop one. What some historians have called the "low intensity" of the German monarchy meant that kings rarely had systematic or efficient communications with, or effective control over, their local servants. The German aristocracy, unlike the aristocracy of England and France, possessed extensive lands that it owned privately and therefore did not hold from the kings. Most of the aristocracy's power base was out of the king's reach, and many nobles had no need even of nominal contact with the king. One way for the kings to achieve some control over the aristocrats was to give them lands that carried obligations of service, but many families were reluctant to accept these. Even when they did, they tended to merge the new lands with lands they already owned privately. Indeed, dynastic territory-building characterized many noble German families in the twelfth century. Even the old tribal duchies, while retaining their former names, became the territories of princely families in the twelfth century and bore little resemblance to what they were before.

Ultimately, the kings of Germany had to leave a great deal of power in the hands of the higher aristocracy, upon whose alliances they depended. This necessity, coupled with the expansion of German power to the east, created a powerful class of princes who effectively governed their smaller territories and expanded their lands into areas in which the kings had less and less authority. The best example of this aristocratic independence is the famous *Drang nach Osten,* the "push to the East," which developed steadily in the twelfth and thirteenth centuries, but under the direction of the princes, not the kings.

A second difficulty faced the German monarchs—that of an elective monarchy versus dynastic succession. With the death of the last Carolingian king of East Francia in 911, the five tribal dukes elected one of their number to become king. This man, Conrad I, died in 918 after nominating his rival, Henry the Fowler of Saxony, to succeed him, and the latter was acclaimed Henry I by the other dukes. Although Henry I's descendants were his son, grandson, and great-grandson, they too were elected formally. Even the Salian dynasty, which succeeded the Saxon dynasty in 1003, was a collateral branch of the family, and the Salians, from Conrad II to Henry V, seemed as much dynastic kings as elected kings and emperors. At the death of Henry V in 1125 the electors had the opportunity once again to seize control of the succession, and in fact they elected a non-Salian, Lothar of Supplinburg, as Lothar III (1125–37). At Lothar's death, however, they turned to a Salian relative, Conrad III of the Hohenstaufen family (1138–52). Conrad was succeeded by Frederick of Hohenstaufen, later known as Frederick I Barbarossa (1152–90), who was descended from both the Salian-Hohenstaufen line and the Welf relatives of Lothar III. Frederick Barbarossa's election appears to have been a compromise between these two dynasties, but Frederick's greatest enemies turned out to be representatives of the latter. Thus the electoral origins of the medieval German monarchy conflicted with the contemporary tendency to make titles the dynastic property of a single family. Although dynasticism may well have been the wisest route for a strong German monarchy, and in fact thrived under the Saxons, Salians, and Hohenstaufen, the electoral principle might be invoked when a direct dynastic line died out or when a strong emperor left a young or powerless heir. The tension between electoral rights and dynastic ambitions was a second problem that the German kings never dealt with successfully.

The imperial title gave the German kings opportunities to exploit territorial and financial resources in Burgundy and Italy, which were not available to them as kings only of Germany. The reign of Frederick Barbarossa suggests how skillfully (although with only limited success) the imperial title might increase the resources of the German monarchy. Because Barbarossa needed the financial resources of the northern Italian cities, he boldly asserted his imperial rights, not only claiming the Saxon and Salian traditions of imperial rule but invoking Roman law and Roman history as well. These imperial claims encountered stiff opposition from the independent Italian cities, which formed the Lombard League against him in 1167, and from the popes, particularly Alexander III (1159–81). Barbarossa had to compromise with both forces at the Peace of Venice in 1177. Barbarossa also attempted to forestall the growth of some of his aristocratic opponents, particularly Henry the Lion, duke of Bavaria and Saxony. By allying himself with other nobles, enriching them, and enhancing their power, Barbarossa succeeded in destroying the vast power of Henry the Lion, but even this triumph resulted in the emperor's recognition of the growing power of the German princes. Although Barbarossa kept control over the German church, one of the chief resources of the monarchy, here too the aristocracy began to acquire considerable authority during his reign.

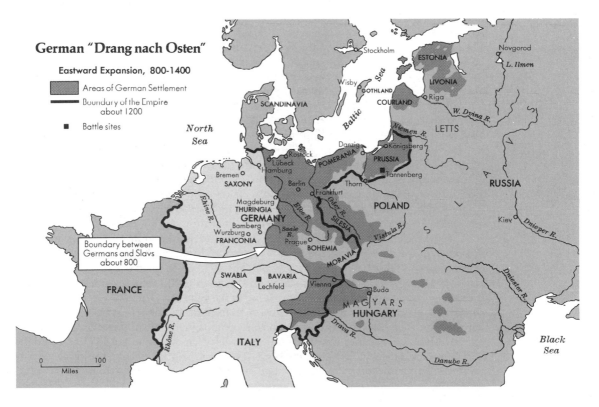

German "Drang nach Osten"

Eastward Expansion, 800-1400

Areas of German Settlement

Boundary of the Empire
about 1200

Battle sites

In 1186 Barbarossa married his son Henry VI to Constance, heiress to the kingdom of Sicily. When Barbarossa died in 1190 on a crusade to Jerusalem, Henry VI succeeded him in Germany, as emperor of the Romans, and, in his own right, as king of Sicily. Although Sicily proved a difficult kingdom to govern, it promised the German kings precisely that base of financial and military power that had largely eluded them in Germany and northern Italy. But the death of Henry VI in 1197 plunged Germany, Italy, and Sicily into a succession crisis. Henry left a three-year-old son, Frederick II, to succeed him, but Frederick's minority and the unleashing of rival forces in Germany and northern Italy plunged both royal offices and the imperial office into chaos. In 1198 Pope Innocent III chose Otto IV, son of Barbarossa's old enemy Henry the Lion, as emperor of the Romans. Supporters of the Hohenstaufen dynasty, the line of Barbarossa and the young Frederick II, revolted, and for ten years the political worlds of Germany, Italy, and Sicily were plunged into discord.

The growing ambitions of Otto troubled the peace of Italy and the empire virtually from the moment of his imperial coronation in 1209. When Otto's forces moved across the border of the kingdom of Sicily in 1210, Innocent excommunicated the emperor. With the collaboration of some of the stronger princes of southern Germany, Innocent then approved the imperial candidacy of Frederick, the young son of Henry VI and the insecure ruler of the beleaguered kingdom of Sicily. Frederick quickly traveled to Germany, rallied more support, and was crowned king of the Romans at Mainz at the end of 1212. In 1213, with the consent of the German princes, Frederick issued the Golden Bull of Eger, a document confirming the autonomy of the Papal States and echoing promises made by Otto IV a few years earlier. Otto was defeated by the king of France, Philip Augustus, at the battle of Bouvines in 1214, and formally deposed in 1215. He died in 1218. After promising to keep the German and Sicilian realms separate, Frederick was crowned emperor of the Romans at Rome in November 1220.

Frederick's insecure boyhood in Sicily and the difficulties of restoring order to the old Norman kingdom posed severe difficulties, and from 1220 on, the emperor directed his immense energies and considerable talents to the restoration of the southern kingdom. Frederick founded the University of Naples in 1224, chiefly to provide his kingdom with the scholars and administrators he needed. Naples was the first university to be established purely out of monarchical interest. In 1231 Frederick issued a remarkable law code for his Sicilian kingdom, the *Constitutions of Melfi*. With the issuance of this document, the development of a strong military and naval force, the recruitment of able administrators, and the imposition of a sound and efficient financial system, Frederick II shaped the kingdom of Sicily and South Italy into the most thoroughly governed, secularized state in Europe within little more than a decade.

Frederick's spirit of adventurous calculation is also reflected in his crusading policies. Although he had agreed to go on Crusade, Frederick was forced to postpone the expedition several times, and in 1227, when he had to postpone it because of illness, Pope Gregory IX (1227–41) excommunicated him. Undaunted, Frederick sailed to Jerusalem the next year and won a remarkable treaty with the sultan al-Kamil of Egypt in 1229. According to the treaty's terms, the holy sites of Jerusalem, Bethlehem, and Nazareth, along with a strip of coastal territory and certain other rights in the city of Jerusalem, were ceded to Frederick. The excommunicated emperor had won more rights in the Holy Land than any other crusader in the past century. The dissension between the pope and the crusading emperor, however, became one of the elements that helped to mute the ideal of the Crusade in western European thought.

The German
and Italian Realms
of Emperor Frederick II,
1212-1250

■ Battle sites

━━ Boundary of the Holy Roman Empire

Kingdom of the Two Sicilies

Papal States

Claimed by papacy

Venetian possessions

North Sea

PRUSSIA

Danzig

Lübeck

Hamburg

Elbe R.

Bremen

Weser R.

POMERANIA

FRIESLAND

SAXONY

BRANDENBURG

Oder R.

POLAND

HARZ MTS

Magdeburg

Goslar

Vistula R.

KINGDOM OF GERMANY

Elbe R.

SILESIA

LOWER
LORRAINE

Cologne

Meuse R.

Aachen

THURINGIA

Rhine R.

Saale R.

Frankfurt

Prague

Trier

Mainz

Main R.

BOHEMIA

MORAVIA

Worms

Würzburg

Bamberg

UPPER
LORRAINE

PALATINATE

FRANCONIA

Ratisbon

F R A N C E

Strasbourg

Danube R.

Augsburg

AUSTRIA

SWABIA

BAVARIA

Vienna

Rhône R.

Saône R.

Constance

STYRIA

KINGDOM OF BURGUNDY
(KINGDOM OF ARLES)

TYROL

CARINTHIA

Drava R.

Danube R.

CARNIOLA

Brescia

Trieste

Legnano

Milan

Adige R.

H U N G A R Y

LOMBARDY

Pavia

Po R.

Venice

Danube R.

Roncaglia

Alessandria

Genoa

Canossa

Ferrara

Avignon

Bologna

Ravenna

ROMAGNA

Zara

SERBIA

Arles

KINGDOM
OF ITALY

Pisa

Florence

Ancona

Adriatic Sea

Siena

Assisi

TUSCANY

Ragusa

CORSICA
(to Pisa)

PAPAL
STATES

Tagliacozzo

Rome

Alaghi

Bari

Naples

Melfi

APULIA

Amalfi

Salerno

Taranto

SARDINIA
(to Pisa and Genoa)

KINGDOM
OF THE
TWO SICILIES
(Hohenstaufen, 1194)

CALABRIA

Palermo

SICILY

Syracuse

M e d i t e r r a n e a n   S e a

Relations between pope and emperor continued to deteriorate, and Frederick's concentration on South Italy and Sicily weakened his power in Germany and led the papacy to forge alliances with the Lombard cities of northern Italy, who also felt their autonomy threatened by Frederick's energies and ambitions in the south. In addition to these political circumstances, Frederick's own royal style tended to cost him sympathy in the north. This splendid court and life in Sicily and South Italy appeared alien and exotic both to Germans and to the citizens of the northern Italian towns. The emperor surrounded himself with immense wealth and splendor, ranging from Muslim bodyguards and a multiethnic court population to the imperial zoo with its elephants and other strange beasts.

Frederick gave wide rein to his considerable intelligence and curiosity. Learned men from all parts of the Mediterranean world—Muslims, Jews, and Christians alike—thronged his court. Michael Scot, a well-known translator of Arabic works and a reputed sorcerer, was Frederick's constant companion. Speaking several languages with ease, Frederick was an integral part of the intellectual life of his court, not merely its pageantry-loving master. He corresponded with the mathematician Leonardo Fibonacci of Pisa. A poet himself, Frederick supported a school of court poets among his courtiers and administrators. So influential was the court poetry of Frederick II and his school that at the end of the century the poet Dante proclaimed Frederick the father of Italian vernacular poetry. A patron of the arts as well, Frederick left a powerful personal legacy throughout South Italy in his castles, public works, and sculptures. Frederick's new golden coins, the *Augustales,* reveal a quality of minting art and a metallic purity of an extraordinarily high character. To his subjects as well as his enemies, Frederick II was a remarkable and enigmatic man who was regarded more in awe and fear than in affection and respect.

Frederick's ambitions in the south led him to make concessions not only to the popes but to the German princes as well. In 1220 his *Confederation with the Ecclesiastical Princes* removed imperial rights of control from episcopal elections, and in 1232 his *Statute in Favor of the Princes* removed several important imperial rights over the great magnates. Although these concessions were not of vital importance as long as Frederick's personal political power was intact, they became immensely influential after the emperor's death and strongly influenced the growth of virtually independent princely power in Germany from the late thirteenth century on.

In 1237 war broke out between Frederick II and the great northern Italian cities. Although Frederick was initially successful, destroying the Milanese army at the Battle of Cortenuova in that year, Pope Gregory IX, alarmed by his ambitions and victories, excommunicated the emperor for a second time in 1239, and Frederick turned his forces against Rome itself. Gregory died in 1241, and his short-lived successor failed to deflect Frederick's ambitions. But the election of the Genoese canon lawyer Sinibaldo Fieschi as Pope Innocent IV (1243–54) seemed to indicate a change in imperial–papal relations. A member of a proimperial family, a superb jurist, and a man wholly lacking in what Frederick II considered the irritable majesty and mystical intractability of Gregory IX, Innocent IV appeared to be an ideal candidate for compromise.

Innocent turned out instead to be Frederick's greatest opponent. Turning the full energies of his mind and office against the emperor, Innocent rallied the Lombard cities and Frederick's other enemies. Escaping to the city of Lyons, he called an ecumenical council and announced the excommunication and deposition of the emperor in 1245. Innocent's decretal deposing Frederick, *Ad apostolice,* summed up fully and eloquently the canon-law tradition of papal authority over the emperor. In spite of a battle of pamphlets designed to wear down papal support—and even a series of complaints against Innocent's action by other European rulers—Frederick was unable to overcome Innocent's opposition. He resumed the war in northern Italy in 1248 and even began a march on the city of Lyons in the same year. But military reversals in the Italian campaign prevented Frederick from capturing the pope, and when the emperor died in 1250 the great German-Sicilian polity began to disintegrate.

Frederick's son, the emperor Conrad IV (1250–54), failed to hold his father's inheritance together. The German imperial electors, freed from the power of the Hohenstaufen dynasty, turned to non-German candidates for the imperial office. The system of electors reflects the transformation of German aristocratic society in the thirteenth century. The succession crisis of 1198–1215 and the conflict of 1245–54 between popes and emperors permitted many lords, clerical and lay, great and small, to assume virtually sovereign power over their own territories while holding only a nominal obligation of allegiance to higher authority. After the death of Frederick II, the *Confederation With the Ecclesiastical Princes* and the *Statute in Favor of the Princes* gave the nobility a free hand. Groups of cities formed mutually protective leagues. The Hanseatic League dominated the trade of the Baltic Sea and the North Sea; the Rhenish League and the Swabian League, founded in 1254 and 1331 respectively, dominated western and southern Germany. With local princes and towns increasing their local authority, the power of the nobles whose votes officially elected the king of Germany increased greatly, although the number of official voters was reduced to seven—four lay and three ecclesiastical princes. With the elimination of the Hohenstaufen dynasty, the electors turned to candidates who could buy votes or submit to control by the electors.

The papacy, now able to separate Sicily from Germany, formed an alliance with Charles of Anjou, brother of Louis IX of France, promising him the Sicilian crown if Charles could drive the last Hohenstaufen, Frederick II's illegitimate son Manfred, out of Italy. At the battle of Benevento in 1266 Manfred's forces were defeated, and Charles of Anjou accepted the crown of South Italy and Sicily. The German electors, with a confusion of imperial candidates, simply left the imperial title vacant from 1254 to 1273 and then elected a series of powerless emperors in the late thirteenth and fourteenth centuries. The old order had come to an end.

ENGLAND: FROM ANGEVIN EMPIRE TO ISLAND KINGDOM

The reign of Henry II Plantagenet (1154–89) illustrates both the building of royal institutions of government and law in England and the wider, less specifically English interests of a Continental lord. Henry II's titles reflect the personal empire of an ambitious and fortunate king in the late twelfth century. Henry inherited the county of Anjou from his father Geoffrey in 1149. He became duke of Normandy in 1151. He became duke of Aquitaine as a result of his marriage to Eleanor, heiress to that territory, in 1152. He inherited the throne of England from his mother in 1154. Later in his reign Henry received the title of lord of Ireland from the pope. In addition, Henry held other territories as a vassal of the king of France: he was lord of Maine, Brittany, Touraine, Berry, Poitou, La Marche, Auvergne, Quercy, and Gascony. As king of England in his own right and as vassal of the king of France for the rest of his lands, Henry II assembled a vast personal empire that included the entire western part of what later became France. He ruled territories that extended unbroken from the Scottish border to the Pyrenees.

Henry's father had advised him to permit local customs and governmental institutions to survive, and in fact Henry's different titles and different rights in different parts of his empire prevented him from creating a homogenized state. Nevertheless, he was a talented and ambitious ruler. His judicial and administrative reforms in England and Normandy began the creation of some degree of uniformity between the two most important territories of his empire. Even though he was a vassal of the king of France for much of his territory, Henry treated this relationship casually. On the other hand, he watched his lands like a hawk. He spent twenty-one years of his thirty-four-year reign as king of England on the Continent, and he spent his energies where he spent his time. If Henry had succeeded in establishing his rule on the Continent more securely, and if his sons had been able to hold his territories together, the present-day political maps of France and England might look very different. But Richard I the Lion-Hearted (1189-99) and John (1199-1216) could not hold Henry's empire together. Not only did they have personal shortcomings as rulers, but they encountered the stiff and successful opposition of two remarkably able and persistent kings of France, Louis VII (1137-80) and Philip Augustus (1180-1223). The relations among these five kings from 1154 to 1216 shaped the internal growth of both France and England and defined the territorial sphere of each king's authority.

The story of the growth and disappearance of the Angevin Empire of Henry II is the framework for the political history of England in the twelfth and thirteenth centuries. Within that framework Henry's governmental reforms and King John's formidable political concessions to his nobles transformed the governance of England. At the outset of his reign Henry faced the immense task of reconstructing royal authority in England after the nearly two decades of civil war and political anarchy caused by the succession contest between King Stephen and Henry's mother Matilda. Royal power had eroded drastically during this period. The English nobles, by changing sides and demanding royal concessions at opportune moments during the conflict, had acquired a degree of independence greater than any the Anglo-Norman aristocracy had enjoyed. In addition, the English church had become involved in the dispute. But with his astute judgment of royal servants, his ruthless drive to impose his authority, and his sophisticated concept of kingly power, Henry reshaped the governance of England and laid the foundations of a new monarchical constitution for the kingdom.

One way of measuring the effects of the anarchy created by the wars between Stephen and Matilda is to note that by 1154, at the outset of Henry II's reign, the royal income had fallen to around ten thousand pounds per year. Not until Henry II's death in 1189 did it attain the level of thirty thousand pounds per year reached in Henry I's reign. In addition, the great magnates who held their lands directly from the king, the tenants in chief, had grown independent between 1135 and 1154. They had also had time to develop a strong hereditary interest in their holdings, regarding their fiefs as a family right that ought to descend to no one but a child of the grantee. These two developments made the Anglo-Norman nobility much more dangerous in 1154 than it had been twenty years earlier, as did the fact that most of the 180 tenants in chief also held lands in Normandy as well as in England. Furthermore, the movement for ecclesiastical independence associated with the Gregorian reform principles came to England early, during the tenure of Saint Anselm as archbishop of Canterbury (1093-1109). During the civil wars of 1135-54, the English church grew even more independent of royal control.

The royal response to these movements within the nobility and the church was at first one of concession. In 1153 the Treaty of Winchester recognized certain hereditary rights among tenants in chief and all vassals of the crown. Henry I had earlier tried to maintain control of the church after the death of Saint Anselm in 1109. But the influence of reform made a strong impact on England, and most of Henry's senior clergy, even though he appointed them from his own household and from ecclesiastical establishments that he patronized, were imbued with reform ideals. During Stephen's reign the church added a practical degree of independence from the king to the theoretical independence that reform ecclesiology had already given it.

Henry II's first task as king was to establish the rudiments of public order in England. From the outset he insisted upon the destruction of unlicensed castles and the curtailment of private warfare. His second problem was that of royal finance. Henry first recovered and then reorganized the income from the lands he ruled directly, the royal demesne. Then he turned his attention to the money due him as overlord of his tenants in chief. He successfully converted the personal military service owed him into scutage—"shield money" paid to the overlord in lieu of this service. Although the costs of war rose rapidly in the second half of the twelfth century, Henry's financial basis for military affairs made him less dependent upon the uncertain resources of his vassals. Henry also made selective grants from his own lands in return for payment, and he increased the fees charged to those who collected taxes locally throughout the kingdom. He sold charters to municipal corporations, although he always distrusted cities and their populations. His legal reforms greatly increased the royal income from fines and pardons. Henry also brought more and more judicial business into his own courts, and thereby helped weaken the judicial powers of his vassals. Henry knew well that royal officials might be even more rapacious than the king, and he supervised them closely. In 1170, for example, he held an investigation of sheriffs, dismissing and fining heavily those whom he found either incompetent or excessively greedy.

Henry also developed an institution begun by Henry I. In 1156 his treasury, the Exchequer, was permanently established at Westminster, outside London, and its practices regularized. By the end of Henry's reign the institution was so efficient in keeping accounts of money paid to the king that one of its officials wrote a treatise about its operations, *The Dialogue of the Exchequer,* the first analytical treatise on institutional operation in European history. Henry's reign witnessed another mark of administrative significance. From 1156 on, the records of royal government survive for the most part in unbroken sequence, and for the period 1156–1220 they are very numerous. Henry II's administrators proved to be able and inventive servants of the king. We can trace their work from year to year in thousands of documents, whose existence makes the reign of Henry II qualitatively different for study from any previous reign in England or elsewhere.

His finances revamped and regularized and slowly growing, Henry II turned simultaneously to legal and ecclesiastical reforms. Of course, the profits of justice and income from the church were part of the royal finances, and Henry's motives for his reforms in these two areas were financial as well as political. Henry II's legal reforms, however, did not consist simply of restoring to the king those judicial rights that most of his predecessors had possessed and had let slip from their hands. As we have seen, the late twelfth century witnessed changing ideas about law and legal procedure in general, and the revived study of Roman law and the increasing sophistication of canon law also influenced legal reform in England. Occurring when they did, Henry II's legal reforms greatly transformed English law in ways that would have been impossible several decades earlier.

The pattern of English law at the accession of Henry II reflects the pattern of the Conquest. Ancient local courts of shire and hundred (some of which had fallen into the private hands of great laymen or ecclesiastics) existed side by side with the feudal courts of the Anglo-Norman aristocracy, for with most grants of land from the king had also gone the grant of jurisdiction on that land. Justice was local, and even the king's courts resembled the courts of any lord, dealing only with those matters that touched upon the king's rights as lord. Judges made their decisions according to local custom or on the basis of extremely limited modes of accusation and proof. For any cause it was necessary for one person to accuse another and for the court to decide between the litigants not on the basis of evidence, but upon the oath of one or the other or the successful outcome of an ordeal, when the procedure called for one. Such courts and procedures were much more instruments of social consensus and control than rational courts of law. For the most part, they regulated personal relations; they cannot be said to have administered ''justice'' in any modern sense of the term.

The king's court was like that of any other lord—with two exceptions. Because in England the king was everyone's ultimate overlord, and because he was the king, possessing certain extraordinary rights, he had slightly more freedom to claim jurisdiction in some cases than any other lord in England or Normandy. Henry I had begun to exploit these conditions, but it remained for Henry II to make a major transformation in the law of the land. In 1166 Henry II issued a set of instructions to a group of royal judges about to set out on a tour of the kingdom. These instructions, the *Assizes of Clarendon,* are a landmark in English law and reflect the knowledge of the law that Henry and his servants had acquired during his twelve years as king of England. The *Assizes of Clarendon* and other enactments of Henry's reign greatly increased the number of offenses that had to be tried in the king's own courts. In this way Henry II brought a great deal of criminal law under his own jurisdiction. Moreover, he required that a local group of landholders in each locality publicly testify under oath as to the criminal activities in their district since the last visit of the royal justices. This finding-jury, the predecessor of the modern grand jury, removed the necessity of a private person's having to bring an accusation against a criminal and put the burden of supervising the peace upon the community itself.

The legal procedures that Henry II developed for the courts of the royal demesne became models of superior efficiency and lesser cost to litigants. By emphasizing the rights of royal officials in shire courts, Henry associated these courts with the procedures in effect in the courts of the royal demesne. This slow legal revolution tended to homogenize the law of the two kinds of courts and constituted the basis of what later came to be called the Common Law of England. By the end of the twelfth century, a royal justice named Ranulf de Glanvill found English law to have become sufficiently rational and systematic that he wrote a treatise *On the Laws and Customs of England.* Like the *Dialogue of the Exchequer,* Glanvill's treatise—and the superior treatise of the same title written by Henry De Bracton in the thirteenth century—reflects the systematization of one of the most important social institutions of twelfth-century England. The large numbers of royal personnel who had to administer English law also testifies to the institutional importance of the laws, as does the establishment of a permanent Exchequer office in Westminster in 1156 and the settling of the Court of Common Pleas at Westminster in 1178. The court of Henry II, like that of the kings of Germany, was largely itinerant, and the placement of these two institutions in a permanent home indicated that the character of monarchical government was in an important process of transformation. Soon the kings themselves would cease to travel and would rule from a capital city.

Not all of Henry's high officials proved as docile as Ranulf de Glanvill and the author of the *Dialogue of the Exchequer.* Thomas Becket, the son of a landowning knight of

London, attended the schools of Paris and entered the service of Archbishop Theobald of Canterbury, where he rose quickly to a position of prominence. When Henry II ascended the English throne he made Becket his chancellor and then archbishop of Canterbury. But Becket proved to be more devoted as a churchman than a king's servant. He experienced years of exile between 1164 and 1170 and earned Henry's hostility for his refusal to conform the English church to the king's legal reforms. In 1170 Becket was assassinated by four of Henry's knights, although without Henry's knowledge or approval. Henry undertook a severe penance for the murder, but his reform legislation overcame both Becket's opposition and the immense popularity of the cult that formed around his martyrdom and sainthood.

Henry's sons nearly ruined their father's work. Richard devoted himself to Continental affairs, to the Crusade of 1187, and to his rivalry with Philip Augustus of France. In Richard's prolonged absences from the kingdom, however, the real strengths of Angevin governance became apparent. The busy, loyal agents who governed England in the king's absence developed the institutional character of English governance considerably. Richard's brother and successor, John, was energetic and intelligent, but a bad general and a tactless and capricious king. John also had the misfortune to lose much of England's Continental possessions to Philip Augustus, including Normandy in 1204, thereby giving his barons an immediate reason for opposing the king such as they had not had since the days of Stephen and Matilda. To make matters worse, John's interference in the election of the archbishop of Canterbury in 1206 permitted Pope Innocent III to intervene and choose Stephen Langton, a brilliant and popular theologian at the University of Paris. When John refused to accept Langton, Innocent placed England under an interdict—an ecclesiastical discipline imposed on a region. While the interdict was in force, from 1208 to 1213, few religious services were permitted and Christian life was publicly suspended.

Having alienated his barons by the loss of Normandy and the pope by his rejection of Langton, John brought further difficulties upon himself by his rapacious attempts to raise money for the recapture of Normandy. When he was defeated at the Battle of Bouvines in 1214 the barons turned on John and, on the field of Runnymede, forced him to issue a charter of privileges that promised to restrain the most offensive features of Angevin governance. The Great Charter, Magna Carta, was surely no Declaration of Independence, and it proved offensive to the pope, to whom John had given England as a fief in 1213. In its sixty-three clauses, however, even those dealing with technical problems of lordly rights, it is possible to discern some important principles. Subjects must be allowed to enjoy their customary liberties in peace; government might be hard, but it must not be capricious, and it must use regular procedures in collecting taxes and administering justice. In short, the king must be consistent, and he must recognize the myriad rights and liberties of his greater subjects. If he was not yet under law, he was now under custom. Although Angevin-style governance was not destroyed, it was brought face to face with principles that rendered its most offensive aspects less harsh.

John was succeeded by his infant son Henry III (1216–72), during whose long minority control of the government was disputed by great barons and papal legates. When Henry came of age he proved to be an ambitious but incompetent ruler. The public servants of the crown became more efficient, and the king took lower-ranking nobles into his service and extended his governance deep into the countryside. But the very efficiency of Henry's government and his use of low- or Continental-born servants outraged many of England's great nobles. Their response went much further than that of their predecessors at Runnymede; they forced the king to accept the Provisions of Oxford of 1258, which permitted royal governance to be controlled by groups of barons. Disputes between the king and the barons led to the intervention of Louis IX of France in favor of Henry III, but the barons, led by Simon de Montfort, rebelled and captured the king at the Battle of Lewes in 1264. A year later, however, Henry triumphed over the rebels at the Battle of Evesham and reasserted the king's supremacy in governance. Henry was succeeded by his son Edward I (1272–1307), one of the strongest English kings. Edward took Wales, fought in Scotland, developed the few Continental possessions left to the English king, and systematically enforced the royal common law of the land. He continually investigated baronial titles to jurisdiction and restricted the acquisition of land by the church.

By stressing the law, rather than royal whim, as the test of rights and liberties, Edward greatly strengthened the political order of England. He continued Simon de Montfort's innovative practice of calling a Parliament—an assembly made up of two knights from every shire and two burghers from every town—to learn of the king's business and assent to his actions. These assemblies had roots in the full sessions of the royal court, which had been held from the twelfth century on. At first Parliament met to give the king advice and to approve royal requests for taxation, but it was also the highest court in the kingdom, and it taught its members something about their common interests, sometimes against the wishes of the king. In the end, the reigns of Henry III and Edward I led England out of the difficulties created by the Angevin style of governance without capitulating to the self-interest of the great nobles or depending upon individual royal whim. Perhaps the phrase that best expresses the character of English governance in the thirteenth century is one that the people of that century invented: "the community of the realm."

The concept of the community of the realm is not as precise as that of the nation-state, but it accurately reflected the results of the innovations of Henry II and the crises under Henry III and Edward I. The scattered communities of early-twelfth-century England had been forced into what some historians have called "self-government at the king's command." Royal justices sat and administered the same law in all parts of the kingdom. Representatives of boroughs and knights of the shires attended Parliament, which was both a court and a representative assembly of the politically aware and financially responsible subjects of the king. In England the law was the medium through which the king and his subjects arrived at definitions of their respective rights and responsibilities. Together, below the law, they constituted the community of the realm. That unique constitutional creation had been shaped by shrewd and greedy kings out of the rough mix of tradition and autocracy that survived the eleventh century. The association of local communal consciousness with a national monarchy was the great result of the Angevin experiment.

THE MOST CHRISTIAN KINGS OF FRANCE, 1108–1328

At the beginning of the twelfth century France was a large kingdom in theory but a small and poor one in fact. Although the kings of France were technically the overlords of the great territorial princes whose vast, thoroughly governed domains surrounded the small royal domain in the Ile de France—the dukes of Normandy and Burgundy and the counts of Anjou, Blois and Chartres, Champagne, and Flanders—their overlordship was usu-

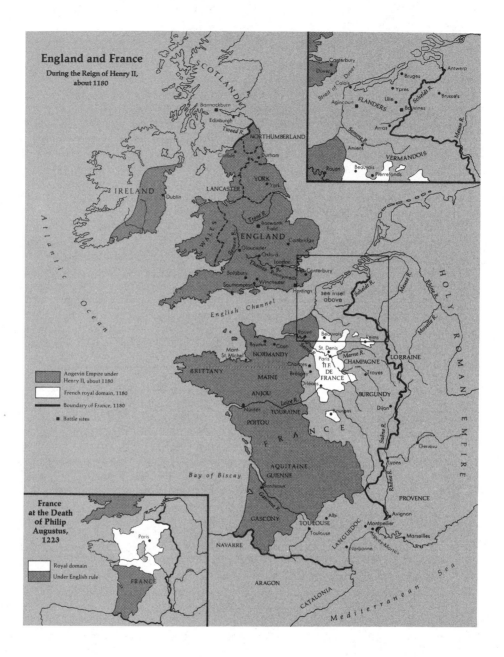

England and France
During the Reign of Henry II,
about 1180

SCOTLAND

Bannockburn
Edinburgh
Tweed R.
NORTHUMBERLAND
Carlisle
Durham

IRELAND
Dublin
YORK
LANCASTER
York

WALES
Bosworth Field
Trent R.
ENGLAND
Cambridge
Gloucester
Oxford
Salisbury
Thames R.
London
Southampton
Winchester
Runnymede
Hastings
Canterbury

Atlantic Ocean

English Channel

Angevin Empire under Henry II, about 1180
French royal domain, 1180
Boundary of France, 1180
Battle sites

Rouen
Beauvois
St. Denis
Paris
Bayeux
Caen
NORMANDY
Mont-St.-Michel
Chartres
Brézigny
ÎLE-DE-FRANCE
CHAMPAGNE
Troyes
LORRAINE
BRITTANY
MAINE
ANJOU
Orléans
BURGUNDY
Dijon
Loire R.
TOURAINE
Nantes
Bourges
POITOU

Bay of Biscay

FRANCE

AQUITAINE
GUIENNE
Bordeaux
Garonne R.
GASCONY
Geneva
Lyons
Rhône R.
PROVENCE
Avignon
TOULOUSE
Toulouse
Albi
Montpellier
Marseilles
LANGUEDOC
Aigues-Mortes
Narbonne
NAVARRE
ARAGON
CATALONIA

Mediterranean Sea

HOLY ROMAN EMPIRE
Moselle R.
Meuse R.
Scheldt R.
Saône R.

see inset above

Inset: Canterbury
Dover
Strait of Dover
Calais
Bruges
Antwerp
Ypres
Lille
FLANDERS
Scheldt R.
Brussels
Agincourt
Arras
Amiens
Somme R.
Meuse R.
Rouen
Beauvais
Pierrefonds
VERMANDOIS

France at the Death of Philip Augustus, 1223
Paris
FRANCE
Royal domain
Under English rule

ally recognized as a mere formality; most of their reigns were spent trying to impose order
on their tiny personal territories. Unlike the kings of England (who were among their
most powerful and troublesome vassals), the kings of France possessed no land that they
ruled directly outside the small royal domain; they controlled the appointment of few
bishops and abbots outside the royal domain; and their courts were peopled by their own

local vassals. Few signatures of powerful lords from the south, west, or east of the kingdom appear on royal documents from the eleventh or twelfth centuries. The best-known image of this diminished royalty is the remark said to have been made by King Louis VII when someone praised the great wealth of Henry II of England: "Now in France, we have only bread and wine and our heart's desire."

At the end of the thirteenth century France was the largest, wealthiest, and most thoroughly governed monarchical state in Europe. Its king contended successfully with the pope and ruled directly a state that was forty times larger than it had been in 1100. Royal officials and relatives ruled most of the old territorial principalities; of the vast holdings of the Angevin Empire only Gascony remained in the hands of the king of England. The city of Paris was an international center of learning and culture, and the kings of France had made it the first capital in modern political history. Toward the end of the thirteenth century the lawyer Jean de Blanot proudly recognized that the king of France had come to possess qualities that had hitherto been attributed to the Roman emperor: "The king of France is emperor in his own kingdom, for he recognizes no superior in temporal affairs." By the end of the century the king of France was indeed emperor in his own kingdom, ruling from a rich capital over a talented and energetic pro-vincial administration, possessing most specialized instruments of governance, and, in spite of his conflict with the papacy, recognized by a title that set him off from all other kings and even the emperor: he was the "most Christian king," ruling a people univer-sally regarded as defenders of the true faith. The bond between king and people in this most Christian kingdom was as strong as that reflected in the English phrase "commun-ity of the realm." The great transformation of the kingdom of France was the result of seven generations of hardworking kings and their servants, the particular configuration of French provincial governments and centers of power, and the rivalry between the kings of France and their powerful vassals, the troublesome kings of England.

The reign of Louis VI (1108–37) illustrates both the limited power and rudimen-tary governmental institutions of the early kingdom of France and some characteristic features of royal policy. Louis struggled chiefly to make his authority recognized throughout the Ile de France, a land full of independent warlords living in virtually im-pregnable towers and owing no allegiance to anyone. Louis's household was ruled by the great officers whose titles ran back to Carolingian Europe: the seneschal, chancellor, butler, chamberlain, and constable. These offices were hereditary in great local families, and the men who held them controlled the local royal administrators, the *prévots*. Such a system had more ceremonial value than practical effectiveness, however, and Louis relied on two other aspects of his authority much more heavily: cooperation with the Church and unremitting warfare within the royal domain. By claiming to be a defender of the Church Louis preserved his own interests and invoked growing ecclesiastical support, witnessed by Abbot Suger's biography of him as a saintly defender of the faith.

The work of pacifying the royal domain and continuing the association between the king and the clergy was brilliantly accomplished by Louis VII (1137–80), who also greatly increased the financial resources of the king and began to make royal authority directly felt outside the royal domain. Louis's patronage of the monastery of St. Denis and its abbot, Suger, gained the monarchy a strong source of support. Louis VII also made fre-quent expeditions outside the domain in order to defend ecclesiastical establishments elsewhere. As a result he acquired as fiefs several important ecclesiastical holdings, and several lay lords as well formally recognized his overlordship. Louis's role as a defender of the Church was reflected in his reputation as a crusader, for although the Second Crusade

(1147–48) covered no one with glory, the portrait of Louis that emerges from Odo of Deuil's *Journey of Louis VII to the Orient* is an admiring one. Louis also helped protect Pope Alexander III from the emperor Frederick Barbarossa.

Besides supporting the Church and receiving its support in turn, Louis began to develop Paris as the royal capital. He gave privileges to the Paris shipping merchants. (Their seal, bearing the picture of a ship, is still the official seal of the city.) Although Louis ruled the rest of the royal domain by the old system of household officers and *prévots,* he defined the powers of officeholders more sharply toward the end of his reign. By then he had increased his income to sixty thousand pounds per year, making himself the wealthiest territorial prince in the kingdom. Although Louis used no administrative institutions outside the royal domain, his presence as king was felt more regularly and with greater impact than that of any other early Capetian ruler.

Louis's son and successor Philip II Augustus (1180–1223) benefited from his grandfather's and father's efforts and greatly increased royal rule and royal wealth in his own right. He is usually regarded as the first great king of France. Only fifteen years of age when he inherited the crown, Philip Augustus had already been associated in the kingship, during the last year of his father's life. By 1190, when Philip Augustus issued instructions for the operation of the kingdom while he was away on Crusade, several marked changes in royal governance are noticeable. First, the *prévots* were instructed to come to Paris to render their accounts three times a year. Second, a new official, the *bailli,* was created to hear cases within the royal domain. Like the *prévots,* he reported three times a year to Paris. Together, the *prévots* and *baillis* brought in royal revenues of around 100,000 pounds for the year 1202–3, according to the first records that survive. Philip's *baillis,* then, were roughly comparable to the traveling justices of Henry II in England. In using Paris as a center of fixed governmental supervision, Philip Augustus continued the tradition established by his father. He made all citizens of Paris free townsmen, governed by a council of six and a provost. In 1185 Philip called an assembly of townspeople to discuss paving the streets of Paris, a considerable achievement of urban development at the end of the twelfth century.

Upon his return from the Crusade, Philip Augustus began to transform the archaic institutions of the royal household into a more modern system of governance. He ceased to fill the great household offices of chancellor (after 1185) and seneschal (after 1191). He drew more upon the services of lesser nobles and less upon those of the great families of the royal domain or nearby principalities. Other great household positions became merely honorific. Philip's increased use of *baillis* and low-born servants created a small, efficient, and loyal central royal court that was very well suited to the new and much larger administrative duties that the last two decades of Philip's reign imposed upon it.

In 1202 King John of England married Isabella of Angoulême, who had been betrothed to another royal vassal, Hugh de Lusignan. Hugh accused John of bad faith before the royal court, and Philip hailed John to appear at a hearing conducted by Philip's other vassals. John refused, and Philip, invoking lordly privilege, declared all John's holdings from him forfeited and invaded Normandy. Philip's able generalship and financial resources soon wore down John's opposition, and Normandy was lost to the English in 1204. Philip enforced his rule in two other parts of the Angevin Empire, Anjou and Touraine, in 1206. Shortly afterwards Philip acquired the large territorial principality of Vermandois and increased his powers in Flanders. These new and very large additions to the territories directly ruled by the king posed considerable problems for Philip. But by adapting his rule to local customs, adopting sophisticated Norman institutions, and sending his *baillis* to supervise the operation of provincial government in the new territories, Philip Augustus developed a full-fledged provincial administration and immensely increased both royal wealth and the prestige of the king of France.

Under Philip's son Louis VIII (1223–26) and his remarkably able and talented queen, Blanche of Castile, royal institutions of governance were extended even farther into the old independent territorial principalities of Poitou and Languedoc. In Languedoc the *baillis* were called *sénéchaux,* but their tasks as provincial representatives of the king remained the same. By the reign of Louis VIII there were three levels of royal administrators. The older offices of *prévot* and viscount had dropped to a second-level status. The new offices of *bailli* and *sénéschal* constituted a senior rank of officials. Drawn from the lower nobility, they were paid a salary and usually posted in provinces where they were not native. At the bottom were numerous local royal servants called *servientes* or *gardes.* By the early thirteenth century, then, the royal governance of France had been greatly transformed, just as the territory directly and indirectly ruled by the king had increased immensely.

The early death of Louis VIII left the young Louis IX (1226–70) in the care of Queen Blanche. For nearly thirty years Blanche was the real ruler of France, both during Louis's formal minority, which lasted until 1234, and during his young manhood. When Louis departed on a Crusade in 1248 Blanche was regent of the kingdom, and she remained in control during Louis's capture and imprisonment in Egypt, which lasted until 1254. Blanche had to fight off coalitions of nobles anxious to take advantage of Louis's minority and the regency of a woman and control the royal government. But together Blanche and Louis successfully resisted baronial opposition and developed even further the administrative reforms of Philip Augustus.

Louis IX depended heavily upon the *baillis,* and in 1247–48 he began to rearrange several of their jurisdictions, making them regularly territorial, dividing some into more manageable territories, and redesigning others. In 1247 Louis also introduced a new office, that of *enquêteur* (inquisitor), a royal official sent out to hear complaints of illegal activities on the part of *baillis* and other officials. Louis relied heavily upon Dominicans and Franciscans to perform this duty, which he had created out of conscience and piety as well as a desire for more institutional supervision. So thoroughgoing were Louis's *enquêteurs,* especially after his return from Crusade in 1254, that Rutebeuf, a satirical French poet, complained that if Louis investigated his Dominicans and Franciscans as carefully as his *enquêteurs* investigated others, he too would find faults and errors. Among Louis's *enquêteurs* was Gui Fulquois, who later became Pope Clement IV.

Personally devout and imbued with a profound sense of royal moral responsibility, Louis IX was regarded for centuries as the ideal medieval ruler. His patronage of the Mendicant Orders, his crusading activities, his passionate desire for justice, and his personal life overshadowed even his administrative successes. Even though he developed his grandfather's institutions and increased royal revenues until they doubled those of Philip Augustus, Louis was remembered as a saintly ruler, and he was canonized at the end of the thirteenth century. Louis's canonization culminated the tradition of ecclesiastical support of the French monarchy. At Louis's death on yet another Crusade in Tunis in 1270, not only did the territory and wealth of the king of France surpass those of every other European ruler, but the prestige of the Capetian dynasty and its most recent and saintly representative had been vastly and permanently increased.

Philip III (1270–85) continued to develop both the royal administration and the royal crusading policy. But it was during the reign of Philip IV the Fair (1285–1314) that the achievements of the Capetian monarchy were put to their most severe tests. Although

PARIS IN THE TWELFTH AND THIRTEENTH CENTURIES

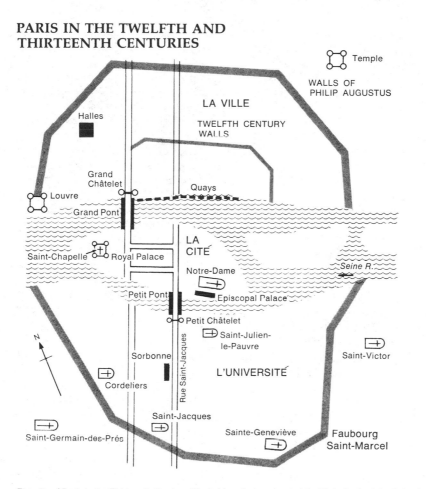

The city of Paris in the Thirteenth Century. The bridges that connected the Right Bank of the Seine (top) to the Ile de la Cité and the Ile to the Left Bank (bottom) linked the three distinctive parts of the town. The walls of Philip Augustus encircled the most important city in France, the center of royal government and the home of the University. Reprinted by permission of the publisher, from *The Scholastic Culture of the Middle Ages 1000–1300* by John W. Baldwin. Lexington, Mass.: D. C. Heath and Company, 1971, p. 28.

the kings of France had added to their territory by warfare in Normandy in 1204 and defended their gains at the Battle of Bouvines in 1214, they fought no major wars for the rest of the thirteenth century. Although their revenues had grown, costs had risen also, and the French king was in no position to make extraordinary military expenditures out of his normal revenues. Finally, France and the papacy had always been particularly close, and the French church had readily cooperated with the French kings without papal interference. But during the reign of Philip IV war broke out once again on a wide scale. Royal finances were strained to the utmost, and the king of France and the pope entered a great contest to determine who in fact ruled the Church in France.

The king who experienced these crises has always been an enigma to historians. Some have argued that Philip the Fair was a rational, calculating ruler who closely supervised all governmental activities; others argue that he was a nonentity whose policies were those of his assistants, particularly the many lawyers with whom he surrounded himself. One school of history regards Philip as a ''constitutional'' king who recognized his duties to the law; another regards him as an autocrat who respected neither tradition nor law. Some regard him as an antireligious tyrant who tried to destroy the papacy and the faith, others as a devout Christian who merely resisted papal encroachments on his traditional rights. Not only the crises of Philip's reign but the problem of his character make his reign at once fascinating and ambiguous.

In 1271 the crown of France had been augmented by the acquisition of Languedoc, and in 1285, upon Philip IV's marriage to Jeanne of Navarre, the crown acquired the rich counties of Champagne and Brie. These immense territorial gains continued the meteoric expansion of the kingdom, but they put considerable strains upon royal institutions and finances and involved Philip more closely in the affairs of English Gascony and in the urbanized region of Flanders. From the outset of his reign Philip had to prepare for war, and his many campaigns against the English in Gascony and the Flemings in Flanders consumed his resources at a great rate.

Not only did Philip ruthlessly push his *baillis* and *sénéchaux,* but he turned the *enquêteurs* into financial agents as well, whose new functions continued into the fourteenth century. Philip tightened control over his financial office, and laid the foundations for its reorganization and permanent settlement in Paris as the Chambre des Comptes. He also systematized his royal court of appeals, the Parlement of Paris, which became the judicial center of the kingdom. Philip drew into royal service townsmen and professional lawyers, usually of urban background and fiercely royalist in their sympathies and loyalties.

In order to increase revenues, Philip began to regularize the principle of the royal right to tax his subjects, at first in cases of the defense of the realm in emergencies, and later on a routine basis. In matters of taxation Philip and his agents dealt with provincial assemblies, because of the strongly localized traditions of legal and financial administration that had prevailed in France during the acquisition of so many new territories. Thus, the large national assemblies that Philip called in Paris in 1303 and 1308—the Estates-General—never acquired the financial or judicial powers of the English Parliament.

Philip IV's financial demands strained every royal resource and led him into areas where no French king had acted before. Although the status of the Jews in France had sharply declined under Louis IX, it became much worse during Philip's reign. In 1306 Philip confiscated Jewish money and property and expelled the Jews from the kingdom, as his contemporary Edward I had done in England in 1292. Philip increased his demands for money and even claimed the right to tax the clergy. Pope Boniface VIII protested Philip's actions, and after a long, drawn-out battle between the two (to be discussed later in this chapter), Philip gained the power to tax the clergy as well as the laity. In his endless quest for more money, Philip also attacked the Order of Knights Templar, one of the most wealthy financial institutions of Europe, and confiscated its resources as well.

Yet for all of his fiscal rapacity and opposition to traditional clerical privileges, Philip IV was not irreligious. Rather, his sense of religion appears to have been inseparable from his awareness of the mission of Christian France and the spiritual obligations his kingship imposed upon him. Cold, impersonal, and distant, he was nevertheless driven by a vision of France as a holy land and its people and king as particularly loved by God. His propagandists and also his subjects appear to have agreed with him. His great appeals to the kingdom were answered favorably by a population whose resources were strained to the utmost by royal demands. The people's acceptance of regular royal taxation marked an important step in the creation of new royal resources and in the growth of their loyalty to the king and the kingdom.

When Philip died in 1314 the kingdom had survived the military, financial, and ecclesiastical crises of his reign, testimony to the achievements of Philip and his royal ancestors. But within a few years the kingdom faced as great a crisis, one from which it was not able to extricate itself as quickly as it had in the early years of the fourteenth century. Philip was succeeded in order by his three sons, Louis X (1314–16), Philip V (1316–22), and Charles IV (1322–28). But none of Philip's sons had a son who survived his father. At the death of Charles IV in 1328 the succession to the throne was a major problem. The aristocracy's resistance to royal centralization complicated the issue, and sent France into the fourteenth century facing what the historian Raymond Cazelles has termed the ''crisis of royalty'' at the end of the eleven generations of Capetian kings.

THE NEW ORDER: THE CONFLICT BETWEEN THE PAPACY AND THE TERRITORIAL MONARCHY

The Great Interregnum of the Holy Roman Empire ended with the election of Rudolf of Habsburg as emperor of the Romans in 1273. Rudolf and his imperial successors, with the striking exception of Ludwig of Bavaria (1314–47), remained content to exercise their powers in Germany and Austria. The popes had succeeded in removing Sicily from the Hohenstaufen dynasty in 1268 through the agency of Charles of Anjou, brother of Louis IX of France, who became king of Sicily in that year. But Charles's rule in Sicily and South Italy excited fear of his power on the part of the Roman curia and resentment on the part of his Sicilian subjects. In 1282 the population of Palermo massacred the French garrison and precipitated a general conflict throughout the northern Mediterranean world. This conflict lasted until the Treaty of Caltabellotta in 1302, which awarded island Sicily to the royal house of Aragon and mainland South Italy to the successors of Charles of Anjou.

Charles of Anjou's grandnephew was Philip IV the Fair, who, in addition to the considerable debts inside his kingdom, faced popular resentment toward France's participation in ecclesiastical vendettas and the diplomatic intricacies of the papal elections of the years 1292–1305. After a two-year vacancy following the death of Pope Nicholas IV in 1292, the saintly hermit Peter Morone was elected Pope. Although many hopes were pinned to Morone, who took the papal name of Celestine V, the burden of the papacy was too much for him, and he resigned the office in December 1294. His successor was an old, wily, and talented papal bureaucrat, Benedetto Gaetani, who took the name Boniface VIII.

It was precisely over questions of royal financial needs and practices that the great quarrel between Philip and Boniface was launched. Although papal permission had long been required in order for temporal rulers to tax their clergy (and even then only in cases of dire necessity), thirteenth-century rulers had often neglected this rule. Facing a war with England and a vexing problem in Flanders, Philip issued new demands for taxes from the clergy in 1296. Boniface responded with a papal letter directing the French bishops not to pay. This letter, *Clericis laicos,* condemned the abuse of temporal authority, and although its legal provisions were on solid ground, its tone was rather more categorical than suited Philip. In the same year, Philip prohibited the export of any money at all, including papal revenues, from France. In 1297, in the letter *Romana mater,*

Boniface qualifiedly suspended the provisions of *Clericis laicos* for France, and in a later letter of the same year, *Etsi de statu,* he withdrew slightly from his earlier position.

In 1297 Boniface faced difficulties on several fronts. An influential segment of the college of cardinals denounced him as a usurper, and Boniface resorted to the unfortunate device of proclaiming a Crusade against them. Supporters of Celestine V further accused Boniface of canonical irregularity. In 1298 Boniface published his great lawbook, the *Liber Sextus,* part of which included texts justifying papal resignation and the procedures for providing a successor to a still-living former pope. In 1297 Boniface had proclaimed the canonization of Louis IX of France, and in 1300 he announced the Jubilee Year, a period in which the pilgrimage to Rome was surrounded with particular spiritual benefits. By 1301 both parties appeared to have recovered from the earlier encounter, and the success of the Jubilee Year must have been encouraging to Boniface.

In that year, however, the second conflict broke out. Philip arrested the bishop of Pamiers, Bernard Saisset, for treason and heresy, condemned him, and wrote to Boniface requesting papal confirmation of his action. Boniface could legitimately have modified his position on taxation, but he could not relax the canonical sanctions against any layman who presumed to try to convict a bishop. Boniface therefore refused, called a council at Rome for 1302, and wrote Philip a long letter, *Ausculta fili,* in which he carefully cautioned the king against abusing the age-old liberties of the Church. Philip's agents circulated a forged version of the letter in which Boniface was made to appear to have claimed complete temporal and spiritual authority. This was one of the first documents in modern propaganda warfare. In addition, in 1302 Philip called a large assembly of nobles, clergy, and people—the first Estates-General in the history of France—to solicit public support in his quarrel with the pope. By the end of the year Boniface had replied with the bull *Unam sanctam,* a long, detailed, and wholly traditionalist exposition of papal authority. This bull, one of the most famous documents in the history of the relations between the papacy and the monarchy, elicited no counterarguments from Philip's supporters. Instead, Guillaume de Nogaret, Philip's chief minister, denounced Boniface as a heretic and blasphemer and marched into Italy, where he took the pope captive at Anagni and attempted to force him to repudiate his earlier statements and renounce the papacy. Although he was released before he was forced to do this, Boniface died a few weeks later, and the questions of the relations between France and the papacy were momentarily suspended.

With the accession of Clement V (1305–14) the relations between France and the papacy were slowly restored, but at a formidable price to the latter. The excommunications against Nogaret and others were lifted, and Philip was formally praised for his devotion in the bull *Rex Gloriae* of 1311. Some of the Boniface's arguments in *Clericis laicos, Ausculta fili,* and *Unam sanctam* were formally repudiated by the pope, and Clement had to work very hard to prevent Philip from engineering a church council that would pronounce Boniface VIII an antipope. These concessions seriously weakened the direct authority of the popes after Clement V, and they presaged an even more remarkable incident, the destruction of the Order of the Templars.

In one sense, Boniface's concern over Philip's claim may well have come from his fear that the territorial monarchies in general were acquiring too much direct power over the clergy in their kingdoms. After all, the machinery of governance and communications was more direct and influential within England or France than throughout all of Christendom, and events of the fourteenth and fifteenth centuries proved that such monarchical control over clergy was a significant threat to the universal claims of the papacy.

No event suggests more clearly the threat constituted by a temporal power than the affair of the Templars. This order, having earned an attractive reputation in the Holy Land, had expanded its role in Europe, particularly in the fields of banking and Crusade financing. The wealth of the Templars and their virtual independence from governmental institutions made them an attractive target for the needy Philip, and their growing concern with financial affairs and their own privileges had doubtless weakened their standing in the eyes of many Christians. Between 1307 and 1314 Philip undertook to destroy the order and confiscate its property. In 1307 his campaign began with the arrest of the Templars on charges of heresy and unspecified but enormous and horrible vices. By 1310 a number of Templars had been burned at the stake as heretics, and in 1314 the grand master of the order, Jacques de Molai, was executed. The financial resources of the Templars were confiscated by the crown, and papal approval was elicited with difficulty after pressure was exerted upon Clement V in the matter of Boniface VIII and the troubles of the first decade of the fourteenth century. Although not all subjects of Philip IV, clergy and laity, concurred in the destruction of the Templars, the king's success marked, along with his successful conflict with the papacy, one moment in the rise of temporal authority in European history. The powers of the king, enhanced by new administrative agents, financial resources, unquestioned Christian orthodoxy, and the growing cult of the kingdom of France itself, were both more immediately visible and more directly effective.

The relations of the papacy with Charles of Anjou and Philip the Fair, the complex problems of the reigns of Boniface VIII and Clement V, and the French king's destruction of the Templars, one of the last vestiges of a kind of supranational Christian society, an event that heralded the civil theology of territorial monarchy, did not of course destroy the traditional authority of the king. The struggle between the two powers was not that between an archaic church and the "modern" state, but rather between spiritual and temporal authorities in the new circumstances of the late thirteenth and early fourteenth centuries. In this sense both powers were still traditional powers. The authority of the clergy and the papacy still counted for much throughout the fourteenth century, and continued to do so until the eighteenth century. Temporal authority, with its resources, claims, and spiritual justification, defined the terms of the new relationship, but still left much room in which spiritual authority could function.

FURTHER READING

Besides the works listed in the general bibliography under *Political History,* see W. L. Warren, *Henry II* (Berkeley and Los Angeles: University of California Press, 1973); Thomas C. Van Cleve, *The Emperor Frederick the Second of Hohenstaufen* (Oxford: Clarendon Press, 1973); William Chester Jordan, *Louis IX and the Challenge of the Crusade* (Princeton, N.J.: Princeton University Press, 1980); Joseph R. Strayer, *The Reign of Philip the Fair* (Princeton, N.J.: Princeton University Press, 1980); and T. S. R. Boase, *Boniface VIII* (London: Constable, 1933).

16

Reason and Imagination
in the Gothic World

THE TRIUMPH OF ARISTOTLE

One of the most important aspects of the new learning of the twelfth century was western Europeans' interest in Muslim and Greek scientific and philosophical thought. With the Christian capture of Toledo in 1085, clerical scholars in Spain and then in Sicily began the process of translating the works of some of the most important thinkers in both alien cultures first from Arabic and later directly from Greek. Peter the Venerable, abbot of the monastery of Cluny, even commissioned a translation of the *Qu'ran* in the mid twelfth century. Among the works of Arabic scholars available to Europeans in Latin versions by the end of the twelfth century were those of Ibn Sina (Avicenna to the Latins; d. 1037) on medicine and philosophy, al-Khwarizmi (d. 850) on mathematics, and Alhazen (d. 1039) on optics. In turn, the Latins received from the Arabs much Greek scientific and philosophical literature, particularly the scientific and philosophical works of Aristotle with the great commentary of the Muslim philosopher Ibn Rushd (Averroës to the Latins; d. 1199).

Thus, after the revival of Aristotelian logical studies had helped to transform the curriculum of the schools in the eleventh and twelfth centuries, a large body of Aristotelian treatises on natural philosophy, ethics, and metaphysics entered those schools in the twelfth and thirteenth. These new philosophical and scientific works added a learned dimension to other trends in twelfth-century legal and social thought that paid new and greater attention to the naturalness of the created universe and the dignity of nature and humanity. They helped to challenge the Platonic-Augustinian tradition of thought that neglected material reality and focused upon invisible forms and ideas in the mind of God that were more "real" than their crude and imperfect earthly copies. The new studies argued instead for the regularity, coherence, and intelligibility of material creation.

The new Aristotelian studies also affected the curriculum. The study of ethics was joined to that of grammar, while the new natural philosophy of Aristotle was attached to logic. Gradually, dissatisfaction with the conventional schema of the liberal arts led to two major changes. First, some of the liberal arts, notably grammar and rhetoric, became preliminary subjects and eventually dropped out of some university curricula altogether. Second, the subjects of the quadrivium, along with logic, grew in importance. In addition, by the thirteenth century the "sciences"—physics, ethics, and metaphysics— became subjects in their own right and were added to the arts. Thus was created the category of "arts and sciences." By the early thirteenth century not only was academic learning a corporate profession with specialized professional curricula and technical vocabularies, but the old arts curriculum was wholly dominated by the study of logic and natural philosophy. Those old liberal arts that did not lend themselves to the requirements of the new disciplines of theology and law tended to be downgraded into merely preparatory subjects; those that did grew to dominate the study of the arts and sciences.

In different medieval universities, of course, the new subjects produced different results. Oxford became prominent in natural philosophy and mathematics, chiefly through the influence of its first chancellor, Robert Grosseteste; Paris concentrated upon metaphysics. Orléans, on the other hand, maintained a respected school of rhetoric, and the University of Bologna became the greatest of medieval schools of law. Not only the flood of new knowledge but the importance of methods of analysis and disputation shaped the thirteenth- and fourteenth-century schools. In general the faculties of the arts and sciences, by now separated from the faculties of theology and law, treated their own specialized subjects with a new freedom and disregard for both tradition and theological caution. Thus, several thirteenth-century thinkers came under attack from theologians who accused them of sharing not only Aristotle's beliefs in natural philosophy but also his pagan ideas about the uncreatedness of the world. They were also charged with failing to account properly for such doctrines as that of the Trinity. Growing friction between theology and philosophy led to several incidents of rivalry within the thirteenth-century universities. In Paris, for example, secular arts masters bitterly resented the arrival of Franciscan and Dominican scholars in university teaching chairs of theology. This rivalry was one of the dominant themes at Paris throughout the century. In addition, the arts faculty was censured several times during the 1200s for teaching philosophical doctrines that ran counter to Scripture and Christian truth. In 1277 Etienne Tempier, the bishop of Paris, issued a condemnation of 219 propositions that he claimed were erroneously being taught at Paris by the arts faculty. This action played a very important role in redirecting philosophy away from pure Aristotelianism, although a strong and articulate school of philosophers committed to the teaching of Aristotle and his Arabic commentator Averroës flourished through the fourteenth century.

It is against this background that the career of Albert the Great, or Albertus Magnus (1193–1280), can best be understood. Albert was born at Lauingen in Germany, entered the Dominican order, and lived at the Dominican convent in Cologne until he was sent to Paris in 1240, where two years later he assumed the Dominican chair of theology. From 1242 until his death, Albert became virtually the model of a learned churchman. From Paris he returned to Cologne to lecture to the Dominicans. He traveled up and down central Europe, from Rome to the Baltic Sea, as head of the German province of the Dominican order. He became bishop of Regensburg and served in other administrative capacities throughout Europe. He attended the Second Council of Lyons in 1274, where he defended some of the work of his greatest pupil, Saint Thomas Aquinas, and he repeated his defense at Paris during the attacks on Aquinas associated with the condemnations of 1277. Although Albert occupies a central place in the history of medieval thought, his career was also that of a competent administrator and experimental scientist.

Albert's greatest efforts were directed at assimilating the body of Aristotle's natural philosophy into a plan of Christian learning without conflicting with revelation and dogma. To do so, Albert distinguished two spheres of knowledge. Theology, he said, dealt with supernatural things and was reached by faith; philosophy dealt with natural things and was reached by reason. Albert argued that these two kinds of knowledge and two ways of knowing were not incompatible, for they led to the same faith and the same truth. Although Albert thought that much of revelation lay outside the realm of reason, he argued that certain topics could be studied by both theology and philosophy. Albert taught in the faculty of theology at Paris from 1242 to 1248, and his most important works are theological. His *Commentary on the Sentences* of Peter Lombard is one of the landmarks of thirteenth-century theology. In his later works, which tended to treat philosophy more than theology, Albert attempted to create a system of natural philosophy that could be tested by reason and experience and proved by purely rational means without dependence upon revelation and theology. By sharpening the distinction between theology and philosophy, Albert, heavily influenced by Aristotle, created one sphere in which reason could claim legitimate autonomy.

SAINT THOMAS AQUINAS AND SAINT BONAVENTURE

The new mendicant orders of the thirteenth century produced not only preachers, saints, and pastoral missions to the populations of the towns, but scholars as well. By the 1250s the theology faculty at the University of Paris was dominated by teachers who were members of these two orders. Of these the two greatest were Thomas Aquinas, a pupil of Albert the Great, and Bonaventure, the most influential representative of Franciscan learning in the thirteenth century.

Thomas Aquinas was born around 1225 to the family of the lords of Aquino in southern Italy. He studied at the monastery of Monte Cassino from 1230 to 1239 and in the arts faculty of the University of Naples. In 1244, against his family's opposition, Thomas joined the Dominican order, began his theological studies under Albert the Great at Cologne, and was sent to Paris as a bachelor in Scripture in 1245. After lecturing upon the text of Scripture, Aquinas went on to lecture on Peter Lombard's *Book of Sentences,* just as Albert and other theologians had. Aquinas's *Commentary on the Sentences* was his first great work. Although Aquinas was prepared to be received by the higher faculty of theology, both he and the Franciscan Bonaventure had to wait, because of secular masters' opposition to the rise of the orders in the university.

Bonaventure was born Giovanni di Fidanza in Italy in 1221. He took his religious name when he entered the Franciscan order around 1240, and he studied at Paris with the great English Franciscan theologian Alexander of Hales (1170–1245). After a distinguished teaching career at Paris, Bonaventure was elected minister-general of the Franciscan order, was the official biographer of Saint Francis of Assisi, and was made a cardinal in 1273. He died at the Second Council of Lyons in 1274.

Although Thomas and Bonaventure were both affected by the resentment in Paris against the rise of the orders, they were not similar thinkers. Aquinas followed his teacher Albert in taking the path of Aristotle and in creating a sphere of activity in which reason was supreme. Bonaventure, on the other hand, was far less an Aristotelian, adhering instead to the older tradition of Augustinian Platonism. Thomas, for example, argued that the question of whether the world was created or eternal could not be answered by reason and therefore had to be answered by faith, which stated that God had created the world. Bonaventure, on the other hand, argued that reason can and does prove that the world was created and could not be eternal. Bonaventure scorned many of the claims made for reason by the Aristotelians, and argued for the primacy of mystical knowledge.

The two thinkers also revealed their differences in their works. Those of Aquinas were chiefly either academic treatises or occasional pieces dealing with philosophy. His *Summa Against the Gentiles* was requested by Raymond of Peñafort, the great Spanish canon lawyer who turned missionary, in order to provide missionaries to the Muslims with logical arguments for Christian faith that did not depend upon revelation. His *Summa Theologiae* was a vast compendium of both philosophy and theology, the monument to Aristotelianism in its Christian form. Bonaventure, besides his academic works, was a contemplative theologian, and his little work *The Mind's Journey to God* is a monument of contemplative theology. Even so, his work as minister general of the Franciscan order took him out into the world and its affairs more than the restricted academic career of Aquinas.

The careers of Aquinas and Bonaventure reflect merely two of the many sides of the rapidly changing world of thirteenth-century thought and testify to the enduring influence of Plato, Aristotle, and Saint Augustine upon that world. In spite of their differences, however, which also reflect some of the differences between their two orders, these two thinkers together suggest much of the variety and power of the philosophical revolution of the thirteenth century.

GOTHIC ARCHITECTURE AND ENGINEERING

One result of the triumph of Aristotelianism was a new degree of confidence in the assertion made by many thinkers that the created universe was intelligible in terms of geometry and mathematics. The appearance of a new interest in mathematics (and the slow introduction of Arabic numerals and mathematical place notation in the late twelfth and thirteenth centuries) influenced aesthetics and carried the concept of the intelligibility of nature into yet other areas. Twelfth- and thirteenth-century thinkers and artists often considered God as a kind of geometer-craftsman using mathematical principles and aesthetic criteria to make physical objects. A famous manuscript illumination of the twelfth century, in fact, shows God setting out to create the world with a geometer's compass in his hand; another of the thirteenth century shows two angels rotating the universe by means of celestial cranks. Neither of these depictions is naive; both represent a courageous attempt to represent immaterial reality in terms of rational principles.

*The Faces of God: The Creation of
Adam.* This sculptured group, from
the north porch of Chartres
cathedral, is a stunning expression
of the Creator's love for his creation, and emphasizes its physical
and material aspects. (Archives
Photographiques, Paris)

This elevation of the dignity and intelligibility of the material world carried over into theology as well, as the art historian Erwin Panofsky has noted:

The human soul, though recognized as immortal, was now held to be the organizing and unifying princi-ple of the body itself rather than a substance independent thereof. A plant was thought to exist as a plant and not as the copy of the idea of the plant. The existence of God was believed to be demonstrable from His creation rather than a priori.[1]

The impact of Aristotelian natural philosophy and metaphysics upon Christian theology was not so much a revolution as a shift in emphasis. Chapter 57 of the *Rule* of Saint Benedict had permitted monks who were craftsmen to work at their crafts as long as

[1] Erwin Panofsky, *Gothic Architecture and Scholasticism* (New York: Meridian Books, 1957), pp. 6–7.

they had their abbot's permission and did not take excessive pride in their work. Around 1120 Theophilus, a monk who believed in the inherent dignity in all labor dedicated to God, wrote a rational account of many artistic processes, *On the Various Arts*. Perhaps the most eloquent expression of this new respect for material creation is the sculpture on the north porch of Chartres cathedral showing a seated, infinitely compassionate and tender God molding Adam out of amorphous clay; Adam's human nature takes physical shape in God's own hands. In this portrayal of creation the soul and body of a human being are undifferentiated visually. Thus, Aristotelian influences extended into theology and the arts, taking up an old strand of Christian thought and making it a dominant theme of philosophy, theology, and the visual arts.

Theophilus's treatise reveals a wealth of artistic talent and rationality in the ideal monastery, but that talent was exercised chiefly upon manuscript copying, illumination, painting, metal sculpture, and the coloring of glass. The greater building arts were probably beyond the capacities of a single group of monks or a single chapter of a cathedral, except for some aspects of design and later decoration of the finished church building. The achievements of Romanesque architects and engineers, however, had revolutionized architecture. In addition, other aspects of building craftsmanship had greatly improved. The increasingly professional use of geometrical principles of design, the development of complex tools such as cranes and hoists, and improved jointing work and stone finishing all contributed to the high quality of the building crafts in the twelfth and thirteenth centuries.

The high degree of technical expertise worked out in Romanesque church architecture was enhanced by new design elements in such Romanesque buildings as the cathedrals of Autun in France and Durham in England. At Autun (1120–32) the pointed arch, contrasting with the round arches of traditional Romanesque style, first appeared in a major church building in western Europe. The Durham cathedral (1093–1104) featured the ribbed vault. Thus, two of the most characteristic features of the style called Gothic appeared in late Romanesque churches. The first church to combine these two elements, which permitted the height of the building to increase greatly and the structural role of walls and columns to be transformed, was the new church at the monastery of St. Denis, constructed by the Abbot Suger around 1140.

The monastery of St. Denis was the religious institution associated most closely with the kings of France. Suger himself, while still abbot, was made regent of the kingdom during the absence of King Louis VII on the Second Crusade. The chronicles of St. Denis were the closest to an official history of the monarchy that France possessed. Therefore, Suger's decision to build a new church was an act of public importance; he was the regent of the kingdom, the biographer of the late King Louis VI, and one of the ablest churchmen and councillors in the kingdom. The new church was to be no mere monastic center; it was the spiritual center of royal France, a pilgrimage site, and the physical illustration of the new twelfth-century spirituality.

Suger was moved to his task by the great churches that most twelfth-century western Europeans knew or knew of—Hagia Sophia at Constantinople and the Temple of Solomon. As he built, almost certainly with the aid of a master builder, the inspiration of these remote buildings became embodied in a structure that employed the newest and most effective techniques that the twelfth century knew. By building the vaults on cross-ribs (arches that stretched diagonally from one column to another and crisscrossed at the center of a bay consisting of four columns), Suger was able to lighten the load of the ceiling. By using pointed arches, he was able to deflect the weight of the roof directly onto

Durham Cathedral, Nave. The nave of Durham cathedral is a fine example of the transition from Romanesque to Gothic church architecture. (Courtesy of The British Tourist Authority)

much thinner support columns. The use of these two techniques meant that the height of the church could be greatly increased and that the thick, formidable walls, piers, and columns of the Romanesque churches could be replaced with slender walls pierced by windows and light, slender columns, and greater length. The aesthetic experience was wholly different from that of the earlier Romanesque style.

The problems of organizing a large-scale building project are illuminated not only by this great new church itself but by Suger's *De administratione,* in which he recounts the story of its creation. Suger tells of the decision to renovate an older, sacred church, the problems of getting stone of the right quality and timbers large enough for his purposes, and of course raising the necessary monies. Organizing the labor on this church and others like it was a considerable task. A master builder had to be found with the technical expertise and the managerial skills to administer the whole project. Masons, carpenters, roofers, metalworkers, glassmakers, and sculptors had to be brought together, often from great distances. For them, the work site became a living site for several years. By the mid twelfth century practical geometry was essential, not necessarily for the patron of a project such as St. Denis but certainly for the master builder. He had to translate suggestions into sketches and mathematically perfect them by basing them on a single modular

The West Facade of Notre Dame, Paris. The most famous, if not the most beautiful of all Gothic churches, was, like many others, an urban church. A long structure, its short transept is barely noticeable. The towered facade, pointed arches, and great rose window are characteristic of the Gothic style. (Trans World Airlines Photo)

measurement, multiples and subdivisions of which became the actual measurements of the design. Sometimes other buildings besides the older church had to be demolished for a new, larger church. The entire project, from plans and early demolitions to the final consecration, could take as long as thirty years.

The organization and financing of the work, the integration of the new building with others nearby, and the quality of engineering and building techniques were striking. A finished Gothic church such as St. Denis or the slightly later cathedrals of Chartres and Notre Dame was the result not only of a new spirituality and aesthetic sense but of applied geometry, engineering, and construction skills of a very high order. The historian Lynn White, Jr., has pointed out that these cathedrals and monastic churches were the first examples of monumental architecture produced by free, paid laborers in the western world. The professional dignity, literacy, and cosmopolitanism of the Gothic architects and master builders helps to explain the spread of Gothic architectural principles and the high regard in which the technical achievements of great builders were held.

The aesthetics and engineering of Gothic architecture are its most striking aspects

Reims Cathedral, Facade. One of the richest Gothic facades, that of Reims cathedral held particular meaning, since it was the church in which the kings of France were crowned. (Marburg Art Reference Bureau)

to one unfamiliar with them. Less clear, but no less important, is the spiritual ideal that the aesthetics and engineering skills of the patrons and builders shaped into physical form. Beneath their high roofs, whose weight was distributed onto slender columns and external buttresses, Gothic churches were full of light. The walls were filled not with thick stone and small windows but with great windows of stained glass, providing images of light and color to those inside. The ceilings soared far higher than any most people had ever seen or could imagine. The naves reached as high as 160 feet, the ultimate physical height of stone architecture before the development of structural steel in the nineteenth century. Light and the impression of fragility of the church fabric, immense height, and the delicacy of window traceries and sculpture are the aesthetic dimensions of Gothic architecture.

In twelfth-century theology the church building was symbolic both of the Church as a whole and of paradise. The elaborately decorated west fronts of twelfth- and thirteenth-century churches were specifically designed to lead the eye and mind of those entering them into a spiritual state in which they could benefit from the experience of the liturgy.

Chartres Cathedral, Nave. The opening of the walls, the great height of the interior, and the rose window all suggest the great enthusiasm for Chartres that is reflected in literature from the twelfth century to the twentieth. (Marburg Art Reference Bureau)

The two main features of Gothic architecture, light and the visibility of structural elements, also played a spiritual role. The light suggested the principle of creation and the gifts of the Holy Spirit; the visible structural members emphasized the order, unity, and coherence of the Church, of belief, and of the spiritual community. The dignity and majesty of the greatest Gothic churches conveyed as well the gifts and richness of a loving God. As a work of art, of engineering, and of spirituality, the Gothic church illustrates the link between reason and imagination in the Gothic world.

THE KNIGHT BETWEEN THE WORLD AND GOD

The new schools and the new churches of the late twelfth and thirteenth centuries were not the only institutional expressions of reason and imagination in the Gothic world. Cities and aristocratic and royal courts also developed new cultural forms, which are reflected in the arts and literature, in building styles, and in styles of life. The style of behavior, status, and values among the higher and lower nobility in the late twelfth century acquired a name of its own, which appeared first in France and quickly spread to the rest of Europe: *courtois, höflich, cortese,* "courtly." Courtly manners, ethics, dress, skills, and values grew out of the rough life of the warrior and warlord. Next to the man who was brave, *preux,* there emerged the ideal of the man who was properly behaved, the *prudhomme.* By the thirteenth century the way of life of the ideal courtier, whether wealthy lord or individual knight, was considered by such different figures as King Louis IX of France and the German poet Wolfram von Eschenbach to be the layman's counterpart to the monk's daily round of prayer and liturgy.

But courtly life and values represented something more than a cultural style. The configuration of noble households and families was changing in the twelfth and thirteenth centuries, and to a certain extent the rules of courtly behavior accommodated this transition and institutionalized new social and emotional dimensions of noble life. The emergence of the noblewoman as the object of erotic and amatory conquest, the elaborate definitions of noble status, and the development of coats of arms and rules for knightly conduct may all be regarded as manifestations of the efforts of both the higher and lower nobility to come to terms with a rapidly changing world. In these courts a secular lay life, an ideal for knights possessing a dignity equal to that of the clergy, was first expressly enunciated. The heavy-handed fighting man of the tenth century and the greedy warlord of the eleventh, who had to do hard penance for killing and whose hopes for salvation were few, slowly turned into the knight, whose initiation into knighthood paralleled the entry into religious life of the clergy. The knight's brotherhood with all other knights discreetly obliterated real social and economic differences among the nobility. The character of a *prudhomme,* as Louis IX once observed, was so dignified and meritorious that merely to say the word "filled the mouth."

The elevation of knightly status and the elaboration of courtly culture are perhaps best reflected in the term *gentleness.* In the late thirteenth and early fourteenth centuries this concept, with its complex earlier meanings in the literature of love and knightly conduct, became imbued with an ethical dignity that was close to virtue and constituted a major landmark in the history of social ideas and relationships. This slow process of transformation of the human concept of self had some of its roots in the changing conceptions of the relations between man and God in the devotional revolution of the eleventh and twelfth centuries, and other roots in the formulation of a secularized ideal of gentlemanly conduct. In this process, which later extended from the courts to the towns and contributed much to an increasing emphasis of human dignity, courtly culture played a considerable role. The knight, like other social types, made a contribution far greater than his picturesqueness, quaintness, and archaic dignity; he helped in his own way to seek a measure of lay life that satisfied both material circumstances and the high demands of moral theology. The knight and the court, just as much as the townsman, merchant, free peasant, and ecclesiastical critic, constitute part of the variety of secular experience that established the legitimacy of lay status in early Europe. Far from being remote, idealized, picturesque institutions, the courts of the thirteenth century legitimated with a new ideal of the self a life of hard activity and much insecurity. Lords, courtiers, retainers, clergy, and poets in these courts absorbed influences from the world outside and created a sense of order and ethical conduct that accommodated their own status and an increasingly secularized world.

The Latin and vernacular love poetry of the twelfth and thirteenth centuries has several themes in common with other kinds of literature, chiefly clerical. Twelfth-century clerical literature was rich in its emphasis upon self-knowledge, whether that knowledge was to be found in Peter Abelard's interest in the role of intention in judging the sinfulness or innocence of an act, or in the treatises on friendship by such monastic writers as Ailred of Riveaulx, the English Cistercian monk who turned Cicero's views on friendship into the language of twelfth-century spirituality. For the clerics too, self-knowledge necessarily meant self-improvement. The individual who explored the inner life, whether that of the emotions or that of the conscience in confession, was regarded as superior. Theologians valued passionate repentance more than routine penance; devotional writers insisted upon the emotional bonds between humans and God, not merely upon the formal bonds of worship and obedience to the law. The surprising number of twelfth-century autobiographies also reflects a heightened awareness of an inner life, and thus a new kind of psychology.

Part of the new vernacular love poetry of the twelfth century can thus be understood as one further reflection of a concern for the self, its relation to others, and the changes made in it by different emotions. The sophisticated erotic poetry of southern France (along with the bawdy songs and stories that the same poets often turned out) found in the amatory emotions a topic eminently suited to the values of an aristocracy whose life and culture were changing from the harsh and crude ideals of the eleventh century to a more mannered and stylized court life.

Birth, training, and the acceptance of a place among the vassals of a great lord made a knight; but knightly status alone was not sufficient to prove a man's quality. Certain virtues had to be added to noble birth in order to make a true knight. Constancy in love, the capacity for love itself, gentleness, humility, bravery, and above all the capacity of the ''gentle'' heart to experience these emotions made the nobly born knight worthy of the love of the nobly born lady. Love indicated that the heart was gentle; a gentle heart indicated elevation above the common run of human beings. When a knight loved ''gently'' he became a better person, and his superiority had to be recognized by others in his society.

A literary setting different from those of the *chansons de geste* (epic poems of heroism and war) was needed for the expression of these values. Writers began to adapt Greek and Roman stories, and then they discovered King Arthur. The legends of King Arthur, scattered obscurely through saints' lives and piecemeal histories, suddenly began to attract a great interest after the mid twelfth century. The Champagne poet Chrétien de Troyes wrote a number of remarkable works in which the court of Arthur served as a focus for knightly adventures that had far more to do with what a modern critic would call the search for an identity than with battles with Saracens or endless feuds over property and privilege. In this world personal identity was discovered through the solution of problems posed by adventure. The court represented order, stability, established identity, and public recognition. Outside the court—in the forests, lakes, and deserts of the literary landscape—lurked the elements of temptation, disorder, uncertainty, paradox, and unintelligibility. There, outside the court, the knight discovered who he was, and his trials legitimized him when he returned to the court to tell his story. In the thirteenth century the stories of Arthur's court expanded. The theme of the Holy Grail, introduced under Cistercian influence, reflects the elevation of knighthood to sacral status. By the early thirteenth century the great *Prose Vulgate* had begun to piece together all the stories linked to Arthur. Versions of this work are found in most European languages. By the mid fifteenth century in England the Arthurian corpus had become a great mine of secular themes, one that contributed political as well as emotional dimensions to Thomas Malory's great epic *Morte d'Arthur*.

The romance based on Arthurian materials expressed a spectrum of courtly concerns. Early in the thirteenth century Gottfried von Strassburg produced the brooding *Tristan and Isolde.* Among his contemporaries were the great German poets von Eschenbach, whose *Parzival* and *Willehalm* contained new speculations on secular values and personal doubts, and Hartmann von Aue, whose *Der Arme Heinrich* and *Gregorius* included analyses of the layman's devotion and the conflict between role and conscience. The love lyrics of Languedoc, the center of lyric vernacular poetry in Southern France, were echoed in Germany, Italy, Sicily, and England.

The history of the tenth-century explorations and settlements in Iceland and Greenland fed a Scandinavian literature of adventure and social concerns—the sagas. Scandinavian mythology, from pagan antiquity to the thirteenth century, contributed to the Eddas, long, complex poems exploring the remote past in the light of thirteenth-century concerns. In Kievan Russia the *Song of Igor's Campaign* was the twelfth-century counterpart to the heroic literature of Scandinavia, early Germany, northern France, and the Spain of the *Song of el Cid.*

Folk literature circulated throughout the European world. Its stories, including those from Islamic, Byzantine, and Buddhist sources, made their way into Latin as well as the vernacular literatures, and they contributed to the language of emotional discourse. In the thirteenth century the Franciscan influence, reflected in the *Little Flowers of St. Francis,* a collection of unique stories about the personality of that individual, extended to other forms of narrative. As we have seen, the new devotional revolution of the twelfth and thirteenth centuries produced different types of saints and holy men, clerical and lay, such as Saint Bernard, Thomas Becket, and Saint Francis of Assisi. Their distinctive lives and personalities expanded the genre of biography. The lives of women saints contributed to the continued exploration of the self in an otherwise traditional genre. *Fabliaux*—comic stories that satirized both townsmen and knights—laid the foundation for the wide range of humorous tales of the fourteenth century, particularly those of Boccaccio, Sachetti, and Chaucer.

There existed also a vast body of literature of which much less is known. Popular songs, tales, verses, and moralizing stories are often neglected by scholars because of their dubious value as "great literature." Yet to the historian of culture they reflect life and interests no less than do the more formally recognized works. The collections of miracle stories of Caesarius of Heisterbach at the beginning of the thirteenth century and Jacobus of Varagine at the end of the century were read by Europeans for centuries. The *exempla,* moral tales used to illustrate and enliven sermons, offer frequent insights into popular life and interests. The stories, jokes, and scurrilous verses quoted in chronicles and memoirs of such thirteenth-century writers as Salimbene offer glimpses of general life that are found nowhere else. From moralizing tales to outright scatology, medieval vernacular literature is a widely varied, rich, and wonderful genre. For the interested reader, these materials heighten and illuminate a level of culture that is attained only incompletely in more formal documents and works of philosophy.

Perhaps two final examples will serve to illustrate these remarks. The *Song of the Nibelungs* is a thirteenth-century epic poem written in Bavaria and based upon materials that date, in their Latin form, from the sixth and seventh centuries. It is the tale of the warrior Siegfried and his people and his wife, Kriemhild, the sister of Gunther, Siegfried's enemy. Following Siegfried's murder Kriemhild plots revenge upon Gunther, and the ensuing action involves the whole world; Attila the Hun, Theoderic the Ostrogoth, and the heroes of the old Latin and German sagas are all drawn together. Yet the Nibelung poet does not revel in the wealth of legend, literary tradition, folklore, and violence he presents, but focuses the action and diversity in a masterly way upon the theme of Kriemhild's revenge. The classification of this marvelous work somewhere among the sagas, *chansons de geste,* and romances reflects both the high command of literary skill that had been reached throughout Europe by the thirteenth century and the complex relationships between medieval vernacular literature and early European society.

The *Song of the Nibelungs* preserves some of the older aspects of heroic literature while emphasizing many of the newer—particularly in its depiction of Kriemhild's psychology. Another work, written around the same time in France, shows another side of courtly values. Around 1235 a French poet named Guillaume de Lorris wrote the first 4000 lines of a poem that he called *The Romance of the Rose.* The poem was in the popular form of a dream-vision, in which the poet dreams he is in a garden peopled by personifications of human behavioral traits—characters with such names as Sir Mirth, the lord of the garden, his lady Dame Gladness, and a helpful woman named Fair-Welcome. The dreamer falls in love with a rose in the heart of the garden (the symbol of a young woman), but his attempts to reach the Rose are blocked by the vices of Shame and Jealousy. These abstractions in the allegorical garden are in one sense all part of a refined analysis of the psychological state of what the author considered the proper way of falling in love.

The Romance of the Rose was immensely popular throughout the thirteenth century. At the end of the century another poet, Jean de Meun, completed the poem with another eighteen thousand lines. But the two approaches were remarkably different. Guillaume de Lorris was a gentle idealist. His figures are painted lightly and gracefully, and the theme of proper love is linked to the theme of the proper social life. Jean de Meun, however, knew other kinds of twelfth- and thirteenth-century thought, and his long continuation of the poem drew upon the methods and interests of academic and legal culture as well. Personifications of various psychological states and human attributes give long and contradictory speeches and argue violently. As the modern English editor Charles Dunn points out, "the entire work portrays an intellectual chain reaction among scholarly specialists occasioned by the Lover's dogged determination to persevere in his pursuit of Love." At the end of the poem, after a military siege of the Rose's castle described by a master of the language of military siege tactics, the Lover wins the Rose, and elevated though they are by the bizarre courtship, the conclusion is clearly sexual. Jean de Meun brought a different mind and different values to the elegant poem of Guillaume de Lorris. It is nevertheless striking that the courtly setting, developed by twelfth-century poets and continued by thirteenth-century romancers, became an appropriate background for his scholastic diatribe.

The *Song of the Nibelungs* and *The Romance of the Rose* encompass a wide range of thirteenth-century courtly literature. Its knightly characters, caught between God and the world, developed an ethos that appeared for a time to satisfy the demands of both, based as it was upon the creative power of love, personal loyalty and conduct, and devotion to God. Even though other cultural values soon clamored for recognition in different settings, courtly literature survived until the eighteenth century. In it the European aristocracy had found its perfect mirror.

THE VITA CIVILE

Others besides the courtly nobility found new sets of values in the twelfth and thirteenth centuries. In northern Italy, France, Flanders, and Germany townspeople created a distinctly urban culture, the liveliest manifestations of which may be found in the large cities of northern Italy—in Lombardy, Tuscany, and Venetia. The term that people used to describe this new urban culture—the *vita civile,* or civic life—is as important as the new courtly culture. Like that culture, with which it shared many values, the *vita civile* represented a predominantly lay approach to the definition and ordering of the good life.

The cities of northern Italy present a variegated picture at the turn of the fourteenth century. They differed widely in size and constitutional structure, in dependence upon other, more powerful towns, in financial, commercial, and diplomatic affairs, in the degree of city control of social and economic life, in the degree of civic consciousness, in relations with the countryside and neighboring towns, and in levels of education and artistic patronage. They were small societies, but the degree of political energy required to mobilize their resources and conduct policy, their high consciousness of the dangers of the surrounding world, and their control of ecclesiastical authority all reflect their precocious development as political societies. The wealth brought in from trade, industry, and finance, the necessity of having a "foreign" policy and a militia, the needs of public financing, and the sense of independence reflected by what a later lawyer called "the city, a prince unto itself," made many of these cities resemble later kingdoms. The political instability and constitutional crises to which the cities were usually prone reflect not so much political immaturity as political creativity. After the Church, the northern Italian towns may be said to have created the first European states.

Population and economic growth, the long struggles for independence, and the very experience of living within the physical city contributed to the development of an urban culture that expressed itself in various ways, from education to history writing, from architecture to public ceremonies. The necessities of town government produced the great town halls that still survive in many of even the smallest towns, as do the carefully planned and maintained public squares. Pride in the physical appearance of the city dates from very early in communal history, and statutes protecting the physical city, from measures concerning hygiene to those dealing with aesthetics, appear on the statute books of many towns. The towns were responsible too for much church building. Citizen committees managed the work and commissioned the artists who decorated the churches. The contacts many cities had with Byzantium and the east and with France and the north and west brought many diverse influences into the towns, and these contributed to the selection and planning of buildings and the artistic themes embodied in them. The cities knew of individual artists by reputation, and many of the greatest works of Duccio di Boninsegna, Arnolfo di Cambio, and Giotto were done on civic commissions. The decoration of churches expressed the spiritual values of the town, and the decoration of public buildings expressed the town's sense of its own history and self-image.

There is no more striking example of the liveliness of urban artistic patronage than the series of frescoes produced by Ambrogio Lorenzetti in the Palazzo Publico of Siena in 1338–40. His frescoes on the subject of good and bad government offer a vast and extraordinarily detailed exposition of the self-image of the city of Siena. Theological personifications and political abstractions are set against a highly intricate depiction of the life of the city and its inhabitants, from masons and carpenters to farmers, traders, hunters, and governing officials. Outdoors, in the towns themselves, fountains, piazzas, public buildings, streets, and bridges provided opportunities for the city to enhance its beauty and reinforce visually and physically the sense of belonging to a well-ordered society.

Ideas, artistic and literary styles, and new forms of urban devotion were other contributors to the *vita civile.* The courts of southern France and Frederick II of Sicily gave birth to literary influences that, adapted by urban Italian poets, shaped the *dolce stil nuovo,* "the sweet, new style," in which amatory, ethical, and philosophical themes were blended in Italian vernacular poetry of a very high order. Lively satirical lyrics and short tales found eager audiences in the towns. So did the stories about Saint Francis of Assisi and his followers, as well as the Latin and vernacular town histories that began to appear early in the thirteenth century. The earliest and one of the greatest of these was the *Chronicle* written by the Franciscan Salimbene of Parma about the events of his day. At the end of the thirteenth century Dino Compagni (1266–1324) of Florence wrote a *Chronicle of Events Occurring in His Own Time,* a vivid account of personalities and political crises in Florence at the end of the thirteenth and beginning of the fourteenth centuries. Another Florentine, Giovanni Villani (1270–1348), wrote a *Chronicle* of Florentine and world history that constitutes an important landmark in the lay writing of history.

This lively cultural world appealed to the eyes, ears, and especially the minds of townspeople in the thirteenth and fourteenth centuries, and it appealed to their spirits as well. Eminent laymen listened to lectures in the Dominican church of Santa Maria Novella in Florence or the Franciscan church of Santa Croce. These two great churches, the cathedral of Santa Maria dei Fiore, and the third circle of the city walls of Florence were all built in the lifetime of Dante Alighieri (1265–1321), the greatest of all Italian poets and men of letters. At the turn of the fourteenth century cities such as Florence had an air not of antiquity but of striking modernity. Florence literally took shape under the eyes of the writers, artists, and preachers who were the most eloquent praisers of the city and its life.

Associations for the building of churches, drinking and gaming clubs, youth associations, masters' guilds, literary circles, and religious confraternities—communal organizations of piety—divided and subdivided the social and cultural life of the towns. By the fourteenth century the life of the city had come to include urban religion as well. The culture of the townsman as well as the culture of the knight and noble acquired a spiritual dimension that enhanced the secular activities that sustained the worlds of court and city.

No single figure represents—indeed transcends—the cultural world of the northern Italian towns more strikingly than Dante Alighieri, and no single literary or artistic work reflects the intellectual and political movements between 1150 and 1300 in greater detail and artistic force than his great poem, *The Divine Comedy.* Dante was born in 1265 to an impoverished family that claimed descent from the earlier Florentine nobility. Though in Dante's youth it had experienced a brief period of economic prosperity through moneylending, its status certainly remained modest. This is indicated by Dante's marriage to Gemma di Manetto, a member of only a minor branch of the great Donati family. Even minor respectability afforded many opportunities to Florentine citizens, however. Dante pursued a course of studies, probably in Florence, and in 1289 he participated in the Florentine defeat of Arezzo at the Battle of Campaldino. By that date his earliest literary work, several lyric poems, had attracted the attention of a talented and influential group of Florentine writers, and his friendships with the great lyric poet Guido Cavalcanti, the chronicler Dino Compagni, and the encyclopedist Brunetto Latini date from these years.

Dante was thus exposed both to a wide literary circle—and the wider circle of acquaintances that a man of letters encountered in the city—and to the new sensibility expressed in contemporary love lyrics. In his own life the figure of Bice Portinari, who was to become the wife of Simone dei Bardi, a prominent citizen of Florence, became his ideal woman; after her death in 1290 Dante wrote a short account of her role in his personal spiritual and intellectual development in verse and prose, *La Vita Nuova* (*The New Life*), which he completed in 1292. Not only are the verses in this work the indication of a major poetic talent, but the development of Bice into Beatrice, Dante's own spiritual guide, foreshadows her role in the *Comedy.*

Dante's development during this period was not solely that of a poet and philosopher. Between 1295 and 1300 he held various political offices and, like other men of letters, enrolled in the guild of apothecaries and physicians. Membership in a guild was essential for holding political office, and there is no evidence that Dante was ever a practicing druggist or physician. The fortunes of Florence were insecure during Dante's terms of public service. Boniface VIII, the Black faction of the Guelf party that dominated Florence, and the royal house of France were involved in complex intrigues, and Dante's term of prior in June and August 1300 revealed to him the dangers surrounding the city. In 1301, while Dante was serving as the Florentine ambassador to Rome, the Black Guelfs seized power, attacked their enemies, and banished Dante from the city *in absentia,* citing several charges of political corruption on his part that would have sufficed for his execution had he returned.

From 1302 to 1304 Dante wandered throughout northern Italy, serving as an adviser to the exiled White Guelf faction in its quest to restore itself to power in Florence. However, Dante broke with his fellow exiles, whose shortsightedness, greed, and self-interest he later denounced bitterly in the *Comedy.* Between 1304 and 1310 he wandered even more widely, moving from court to court and experiencing both the pain of exile and the fitful patronage of local princes. When Emperor Henry VII descended into Italy, Dante joined his cause and became a spokesman on his behalf. The early years of his exile had produced the unfinished treatise on the Italian vernacular, *De vulgari eloquentia,* and the long, unfinished collection of philosophical poems and commentaries, *Il Convivio.* Dante's letters on behalf of Henry VII contain a more prophetic strain, and his later letters, written when Henry's cause had failed, contain bitter denunciations of those whom Dante held responsible not only for the emperor's failure but for the chaos of Italian life.

From 1310 to his death in September 1321 Dante lived at the courts of various patrons, most notably that of Can Grande della Scala at Verona and that of Guido da Polenta at Ravenna, where he died and is buried. During the last decade of his life, and possibly earlier, he worked on the *Comedy,* a vast vision of hell, purgatory, and heaven in which he organized and analyzed the events of his life and his time with a vast intelligence and one of the greatest poetic voices the world has ever known.

Several times he attempted to negotiate with Florence for his return to the city, but the parties never reached terms that Dante could accept. His exile and pilgrimage became for him a metaphor of justice; *exul immeritus,* "an undeserving exile," he called himself, condemning in passionate and eloquent language the disorder of justice that in his vision prevented humankind from governing itself properly. From his exile there emerged the great poem that embodies his visionary genius. Citizen, scholar, man of letters, philosophical lover, and exile, Dante illuminates, not as a type but as a distinctive, compelling individual, the life of the cities in which he lived and the force of the culture that he shared and helped shape.

FURTHER READING

The literature on philosophy and theology in the thirteenth century is vast, and the beginning student will want as easy a guide through it as possible. M.-D. Chenu, *Toward Understanding St. Thomas,* trans. A. M. Landry and D. Hughes (Chicago: Henry Regnery, 1964), is an ideal student's guide to the period in general as well as to Aquinas himself. A good recent biography of Thomas is James Weisheipl, *Friar Thomas d'Aquino: His Life, Thought and Work* (New York: Doubleday, 1974). For Saint Bonaventure, see J. Guy Bougerol, *Introduction to the Works of St. Bonaventure,* trans. José de Vinck (Paterson, N.J.: St. Anthony Guild Press, 1965). John W. Baldwin, *The Scholastic Culture of the Middle Ages, 1000–1300* (Lexington, Mass.: Heath, 1971), is a good general introduction, and David Knowles, *The Evolution of Medieval Thought* (New York: Random House, Vintage Books, 1962), is somewhat more complex and thorough.

On the Gothic movement in the arts, see George Henderson, *Gothic* (Baltimore: Penguin, 1967), and Otto von Simson, *The Gothic Cathedral* (reprint ed., New York: Harper & Row, 1964). See also the stimulating essay by Erwin Panofsky, *Gothic Architecture and Scholasticism* (New York: Meridian, 1957) and, for a single example, Robert Branner, *Chartres Cathedral* (New York: Norton, 1969).

On chivalry, besides the works cited in the general bibliography under *Social History,* see Roger Sherman Loomis, ed., *Arthurian Literature in the Middle Ages* (Oxford: Clarendon Press, 1959). The best study of thirteenth-century society is John H. Mundy, *Europe in the High Middle Ages, 1154–1309* (reprint ed., New York: Longmans, 1973). A brilliant study is Georges Duby, *The Three Orders: Feudal Society Imagined* (Chicago: University of Chicago Press, 1980).

Besides the works in the general bibliography dealing with Italy, see John Lardner, *Culture and Society in Italy, 1290-1420* (New York: Scribner's, 1971), and Hélène Wieruszowski, *Politics and Culture in Medieval Spain and Italy* (Rome: Edizioni di Storia e Letteratura, 1971).

PART VI

THE LATER MIDDLE AGES

17

Material Civilization:

Crisis and Recovery

THE FOUR HORSEMEN OF THE APOCALYPSE

In the book of Revelation, the last canonical book of the New Testament, the Four Horsemen let loose to afflict the earth were associated with death, famine, pestilence, and war. The art of the fourteenth and fifteenth centuries abounds with the depiction of these figures, and in the former century famine, pestilence, and war plunged material civilization into a crisis. Population levels fell, land turned to waste, and the overextended system of agricultural production virtually collapsed.

The mild climate that Europe had enjoyed since 100 B.C. began to change in the thirteenth century. This did not mean instantly colder temperatures, shorter summers, and more severe winters. The signs of change came, rather, in increasingly unpredictable weather patterns. Extremely good years were followed by inexplicably bad ones; a series of heavy rains that rotted crops and leached the earth might last for several years, to be followed by improved weather for a decade or more; intermittent severe conditions might freeze or inundate vineyards and grain fields for a season or two.

The effects of such changes were felt most quickly in the former marginal lands that required intensive cultivation and whose margin of productivity was small in the best of times. Famine had been a constant danger, even in periods of prosperity, and from 1290 on, it appears to have occurred more regularly. Although from 1309 to 1314 extremely poor crops and a series of long, destructive rains posed a threat of famine in a few places,

241

The Labors of the Months. Scenes showing the different occupations appropriate to different months of the year often decorated astronomical manuscripts, as in this tenth-century example. (Bild-Archiv der Österreichischen Nationalbibliothek, Vienna)

the general shortage of food everywhere and the immediate impact of climatic change on marginal land mark the first of the fourteenth-century crises. The tenuous balance between population and agricultural productivity was particularly threatened. The seed-to-yield ratio of even the best-tended and most productive fields was relatively low, and even a small decline in that ratio had serious consequences for the total agricultural output of a region. On lands requiring intensive labor for prevention of erosion or maintenance of drainage, a higher population level was needed than elsewhere; agricultural output had to remain high if it was to sustain that population.

The famine was greatest from 1315 to 1317. Grain prices soared astronomically, regions that depended on distant places for their food suffered a drastic population loss—as high as 10 percent in some towns—and the seed-to-yield ratio fell, in some cases by half. The 1315–17 famine was the greatest that Europe experienced, but it was not the only one. The fragile agricultural system, even if it had not achieved its potential output, had nevertheless proved incapable of feeding Europe without profound revision. Moreover, nearly every succeeding decade of the fourteenth century witnessed either regional or more widespread famine, and hunger became a universal and perennial scourge for the first prolonged period since the end of antiquity.

Hungry people die—or move. In the fourteenth century, land that could no longer be worked—because of soil exhaustion, population loss, the ravages of war, or the frequency and extent of pestilence—was abandoned. The fourteenth century produced an increasing number of deserted farming settlements and towns, many of which were never settled again. People moved to monasteries, towns, or more productive regions, there to seek food through charity, wage labor, or the assumption of servile status. The migrations provoked by famine raised other crises. The new arrivals could contribute little to the quality of town or city life, and they strained urban food supplies. As we will see later in this chapter, fourteenth and fifteenth century warfare also disrupted agricultural life. And on the heels of famine and war followed pestilence.

The dangers of reduced harvests, rising grain prices, and widespread famine are many. Death by starvation is not the only consequence of famine, nor is it the most far-reaching. Medieval people knew little about the different properties of foods, and medieval nutrition was uneven even in the best of times. The wealthy tended, even as late as the seventeenth century, to eat more animal protein and fewer vegetables than they needed, and the poor tended to eat far less animal protein and—because these foods were more readily available—far more vegetables and starch foods. Animal protein, always expensive, was usually available only in late fall and early winter, when animals were slaughtered. As winter progressed meat was salted more and more heavily and spiced to prevent rancidity.

Besides producing such diseases as gout, a diet of too much meat raises the dangers of a host of other diseases and severe vitamin deficiency. Wealthy or moderately prosperous Europeans ran these risks until well into modern times. On the other hand, a deficiency of animal protein produces tuberculosis, dysentery, and other maladies, and stunts growth substantially. Vitamin deficiency generally produces enormously painful and prolonged physical conditions—scurvy, rickets, gallstones. Thus the European diet, even in the most prosperous of years, created physiological imbalances that afflicted many people, although their causes were not generally known until the eighteenth century. Starvation and malnutrition raised equally severe problems, and the period between 1300 and 1850 witnessed the greatest effects of malnutrition on the greatest number of people. Starvation and malnutrition kill the old and the weak and, as we now

know, maim those who experience them in childhood. They produce a drastic change in
the demographic composition of society. The number of old and sick drops, infant mortality increases, and the birth rate decreases. Women die during their most fertile years,
or those who survive leave the area, taking with them another generation, one that will be
born elsewhere. Thus, the depopulation of many farms, villages, and towns does not last
merely for the duration of the period of famine, but for two or three generations, and
sometimes forever.

THE PALE HORSEMAN:
PLAGUE IN LATE MEDIEVAL EUROPE

Those who suffer malnutrition lack resistance to disease. Widespread starvation and
malnutrition had already begun to reduce the population of Europe when the next of the
Four Horsemen—pestilence—struck with unprecedented fury. It struck a population
weakened by hunger and lack of resistance, crowded into cities, more mobile than in any
period of Europe's history since the fifth and sixth centuries, and thus extremely prone to
contagion—a principle it did not understand—carried by a bacillus that was not identified until 1918.

The history of widespread epidemic disease and human society has barely been
written. The great plague described by Thucydides in Athens during the Peloponnesian
War, the plague brought back to Italy by Marcus Aurelius' troops in the late second century A.D., and the great plague that struck Constantinople and the west in 542–43—these
were the most striking and best-known epidemics in early European history. Although
the great epidemics of cholera, smallpox, and influenza in nineteenth- and twentieth-
century Europe have been better described and analyzed than earlier epidemics, the
plague of 1348–50, and its subsequent outbreaks between the mid fourteenth and the late
seventeenth centuries, stands as the most memorable and destructive of all. Although its
ravages were regional, it reduced the population of Europe by one third, completely
depopulated some regions and towns, and further aggravated the earlier effects of
agricultural shortcomings, famine, and demographic rearrangement that had begun by
the last years of the thirteenth century. It was also a prodigious test of the resiliency of
European society. The recovery of fifteenth-, sixteenth-, and seventeenth-century
Europe in terms of population, agricultural output, and living conditions offers eloquent
testimony to the vigor and recuperative powers of that society. The roots of this recovery
surely lay in the agricultural, technological, and economic innovations of the tenth
through the early fourteenth centuries.

Bubonic plague, carried by the fleas on black rats, appears to have struck first in
China around 1333. By 1340 it had reached Lake Baikal in Siberia, and by 1346 it had
crossed the Caucasus and struck the Crimea, the great port center on the Black Sea. Carried by the rats on an Italian fleet from the Black Sea to the Mediterranean, the plague
struck first in Europe in Messina and Sardinia in 1347. The next year it hit Genoa and
Venice, the greatest ports of the west, simultaneously. From the ports the plague followed
the trade routes. In February 1348 both Lucca and Avignon reported outbreaks, and two
months later Siena and Perugia in Italy and Cerdaña and Rousillon in southwestern
France were struck. In May, Ancona, Orvieto, and Rimini in Italy and Barcelona and
Catalonia in Spain were afflicted, followed in July by Paris and Antioch and a year later
by Germany and Tunisia. By September of 1349 the plague had reached England, by

1350 Prussia, Bremen, and the eastern Netherlands, and by 1351–52 western Russia. The indescribably swift spread of plague, its erratic destructiveness of human life, and the utter incomprehension of European society not only provoked severe loss of life and economic disruption on a vast scale but struck the European Christian mind and imagination with a terrible force. The consequences of the plague were echoed in literature, devotional styles, and the visual arts, as well as in depopulated farms and villages, devastated cities, and disordered economic institutions. Moreover, survival of the 1348–51 crisis did not guarantee immunity to later outbreaks.

Quickly joining the widespread bubonic form of plague were the vastly more contagious and deadly pneumonic and septicemic strains. In these three forms the plague attacked a population that was crowded into towns and ecclesiastical centers under the worst possible hygienic conditions, possessed uncertain food supplies, and already lacked a full complement of women of childbearing age. Those who survived one attack of plague were, of course, vulnerable to other infectious diseases, such as tuberculosis.

The years 1362 and 1375 witnessed epidemics as severe as that of 1348, and plague returned at least once in every decade until 1497. The great plague cycle begun in 1348 did not end until the late seventeenth century. Pestilence, then, followed hunger and malnutrition in the experience of fourteenth- and fifteenth-century men and women.

The birth rate usually increases after great population losses, as if to offset them. After the mid fourteenth century, however, the frequent recurrence of plague and famine prevented the birth rate from increasing the population. Indeed, most of the population increase in Europe after 1100 was wiped out. But such population loss did not occur uniformly everywhere. Population densities were redistributed considerably, villages were deserted for centuries, new villages were founded, and the proportion of urban to rural dwellers increased. Cities recovered their populations faster, not through an increased birth rate but by drawing off the rural population increase. The countryside had to populate both itself and the cities.

THE RED HORSEMAN: WAR AND SOCIETY

Famine and plague strike most severely at those least able to provide for themselves. In fourteenth- and fifteenth-century Europe, a society in which material resources had been stretched to their limits, a series of wars broke out between 1337 and the late fifteenth century. Their duration and character were different from those of earlier wars, which had consisted generally of infrequent pitched battles between small armies that were not assembled for long periods of time. Such wars usually troubled the noncombatant population relatively little, because they did little permanent damage. The wars of England and France, Castile, and northern Italy in the fourteenth and fifteenth centuries, however, had a different character. Recurring campaigns made battlefields out of plowed fields year after year. Some elements of agricultural life, such as mills and barns, could not be quickly replaced, because they required substantial capital and labor investment. The temporary but often regular destruction of crops and the prolonged effects of the destruction of mills and barns framed the circumstances of warfare. An invading fourteenth-century army, rather like a small expeditionary force, struck into enemy territory on a swift raid, a *chevauchée,* supporting itself from enemy land, capturing enemy towns, and destroying opposing forces. The invaded country, its inhabitants temporarily crowded into fortified towns and castles barely large enough to contain them, could only destroy the food in its own fields so that it did not fall into enemy hands, and hold out until the invaders, frustrated and hungry, moved on. The open country of northern France was particularly vulnerable to this kind of warfare, and the frequent slowing down of military campaigns by prolonged sieges increased the dangers to the noncombatant population considerably. Enemy armies, particularly when they wished to demoralize a hostile population, could themselves destroy fields and crops, exact large ransoms and bribes, and fail to keep their armies from looting.

The duration, frequency, and style of warfare proved particularly disastrous to noncombatants, and so did the composition of fourteenth-century armies. Soldiers were paid little, and their pay was frequently late if it came at all. Soldiers were usually recruited from the poorer and less stable elements of society, and regarded military activity as a means of self-enrichment. Prisoners were taken for ransom, towns and castles were plundered, and agricultural lands were held for tribute. Financial needs usually demanded that armies be disbanded as soon as possible, and large bands of discharged soldiers wandered around the countryside during truces, plundering and terrorizing the population. These groups, called *routiers* in the fourteenth century and *écorcheurs* in the fifteenth, posed continual problems. Sometimes they were reabsorbed into armies when the wars broke out again, and sometimes they sold themselves to the highest bidder in local conflicts. France and Italy were plagued the most severely by them, until the end of the fifteenth century.

Closely related to the activities of discharged or deserted soldiers was the increasing prevalence of banditry in the late fourteenth and fifteenth centuries. *Ecorcheurs* took over territory around fortified places they had captured on their own, ransomed those they kidnaped, demanded entire harvests, and required "protection" payments from all whose lives they touched. Impoverished and undisciplined lords of castles found it profitable to raid neighboring areas, particularly after acquiring some military experience—and probably some military personnel—in the numerous wars of the fourteenth century. Both nobles and displaced peasants sometimes formed their own bands or joined larger gangs in the French provinces and the north of England. Finally, robber bands seem to have formed among the poor, as well as among individuals of yeoman status. From the fourteenth century to the nineteenth, banditry became a ubiquitous and, to those already ravaged by famine, plague, and war, a particularly dangerous aspect of life.

A final aspect of late medieval warfare ought to be discussed. Earlier wars had been fought by professional knights and men-at-arms, and were caused by the arguments of princes and kings. They were small in scale and generally short. By the fourteenth century, however, wars touched the noncombatant population more regularly, not only through their destructiveness but through their financing and recruitment as well. The affairs of kings and princes drew upon a wider circle of resources and personnel. The organization of late medieval warfare and its power to mobilize extensive social and material resources made war a more prominent part of both social and economic history and an important part of political and constitutional history as well.

Philip IV the Fair of France won his first conflict with Pope Boniface VIII on the grounds that a king's obligation to defend his kingdom overrode his conventional obligations to churchmen and their finances. As other kings and rulers found that financing warfare was growing more and more expensive, they too tended to neglect traditional restraints in their dealings not only with the Church but with their other subjects. Royal administrators, judges, and tax collectors had made the king's power known throughout his kingdom; so now did military recruiters and suppliers. In this way, then, late medieval warfare made people more aware that they were the subjects of a territorial monarch and that this status entailed certain obligations.

THE BLACK HORSEMAN: FINANCIAL COLLAPSE AND RECOVERY

Among the earliest consequences of the changes in material life between 1270 and 1350 in the agricultural sector of the economy were the stabilization and decline of cereal-grain prices, a rise in the prices of manufactured or crafted goods, a considerable jump in the prices of commercial agricultural products, and an increase in the size of sheep herds at the expense of agricultural land. Over the fourteenth century the increasing demand for meat led to the raising of meat prices and to the importation of cattle from northern and eastern Europe. The new mobility of peasant families and the new demands for labor contributed to changing patterns of inheritance among the peasant population and to the practice of leasing vacant land at a fixed rent for a short period and subcontracting a labor force to work it. High urban labor costs and the search for cheap sources of power of the urban craft guilds led entrepreneurs to take different stages of wool production into the countryside, where they found an unregulated labor force in need of income. In much of England, western Germany, the Low Countries, and Savoy the growth of rural craft industry became prominent. The material crises of the fourteenth century opened much land to the profitable vocation of sheep raising, and in Castile an organization of wealthy sheepherders, the *Mesta,* grew quickly after 1273. Great herds of fine merino sheep were driven north across the vast Castilian tableland in the spring and south in the fall, and this restricted the development of the Castilian agricultural economy.

To the peasants who survived famine, plague, and war, the new economic opportunities were in some places considerable. The price of labor in a reduced labor force had gone up. If old lords were unwilling to renegotiate the price and conditions of service, other lords or prosperous peasant proprietors would. Statutes against wage increases proved incapable of controlling labor costs, and there appeared thriving peasant agricultural entrepreneurs who became employers of the available rural wage labor. The old haphazard scatterings of settlements on good land and bad that had spread unchecked between the tenth and the fourteenth centuries began to be tightened into compact new villages. Field systems were reorganized. Large farms appeared, owned and worked by a single peasant family with its own employees and servants. These peasants were increasingly resentful of demands made by old lords and royal tax agents, and of the successful enterprise of townspeople and middlemen that seemed to keep grain prices down and allow the towns to grow rich at the expense of rural labor. The new conditions of rural enterprise and the markets of the wider world contributed to the heightened tensions of society.

The good fortune of some peasants must not obscure the miserable lot of others. Wage laborers had been forced to trade the security of servile tenure for the instability of a world in which there was opportunity both to earn and to lose money. The increase in the number of wage laborers in the countryside who had no possessions or security led to a widening of the spectrum of the peasant population and to a differentiation of social and economic relationships. For instance, the cereal-grain farmer was generally closer to his employees and servants than the commercial farmer or the stock raiser. The new conditions of economic exchange further eroded the old social and economic bonds of dependence and security that had characterized much of rural society before the mid fourteenth century.

The crisis in grain prices and the growth of industry in the fourteenth and fifteenth centuries increased the spread of commercial agriculture. Barley and hops for the brewing of beer brought better prices than wheat and rye. Flax, hemp, woad, and madder—fiber and dye crops—all increased in value as wheat prices remained stable or declined. Some of the changes in late medieval agriculture ultimately proved beneficial. The retreat of grain cultivation to good land rather than marginal or poor land concentrated the remaining labor force on the most productive lands. The increase in crop rotation and the generally greater proportion of leguminous crops meant that the soil received more nitrogen, animal and human diets improved, and land that grew grain crops after having produced legumes required somewhat less animal manure to fertilize it. The cultivation of fodder crops, which increased after the fourteenth century, decreased the frequency of necessary fallow periods, in many areas from one year in three to one year in five or six.

The city was the module of nonagricultural society, and although its population remained small and its political significance often dwindled in the face of the increased power of royal authority, it remained the hub of the European economy. Moreover, between the fourteenth and the seventeenth centuries the city replaced the rural castle as the seat of royal government. In spite of the catastrophes in the agricultural, industrial, and commercial sectors of the fourteenth- and fifteenth-century economy, the importance of the city increased. While territorial monarchies were being shaped, the cities became the critical components of larger states, and the life of the late medieval city influenced the psychology, politics, and economy of larger regions. The study of the nonagricultural sectors of the late medieval European economy begins, then, with the cities.

The Walled City of Carcassonne. Built in the thirteenth century primarily as a trading and manufacturing center, Carcassonne was extensively restored in the nineteenth century. The restoration has perhaps given it a more quaint and romantic look than it originally possessed; it was far more busy than picturesque. (Peter Buckley)

The density of population in a medieval city permitted the concentration not only of a productive labor force but of economic activities on both a large and a small scale. Venice, Genoa, Milan, and Florence became the principal centers in Italy of international trade and finance; in England, London and Bristol; in Flanders, Bruges; in the south of France, Marseilles and Avignon; and in the north, the Hanseatic towns of Danzig, Riga, Stralsund, Rostock, Lubeck, Hamburg, and Bremen. These were the international as well as the regional centers of the European economy, and they controlled the economy in their immediate vicinity: Venice, the Adriatic Sea and increasingly the towns in the Trevisan March; Genoa, the Ligurian coast and what is now the Riviera, with a growing influence in southern Spain; Milan and Florence, the center and north of Italy; London and Bristol, the productive wool trade of southeastern and southwestern England. In international affairs these cities prospered because of their strong coinage, the exclusivity of their control, and the supporting services they offered their merchants and bankers. In regional affairs their strong political control of the countryside and their relative prosperity made them local capitals as well. Powerful rulers of large territories transformed such cities as Paris, London, Dijon, Avignon, and Naples into political capitals, thereby enhancing their economic prominence and drawing people to them. Although many medieval cities preserved their traditional character and their customary political divisions, the economic boom of the twelfth and thirteenth centuries, the growing concentration of political authority, and the stabilizing of local and long-distance trade and finance caused the greatest cities to grow even greater.

Sophisticated and extensive recording and accounting systems created new kinds of information about the economy. Public as well as commercial finances were watched more carefully and more expertly. In the fifteenth century the kingdom of France produced the first modern budget constructed according to sound accounting principles. A good example of this new economic instrumental rationality is to be found in the history of late medieval banking. The word "bank," like the legal term "bench," derives from the Latin *bancus,* the bench on which simple bankers and judges did their work. But neither law nor finance remained simple. Large amounts of capital in the hands of Italian merchant bankers of the thirteenth century were let in the form of large loans, sometimes to individuals or companies but more often to those who could offer more substantial security—the rulers of the principalities and territorial monarchies. As we shall see, the fiscal and political crises of the early fourteenth century caught European rulers with antiquated fiscal systems in a dilemma: rulers had come to depend on large loans as a regular part of their revenue, and the retarded development of public finance in the late thirteenth and early fourteenth centuries met the new flood of private commercial capital and engorged it indiscriminately.

One of the most striking political changes in the late fourteenth and fifteenth centuries was the restructuring of public finances and their influence on political life. The large amounts of capital available to underfinanced rulers in the late thirteenth and early fourteenth centuries led them to borrow on anticipation of revenues, to assign future revenues to their creditors, and to issue monopolies inconsiderately. Even these unwise measures failed to produce enough money for repayment of debts, and they further decreased operating revenues. Consequently, the kings of England and France, faced with extensive financial needs because of their mobilization for war, refused many of their obligations to the Italian and Flemish bankers who had loaned them money. Thus, in addition to demographic, epidemic, and military crises Europe experienced a financial crisis of previously unheard-of dimensions. Banks whose revenues had been committed

The Market. In Italian towns no aspect of social life was too modest to be depicted in bright frescoes. The stalls, shops, and houses of merchants were anchors of civic life. The shops depicted here are from two fourteenth-century frescoes in northern Italy. (L'Italia Magazine, Rome)

to government loans quickly failed. The great banking houses of Siena collapsed in 1339; in 1343 and 1346 the great Florentine banks of the Peruzzi and the Bardi went under. The crisis of the great early banking houses not only incapacitated public finance for most of the century and turned the rulers of Europe to new means of raising money; it also transformed banking itself. Investments in even the most wealthy territorial monarchies had proved to be no more secure than investments in private enterprises. Banks had to take two steps: first, to find a way of minimizing their risks, and, second, to find new investments for their diminished capital.

Until the seventeenth century the banking houses that survived the crash of the mid fourteenth century operated generally on a smaller scale than their great predecessors had. The new banks that rose in the wake of the mid-fourteenth-century failures—in Italy, those of the Medici, the Casa di San Giorgio in Genoa, and the Banco di San Ambrogio in Milan—became semipublic, absorbing shares of the increasingly common funded debts (publicly guaranteed, interest-paying bonds) of the cities and acquiring political power that made their investments more secure than they had been in the thirteenth century. The surviving banks and the newer institutions were aided by an increasing tendency to make monetary values homogeneous over wider regions. With this alignment of currencies one of the most vexing and time-consuming activities of early medieval money changers and bankers was slowly overcome. Some areas also insisted on evaluating different currencies according to a stable gold standard determined according to weight. Currency speculation had long provided a profitable area of investment, but unstable currency had increased economic risks, and "bad money" persisted in driving out "good money." The great stable coins of the twelfth and thirteenth centuries—the Byzantine *solidus,* the Venetian *ducat,* the Florentine *florin*—all succumbed in the fourteenth century. By the end of the fourteenth century Italian banks had begun to issue paper currency, but the spread of this new form of money was slow and uneven. Early modern Europe operated on a metallic currency, and the scarcity or promiscuity of bullion altered considerably the economic activity of regions, cities, and kingdoms.

The history of the wool industry in the fourteenth and fifteenth centuries illuminates one aspect of late medieval trade: shifts in the areas of production, finishing, and sale and the consequent economic, social, and political changes in those areas that lost and those that gained from such shifts. The rise of the English cloth industry, its relative freedom from restriction, the decline of Flanders, and the weakening of Italian trade all suggest an aspect of late medieval economic life that has long been misunderstood—the economic reorganization within a complex system that many historians have insisted must be labeled uniformly as a decline. To be sure, there is remarkable evidence of many sorts of decline—from financial to agricultural—during this period. But there are also compelling indications that the rearrangement of the European economy—from finance to agriculture—not only increased prosperity in some places and among some social groups, but ultimately laid the groundwork for the social and economic changes of the seventeenth and eighteenth centuries. The new freedom of different kinds of entrepreneurs, new means of record keeping and accounting, the increasingly prominent role of political authority in economic activity, and the rapidly changing prosperity of many areas offer a confusing picture, but not one that can casually be labeled as uniform decline. Regional variations were still the predominant characteristic of European economic life until well into the eighteenth century, and the decline of one region, town, or family usually meant the rise of another.

Most of these economic changes were misunderstood: they were interpreted as acts of God, as signs of the corruption of political or ecclesiastical authority, as the result of greed (the predominant vice in late medieval moral philosophy), or as the consequences of a world turned upside down. Economic complaints were joined indiscriminately to other kinds of complaints and sometimes to the literary or artistic preoccupations of late medieval society. The resulting picture of unrelieved gloom and totally unchecked self-interest is a common portrayal but certainly not a uniformly accurate one. It does little justice to those who in bettering their lot, however novel and incomprehensible their activities, *did* attempt to be useful to society, to serve their rulers loyally, to be good Christians, and to accommodate as best they could the deepest and most enduring values their society held.

FURTHER READING

See especially Denys Hay, *Europe in the Fourteenth and Fifteenth Centuries* (New York: Longmans, 1966); George Holmes, *Europe: Hierarchy and Revolt, 1320–1450* (New York: Harper & Row, 1975); John Hale, Roger Highfield, and Beryl Smalley, eds., *Europe in the Later Middle Ages* (Evanston, Ill.: Northwestern University Press, 1965); Margaret Aston, *The Fifteenth Century* (New York: Harcourt Brace Jovanovich, 1968); F. R. H. Du Boulay, *An Age of Ambition* (New York: Viking, 1970); and Johann Huizinga, *The Waning of the Middle Ages* (New York: Doubleday, 1953).

On the plague and its consequences, see Philippe Ariès, *Western Attitudes Towards Death* (Baltimore: Johns Hopkins, 1975); Philip Ziegler, *The Black Death* (New York: Harper & Row, 1969), and the brilliant cultural study by Millard Meiss, *Painting in Florence and Siena after the Black Death* (New York: Harper & Row, 1964).

On warfare, see J. F. Verbruggen, *The Art of Warfare in Western Europe During the Middle Ages* (Amsterdam: North Holland Publishing Co., 1977); John Keegan, *The Face of Battle* (New York: Random House, 1977); Kenneth Fowler, ed., *The Hundred Years' War* (New York: St. Martin's, 1971); and John Barnie, *War in Medieval English Society* (Ithaca, N.Y.: Cornell University Press, 1974).

On commerce and finance, see the general bibliography.

See also Michel Mollat and Philippe Wolff, *The Popular Revolutions of the Late Middle Ages* (reprint ed., Winchester, Mass.: Allen & Unwin, 1973).

18

The Church and the World

THE REFORM OF THE WORLD

From the thirteenth century on, the work and the thought of churchmen were exercised in a world much wider than that of the earlier Middle Ages. One cause of this change was the development of European society itself and the demands it made upon the Church. Another was the change in the relations between Latin Christians and the Byzantine, Muslim, and pagan world around them. Examples of this change may be seen in the history of the Crusader states, the Byzantine Empire, and the Mongols.

The kingdom of Jerusalem had fallen to the Muslims in 1187. The Third Crusade, launched in 1190, failed to recapture it. Although many plans for crusades were drawn up and several were launched in the thirteenth century, the movement failed. With the fall of the city of Acre to the Muslims in 1291, the last Christian territory in the Holy Land was lost. The kings of Jerusalem moved to the island of Cyprus. Some of the military orders also moved. The Teutonic Knights shifted their activities to the Baltic and northeastern Europe. The Knights of the Hospital of St. John conquered the island of Rhodes in 1308 and held it until the sixteenth century. The Templars, as we have seen, remained in France, where they were destroyed by Philip IV the Fair between 1307 and 1312. The great idea of Pope Urban II, the event that the historian Edward Gibbon termed "the world's debate,'' had indeed brought Latin Christians into a new world, but it failed to keep them there.

In 1198, when Pope Innocent III preached yet another Crusade to recover Jerusalem, an army assembled and sailed from Venice. The army's inability to pay the fleet of Venice for its transportation to the Holy Land, however, and several political intrigues led the Crusaders not to the Holy Land but to Constantinople, which they conquered in 1204. A Latin Empire was established, and Latin rites and observances were forced upon the Greek Christians. Further deterioration of relations between Latin and Greek Christians was the result. The Latin princes who carved out territories for themselves behaved ruthlessly toward their Greek subjects. The city of Constantinople was looted of both its wealth and its treasury of relics. But the Latin Empire failed too. From 1204 until its collapse in 1261 it struggled with its own rebellious Latin subjects and with Byzantine resistance, kept up in a few territories that the Latins had not managed to capture. In 1261 the emperor Michael VIII Palaeologos recaptured the city of Constantinople and drove the Latins out of part of his empire. But Greece itself was lost to the Byzantines. From 1261 the weakened and shrunken Byzantine Empire struggled between pressure from the Latins and pressure from the continuing power of the Islamic world close by.

The third and most dangerous challenge to the frontiers of the Christian world was the rise of the Mongol Empire from the early thirteenth century. Under the inspired leadership of Genghis Khan, several central Asian peoples joined together in a vast military empire that struck at China and Europe simultaneously. Moving westward, the Mongols destroyed Kiev in 1240 and struck deeply into Hungary and Poland. Mongol armies also assaulted the Islamic world, and the destruction of Baghdad in 1258 indicated the presence of a threat to the Christian and Islamic worlds alike. But the unity of the Mongol Empire broke up after 1258. One part of the empire, the Golden Horde, established itself in Russia, where it remained until the fifteenth century. In 1266 Kublai Khan established a powerful Mongol empire in China, with its capital at Peking. Kublai's brother Hulagu Khan established the empire of the Ilkhans of Persia and was responsible for the sacking of Baghdad. He was prevented from moving further west by his defeat at the hands of the Mamelukes of Egypt at the great battle of Ain Jalut in 1260. Although Mongol power weakened after the middle of the fourteenth century, the Mongols had transformed the eastern frontiers of Christendom.

The failure of the Crusade movement, the capture and loss of Constantinople, and the arrival of the Mongols transformed not only the circumstances but also the consciousness of the Christian world. God's plans had seemed to go awry, in terms of both the recovery of the Holy Land and the reunification of the Latin and Greek communions. A mysterious people, neither Christian nor Muslim, had appeared out of the east like the avenging armies of the Apocalypse. Among the many consequences of these events two in particular stand out: the opening of Asia to European missionaries and traders, and the transformation of the European view of the world. The first of these will be considered in Chapter 20. Here, we must consider the second.

The point of view from which the Latin Christian world regarded the arrival of the Mongols and the disasters in Constantinople and Palestine was deeply colored by a prophetic movement that had begun in thirteenth-century Italy. It is associated with the figure and writings of Joachim of Fiore. Joachim was the Cistercian abbot of a monastery in Calabria in the second half of the twelfth century. In a series of commentaries on the

Bible Joachim professed to see a new division of divine and human history, and his speculations, which included prophecies, spread beyond the walls of his order. His writings were edited by Gerardo of Borgo San Donino, a Franciscan, around 1250, and they became very influential in the radical wing of the Franciscan order. This wing, later known as the Spiritual Franciscans, opposed what it considered the worldliness of other Franciscans and claimed that it alone preserved the true instructions of Saint Francis. Among Joachim's prophecies was one concerning a new monastic order of holy men, and some of the Spiritual Franciscans identified themselves as this new order. The spread of Joachim's prophetic ideas influenced powerful thinkers in the order, men such as the scholar Peter Olivi and the polemicist Ubertino da Casale.

Others were influenced by Joachim's thought. Arnald of Villanova, a lay theologian, physician, and counselor of popes and kings, also wrote on prophecy and the coming end of the world. Among the strongest influences of Joachimic thought was its notion that a new age of the world had begun with the Franciscan order, an age when the new spiritual men would convert Jews and Muslims without the need of the sword or temporal power. Thus, from several different directions the historical failure of the Crusade movement and new idealistic hopes about the immediate future converged to create a new vision of the future, a vision whose emphases on reform, the coming of the millennium, and the miraculous conversion of non-Christians became common topics of discussion in many clerical and lay circles.

One of the most striking figures in this movement was the Catalan noble Ramon Lull (1232–1316). A gifted poet and a prosperous man, Lull was moved by the example of Saint Francis of Assisi around 1263. Renouncing marriage and the world, he set out to learn Arabic, found training schools for missionaries, and become a missionary to Muslims himself. Lull attended school in Italy and Paris, patronized the Franciscans, founded schools for training missionaries and teaching them Arabic, and produced many literary works of great influence. He died, possibly in North Africa, on a conversion mission. His ideas and works continued to circulate widely, and he is one of the most important figures in late medieval devotional literature.

Such aspects of Christian practice and theory as the problem of the rights of non-Christians, the conversion movements, and the problem of the reunion of the divided Greek and Latin churches dominated much of Christian thought from the mid thirteenth to the mid fifteenth century. The emotional pitch of this concern was very high, for lay people and clerics alike feared that their efforts had been too few and that hope for reform had dawned too late. The Council of Vienne in 1312 decreed that schools of Arabic and other non-Christian languages ought to be established, and popes and lawyers attempted to institutionalize these concerns in their decretals and administrative practices. At a very different level, such laymen as Arnald of Villanova and Ramon Lull responded to these same concerns in their own inventive ways. Behind both institutional and personal activity lay the fear that the last age of the world was coming soon, or was already upon humanity. The prophetic strains of Joachism were echoed in many places in the fourteenth and fifteenth centuries, and they form a characteristic background to the hope, fearful anticipation, and sense of duty that mark the efforts of so many thinkers between the mid thirteenth and mid fifteenth centuries. They also shaped the attitudes with which people responded to the crises of the later fourteenth century—the failure of Greek and Latin reunion, the Avignon papacy, the Great Schism, the conciliar movement, and the new forms of devotion that were to grow up in the fifteenth century.

THE REVOLT AGAINST ARISTOTLE AND AQUINAS

From the first appearance of Aristotle's works of natural philosophy and metaphysics in the late twelfth century, opposition to Aristotelian thought developed among Christian theologians, just as it had among earlier Muslim theologians. Aristotle's picture of an uncreated universe and a single collective intellect for the human race, the failure of his theology to account for the Trinity, and his theory that God acted from necessity rather than freedom encountered bitter opposition from theologians and led to the condemnation of many of his works and ideas (and their Arabic explanations) from 1210 to 1277. Indeed, the condemnation of many Aristotelian and Averroistic theses by Stephen Tempier, the bishop of Paris, in 1277 has often been considered the watershed of medieval intellectual history. But others besides theologians had attacked Aristotle, and even the expositions of Albertus Magnus and Saint Thomas Aquinas came under heavy fire, from outside and inside the Dominican order.

Roger Bacon, (1214–92), a teacher of natural philosophy and a lay member of the Franciscan order, bitterly attacked Parisian scholars for their unthinking acceptance of Aristotelian natural philosophy. Other natural philosophers, including Robert Grosseteste, developed original scientific approaches to problems that Aristotle had generally left unsolved or had treated inadequately, such as the nature of rainbows and the problem of local motion. The condemnations of 1277, which were primarily theological and aimed at restoring the liberty of God from Aristotelian necessity, were also important for prying loose Aristotelian authority in general and consequently permitting the work of such natural philosophers as Grosseteste and Bacon to be continued in the schools with much greater independence.

The condemnation of many Aristotelian and Thomistic principles at the University of Paris in 1277 produced a revolt not only against a theology based upon Aristotle, but against Aristotelian natural philosophy as well. Although a few schools, notably those of theology and natural philosophy at the University of Padua, remained close to Aristotelianism and Averroism (too close, many thought), and although the Dominican order tried (ultimately successfully) to preserve the authority and reputation of Saint Thomas, a number of thinkers set off in new directions in both theology and natural philosophy.

John Duns Scotus (1265–1308), an immensely complex theologian in the Augustinian and Franciscan traditions, criticized the Aristotelian tendency to make God less transcendent by attributing to him rationality and a kind of intelligibility that made him accessible to human reason. Duns Scotus argued that such a view of God diminished God's transcendence and majesty. He therefore emphasized the divine will, rather than divine reason, and the ultimate unknowability of God. Reason, Duns Scotus argued, can give no reliable information about God at all.

Although William of Occam (1285–1349) criticized much of Duns Scotus's work, he agreed that God was transcendent, omnipotent, and infinitely free. Only faith and revelation tell us about God's nature and will. Reason, on the contrary, informs us only of the observable world. Although Occam's rationalism may appear to represent a step backwards in its reversion to a mystical theology from a rational one, it is probably wiser to regard his and Scotus's theology as correcting a movement toward rationalism that had gone too far. On the other hand, by insisting upon the supremacy of reason in the field of observable phenomena, Occam gave a new and separate degree of authority to rational and scientific analysis. Having deprived reason of all power to inform us about God, Occam gives it every power to inform us about the phenomenal world. Since in Scotus's and Occam's theology God's will may interrupt the phenomena of the material world at virtually any time, reason describes only the regular operation of that world before God intervenes.

Out of this division of religious and philosophical consciousness, reflected in other theologians and scientists between the fourteenth and the seventeenth centuries, there emerged the twin currents of divine voluntarism and rational authority in explanations of the material world. In the case of voluntarism, God's will, unbounded and incomprehensible, characterized the Divinity. Mystical theology, mystical devotion, pious private prayer, interior spiritual development, a revival of symbolic thought and expression, and a new interest in contemplation came to characterize religious sensibility after the mid fourteenth century.

In the case of rational natural philosophy, Scotus and Occam opened the door to the idea that if reason is of no value in ascertaining truths about God, it may be of supreme and uncontestable value in ascertaining truths about the observable world. If reason has no validity in clarifying the spiritual realm and must thereby defer to faith, revelation, and mysticism, conversely these three may not validly ascertain truths about the material world. This last point, developed more fully by thinkers of the fifteenth and sixteenth centuries, created a much smaller realm, but a much more manageable and verifiable one, for rational empiricism. Finally, both voluntaristic theology and rational empiricism, having developed in common as a reaction to Aristotelianism and Aquinas, were mutually acceptable to each other. One finds many late medieval thinkers of a strongly mystical theological bent holding obviously rational ideas about the material world. By removing reason from metaphysics and theology, Scotus and Occam made it acceptable to both theologians and natural philosophers.

While Franciscans were attacking Aristotle and Aquinas, several fourteenth-century thinkers revived the thought of Saint Augustine into a dominant influence. Thomas Bradwardine, archbishop of Canterbury (d. 1349), relied heavily on Augustine's writings in his treatise *On the Cause of God Against Pelagius,* which emphasizes the importance of faith in the achievement of salvation. Bradwardine was also associated with a group of mathematicians at Merton College, Oxford, and in his scientific studies of dynamics and local motion he strongly criticized Aristotelian dynamics and brought to bear on Aristotle's generally nonmathematical physics a new mathematical sophistication that further eroded the prestige of Aristotelian natural philosophy.

Thus, the revolt against Aristotle and Aquinas gave new impetus to the evolution of theology and natural philosophy alike. The marvelous synthesis of Aquinas came under attack from many directions, and the vast resources of theological thought and feeling, as well as the new interest in experimental natural philosophy—incompatible as these movements may appear to a modern mind—shaped the spiritual and scientific direction of late medieval thought and began to forge the links (which historians are still exploring) between the late medieval and modern worlds.

THE POPES AT AVIGNON

Not only did Greek and Latin Christianity fail to find union, but internal changes in the Latin church itself marked the fourteenth and fifteenth centuries. The Avignon papacy was perhaps the most striking manifestation of these changes.

Boniface VIII died at Rome in 1303. His successor, Benedict XI (1303–04), died at Perugia. Benedict's successor, Clement V (1305–14), was not in Italy when he was elected, and was crowned pope in Lyons. Mediation between the kings of England and France and the Council of Vienne in 1311–12 kept Clement out of Italy, and the press of business and turbulence in Italy kept his successor, John XXII, in the south of France. From the pontificate of John XXII (1316–34), the popes took up residence in the city of Avignon, in which they purchased first the bishop's palace and in 1348 the city itself from its owner, the king of Naples, a papal vassal.

To a great extent the Avignon residence aided the papacy in its task of directing the spiritual life of Christendom. It is ironic that although the popes at Avignon were more disposed, better equipped, and more efficiently financed for the task of directing Christian society than ever before, their residency there was regarded by many as the "Babylonian captivity" of the papacy. There were reasons for this. The increasing friction between the kings of France and England always tended to place the mediating popes in great disfavor with parties who opposed their activities. The struggle between the Avignon popes and the emperor Ludwig of Bavaria (1313–47) has often been regarded as high-handed and autocratic on the part of the popes. Indeed, the Avignon residency was long widely heralded by contemporaries and later historians as the symbol of the breakup of medieval Christendom. Only recently have scholars clarified its real accomplishments, estimated the dedication of popes and curia, and begun to appreciate the work of some of the fourteenth-century popes as highly as it deserves.

The Avignon popes put papal, financial, and administrative practices on a sounder footing than ever before. The Palace of the Popes at Avignon appears to have been designed and built specifically to facilitate papal business; it may be regarded as the first building in Europe devoted to large-scale administrative functions. The care with which papal archives and records were kept, the intelligent design and decoration of the palace, and the increasing consistency of papal policy during this period mark the Avignon papacy as a time of vigorous application of rationality to the stubborn problems of rule rather than a captivity, a concession to the kings of France, or the expression of a frustrated monarchical political theory.

As the fourteenth century wore on, pressures on the popes to return to Rome grew stronger. But the enormity of the task of moving the papal administration, household, and records postponed such a move (except for a very brief visit by Pope Urban V) until 1377, during the papacy of Gregory XI (1370–78). The conflicting opinions concerning the return of the papacy to Rome proved to be the prelude to a great crisis, the double papal election of 1378.

THE GREAT SCHISM
AND THE COUNCIL OF CONSTANCE

The pressures on the conclave of cardinals voting in Rome in 1378 were strongly in favor of an Italian pope. Conflicting opinions between Italian and French cardinals led to the election of an Italian from outside the curia, Bartolomeo Prignano, archbishop of Bari, who took the title of Urban VI. But Urban's high-handed treatment of the curia led a dissident group of cardinals to flee Rome, denounce the papal election as uncanonical, and elect as their own pope, Cardinal Robert of Geneva. These two popes, the "Roman" Urban VI (1378–89) and the "Avignonese" Clement VII (1378–94), divided the Christian Latin world into two conflicting camps. Their rivalry destroyed the nonpartisan status of the papacy in mediating international conflicts, diverted the papacy's attention from the needs of Christendom to those of personal predominance, and led to a virtual duplication of papal governing apparatus as each pope strove to force his rival and his rival's supporters to capitulate.

The schism endured. Various steps were taken by kings, theologians, canon lawyers, and prelates to pressure the two sides to compromise. Between 1399 and 1403 the king of France declared a "subtraction of obedience" from both sides and gave the French church an early experience of that independence from Rome that, in the form of special agreements between the king of France and the papacy, was to help create the highly autonomous Gallican church of the sixteenth and seventeenth centuries. In 1409 a council at Pisa deposed both papal rivals and elected yet another pope, thereby widening the contest to a field of three. The next six years were spent in a series of dramatic attempts to resolve their conflicting claims, and only the persistence of a number of prelates, the universities, and the emperor Sigismund (d. 1437) determined the direction in which a solution to the dilemma might be found. It was decided that this, the greatest of all ills in the history of the Church, must be solved—could *only* be solved—by an ecumenical church council. The council, called to meet at Constance in 1415, was to be the Church's last opportunity to restore unity to a faction-ridden world and to place once more a single universal pope on the Throne of Saint Peter.

The Council of Constance (1415–18) managed to remove the three contending popes and elect a fourth pope, Martin V (1417–31), who spent his pontificate trying to restore the pope's rights and security in the city of Rome and recover the papacy's lost prestige throughout Europe. The council also burned the Bohemian ecclesiastical reformer John Hus, who was accused of unorthodox views on the Church hierarchy, excessive criticism of clerical abuses, and heresy. Hus had been a major figure in Bohemian spiritual and cultural life, however, and after his execution Bohemia was torn by civil wars until 1434. Finally, the council voted that general councils be called regularly. But the suggestion of the most extreme supporters of this view, the Conciliarists, that a general council might be superior to a pope, generated papal opposition to the notion of regular councils. From the pontificate of Martin V on, the popes grew more preoccupied with settling affairs within the Papal States and Italy, ruling the Church alone with the help of the curia, and, by opposing councils, turning the loyalties of many churchmen to local temporal powers instead of to Rome. Up to the beginning of the sixteenth century these popes found that the return to Rome and the local political rivalries in central and northern Italy occupied far more of their time and attention than they could readily spare from dealing with the remnants of a universal Christian society and its pressing spiritual and material needs.

VARIETIES OF DEVOTION
ON THE EVE OF THE REFORMATION

Historians have often assessed the religious culture of the period between 1350 and 1500 by comparing it with what followed—the Reformation of the sixteenth century and the Counter-Reformation. Recognizing the spiritual vitality and conflict of the sixteenth century, many of them have casually criticized late medieval religious culture as being formalized and devoid of spiritual intensity or clear theological thought. Much recent research has sharply altered this picture of the spiritual life of the later Middle Ages. Attempts at church reform are surprisingly numerous after 1350, and the intensity of the lay people's search for spiritual comfort and assurance is notable. Fourteenth-century English bishops, for example, made substantial attempts to administer their dioceses and care for the spiritual life of their congregations. The appearance of such guides for parochial clergy as William of Pagula's *Occulus Pastoralis* in the fourteenth century and John Mirick's *Instructions for Parish Priests* in the fifteenth marks the first stage of the slow process by which thirteenth-century theology, morality, and canon law began to filter down to the parish level, and there generate a pastoral revolution, just as the occasional influence of the Franciscans and Dominicans was beginning to wane. The early-fourteenth-century compendium by John of Freiburg, the *Summa Confessorum,* became the standard handbook of theology for most fourteenth- and fifteenth-century clergy with any pretense to learning at all. In the mid fourteenth century Pope Benedict XII made an extensive effort to reform monasticism, the first such attempt since the Cistercian revolution two centuries before, and the last until the mid sixteenth century.

In the fourteenth century a pastoral ideal took shape that is perhaps best illustrated by the parson in Chaucer's *Canterbury Tales,* a figure certainly not invented by Chaucer himself. A genuine sense of responsibility for the souls of individual Christians at all levels of society—aided by ideals of clerical behavior, handbooks of instruction for laity and clergy alike, and helps for sermon writing and delivery—was one of the greatest legacies of the thirteenth century. That sense of responsibility was sometimes impossible to activate, however, and it is more remarkable in isolated centers than in dioceses with consistently applied and supervised regulations.

The fourteenth and fifteenth centuries also witnessed a new sophistication and acuteness of conscience on the part of many individuals, laity as well as clergy. Confraternities spread through the towns as urban spiritual needs came to be perceived as different from the needs of the rural population. The Brethren of the Common Life at Deventer in the Netherlands offer a different example. A devoted organization of lay people from all walks of life, they explored the inner spiritual life by means of pietist contemplation. Saint Brigit of Sweden, Saint Catherine of Siena, San Bernardino of Siena, and Thomas à Kempis— some of the most remarkable religious figures of the fourteenth and fifteenth centuries—shared this concern for devotional purity and its pollution by secular abuses.

Another powerful force in the religious sensibility of the later Middle Ages was the growing sophistication of the European vernacular languages. Although prayers and sermons had always been part of vernacular expression, Latin Christian society heard masses and other forms of the liturgy in Latin, and the formal administrative affairs of the Church, as well as all higher learning and much law, were conducted in that tongue. The universality of the Latin language made it easier for universal institutions such as the papacy and universities to draw upon a wide range of peoples for administrators and staff members. It was also a linguistic reflection of a kind of Christian European unity. Finally, it permitted sophisticated thought to find expression at a time when vernacular languages were not sufficiently developed to do so.

The European vernacular languages developed quickly and irregularly after the eighth century. Two generations after Charlemagne the Frankish language was giving way to Old French and Old High German. In the Strasbourg oaths of 842, the grandsons of Charlemagne swore mutual oaths of respect in the Old French and Old High German languages of their followers, and the chronicler Nithard recorded these vernacular statements. But medieval linguistic development reflected the particularization of

Europe. In the territory of France, for example, the language of the north, the *langue d'oïl*, was very different from the language of the south, the *langue d'oc*. But dialects and smaller regional differences also survived, as did the different languages of Catalan in the southwest and Breton in Brittany. A variant of the *langue d'oïl* traveled with the Normans to England in 1066 and helped create the Anglo-Norman language of the Norman aristocracy, which displaced vernacular Old English to a socially inferior status. The Anglo-Norman tongue contributed to the shaping of yet another language, Middle English, which appeared in the twelfth century.

Not until the reign of King John (1199–1216) could a post-Conquest king of England speak English. Not until 1349 was English used as a medium of teaching, and not until 1362 was it made the language of law. In the latter year English was first used in a speech in Parliament. What Basil Cottle has called the triumph of English took place between 1350 and 1400.

The slow development of vernacular languages made churchmen hesitant to permit translations of Scripture into European vernaculars on the often justified grounds that theological errors might crop up as a result of linguistic incapacity. But much devotional literature, especially after 1200, did make its way into common languages. Stories about Saint Francis of Assisi, stories for use in sermons, meditative literature, and poetry all conveyed religious sentiments to wider circles of people. By the fourteenth century the hunger for vernacular Bibles had led to several English translations and versions in other languages as well. John Hus wrote several pieces of religious literature in Czech, thereby doing for literary Czech what Martin Luther's German bible would do for literary German early in the sixteenth century. Vernacular biographies of Jesus also appeared, supplementing the Latin Gospels. The coming of age of the European languages had a great impact upon religious sentiment and expression during the fourteenth and fifteenth centuries. Joan of Arc, for example, although she was illiterate, could articulate her powerful sense of her religion and her keen awareness of what it meant to be a subject of the king of France.

A heightened sense of pastoral obligation, a broad awareness of the need for reform, the insistence upon self-awareness through confession, the spread of religious fraternities, the growing self-consciousness of the laity, and the rise of vernacular religious literature—all are eloquent testimony to the spiritual condition of Europe on the eve of the Reformation. The fragmented ecclesiastical organization of the fifteenth century could not deal adequately with these movements as a whole and had only occasional contact with them in particular localities. The death of Pius II (1458–64) as he was setting out on a crusade against the Ottoman Turks—the first great humanist pope setting out on the last crusade—may well have marked an end to one formal phase in the history of the idea of Christendom.

FURTHER READING

Most general histories of late medieval Europe deal in some way with the problems of reform, reunion, and prophecy discussed in the first section of this chapter. Several works, however, are good guides to some of the most interesting aspects of the period. E. Randolph Daniel, *The Franciscan Concept of Mission in the High Middle Ages* (Lexington: University Press of Kentucky, 1975), and Marjorie Reeves, *The Influence of Prophecy in the Later Middle Ages* (Oxford: Oxford University Press, 1969), offer sensitive treatments of the prophetic mentality from a wide variety of sources. Delno C. West, ed., *Joachim of Fiore in Christian Thought*, 2 vols. (New

York: Burt Franklin, 1975), is a good collection of essays on different aspects of Joachism. C. M. D. Crowder, *Unity, Heresy and Reform, 1378–1460* (New York: St. Martin's, 1977), is a fine collection of translated and annotated documents illustrating many of the aspects of the problems discussed in this chapter.

On the Avignon papacy, see Yves Renouard, *The Avignon Papacy, 1305–1403* (London: Faber & Faber, 1970). See also Walter Ullmann, *The Origins of the Great Schism* (reprint ed., Hamden, Conn.: Archon Books, 1973); W. A. Pantin, *The English Church in the Fourteenth Century* (reprint ed., Toronto: University of Toronto Press, 1980); Louise Ropes Loomis, *The Council of Constance,* John H. Mundy and K. M. Woody, eds. (New York: Columbia University Press, 1961); and Matthew Spinka, *John Hus: A Biography* (Princeton, N.J.: Princeton University Press, 1968).

Fine recent general studies of the period are Francis P. Oakley, *The Western Church in the Later Middle Ages* (Ithaca, N.Y.: Cornell University Press, 1980) and Steven Ozment, *The Age of Reform* (New Haven: Yale University Press, 1980). On the pastoral concerns of the period, see Leonard E. Boyle, *Pastoral Care, Clerical Education and Canon Law, 1200–1400* (London: Variorum, 1981).

19

Power and Order

THE POLITICAL COMMUNITY

The "history" of modern states is often extended backwards in time to remote periods and based upon an idea of the political community that was developed only in the nineteenth and twentieth centuries. The main components of modern political societies are continuity in space and time, community of language, impersonal institutions of governance and the impersonal loyalty of subjects and citizens, political sovereignty, and the various aspects (some nonpolitical) of "national consciousness." Neither nationalism nor the modern sovereign state appeared in the twelfth and thirteenth centuries, but some extremely important elements of them did. These were strengthened over the enormous span of time in which European political communities could develop without massive outside interference. Such diverse elements of a political community as the awareness of a common history and language, uncritical loyalty to a legitimate ruler, and even the common notion of being subject to a king coalesced with the claims of kings and helped to identify kingship with the idea of the state. The mobilization of state resources, a general test of modern states, occurred on a far smaller scale and for shorter periods of time in medieval polities. The concept of patriotism and, conversely, that of a state with resources so great that universal coercion was possible for its rulers were both far in the future. The words *politics, polity,* and *policy* appeared in most western languages in the late thirteenth and fourteenth centuries, but it took them a long time to become part of people's common vocabulary.

By the end of the tenth century the older tribes, war bands, *gentes,* and *populi* of early medieval society had virtually disappeared as political societies. The idea of a single Christian people, the *populus Christianus,* one of the legacies of the age of Charlemagne, still survived, and both popes and emperors claimed certain ordinary governmental rights (and at the very least a kind of honorific preeminence) in respect to it. But neither the regional principalities nor a universal Christian society constituted the dominant political forms of Europe between the twelfth and the fourteenth centuries. That distinction was reserved for the city-republics, especially those of northern Italy, and the territorial monarchies of England, France, and the Iberian peninsula, which emerged with a new kind of political culture. Apart from these examples of early development and failure, some kingdoms simply disappeared, as did the old Carolingian Middle Kingdom and Burgundy, which was absorbed into the Holy Roman Empire. Other kingdoms, many of them much smaller and with fewer resources, survived vigorously into early modern times. A good example is Scotland, which developed strong national feelings in spite of its relative weakness in comparison with England or France.

For much of the twelfth century, great territorial principalities such as Normandy, Lorraine, Bavaria, Poitou, Flanders, and Champagne remained strong and proved indigestible to centralizing monarchies. This is but one indication that the road from medieval monarchy to modern nation-state was long and difficult. The transformation was not inevitable. In the examples considered in the rest of this chapter, which focuses upon kings and their servants, the two streams—political and nonpolitical—in the evolution of a political society should be kept in mind. For only by developing monarchical power on the one hand, and on the other a collective consciousness of belonging to a political community on the part of a widening circle of classes and individuals, did the medieval kingdom lay the foundations of the modern state.

Along the periphery of Europe, from Ireland to the Iberian peninsula, Cyprus, and Constantinople, from Scandinavia to Poland, Bohemia, and Hungary, political centralization was retarded by the successes of warrior aristocracies whose political vision was as limited as their response to economic and social change. Much of the work that in Italy, France, and Germany was done by the native populations was in these kingdoms done by outsiders who were never integrated into the political community. Merchants and traders passed through these areas; they did not stay. The vast lands, military culture, and restricted royal means of governance in these kingdoms allowed their nobles great power, but did not permit the aggressive state building that took place in the northern Italian cities, France, and England. There, political communities were formed that linked rulers and subjects in sophisticated and novel relationships, some pragmatic and financial, some theoretical and hard to pin down. The kingdoms and communities on the European frontier, though, were delayed in political development at exactly the moment when this large-scale state building took place.

One of the most striking features of political culture between the twelfth and the nineteenth centuries is the success temporal rulers achieved in establishing and legitimizing the secular bases of civil life. In the late eleventh and twelfth centuries the political ideas of Gregorian reformers deprived European lay rulers of their sacramental and sometimes priestly status and forced them to seek a new kind of legitimacy. As this book has shown—for example, in the prestige of Saint Louis IX of France, lay people's recognition of the sacredness of royal anointing and coronation, and Philip IV the Fair's propaganda portrait of France as a holy land and a most Christian people—rulers sometimes found that legitimacy very close to its ancient sources. At other times they had to seek it farther afield, in the expansion of the areas of contact between ruler and people in day-to-day administration, in the idea of the king as defender of the law, and in the exploitation of the idea that civil society was a natural good in the tradition of Aristotle. Some rulers benefited from the application to themselves and the communities they ruled of ideas that had once applied only to the universal authority of the Roman emperor. Others found increased support in the growth of social and cultural bonds that were at first not political at all, such as a common vernacular language, the institutions of a national law, and the idea of a common history.

Although many ecclesiastical political thinkers continued to approach political thought from the point of view developed by canon lawyers and papal political propaganda in the thirteenth century (a point of view that in some respects was accepted until the nineteenth century), many more political theorists developed new approaches to the problem of political order and legitimacy. And in practice the worlds of the royal court and the town hall became something more than private lordly households and limited patrician assemblies. Both worlds articulated the public functions of their members. Both exploited high, formal political theory and the increased institutional and financial resources of the late medieval political community to extend and increase their power and further support their claims to legitimacy.

One of the best examples of the potential of political discourse in the late-thirteenth- and fourteenth-century Europe is Marsiglio of Padua's treatise *The Defender of the Peace*. Marsiglio (1275–1342) set out to solve the problem of the loss of civil peace in the Italian cities of the late thirteenth and fourteenth centuries, a problem that inspired some of the most dramatic and influential political discourse in European history and gave Italian writers a predominance in political theory until the end of the sixteenth century. In his greatest work, *The Defender of the Peace* (completed in 1324), Marsiglio drew upon the political thought and culture of the northern Italian cities, which had had to justify their independence not only from ecclesiastical authority (as had Philip the Fair of France), but from imperial authority as well. The Italian city-republics, consequently, made greater and wider use of Aristotelian political theory than did most transalpine thinkers, and they discovered and wrote much earlier than others about an organic concept of the political community. *The Defender of the Peace* is therefore the first European political treatise to offer a comparative vocabulary of political concepts and constitutional principles applicable to all political communities in general, not merely to particular monarchies, the Holy Roman Empire, or individual city-republics.

For Marsiglio, political order is a natural and beneficial attribute of human society. Its end is the formation of a new kind of political community, one whose members participate freely and productively in a society ordered on the basis of civic peace. Marsiglio's analysis of such a society is certainly not "liberal" in the modern sense of the term, but it may truly be called philosophically liberal. He drew upon many diverse strands of earlier political thought and the unique experience of Italian city-republics to describe a universal set of political principles based upon the overriding rights of an essentially lay community.

THE *RECONQUISTA* RESUMES

Although the three great Iberian kingdoms of Portugal, Castile, and Aragon developed differently, they all took part in the *reconquista*.

Twelfth-century Iberian Christian rulers were able to continue expanding southward, although at a slower rate. Sometimes they had remarkable success. Alfonso I of Aragon and Navarre (1104–34) had to face both civil wars and the Almoravids, but he managed to capture several important towns in a series of able campaigns. In 1118, with help from southern France, he captured Saragossa. In 1119 Tarragona fell to him, and in 1120 Calatayud. This continued expansion and consolidation of territories already conquered created in Iberia a tough, highly mobile frontier society that developed differently from societies in England and France.

In 1229 James the First of Aragon captured Majorca and the other Balearic Islands. In 1236 Ferdinand III of Castile captured Córdoba. In 1238 James captured Valencia, and in 1247 Ferdinand captured Seville. By 1247 only the Nasrid kingdom of Granada was left under direct Muslim rule, protected by its contacts with the strong Moroccan kingdom and the many enclaves of Muslim power and population in reconquered Christian Spain. By the middle of the thirteenth century the *reconquista* was nearly complete. The remaining Christian triumphs extended over two centuries—the capture of Algeciras in 1344 and the capture of Granada itself in 1492.

The *reconquista* was attended everywhere by two problems—a shortage of manpower for repopulation and the need of the kings for money to finance their long and often costly campaigns. Apart from these common problems Castile and Aragon produced very different political cultures, and it is worth taking a look at how they developed.

The development of Christian kingdoms on the Iberian peninsula may be seen as a result of the ways in which land was conquered and became available for settlement and governance and the particular characteristics of Iberian societies. Almoravid power lasted in Spain until the 1140s, when another Muslim sect, the Almohades, invaded the peninsula. They remained the dominant force in Islamic Spain until the Christian victory at Las Navas de Tolosa in 1212. With this battle Muslim power in Spain was broken, except in the south, and Iberian society began to develop its distinctive forms. In Castile the powers of the warrior aristocracy and the privileged towns and associations of sheepherders grew great at the expense of both large-scale agriculture and commercial trade. The kings of Castile, lacking a permanent administrative class of servants, were subject to a rebellious aristocracy and an ambitious church. They did control the Cortes, the representative assembly that had met since 1188, and occasionally succeeded in demonstrating potentially extensive royal power. Alfonso X El Sabio (1252–84), for example, issued elaborate and ambitious codes of law, patronized a cultural revival, and offered himself as a candidate for the imperial title. But his reign ended in succession quarrels, and once again the privileged aristocracy and the economically underdeveloped countryside and towns failed to provide a workable basis for political centralization.

In spite of Aragon's expansion into the Mediterranean, to Sicily, and even to Greece and the Levant in the fourteenth century, its nobility and townspeople regularly opposed the king, limited royal authority severely, and defended their local immunities and customs. Two institutions in particular limited the authority of the king. The office of *justicia,* created in 1265, was a legal mediator between the nobility and the king of Aragon.

The Cortes of Aragon, unlike that of Castile, also limited royal authority. Such restraints on the ruler constituted an important aspect of medieval political culture.

Political instability, succession crises, and economic disorder plagued the Iberian kingdoms in the fourteenth and fifteenth centuries. However, the small frontier principalities in the northern part of the peninsula that had set out to "reconquer" Iberia from the Muslims in the eighth century had managed to create large, generally prosperous kingdoms. Under the banner of *reconquista* these kingdoms slowly became diverse political communities possessing the most complex ethnic and historical legacy in Europe.

PRINCES AND CITIES

The decline of imperial authority, the growth of princely independence, the leagues of towns, and the eastward expansion of German power mark the late thirteenth and fourteenth centuries. The excommunication of Frederick II and the death of Conrad IV in 1254 marked the triumph of the papacy over Hohenstaufen ambitions in South Italy and Sicily. Conrad's death also began a nineteen-year period in which there was no person with a clear title to the emperor's throne, though such non-German figures as Alfonso X of Castile and Richard of Cornwall, brother of Henry III of England, were active candidates. During these years both great and small princes and cities took full advantage of the autonomy that had been granted them by Frederick II, administering justice and issuing coinage wholly independently of any outside power. The imperial succession, which had been broken in Italy, was at the disposal of the electors. These were the leaders of the lay and ecclesiastical princes who had benefited from Frederick II's great political concessions of 1220 and 1232, the *Constitutio in favorem principum*. In time three clerical electors—the archbishops of Mainz, Trier, and Cologne—and four lay electors became the college of electors of the emperors. In 1273 this body elected Rudolf of Habsburg emperor. The scarcity of imperial resources forced Rudolf to concentrate upon building a family territory to support his monarchy. By marrying his sons to heiresses in Austria and Styria he built a basis of family wealth and land in southern and southeastern Germany, and the Habsburg emperors of the fourteenth and fifteenth centuries made these territories the center of their rule.

Even Rudolf's modest territorial gains displeased the electors, and at his death they elected an even weaker noble, Adolf of Nassau, who was deposed and killed in 1298. The election of Henry VII (1308–13) of the house of Luxembourg pleased Dante and other imperial idealists, but Henry's political ambitions in Italy undermined his support and drew the opposition of the northern Italian cities. Henry's successor, Ludwig of Bavaria (1313–47), also pretended to imperial grandeur, and he too encountered resistance from both electors and the papacy.

In 1346 the electors nominated Henry VII's grandson, Charles IV of Luxembourg, as emperor. Ten years later Charles issued the Golden Bull, which validated the power and status of the seven electors, and confirmed that election by them alone made an emperor. The electors' territories were declared inalienable, and litigants could not appeal a decision made in an elector's court to the higher judicial authority of the emperor's court. With the concentration of Charles IV's interests in Bohemia and the establishment of his capital at Prague, the history of Germany becomes the history of its principalities.

The interests and resources of the emperors remained in the southeast, under the next few Luxembourg emperors and their Habsburg successors. The office of emperor had virtually disappeared as a political force in Italy and Germany; the age of the principalities had arrived.

The long history of northern Germany as a base for territorial expansion to the east and for missionary efforts to convert pagan Scandinavians, Balts, and Slavs is the main political and cultural theme of northern European history from the tenth to the fifteenth century. With the foundation of the archbishopric of Lund in 1108, Scandinavian Christians developed an independent ecclesiastical center, free of German episcopal control. The German bishoprics of Magdeburg, Bamberg, and Hamburg-Bremen all launched missionary efforts in pagan Slavic lands, sometimes creating friction with the Christian Slavic kingdoms of Poland and Bohemia. In 1147 Saint Bernard of Clairvaux obtained papal permission for German Crusaders to battle the pagan Wends instead of going to Jerusalem.

Warriors followed missionaries, as did merchants and settlers. The expanding population of western Europe permitted not only the internal colonization of older territories but expansion into new ones. The Cistercian monks were particularly zealous in settling remote lands. The founding of Lubeck in 1158–59, the development of a community of merchants in Gotland during the twelfth century, the success of Albert, bishop of Livonia (1199–1229), in founding bishoprics and monastic orders in the newly conquered lands and establishing military orders to support them, and the territorial ambitions of Henry the Lion, duke of Saxony and Bavaria, and the margraves of Brandenburg furthered the expansion.

By the early twelfth century, trade was flourishing in the North Sea, the Baltic Sea, and the Rhine valley. This trade linked England, the Low Countries, Denmark, Sweden, the towns along the Baltic coast, and Novgorod in northern Russia. The economic developments attending this trade, the growth of towns along the Baltic shore, and the large markets of Poland and Russia underwrote the great financial cost of the new German expansion and colonization.

In 1226 the Teutonic Knights, one of the many military orders in the Holy Land, moved to northeastern Germany, where, with the support of Emperor Frederick II and under the leadership of Grand Master Hermann von Salza, they conquered and occupied Prussia. In 1236 the Knights incorporated the Livonian orders, and from the mid thirteenth century on they governed Prussia and pushed frequently into Poland and Russia. In 1309 the city of Marienburg became their headquarters and the seat of the grand master.

The military aspect of German eastward expansion was not dominant everywhere, nor did conquest allow the mass immigration of German settlers. Migration and settlement were more often peaceful than forceful, and the competition for settlers was brisk among lords of all sorts. By the thirteenth century a specialized group of men known as *locatores* were organizing movements of settlers in western Europe and being rewarded with privileges in the new settlements. By the end of that century the balance of wealth and political power in Germany had shifted from its Rhineland origins far to the east. This movement was signaled by the rise in power of the king of Bohemia, the growth of Prussia, the influence of Cistercian ideas on eastern Germany, and the rapidly growing wealth of the Baltic and Rhenish cities and the city-foundations of Danzig, Riga, and Breslau. The rise of the Bohemian and Polish kingdoms and the eastward expansion of Germans during the twelfth and thirteenth centuries was thus a complex process, one that

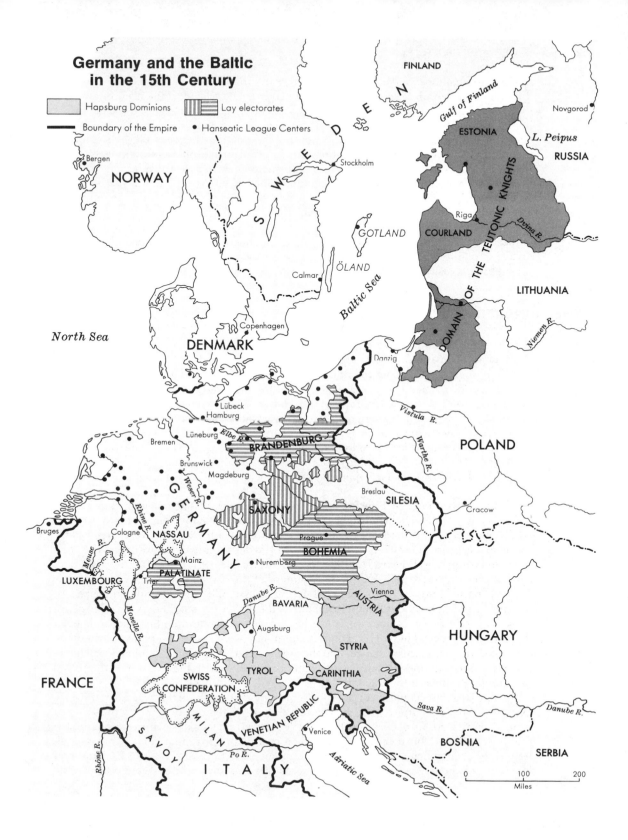

Germany and the Baltic in the 15th Century

Hapsburg Dominions
Lay electorates
Boundary of the Empire
● Hanseatic League Centers

FINLAND

Gulf of Finland

Novgorod

ESTONIA

L. Peipus

RUSSIA

Bergen

NORWAY

S W E D E N

Stockholm

GOTLAND

ÖLAND

Calmar

Baltic Sea

Riga

COURLAND

Dvina R.

DOMAIN OF THE TEUTONIC KNIGHTS

LITHUANIA

Niemen R.

North Sea

Copenhagen

DENMARK

Danzig

Vistula R.

POLAND

Lübeck
Hamburg

Bremen

Lüneburg

Elbe R.

BRANDENBURG

Weser R.

Brunswick

Magdeburg

Warthe R.

Rhine R.

Breslau

SILESIA

Cracow

SAXONY

Cologne

NASSAU

Bruges

Meuse R.

G E R M A N Y

Prague

BOHEMIA

Mainz

● Nuremberg

LUXEMBOURG

Trier

PALATINATE

Moselle R.

Danube R.

BAVARIA

Augsburg

Vienna

AUSTRIA

HUNGARY

STYRIA

FRANCE

SWISS CONFEDERATION

TYROL

CARINTHIA

Sava R.

Danube R.

Rhône R.

SAVOY

MILAN

VENETIAN REPUBLIC

Venice

Po R.

I T A L Y

Adriatic Sea

BOSNIA

SERBIA

0   100   200
Miles

has far more political and economic characteristics than ethnic or racial ones. Dynastic difficulties and a limited economy, more than German hostility or influence, contributed to the weakening of the Polish Premyslid dynasty in the thirteenth century and the growing local Bohemian resistance to it in the fourteenth.

By the middle of the fourteenth century the relations between Germany and its neighbors had been transformed, as had the internal structure of Germany itself. The new world of reduced imperial power, great principalities, leagues of cities, and a newly prominent eastern Germany contained both economic vitality and political chaos. The settlement of new lands greatly increased productivity and colonization. Planned towns and villages linked the new territories in an efficient trading network. New principalities and new laws offered increased freedom to the settlers in the east. The impotence of the emperors and the self-interest of the electors made the fourteenth and fifteenth centuries an age of political experimentation in hundreds of independent principalities and cities throughout a vastly expanded Germany.

THE HUNDRED YEARS' WAR

Rivalry among Italian city-republics, the conflict between the emperor Ludwig of Bavaria and Pope John XXII, and the political growth and development of most territorial monarchies in the fourteenth and fifteenth centuries are all manifestations of the political problems that concerned Marsiglio of Padua and other political theorists. But there is no better or broader example of the relation between old and new political theory and old and new political experience than the long war between the rulers of England and France that lasted from 1337 to 1453 and acquired the dramatic but erroneous name of the Hundred Years' War. Like most medieval conflicts, it began as a private war between rival kings. It ended by consuming resources and people on a national scale, transforming the political culture of its participants, and influencing the affairs of other powers drawn into it.

The heavy hand of Edward I of England had suppressed rebellions against his father, Henry III, and held down the turbulent English aristocracy during his own reign. Resurgence of the aristocracy in the wake of Edward's death and the incompetence of his successor, Edward II (1307–27), led to Edward II's deposition and murder and the placing of his young son, Edward III (1327–77), on the throne in his place. In France the succession crises of 1314–28 led to the replacement of the Capetian dynasty by the Valois dynasty in the person of Philip VI (1328–50). The instability in England and the lack of unanimity in France about Philip's legal title to the throne prompted Edward III to claim the crown of France as his own, since his mother and grandmother had both been daughters of French kings. His claims to legitimacy were made in a period of financial crisis and aristocratic ascendance, and they influenced governmental policy in such territories as Gascony and Brittany, which, although they were in France, were either ruled or strongly influenced by England.

The English occupation of Gascony represented virtually all that was left of the once extensive Angevin empire. Technically the king of England was vassal to the King of France for his lordship of Gascony, but the roles of lord and vassal became very strained in the thirteenth and fourteenth centuries when both happened to be kings. Theorists on both sides argued that "the king shall be no man's vassal." The kings of England had long administered Gascony in much the same way that they administered other crown

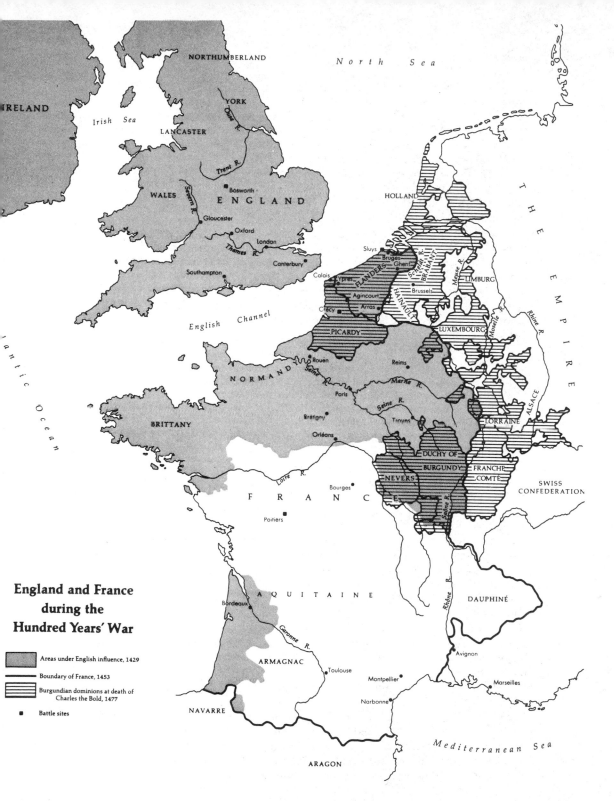

NORTHUMBERLAND

North   Sea

IRELAND

Irish   Sea

YORK

Ouse R.

LANCASTER

Trent R.

Bosworth

Severn R.

WALES

E N G L A N D

Gloucester

Oxford

Thames R.

London

Canterbury

Southampton

HOLLAND

Sluys

Bruges

Ghent

Scheldt R.

BRABANT

Meuse R.

LIMBURG

Calais

Ypres

FLANDERS

Brussels

Agincourt

HAINAULT

LUXEMBOURG

Crécy

Arras

Moselle R.

Rhine R.

PICARDY

THE   EMPIRE

English   Channel

Rouen

Reims

Seine R.

Marne R.

NORMANDY

Paris

Seine R.

LORRAINE

ALSACE

Brétigny

Troyes

BRITTANY

Orléans

DUCHY OF BURGUNDY

FRANCHE COMTÉ

Loire R.

NEVERS

Bourges

F R A N C E

SWISS CONFEDERATION

Poitiers

Saône R.

Atlantic   Ocean

**England and France
during the
Hundred Years' War**

AQUITAINE

Bordeaux

Garonne R.

Rhône R.

DAUPHINÉ

Areas under English influence, 1429

Boundary of France, 1453

Burgundian dominions at death of Charles the Bold, 1477

ARMAGNAC

Avignon

Battle sites

Toulouse

Montpellier

Marseilles

Narbonne

NAVARRE

ARAGON

Mediterranean   Sea

possessions to which they had absolute authority. Moreover, Gascon wine was part of a complex English economy that included free access to Flemish wool centers, Breton salt processing, and Portuguese trade. The conflict between lord and vassal over Gascony is simply one way of looking at a set of problems that possessed equally critical economic and diplomatic dimensions. The lord-vassal relationship, if pressed too strictly, was no longer capable of accommodating these problems successfully.

The French pressure on Gascony and the English claim to the French throne heightened tensions between the two monarchs, which were exacerbated by the French alliance with Scotland. In 1340 the English destroyed a French fleet at Sluys, and from then until the Treaty of Brétigny in 1360 the English had the upper hand in the war. England launched armed expeditions into France, winning pitched battles at Crécy and Poitiers in 1346 and 1356, capturing the Channel Islands in 1345 and the great port of Calais in 1347. The war proved difficult to control and very expensive. Moreover, both kingdoms were devastated by the Black Death of 1348. The early English triumphs helped strengthen the prestige and the power of Edward III, but the French losses, culminating in the capture of King Jean II in 1356, precipitated intense factionalism among the nobility and in 1356–58 a social revolution in Paris itself, led by Robert LeCoq, bishop of Laon, and Etienne Marcel, provost of the merchants of Paris.

The reign of Charles V (1364–80) witnessed significant improvements for France. Between the capture of his father Jean II and Jean's death in 1364, Charles was the regent of France. In that capacity he first subdued the rebels of 1358 and then successfully negotiated his father's ransom and release. By 1369 Charles's administrative and financial reforms had allowed him to resume the war, in which he profited from the senility of Edward III, the deaths of Edward's son the Black Prince in 1376 and of Edward III himself in 1377, and the minority of Richard II (1377–99) to gain a truce. (Charles's fiscal and military reforms were only part of his success. His artistic and literary patronage helped inaugurate the role of the French crown as a leader in intellectual and artistic as well as political life.) However, Charles's son Charles VI (1380–1422) was a minor at his accession, and his long reign was also troubled by his periodic insanity after 1392. While the great noble families were contending for power over Charles VI, the ducal house of Burgundy allied with England. Upon the English resumption of the war in 1415, then, France was plunged into far greater misery than it had experienced from 1340 to 1360.

England had made little use of its early victories in the war, and forces of discontent built during the last years of the disabled Edward III. The loss of the popular Black Prince and the troubled minority of Richard II permitted great nobles, particularly Edward III's younger brother John of Gaunt, duke of Lancaster, to assume ascendancy over the crown and wage the economic policies that helped precipitate the Peasants' Revolt of 1381. Richard II's peace policy and his intelligent but autocratic attempts to restore royal control over the government and nobles led to his deposition and murder in 1399, the usurpation of the throne by Henry IV (1399–1413), son of John of Gaunt, and the beginning of the royal house of Lancaster. Henry IV and his son Henry V (1413–22), facing rebellions in the north and discontent at home, reopened the war with France in 1415, and the English forces sustained a major victory at Agincourt in 1415. At the Treaty of Troyes in 1420, Henry V's title to the throne of France was guaranteed. When Charles VI of France died in 1422, he left a shattered kingdom with an English king on its throne, an empty treasury, bitter resentment against the crown and the higher nobility, and a legally disinherited son, the Dauphin Charles, ruling a small part of southern France from an empty, borrowed palace in the old city of Bourges.

Between 1415 and 1453 the tone of the war changed. The length of the conflict, its social and economic consequences, the political instability that ensued, and the character of the fighting made it considerably more savage than earlier wars, and France, the invaded land, bore the brunt of these effects first. The complete and efficient occupation of a conquered nation is difficult in the twentieth century, and it was impossible in the fifteenth. Although England began the fifteenth century by ruling most of northern France, it had neither the population nor the ability to "occupy" the kingdom, nor could it support indefinitely an expensive expeditionary force in an economically depleted country. Intimidation of the population had become a matter of English policy, and the economic and social consequences of this intimidation influenced the character of English rule. Thus, as the character of the war changed and the costs of war mounted, opportunities for dissension increased considerably, whether over traditional problems such as privilege and status or over novelties such as the burden of taxes and the less tangible circumstances of shifting fortunes. France's internal stresses between 1340 and 1430 prefigured the internal conflicts of 1380 to 1480 in England. The shifting aims of war, changing political circumstances, and the mutual reluctance of France and England to surrender, respectively, sovereignty and the claim to the French throne, revealed that there was no clear way of ending the conflict that might satisfy all interested parties.

PATTERNS OF RECOVERY

In spite of England's initial triumphs, the toll of prolonged war and the poverty of English institutional response to its social and economic crises threatened its hold on France. Not the least important element of French resistance was the disinherited prince himself. Charles VII (1422–61), weakened by the Treaty of Troyes and suffering from the added imputation of illegitimacy, was an unlikely reformer. Sickly, personally unattractive, completely unwarlike, and dominated by ruthless favorites, he helplessly witnessed the English armies proceed south from 1422 to 1428 through Maine and Anjou toward his temporary residence in Bourges. But in 1428 French military resistance stiffened. Among the complex causes for this new resistance was the appearance of a young woman named Joan of Arc from a small town in Champagne. Arriving at Charles's court at Chinon in 1429, Joan claimed that Saints Michael, Catherine, and Margaret had "told me of the pitiful state of France and told me that I must go to succor the King of France." In April, Joan and the leaders of the French army relieved the English siege of Orléans, and in July Charles was able to proceed to Reims for his coronation. Joan's capture by the Burgundians and burning at the stake by the English only reinforced the anti-English course that the war had taken.

In 1434 Charles VII's legitimacy was pronounced by the Council of Basel, and in 1435 at the Council of Arras he was formally reconciled with Philip the Good, successor to John the Fearless as duke of Burgundy. By 1453 Charles had won back most of northern France, Normandy, and Gascony and had begun to restore many of the reforms instituted by his grandfather, Charles V. In 1456 he initiated the overturning of the verdict of heresy upon Joan of Arc. The last years of Charles's reign were spent restoring royal fiscal and political dominion over a drastically weakened kingdom against the discredited nobility and the rebellious burghers. When he died in 1461, Charles VII had laid the foundations for the growth of monarchical power and national order.

Joan of Arc was the most dramatic but not the most efficient servant of Charles VII.

Over the long process of recovery and reform Charles was also served by the great financier Jacques Coeur. A wealthy merchant of Bourges, Coeur traveled and traded in the Mediterranean and returned to France to be made master of the royal mint at Paris in 1436. In 1437 Charles made Coeur his treasurer, and in this post Coeur became the king's chief commercial and financial entrepreneur. Coeur helped restore the financial stability of the French crown, and his own private trading network helped open the Mediterranean to French trade, in which Coeur also had a hand, trading cloth, salt, silver, copper, leathers, and furs. Like many successful traders, he operated money exchanges as well. Coeur grew so wealthy that he was personally able to lend Charles 200,000 gold crowns in 1449, enabling the king to begin the reconquest of Normandy. The services of Joan of Arc and Jacques Coeur gave Charles VII the epithet by which he is known to history, Charles *le Bien Servi*—Charles the Well-Served.

Charles's son Louis XI (1461–83) built upon his father's successes in striking ways. A rebel against Charles as a youth, Louis had lived a complex and anxious life for many years. Of this period Louis's biographer Philip de Commines once remarked: "What he did in his youth, when he was a fugitive from his father under the Duke of Burgundy, was very valuable to him, for he was compelled to please those of whom he had need, and this benefit taught him the meaning of adversity." Louis's capacity for finding out information, dissembling his real intentions, and controlling the French nobles gave him the nickname of "the Spider King," a reputation that Louis himself did little to discourage.

But Louis also worked. Commines elsewhere remarked: "I think that if all the good days he enjoyed during his life, days in which he had more pleasure and happiness than hard work and trouble, were carefully numbered, they would be found to be few; I believe one would find twenty days of travail and worry for every one of ease and pleasure." Louis fully developed the use of royal authority to alleviate the economic problems of his kingdom. He encouraged industries and domestic trade, continued his father's practice of abolishing internal tolls and tariffs, and sponsored fairs that brought the money of others into France and prevented a financial drain on the kingdom. On the other hand, Louis continually collected old taxes and levied new ones. He waged economic warfare abroad and practiced economic protectionism at home.

Louis XI was one of the first monarchs in European history to possess an accurate sense of the potential economic power of the royal government in alliance with a national economy. At his death in 1483 France had greatly improved its economic position, both internally and in relation to other kingdoms, the great nobles had generally been humbled, and the income of the crown had nearly quadrupled. Charles VII had left Louis an income of 1,800,000 pounds per year. Louis left his successor Charles VIII an income of 4,700,000 pounds per year, a full treasury, a strong diplomatic position, a kingdom at peace, and a restored throne.

England recovered less quickly than France, and in a different way. The overstrained English governmental institutions were not improved by Lancastrian rule, and the collapse of the English occupation of France, coupled with the early death of Henry V in 1422 and the long minority of Henry VI (1422–61), precipitated political and military struggles that lasted nearly to the end of the fifteenth century. The costs of the wars had been enormous compared with the returns from English victories, and the resulting strain imposed on English finances had led to violent clashes within the high aristocracy. The reign of Henry VI witnessed fiscal and political collapse, and the reversals of English fortune in France plunged England into the dynastic conflicts commonly called the Wars of the Roses (1454–85). The economic, military, and social consequences of these over-romanticized wars were quite small. Even more important than the changes of dynasty that placed Edward IV on the throne in 1461 and then Henry VII in 1485 was the ability of the English monarchs after 1461 to capitalize upon the end of expensive foreign wars and to reorganize both royal finances and aristocratic factionalism in favor of a stable but not particularly strong royal rule.

FURTHER READING

The work of Marsiglio of Padua may be read in a translation by Alan Gewirth, *Defensor Pacis* (reprint ed. Toronto: University of Toronto Press, 1980).

On Spain, besides the works in the general bibliography, see Angus MacKay, *Spain in the Middle Ages: From Frontier to Empire* (London: Macmillan, 1977), and R. I. Burns, *The Crusader Kingdom of Valencia,* 2 vols. (Cambridge, Mass.: Harvard University Press, 1967).

On Germany, see the work of Joachim Leuschner and Philippe Dollinger cited in the general bibliography; also Gerald Strauss, *Manifestations of Discontent in Germany on the Eve of the Reformation* (Bloomington: Indiana University Press, 1971).

For the Hundred Years' War, see the classic work of Edouard Perroy, *The Hundred Years War* (New York: Oxford University Press, 1951) and Kenneth Fowler, ed., *The Hundred Years War* (New York: St. Martin's Press, 1971). John Barnie, *War in Medieval English Society* (Ithaca, N.Y.: Cornell, 1974) describes the social impact of the war. On Joan of Arc, see Regine Pernoud, *Joan of Arc* (New York: Stein and Day, 1966). For France's recovery, see P.S. Lewis, ed., *The Recovery of France in the Fifteenth Century* (New York: Harper & Row, 1972). On England, see J. R. Lander, *The Wars of the Roses* (New York: Capricorn, 1967), and H. S. Bennett, *The Pastons and Their England* (Cambridge: Cambridge University Press, 1970).

20

Frontiers and Horizons

THE WORLD ON THE LAST DAY

In the late fourteenth and fifteenth centuries a new Turkish invasion swept into Asia Minor and the Balkans, and in 1453 Constantinople, the last, shrunken symbol of the idea of a universal Christian empire, fell to the Turkish armies of Sultan Mehmet II. Byzantine resistance to western demands for ecclesiastical reunion and the vastly diminished resources of the restored empire of Michael VIII Palaeologos after 1261 had reduced Byzantine power considerably. A fifteenth-century English chronicler who had observed Emperor Manuel II's visit to the west for aid sadly commented, "How grievous it was that this great Christian prince should be driven by the Saracens from the furthest East to these furthest Western islands to seek aid against them. . . . Oh God, what dost thou now, ancient glory of Rome?" In the fourteenth century the vigorous kings of Serbia, particularly Stephen Dusan (1331–55), threatened the empire's existence, and the growth of Catalan and Aragonese power in the eastern Mediterranean also reduced Byzantine strength. In the early years of the fourteenth century the Catalan Grand Company brought the first Ottoman Turks to Europe as mercenaries, and in the next several decades the expansion of the emirate in Anatolia and the growing reputation of the Ottoman sultans as supporters of Sunnite orthodoxy increased Ottoman power and prestige in the Islamic world.

In 1354 the Turks conquered Adrianople, the site of the emperor Valen's defeat at

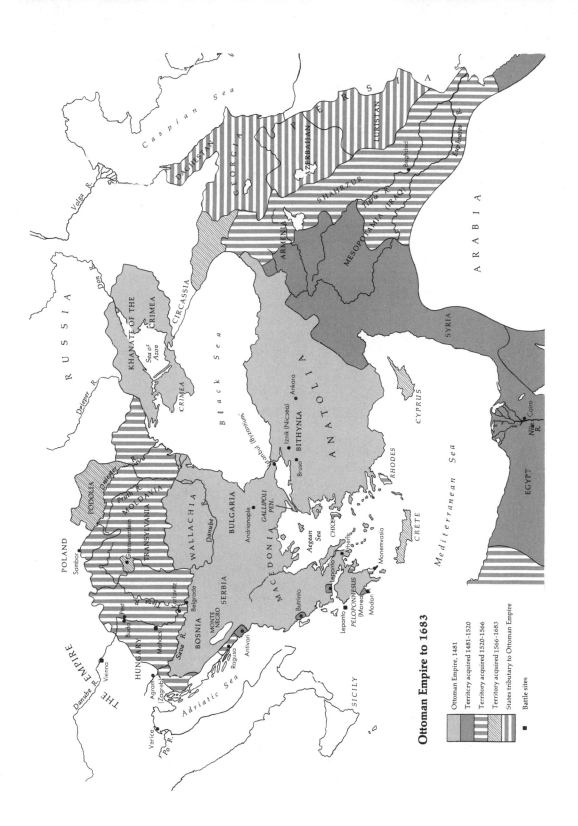

Ottoman Empire to 1683

Ottoman Empire, 1481

Territrcry acquired 1481–1520

Territory acquired 1520–1566

Territory acquired 1566–1683

States tributary to Ottoman Empire

■ Battle sites

Map labels (clockwise/geographic):

Caspian Sea

Volga R.

Don R.

Dnieper R.

RUSSIA

POLAND

Sambor

THE EMPIRE

Vienna

Danube R.

HUNGARY

Agram (Zagreb)

Venice

Po R.

Adriatic Sea

SICILY

Buda

Pest

Mohacs

Grosswardein

Carlowitz

Sava R.

Tisza R.

Drau R.

Prut R.

PODOLIA

MOLDAVIA

TRANSYLVANIA

WALLACHIA

Danube R.

BULGARIA

SERBIA

Belgrade

Nissa

BOSNIA

MONTE NEGRO

Ragusa

Antivari

MACEDONIA

Andrianople

GALLIPOLI PEN.

CHIOS

Aegean Sea

Athens

Lepanto

Bufrinto

PELOPONNESUS (Morea)

Modon

Monemvasia

Lepanto

KHANATE OF THE CRIMEA

Sea of Azov

CRIMEA

CIRCASSIA

Black Sea

Istanbul (Byzantium)

Bruça

Iznik (Nicaea)

BITHYNIA

Ankara

ANATOLIA

CYPRUS

RHODES

CRETE

Mediterranean Sea

DAGHESTAN

GEORGIA

AZERBAIJAN

LURISTAN

ARMENIA

SHAHRZUR

MESOPOTAMIA (IRAQ)

Baghdad

Tigris R.

Euphrates R.

PERSIA

SYRIA

ARABIA

EGYPT

Cairo

Nile R.

the hands of the Visigoths nearly one thousand years before. The powerful and well-organized Ottoman armies assaulted Constantinople in 1396 and 1422. In 1453, when Mehmet II assaulted the city by sea and land with vast armies and massive artillery pieces, the city was defended by only five thousand troops and two thousand foreigners. The assault breached the great Theodosian walls on May 29, and Constantine XI, the last emperor, died fighting in the streets of the sacred city. The principalities in the Peloponnesus and Trebizond capitulated to the Turks shortly after the fall of Constantinople, and the great city became the capital of a new Turkish empire. Control of the Black Sea and new influence in South Russia and Poland, as well as in the Balkans and most of Hungary, passed into the hands of the sultan. The eastern borders of Europe had suddenly become very clear indeed.

In a famous letter, Pope Pius II (1458–64) complained of Europe's failure to restore Constantinople and blamed the particularism of the Latins for their reluctance to challenge the Turkish lords of southeastern Europe: "Who will understand the different languages? Who will rule the diverse customs? Who will reconcile the English with the French, or join the Genoese to the Aragonese, or conciliate the Germans to the Hungarians and Bohemians?" The resources of Christendom as a collective society seemed to have disappeared with Constantinople. Latin Europe indeed fought battles against the Turks, but these were defensive battles. The last emperor was dead, and the new patriarch of Constantinople, George Scholarios Gennadios, was an appointee of the sultan.

In spite of papal urging and diplomatic activity it became clear during the next century that Constantinople would not be won back and that the Turks would advance even further into southeastern Europe. Only very small enclaves preserved something of the vanished Byzantine past, such as the fortress city of Mistra on the Greek peninsula, which was not taken by the Turks until 1824. But the power of Byzantine civilization survived in other places: in Venice, whose very fabric was built from Byzantine influences; in Russia, which became the heir of Byzantine religious orthodoxy and culture; in the new concern for the Greek language and Greek scholarship in western Europe; in the somber and mysterious pictures painted in faraway Spain in the sixteenth century by the Greek painter Domenikos Theotokopoulos—El Greco. The Byzantine writers themselves preserved a different memory—a vision of the sacredness of the city that not even the Turkish conquest could pollute. Several later chroniclers tell of the last free religious service held at the Church of Hagia Sophia, on the day the Turks took the city. The crowd huddled together and the service began. But the Turkish soldiers burst through the doors of the great church and began to slaughter the congregation mercilessly. The priests, however, continued the service, and at the last minute took up the sacred instruments of the Mass and walked toward the wall of the sanctuary. The wall, the chroniclers say, then opened to let the priests in. It is said that they will emerge to finish their service when Constantinople is once again a Christian city.

THE THIRD ROME

The Mongol occupation of Russia had virtually cut that land off from both Byzantium and the west. In 1300 the metropolitan of Kiev established himself in Vladimir, to the north of Kiev, and then in 1328 in the town of Moscow. The Russian revival of the fourteenth century that brought it once again into active contact with Byzantium began with the rise of the principality of Muscovy and signaled a change in the relations between the Russians and the Byzantines.

Muscovy's greater distance from Constantinople, its long period under Mongol domination, and its ecclesiastical rivalry with Lithuania all helped weaken the bonds between Byzantium and the most faithful of its cultural dependents. The alternations between Greek and Russian metropolitans of Kiev after 1250, however, helped maintain relations between the two peoples, and the steady stream of Russian pilgrims to Constantinople continued to testify to the great city's religious attraction in the north. In addition to its rivalry with Lithuania over the question of the metropolitan, however, Muscovy began to criticize Constantinople itself after 1439. The Council of Florence, at which union between the Greek and Latin churches was proclaimed, seemed to the Russians a breach of the faith. The Greek metropolitan of Kiev, Isidore, was arrested after his attempts to introduce the Latin rite upon his return to Muscovy. In 1448 a synod of Russian bishops took the unprecedented step of electing a metropolitan of Kiev without Byzantine initiation. Although this step must be considered in terms of Russian resistance to Byzantine unionization, it may also be considered as a reflection of the vigor of the Russian church.

The rule of Grand Duke Ivan III (1462–1505) traditionally marks the full coming of independence to Muscovy. Under Ivan's energetic and ambitious rule, the breakup of the Mongol khanate and the western interests of Lithuania were both exploited to Muscovy's advantage. By the mid fifteenth century the Golden Horde had splintered into three separate khanates, one at Kazan, one in the Crimea, and a third on the lower Volga. Ivan III became the first grand duke of Muscovy to assume his rulership without Mongol permission, and he soon began to exert Muscovite control over other northern Russian principalities. Between 1456 and 1473 the great city of Novgorod, hitherto dependent upon its economy and its Lithuanian neighbors for support, fell to Ivan's armies. The rise of Muscovy to the domination of all Russia had begun.

The strained ecclesiastical relations between Russia and Byzantium in the fourteenth and fifteenth centuries, the vigor of the principality of Muscovy, and the success of Grand Dukes Vasili (1425–62) and Ivan III in the face of Lithuanian-Polish, Mongol, and other Russian opposition—all led to the development of considerable economic and political power within the Muscovite state, as well as to a fierce sense of pride and divine approval. Thus, in 1460 the metropolitan of Moscow could firmly observe that Constantinople had fallen because of God's disapproval of the union of the churches at the Council of Florence. Certainly the new Muscovite dominance was a heady experience, and the success of the grand dukes of the fourteenth and fifteenth centuries had acquired for them a preeminence even among the *boyars,* which hastened political consolidations. Like the earlier rulers of Serbia, Bulgaria, and the Romanian principalities, the grand dukes of Muscovy began to adopt the outward signs of Byzantine imperial rule. In 1472, partly through the agency of the pope, Ivan III married Zoe Palaeologina, the niece of the last Byzantine emperor. Although the pope may have hoped through this marriage to effect the 1439 provisions in Russia, Ivan and the empress, renamed Sophia, adopted an elaborate Byzantine court ceremonial and the imperial device of the double-headed eagle. Under this rule the grand dukes of Muscovy began to evolve into the tsars of Russia (*tsar* is the Byzantine equivalent of *Caesar*). Muscovite self-confidence went even further in certain areas. In 1492 Moscow was proclaimed the "New Constantinople"; in 1510 the monk Philotheus of Pskov declared it the "Third Rome."

THE FIRST ROME

As the Muscovite principality claimed its place in the sequence of centers of Christendom many western European thinkers also turned to the idea of Rome, but not in search of a successor state to old Rome and Constantinople. From the twelfth century on, western Europeans had begun to acquire a greater appreciation of some of the achievements of ancient Roman culture and civilization. This new appreciation was not exclusively the result of greater familiarity with ancient Latin literature, although reading the classics was certainly one important part of it.

R. W. Southern has suggested some of the conditions of twelfth- and thirteenth-century western European culture that supported a new interest in the Roman past. Among them are a concern with the dignity of human nature and the dignity and intelligibility of the natural order. The new twelfth-century devotional exercises that led to the search for God into the soul and the inner self are one consequence of the new attitudes. The recognition by theologians and pastors of the spiritual life of the laity, particularly that of the lay population of the growing cities, is another. The increasing complexity of legal relationships made the rationality, order, and systematic character of Roman law appealing to judges and political leaders as well. In short, as medieval European society grew more complex, the old and profound differences between the new Christian world and ancient pagan Rome appeared to be less important than other elements that the two societies were perceived to have had in common: a respect for precise language, a search for civic morality, principles of political order, and a new and wholesome respect for the intellectual rather than the purely religious virtues of classical Latin literature and the writings of the early Fathers of the Church.

To be sure, the considerable literary achievements of European writers in the twelfth century had led some writers to take great pride in the achievements of their own time. Chrétien de Troyes, the greatest of the French writers of knightly romances, went so far as to claim for France the sum total of all the virtues of the past:

> Greece once had, for chivalry,
> The greatest honor, and of clergy.
> Then chivalry passed on to Rome,
> And clergy too. But now their home
> Is France.

Next to the papal ideal of the *translatio imperii,* the translation of legitimate empire from Greece to Rome to Germany, and the university ideal of the *translatio studii,* the translation of learning from the east to the west, there emerged the secular idea of the translation of culture, not merely from the lands of the east to those of the west but from the societies of antiquity to those of twelfth- and thirteenth-century western Europe.

Europeans also discovered that antiquity held treasures that had not yet been understood. Among these were the writings of the fourth-century Church Fathers, particularly Saint Jerome and Saint Augustine. Besides the theology of the Fathers, however, fourteenth-century thinkers discovered their Latin prose style, which was modeled upon the clarity and elegance of earlier Latin writers such as Cicero. Just as philosophers were drawn away from Aristotle toward Plato, so theologians and writers were drawn from the thirteenth-century scholastic thinkers to the eloquent Church Fathers. Since the Fathers themselves had been strongly influenced by Plato, the works of that philosopher began to be translated. The fifteenth century saw the acquisition of other

Greek manuscripts by Latins, some of them from Constantinople and from Greek scholars traveling in western Europe. The new interest in the thought of Plato and other Greeks also led to greater study of Greek language in western Europe, first in northern and southern Italy and later across the Alps.

But the linguistic focus of fourteenth- and fifteenth-century thinkers was Latin, and their initial coloring was moral. Perhaps the most characteristic of the new thinkers was the Florentine scholar and man of letters Francesco Petrarca (1304–74), whose importance lies as much in his later influence as in his own considerable achievements. Petrarca was raised in Avignon and was sent to study law at the universities of Montpellier and Bologna. Unlike many of his contemporaries, however, Petrarca felt no love for the law. Indeed, he bitterly criticized the flat technical jargon not only of legal studies but of logic and medicine as well. Petrarca's ambitions were literary rather than legal, and he never finished his legal studies. From early in life he had studied Latin, particularly the prose of Cicero, which he admired immensely and read more carefully than anyone before him. Petrarca's excellent ear for the intricacy and subtlety of Ciceronian Latin was matched by a careful eye and a critical intelligence of considerable merit. As he read he became aware of the errors that had crept into ancient texts because of scribal carelessness or incomprehension over many centuries of recopying. With other scholars in Avignon, Petrarca began to search for more and more manuscripts, developing his study of Latin philology and textual editing into a fine art. These two activities led to Petrarca's own development of a fine Latin prose style, flexible and elegant, which stood in sharp contrast to the dullness and formality of the academic and professional language he had come to despise. Petrarca's interest in searching out manuscripts turned up not only more Latin literature than had previously been known to exist, but brought to light literary works that had been little used since the twelfth century.

The renovation of Latin prose and the beginning of the search for antiquity through the study and collection of ancient manuscripts were two of Petrarca's most important achievements. But his real greatness lay in two other areas. Having rejected the profession of law—and indeed the very idea of a profession in the fourteenth-century sense—Petrarca became a poet and man of letters, perhaps the first such figure in European history. But he did not do so solely out of a love for literature. In Cicero's and Augustine's works Petrarca found a personal and social moral theory that appealed to him far more strongly than the theology and social ideas of his contemporaries, and he insisted that the study of Latin and the practice of letters had primarily a moral end. His own early works investigate his own personality. Petrarca was not reluctant to reveal his shortcomings as well as his virtues. Indeed, this search for the true self, inspired by Cicero and Saint Augustine, was one of Petrarca's great contributions to the history of European thought. Besides seeking the true self Petrarca searched for the ideal society, and he claimed to have found it in the civilized, moral world of Cicero's Rome. Clarity, eloquent language, friendship, and cultivated leisure—these for Petrarca were the elements of the ideal life, and he pursued them in his own life and writings, particularly in his many letters and treatises. In so doing he opened a new vista not only upon scholarship and literature but upon individual and social morality.

This practical use of the Latin classics, coupled with Petrarca's thoroughgoing Christian values, immensely influenced the next several generations of scholars and writers north and south of the Alps. By claiming for Roman morality a degree of virtue that no Christian writer had ever accorded it, Petrarca opened new avenues for later generations to explore, especially in literature and moral thought. This combination of literary study, exact scholarship, and the ideal of the life of dignified leisure has generally been labeled humanism, and Petrarca was acclaimed the first humanist by later scholars. As we have seen, Cicero himself had defined the liberal arts, and chiefly literature, as those arts befitting a free man—that is, a leisured, conscientious Roman citizen with aristocratic status and good taste. Cicero's idea of humane studies strongly appealed to Petrarca's secularized psychology, and although strong claims have been made for a medieval ideal of humanism, tradition still attributes to Petrarca the title of the first humanist.

Petrarca's interest in ancient Rome did not end with imitating its literary language and appreciating its morality. On his visits from Avignon to Rome (where he was awarded the ancient laurel crown for poets in 1341), Petrarca was stunned by the desolation of the city, abandoned by its popes as it had once been abandoned by its ancient emperors. When a young Roman, Cola di Rienzo (1313–54), created a revolutionary government in the city and designated himself its tribune—the ancient civic title of Rome's republican leaders—Petrarca praised Cola eloquently. Even Cola's early death and the failure of the "Roman Republic" did not dissuade Petrarca from his fascination with the ancient greatness and present desolation of the city. Rather, it led him to the study of history. In 1343, two years after his poetic coronation amid the ruins of Rome, Petrarca wrote to his friend Giovanni Colonna:

As we walked over the walls of the shattered city [of Rome], or sat there, the fragments of the ruins were under our very eyes. Our conversation turned toward history, which we appear to have divided up between us in such a way that in modern history you, in ancient history I, seemed the more expert. Ancient were called those events that took place before the name of Christ was celebrated in Rome and adored by the Roman emperors. Modern, however, [were called] the events from that time to the present.

Petrarca's sense of a major division of history, marked by the Christianization of the Roman Empire in the fourth century, was the result of his veneration of ancient Latin literature and morality. But it proved to be very influential in the following three centuries, when Petrarca's own role in "reviving" the culture of antiquity was regarded as the beginning of a rebirth—in French, a *renaissance*—of the world of antiquity. As closely related as his thought was to the devotional and scholarly trends of the fourteenth century, Petrarca's vision of history was later regarded as itself beginning a new age in European civilization, the "Age of the Renaissance."

But the rediscovery of the first Rome was not an achievement of Petrarca alone, nor of Italian scholars exclusively. Richard de Bury, (1281–1385), tutor to King Edward III of England and author of the *Philobiblon,* was also a fine Latin scholar, collector of manuscripts, and connoisseur of Roman civilization. In France the great moralist Nicholas de Clamanges shared the literary and cultural interests of Petrarca, Richard de Bury, and other humanists. By the end of the fourteenth century the new interest in Latin literature and the morality of ancient Roman and Greek civilization that had been created by Petrarca and others had brought the first Rome before the eyes of curious and interested Europeans. By revealing, sometimes painfully, the differences between the civilization of ancient Rome and that of fourteenth- and fifteenth-century western Europe, the humanists sharpened Europeans' sense of the past as they began to provide more and more accurate information about that past. The image of the first Rome gradually became grander, more dignified, and more profound than contemporary culture, and European thinkers began to speak of Petrarca's "modern history" as if it were a great decline from the glories of Rome. For the next three hundred years that period of the European past extending from the fourth to the fourteenth century had to defend itself against the formidable attacks of the humanists as one by one its own achievements were either ignored or dismissed as errors. With the rediscovery of the first Rome there also occurred the invention of the Middle Ages.

ANCIENTS AND MODERNS

Those writers who praised the virtues of ancient Greece and Rome at the expense of the Middle Ages made possible another point of view, one that regarded the fifteenth century and later as superior even to the glories of Greece and Rome. Such a view, which did little to change the attitude of people toward the Middle Ages, grew out of certain late-medieval achievements in culture and technology. By the seventeenth and eighteenth centuries the debate between those who praised Greece and Rome as the greatest cultural achievements of humanity and those who claimed that distinction for the period between the fifteenth and eighteenth centuries had produced a literary and philosophical argument that is generally called the Quarrel Between the Ancients and the Moderns. Although ancients and moderns both used examples from literature, morality, the arts, and the sciences in their arguments, the moderns had an edge that the ancients could not claim—the results of late-medieval and early-modern developments in technology.

As we have seen in earlier chapters, one of the most distinctive features of early medieval society was its free use of new techniques and machines to open the forests and scrublands of northern Europe to extensive agricultural development. The spread of the water mill from the sixth century, the heavy plough after the seventh, the three-field system after the eighth, and the new developments in the breeding, shoeing, and harnessing of horses after the ninth enabled northern Europeans to make great strides toward the settlement of hitherto empty parts of Europe and increased the productivity of settled parts. After the tenth century, developments in agricultural technology began to influence other areas of economic activity, chiefly manufacturing. The water mill produced about three and a half horsepower, which after the tenth century was applied to the brewing of beer, the fulling of cloth, the sawing of wood, and the making of paper. The windmill, which appeared in western Europe around 1200, generated around twenty-five horsepower. Mounted on a large shaft, it could be turned to face the wind. The power of the windmill was also applied in areas besides the grinding of grain. Sixteenth-century writers were well aware that the Romans had not known of the windmill, and they took pride in this achievement of the "moderns."

But the development of new techniques in agriculture and new sources of nonanimal and nonhuman power was not the only medieval contribution to the arguments of the moderns against the ancients. Much more striking was the application of machines from one area of economic activity to others—from the farm to the cloth mill, from the rural monastery to the smithy, from the grain mill to the sawmill. The best historian of medieval European technology, Lynn T. White, Jr., has argued persuasively that one of the most distinctive features of medieval European culture is precisely this machine-mindedness, the assimilating ability—and willingness—of Europeans that made them the most technologically developed people in the world at the end of the Middle Ages: "During the later Middle Ages there was a passion for the mechanization of industry such as no culture had known. . . . The Europe which rose to global dominance about 1500 had an industrial capacity and skill vastly greater than that of any of the cultures of Asia—not to mention Africa or America—which it challenged.''[1] The windmill and the printing press were simply two of the many machines that made Europeans, however great their reverence for Greece and Rome, vastly different from their ancient predecessors.

"Every day new arts are discovered," observed a Florentine preacher in 1306. Friar Giordano da Pisa particularly admired (as scholars have ever since) the invention of eyeglasses, which had taken place around 1280. He went on to note

There are [even] many [arts] which have not yet been discovered. Every day you could find one, and there would still be new ones to find. . . . It was not twenty years since there was discovered the art of making spectacles which help you to see well, which is one of the best and most necessary [arts] in the world. I myself saw the man who discovered and practiced it, and I talked with him.

As White concisely observes, "Here was a mood without historical precedent: . . . the invention of invention as a total project. It was the mood of Europe's technicians from the later thirteenth century onwards.''[2] Although White and other historians of technology and science have differed over which qualities in European culture of the period between the sixth and the fourteenth centuries made Europeans so machine-minded, most agree that the causes are cultural, the product of distinctive human attitudes towards labor, the material world, mathematics, and efficiency. Not only did Europeans borrow, modify, and invent machines, they put them into works of art and imagination. As they discovered Roman ruins and artistic monuments they found that they possessed cultural traits that the Romans lacked, and they took pride in them.

And they spread them. Individual technological developments were spontaneously invented in several different places. Communication was another integral part of European technological development. From the thirteenth to the seventeenth century most of the improvements in land communication and transport consisted of refinements of techniques that had been developed in the twelfth and thirteenth centuries. New techniques in harnessing and shoeing horses, more maneuverable wagons with better suspension, and improvements in road and bridge building brought European technology in this field to a state that remained essentially static until the extensive road-building programs and the development of the steam engine in the eighteenth century. Networks of information, in merchants' companies and in kingdoms and other political units, improved the regularity and speed of some communications. By the early fourteenth century cart roads were being built in the Alpine passes, and in 1480 gunpowder was used in the Tyrol to blast rock for the widening of roads. Slowly the pack animal gave way to the wagon, the track to the road. The increasingly sedentary character of large governments made capital towns and cities centers of new communications networks, from papal Avignon in the fourteenth century to Vienna and Madrid in the sixteenth.

As the means of sending information and goods improved in this period, so did the means of preserving information. Improvements in the making of cheap paper, the invention and development of movable type, investment in printing, and the growth of a literate public propelled the book trade into a prominent place in fifteenth- and sixteenth-

---

[1] Lynn T. White, Jr., *Medieval Religion and Technology: Collected Essays* (Berkeley and Los Angeles: University of California Press, 1978), p. 221.

[2] Ibid.

century life. Not only books, of course, but laws and lawbooks, newsletters, and official and unofficial printed matter of all kinds helped accelerate the dissemination of information. Frequent large-scale public assemblies, from regional gatherings to the great international congresses and councils, drew people together and then returned them to their places of origin, their heads full of what they had seen, read, and heard.

By 1360, after more than a century of development, fully operative mechanical clocks had come into being. Once developed, they were widely incorporated in public buildings, first at the church of St. Eustorgio in Milan in 1309 (just three years after Giordano da Pisa's sermon in praise of eyeglasses) and by 1370 in the palace of King Charles V of France. As in other aspects of social and cultural relations, notably weights, measures, and coinage values on the one hand and practical and speculative mathematics on the other, towns and lay authorities in general transformed the measuring of time.

Besides affecting productivity, measurement, good order, and peace, European technology transformed the face of war. Gunpowder was brought to Europe from China at the end of the thirteenth century, and by the fourteenth it was being used on a very small scale in warfare. The development of heavy metal casting in the manufacture of bells soon provided a means of containing gunpowder and projectile in a single cannon. The use of the cannon—at first as a kind of superior catapult—increased during the 1400s, and by the end of that century the mobility and destructiveness of field cannon was causing great consternation among those who depended upon thick castle walls to protect them from the enemy. The guns burst the walls, and the inhabitants had to find ways to redesign them. By making the walls thinner but building out from them angle bastions that would deflect cannon fire and cover the breaches in the walls by means of enfilading fire, military architects transformed the thick-walled medieval castle into the geometrically calculated fort of early-modern Europe. They did so by mathematical calculations that were just as careful as the calculations necessary in making large guns and projectiles.

From the heavy plow to the cannon, the water mill to the angle bastion, the water clock to the mechanical clock, European technology knew little of the conventional divisions of medieval, renaissance, and early-modern history. As the "moderns" knew well, the technical achievements and the technology-mindedness of Europeans were very different from those of the ancient Greeks and Romans. In this one area at least, the moderns surpassed the Greeks and Romans and held their own in debates about which period of history was preferable. Petrarca had said that he would have chosen to live in the period of Cicero if he had had the choice. By the end of the fifteenth century, in spite of their fondness for the revival of antique culture, many other Europeans knew exactly which advantages their own time held over that of Cicero. Research into the history of technology has shown just how much those advantages owed to the farmers and craftsmen and artists of medieval Europe, not only on land but on the sea as well.

"HERE THERE BEE TYGRES"

In 1298 Rustichello of Pisa, a writer of knightly romances, shared a Genoese prison cell with a Venetian captive named Marco Polo, who told the writer of his eighteen years in China in the service of the Great Khan. Rustichello wrote the stories down in a book that came quickly to be called *Il milione,* "The Million," because of its tales of the fabulous wealth of Asia and possibly also because Marco Polo was alleged to have brought back great wealth. Thirty years earlier, regular Genoese and Venetian fleets had sailed out of the Mediterranean Sea and into the Atlantic to make commercial connections with the trade networks of northern Europe. In 1294 two brothers of Genoa, the Vivaldi, had out-fitted several ships and sailed west to seek new trade routes. The travels to Asia, the establishment of regular maritime contact between the Mediterranean and the Atlantic, and the mystery and interest generated by such adventures as those of the Vivaldi, who disappeared, and Marco Polo, whose story quickly became widely known, suggest a new interest by some Europeans not only in the wonders of the unknown parts of the world but also in the possible material value of the unknown world. The time between the papal missions to the Mongols of John del Piano Carpini in 1245–47 and William of Rubrouck in 1253–55 and the establishment of regular sailing routes to the west was very brief. By the 1270s others had begun to travel to Asia.

The traditional geographical knowledge of Europeans before the thirteenth century was most accurate close to home and progressively more imaginative the further from Europe it strayed. In the thirteenth century, however, Europeans learned much about the rest of the world, and their commercial ambitions, systems of communications, and travel reports accumulated more and more geographical knowledge. This knowledge was not, of course, immediately and universally absorbed, but it represented an enormous increment that began to chip away at the tradition of geographical thought received from eleventh- and twelfth-century Europe. That knowledge was a learned and nonexperimental amalgam of several distinct traditions. The knowledge handed down by Roman literature, from Pliny through Isidore of Seville, constituted one such tradition. A second comprised the speculations on such problems as the size and shape of the earth, its habitable and nonhabitable areas, and their climate—problems that had emerged in centuries of commentary on the description of the creation of the world in the Book of Genesis. Third, the efforts of twelfth-century thinkers to describe natural phenomena in terms of Platonic cosmology led to other speculations concerning the nature of the world and its inhabitants. Fourth, there grew up in the twelfth century a large body of literature, ranging from travel accounts to stories of the legendary journeys of Alexander the Great and others, that made much of each of these traditions available to a wider circle of readers.

The one truly impressive body of geographical knowledge developed between the ninth and the thirteenth centuries, that of the Muslim geographers, was virtually ignored in the west, and the legendary travel stories, including even Marco Polo's book, tended to be ignored by the learned. These individuals, for many of whom geography was a branch of theology, tended to regard geographical knowledge as useful insofar at it was consistent with the data from other branches of learning and insofar as it was morally edifying. Jerusalem was at the center of the world, Europe occupied precisely one quarter of the world, and the Mediterranean Sea neatly divided the sections of the world in such a way as to make the land areas resemble a T within a large circle. The resulting O-T maps constituted the basis of formal geographical knowledge, and the history of their slow transformation during the fourteenth and fifteenth centuries is one reflection of the new impact of naturalistic geography upon the traditional learning of the twelfth and thirteenth centuries.

The stream of legates, missionaries, adventurers, and merchants who followed John del Piano Carpini into Asia after 1247 swelled quickly. As early as 1260 two Venetian brothers, Maffeo and Nicolo Polo, left the Venetian settlements in the Crimea and traveled with merchandise to the Mongol court at Sarai on the Volga. They then made their way to Bokhara and, in the company of one of Kublai Khan's envoys, to Shangtu in China. By 1269 they had returned to the west with messages and gifts from Kublai Khan to the pope. Their son and nephew Marco (b. ca. 1254) departed with them on another trip to China, which they reached in 1275. The Polo brothers had begun as merchants and traders, but the success of their first journey to China, the Khan's welcome, and their return journey with Marco transformed them from traders into gentlemen ambassadors. As a diplomat and administrator, Marco Polo served the Great Kahn for eighteen years.

The Polos returned to Italy in 1295, a year after the Franciscan John of Monte Corvino arrived in Peking, of which he became the first Christian archbishop, in 1307. Marco Polo settled in Venice as a moderately wealthy nobleman, spent several years in a Genoese jail as a war prisoner, was released in 1299, and died in Venice in 1324, his mission as papal emissary to the court of the Great Khan unfulfilled. The book about him, *Il milione,* was widely known, and when Christopher Columbus began to record his plans to reach China two centuries later, he regarded himself as following in Marco's footsteps.

The failure of the Vivaldi expedition was counterbalanced by the success of Genoese and Venetian voyages into the Atlantic, their links with the trade routes of the northern seas, and the increased maritime prosperity of European trade. The success of the Polos and the sense of wonder and entertainment in Marco's book was also followed by practical enterprises. In 1340 Francesco Balduccio Pegolotti wrote a treatise commonly called *La Practica della Mercatura,* in which he described very soberly all the things a merchant would need to know in order to do business among the Mongols. The work included a remarkable description of the overland route to China (Pegolotti found it much more secure than it has ever been since). As Leonardo Olschki has observed in comparing this work and *Il Milione,* "For the Florentine, the whole earth is one vast market. For the Venetian, the world is a spectacle, which he portrays as best he may and recalls in great variety and a multiplicity of manifestations."[3]

As long as it was forced to remain within the upward limits of animal and human power, land transportation remained generally unchanged between the thirteenth and the nineteenth centuries. On the sea, however, technological and economic influences quickly expanded Europeans' capacities for long-distance travel. Early European ships were of two types, neither very satisfactory. The round-bottomed cog with a square sail was roomy but slow, and the long, narrow, oar-powered galley was fast but had too large a crew for effective cargo transportation. In the fourteenth century the great hulk was developed in the Baltic. It had a greater carrying capacity but no more speed. At the beginning of the fifteenth century, however, the caravel appeared. The stern rudder, the increased proportion of beam to length, the use of two masts, one of which carried a triangular lateen-rigged Mediterranean sail, the superior hull construction, the reduced crew, and the enormous cargo capacity of around four hundred tons produced the most efficient ship the west had ever known and the most profitable ship afloat. It was also the fastest. The caravel's speed under full sail was exceeded only slightly by the clipper ships of the nineteenth century. By the end of the fifteenth century not only had sail gone far to replace oar but the upward limits of commercial sailing speed had very nearly been reached.

Marine technology and practical navigation quickly outreached geography and cartography. Celestial navigation and the geographical and cartographical knowledge that characterizes more recent marine technology and theory did not come for a century.

---

[3] Leonardo Olschki, *Marco Polo's Asia* (Berkeley and Los Angeles: University of California Press, 1960), p. 98.

But the compass, the minutely accurate local charts called portolans, and practical trigonometry for course correction—all of which developed by the end of the thirteenth century—gave European mariners impressive tools. Baltic, North Sea, and Atlantic sailing routes had all been developed by the end of the thirteenth century. During the Spanish *reconquista* sugar-cane-producing settlements on the Atlantic islands of the Canaries and Madeira developed in imitation of the Venetian and Genoese colonies in the eastern Mediterranean. In spite of these practical achievements, however, knowledge of geography and anthropology was still restricted to the descriptions of Marco Polo and the fabulous account of Sir John Mandeville's travels in the Near East between 1332 and 1366, which featured semihuman creatures and the catchall warning *hic sunt leones*—"here there bee tygres," as the Elizabethans later translated it. Not until Poggio Bracciolini's *Dialogue on Geography,* written in 1447–48, was there an attempt to link informal, learned geography with the actual experience of travelers and sailors. Indeed, there was no word for "explorer" in any European language.

In the late thirteenth and fourteenth centuries climatic change and economic interests focused Scandinavian maritime activity in the Baltic and North seas. In 1291 the brothers Vivaldi were lost in the first modern attempt to navigate the western coast of Africa, and in 1346 the Catalan Jaume Ferrer probably reached the coast of Senegal before he too disappeared. In 1268 and 1291 Christian forces captured Cadiz and Seville, the greatest ports in southern Spain, and the expansion west and south into the Canaries and Madeira developed Castilian maritime techniques considerably. That technical experience took place in a fortunate location—the eastern end of the most climatically favorable route for sailing west, between 35 and 42 degrees north latitude, an area in which the winds and currents flow west for nine months of the year.

At first, however, the southward thrust of Spanish and Portuguese maritime power turned not to exploration but to recognized trade routes. By 1277 Genoese and Venetian fleets were sailing from the Mediterranean to the Altantic, and the great northern and southern European maritime trade routes were finally connected at England, Normandy, and Flanders. Along the new Altantic routes, as we have seen, the discovery and exploitation of the Canaries and Madeira in the first half of the fourteenth century brought Iberian sugar into the European market.

By the late fourteenth century the Mediterranean–Atlantic routes had raised Castilian and especially Portuguese interests in yet another area, North Africa. Since the tenth century the Maghreb, the western coast of North Africa, had been the northern destination of the gold caravans that originated in Ghana and crossed the western edge of the Sahara to Ceuta, Oran, Algiers, and Tunis. Copper and salt also came up this route. These products, along with North African wheat, enriched the North African cities and made them attractive—for trade, conquest, or both—to other Mediterranean powers, from Norman Sicily in the twelfth century, to the Italian maritime cities in the thirteenth and fourteenth, to the Crusading army of Saint Louis of France in 1270, and finally to the Castilian and Portuguese rulers in the fourteenth and fifteenth centuries. In the fourteenth century the gold of the Sudan became a particularly important prize among Christian and North African Muslim powers, and Christians began to obtain clearer information about its sources. A Majorcan portolan map of 1339 noted, "Below the Sahara, on the banks of a river that is the Niger, there is a king whose riches are counted in gold; it is the king of Mali." One chronicler's account of Jaume Ferrer's voyage to West Africa in 1346 stated that his purpose was "to go to the river of gold." By the mid fourteenth century, Europeans knew that the source of the gold traded in the cities of the Maghreb was in the West African part of the Sudan and that it was extracted from rivers by black men, about whom a number of legends had circulated among Muslim traders. Europeans also knew that there were powerful, advanced black kingdoms in West Africa whose strength rested upon their rulers' control of the gold trade. The great kings of Ghana and Mali controlled access to the gold-mining natives and permitted only their own subjects to trade salt for gold, which they then carried north and traded to the North African caravan merchants.

The greatest of all black Muslim rulers of this period was, as the Majorcan map of 1339 had observed, the king of Mali. By 1375, when Abraham Cresques drew his great Calalan atlas, the brief reference of 1339 had been expanded to a large picture of the black king seated on a throne, holding a globe and (somewhat improbably) the royal scepter of France with a fleur-de-lis at its end. The new legend read, "This black lord is called Musa Melly, lord of the blacks of Guinea. This king is the richest and most noble lord by reason of the abundance of gold that is found in his country." The black king of the 1339 and 1375 Catalan maps was Mansa Musa, who had made a pilgrimage in 1321 to Mecca. There his display of wealth and piety astonished his Muslim coreligionists.

The financial crisis of the late fourteenth century had drastically increased Europeans' need for gold, and the new knowledge of the sources of West African gold raised the possibility of circumventing the Saharan–Maghreb trade routes by sailing directly to the source of the gold. The new maritime importance of Castile and Portugal on the Mediterranean–Atlantic trade routes, the new security of Christian Iberia, and the production of sugar-cane in the eastern Atlantic islands had greatly increased Iberian maritime experience and skill and had also brought the enterprising genius and technological skills of the Italian city-republics to bear on the peninsula. Finally, in Portugal and later in Castile the gap between practical maritime experience and scholarly knowledge appears to have been less than elsewhere.

The central, but still obscure, figure in the first Portuguese voyages to the west coast of Africa was Prince Henry the Navigator (1394–1460), the son of King John I of Portugal. Little different in world view or character from other fifteenth-century princely knights, Henry appears to have been particularly interested in the legends of mysterious lands in Africa, especially the reports that Prester John, the legendary Christian king, was to be found in Africa, perhaps in Ethiopia. Interested in measuring the extent of Muslim power and imbued with the Crusade mentality that had driven the earliest stages of the *reconquista,* Henry also thought that his own dynasty and kingdom might be the first to tap African gold at its source. With this mixture of motives—none of which was particularly "scientific" or "modern"—Henry spent vast sums of his own wealth in assembling at Sagres a group of cartographers, scholars, and sailors of all faiths and many languages. Henry was driven by an important youthful experience. When he was twenty-one a military expedition under his father had captured Ceuta on the North African coast, the first Christian landfall in Muslim Africa. For the rest of his life Henry considered that event the beginning of Portuguese expansion, as much for the injury to Islam as for any particular increases in scientific knowledge that it might promote. By 1431 Portuguese had discovered and settled in the Azores and Henry, armed with royal and papal privileges to carry on the *reconquista* in Africa, had begun his annual dispatches of fleets to the west coast of Africa. Shortly after mid-century Portuguese sailors landed in Guinea and began to exploit the gold reserves and the large numbers of slaves, a right that had once belonged exclusively to the Muslim Sahara caravans. By the time Henry died he had fulfilled many of his ambitions. Gold had begun to flow into Portugal, and just before his death Portugal had issued its first gold coin, appropriately called the *crusado.*

The beginning of Portuguese exploitation of the Gold Coast of Africa had two remarkable consequences: the direct acquisition by the Portuguese of large amounts of gold and the beginning of the trade in black slaves that was to remain a source of income first in Mediterranean and transalpine Europe and later, and to a much greater degree, in the ranching, agricultural, and mining settlements in the Spanish New World.

THE AMBASSADORS

In 1533 the Augsburg painter Hans Holbein the Younger painted the portrait of two young French ambassadors in London, the noble Jean de Dinteville (1504–55) and the bishop-elect of Lavaur, Georges de Selve (1509–41). The painting serves as a convenient object around which to draw many of the themes in this book.

Jean de Dinteville, on the left, was Francis I's ambassador to England. He came from an old noble family near the city of Troyes in Champagne, was the local lord of the town of Polisy, and held the ancient office of bailli of Troyes. The prominence of the French nobility in royal service was apparent in the early sixteenth century, and the lay noble, rather than the cleric alone, participated in those royal affairs that touched other parts of the world besides the kingdom itself. Georges de Selve, son of the president of the Parlement of Paris, was one of six brothers, five of whom were ambassadors in the service of the king of France.

The portrait had come of age in the fifteenth century, and from that period on it is possible to *see* the figures of history in ways that were virtually impossible earlier. In general, medieval artists, like medieval biographers, tended to portray an ideal type rather than a particular individual. But the artistic triumphs of the Romanesque and Gothic movements allowed greater artistic freedom and a greater degree of naturalism, and by the end of the thirteenth century first in tomb sculptures and later in portraits of the donors of churches, there is a clear attempt to record the actual physical appearance of individual subjects. Holbein's portrait catches an important aspect of late medieval artistic technique.

The office of Holbein's subjects had emerged out of the earlier offices of papal legate, personal messenger, and herald. The status and functions of these individuals had become more regularized and more recognized in the early fifteenth century. In 1436 Bernard du Rosier, later bishop of Toulouse, completed the first analysis and description of diplomacy in European history, *The Short Treatise About Ambassadors*. It is difficult for a modern reader to imagine a world of strong and thoroughly governed states touching each other's borders and necessarily having business with each other but not possessing a regular network of formal and informal communications. Such a practice, though, was the invention first of the papacy and in the fourteenth and fifteenth centuries of the western European states. Among the earliest and best-known records of this new institution are the reports of Venetian ambassadors, for Venice, like the papacy, had business everywhere and demanded information as much as any larger power—more strongly, indeed, than many. Not only the circumstances of late medieval states, however, but their unique capacity to borrow from tradition—from Roman law, canon law, chivalric practice, political expediency, and public relations—combined to form the idea, the status, and the office of the late-medieval ambassador. Holbein's picture shows us an institution that grew out of many different sources and that by the early sixteenth century was a recognized fixture in the political and diplomatic world of western Europe.

On the two levels of the table that occupies the center of the picture is a collection of

Hans Holbein; The Ambassadors (1533). (National Gallery, London)

objects that illustrate, literally and symbolically, the ambassadors' world. Each of the astronomical and navigational instruments in the picture can be identified, either with objects whose maker is known and that are presently in the world's museums, or with common types known to have been made around the time of the portrait. Holbein was fascinated with measuring devices, and their presence here both reflects our earlier notice of the tool-mindedness of late-medieval Europeans and suggests just how wide the world of the ambassadors had become. The late-fifteenth-century voyages of Vasco da Gama and Columbus had immensely widened that world, and Europeans in turn began to produce instruments and maps to describe it. The celestial globe by Dinteville's left hand matches the terrestrial globe by his left leg. The book in front of the terrestrial globe has also been identified: it is Peter Apian's *Well-Grounded Instruction in All Merchant's Arithmetic*. Apian was a professor of mathematics and astronomy in Bavaria, and he made the celestial globe on the higher level of the table.

The open book in front of the lute shows on one page the German words and music of Martin Luther's translation of the hymn "Veni Creator Spiritus," a popular hymn in both reformed Protestant and Roman Catholic churches. It was a hymn particularly associated with church councils, and by extension with universal harmony under the guidance of the Holy Spirit. The lute, too, was a symbol of musical and hence universal political harmony, and its broken string, meticulously depicted by Holbein, suggests the discord of states in Europe. When William Shakespeare, in writing *Troilus and Cressida*, wished to describe the chaos that comes upon human society when the hierarchical order is dissolved, he also used the familiar musical metaphor:

> The heavens themselves, the planets, and this center
> Observe degree, priority, and place,
> Insisture, course, proportion, season, form,
> Office and custom, all in line of order. . . .
>   How could communities,
> Degrees in schools, and brotherhoods in cities,
> Peaceful commerce from dividable shores,
> The primogenitive and due of birth,
> Prerogative of age, crowns, sceptors, laurels,
> But by degree, stand in authentic place?
> Take but degree away, untune that string,
> And, Hark! What discord follows.

Harmony in music and harmony in the affairs of men and women was a medieval commonplace that later centuries preserved and used themselves, in spiritual as well as human affairs. The fifteenth-century Netherlands music theorist Johannes Tinctoris once wrote that Jesus Christ was the greatest of all musicians, because he had brought into harmony the great discord between God and humankind. Holbein's portrait is thus capable of being "read" as well as looked at. It preserves many of the themes and characteristic features of the culture that took form in the preceding centuries.

This book began with some predecessors of Dinteville and de Selve—the Phoenician and Greek sailors and migrants who set out westward across the Mediterranean Sea to found colonies, spread their way of life and thought among other peoples, and gain wealth and land for themselves. By the beginning of the sixteenth century Europeans were ready to step out across a far wider sea, regardless of whether or not the people who lived beyond it were ready for them. The peoples who encountered the European explorers, colonists, soldiers, and ambassadors have been dealing ever since, in one way or another, with the consequences of their visits. Parts of the land laws hammered out in twelfth- and thirteenth-century Castile still survive in the laws of South America, Texas, and California. The institutional descendants of Henry II's grand jury still assemble in Canada, Australia, Hong Kong, and the United States. The medieval university still has not been replaced as the most efficient means of organizing and desseminating knowledge. States and ambassadors still wrangle about the means of restoring concord to a discordant world. The difference between the world into which the Phoenicians and

Greeks stepped and that of the sixteenth century explorers and ambassadors is one measure of the achievement of medieval civilization. It is a powerful and impressive measure. For Dinteville and de Selve and others like them stepped not only into a far wider world but into time itself. And the culture they brought with them was the foundation of the modern world.

FURTHER READING

On Byzantium, see Donald M. Nicol, *The Last Centuries of Byzantium, 1261–1453* (London: Hart-Davis, 1972), and *The End of the Byzantine Empire* (New York: Holmes & Meier, 1981). See also the well-told story of Steven Runciman, *The Fall of Constantinople, 1453* (Cambridge: Cambridge University Press, 1965). The best survey of early Ottoman Turkish history is Halil Inalcik, *The Ottoman Empire: The Classical Age, 1300–1600* (London: Weidenfeld & Nicolson, 1973).

On Russia and the Mongols, see J. A. Boyle, *The Mongol World Empire, 1206–1370* (London: Variorum, 1977); Christopher Dawson, *Mission to Asia* (reprint ed.: Toronto: University of Toronto Press, 1980); and George Vernadsky, *The Mongols and Russia* (New Haven: Yale University Press, 1953). A classic study is A. E. Presniakov, *The Formation of the Great Russian State* (Chicago: Quadrangle, 1970).

On Rome, see Richard Krautheimer, *Rome: Profile of a City, 312–1308* (Princeton, N.J.: Princeton University Press, 1980).

On the changing face of the first Rome, see Charles T. Davis, *Dante and the Idea of Rome* (Oxford: Clarendon Press, 1957), and *Dante's Italy* (Philadelphia: University of Pennsylvania Press, forthcoming). There is a large literature on humanism. See in particular Erwin Panofsky, *Renaissance and Renascences in Western Art* (reprint ed.: New York: Harper & Row, 1972).

On technology, see the general bibliography; see also Jacques Le Goff, *Time, Work and Culture in the Middle Ages* (Chicago: University of Chicago Press, 1980).

On European expansion, see E. W. Bovill, *The Golden Trade of the Moors* (New York: Oxford University Press, 1970), and Pierre Chaunu, *European Expansion in the Later Middle Ages* (Amsterdam: North Holland Publishing Co., 1978).

A. G. Dickens, ed., *The Courts of Europe* (New York: McGraw-Hill, 1977), portrays the ambassadors' world, as does Donald Queller, *The Office of Ambassador in the Middle Ages* (Princeton, N.J.: Princeton University Press, 1967).

On the idea of the Middle Ages, see Bryce Lyon, *The Origins of the Middle Ages* (New York: Norton, 1972), and Wallace K. Fergusson, *The Renaissance in Historical Thought* (Boston: Houghton Mifflin, 1948).

Appendix

POPES AND RULERS

The following tables contain the names and dates of popes and rulers of medieval European states. Tables II–VI are in genealogical form, although not all family members are shown.

295

TABLE I. THE MEDIEVAL POPES (ANTIPOPES OMITTED)

Sylvester I, 314–335
Mark, 336
Julius I, 337–352
Liberius, 352–366
Damasus I, 366–384
Siricius, 384–399
Anastasius I, 399–401
Innocent I, 401–417
Zosimus, 417–418
Boniface I, 418–422
Celestine I, 422–432
Sixtus III, 432–440
Leo I the Great, 440–461
Hilary, 461–468
Simplicius, 468–483
Felix III, 483–492
Gelasius I, 492–496
Anastasius II, 496–498
Symmachus, 498–514
Hormisdas, 514–523
John I, 523–526
Felix IV, 526–530
Boniface II, 530–532
John II, 533–535
Agapitus I, 535–536
Silverius, 536–537
Vigilius, 537–555
Pelagius I, 555–561
John III, 561–574
Benedict I, 575–579
Pelagius II, 579–590
Gregory I the Great, 590–604
Sabinianus, 604–606
Boniface III, 607
Boniface IV, 608–615
Deusdedit, 615–618
Boniface V, 619–625
Honorius I, 625–638
Severinus, 640
John IV, 640–642
Theodore I, 642–649
Martin I, 649–655
Eugenius I, 654–657
Vitalian, 657–672
Adeodatus, 672–676
Donus, 676–678

Agatho, 678–681
Leo II, 682–683
Benedict II, 684–685
John V, 685–686
Conon, 686–687
Sergius I, 687–701
John VI, 701–705
John VII, 705–707
Sisinnius, 708
Constantine, 708–715
Gregory II, 715–731
Gregory III, 731–741
Zacharias, 741–752
Stephen II, 752–757
Paul I, 757–767
Stephen III, 768–772
Adrian I, 772–795
Leo III, 795–816
Stephen IV, 816–817
Paschal I, 817–824
Eugenius II, 824–827
Valentine, 827
Gregory IV, 827–844
Sergius II, 844–847
Leo IV, 847–855
Benedict III, 855–858
Nicholas I the Great, 858–867
Adrian II, 867–872
John VIII, 872–882
Marinus I, 882–884
Adrian III, 884–885
Stephen V, 885–891
Formosus, 891–896
Boniface VI, 896
Stephen VI, 896–897
Romanus, 897
Theodore II, 897
John IX, 898–900
Benedict IV, 900–903
Leo V, 903
Sergius III, 904–911
Anastasius III, 911–913
Lando, 913–914
John X, 914–928
Leo VI, 928
Stephen VII, 928–931

John XI, 931–935
Leo VII, 936–939
Stephen VIII, 939–942
Marinus II, 942–946
Agapitus II, 946–955
John XII, 955–964
Leo VIII, 963–965
Benedict V, 964–966
John XIII, 965–972
Benedict VI, 973–974
Benedict VII, 974–983
John XIV, 983–984
John XV, 985–996
Gregory V, 996–999
Sylvester II, 999–1003
John XVII, 1003
John XVIII, 1004–1009
Sergius IV, 1009–1012
Benedict VIII, 1012–1024
John XIX, 1024–1032
Benedict IX, 1032–1044
Sylvester III, 1045
Benedict IX, 1045
Gregory VI, 1045–1046
Clement II, 1046–1047
Benedict IX, 1047–1048
Damasus II, 1048
Leo IX, 1049–1054
Victor II, 1055–1057
Stephen IX, 1057–1058
Nicholas II, 1059–1061
Alexander II, 1061–1073
Gregory VII, 1073–1085
Victor III, 1086–1087
Urban II, 1088–1099
Paschal II, 1099–1118
Gelasius II, 1118–1119
Calixtus II, 1119–1124
Honorius II, 1124–1130
Innocent II, 1130–1143
Celestine II, 1143–1144
Lucius II, 1144–1145
Eugenius III, 1145–1153
Anastasius IV, 1153–1154
Adrian IV, 1154–1159
Alexander III, 1159–1181
Lucius III, 1181–1185

TABLE I. (CONT.)

Urban III, 1185–1187
Gregory VIII, 1187
Clement III, 1187–1191
Celestine III, 1191–1198
Innocent III, 1198–1216
Honorius III, 1216–1227
Gregory IX, 1227–1241
Celestine IV, 1241
Innocent IV, 1243–1254
Alexander IV, 1254–1261
Urban IV, 1261–1264
Clement IV, 1265–1268
Gregory X, 1271–1276
Innocent V, 1276
Adrian V, 1276
John XXI, 1276–1277

Nicholas III, 1277–1280
Martin IV, 1281–1285
Honorius IV, 1285–1287
Nicholas IV, 1288–1292
Celestine V, 1294
Boniface VIII, 1294–1303
Benedict XI, 1303–1304
Clement V, 1305–1314
John XXII, 1316–1334
Benedict XII, 1334–1342
Clement VI, 1342–1352
Innocent VI, 1352–1362
Urban V, 1362–1370
Gregory XI, 1370–1378
Urban VI, 1378–1389
Clement VII, 1378–1394

Boniface IX, 1389–1404
Benedict XIII, 1394–1423
Innocent VII, 1404–1406
Gregory XII, 1406–1415
Alexander V, 1409–1410
John XXIII, 1410–1415
Martin V, 1417–1431
Eugenius IV, 1431–1447
Nicholas V, 1447–1455
Calixtus III, 1455–1458
Pius II, 1458–1464
Paul II, 1464–1471
Sixtus IV, 1471–1484
Innocent VIII, 1484–1492
Alexander VI, 1492–1503.

TABLE II. THE FRANKISH KINGDOMS AND EMPIRE, 680–987

Pepin II of Heristal (680–714)
Mayor of the Palace

|

Charles Martel (714–741)
Mayor of the Palace

|

Pepin III (741–768)
Mayor of the Palace
King of the Franks, 751–768

|

Charlemagne (768–814)

Louis the Pious (814–840)

Lothar (840–855)
Emperor, the Middle Kingdom

Louis' the German (840–876)
East Francia

Charles the Bald (840–877)
Emperor, West Francia

Louis II (855–875)
Emperor, Italy

Charles the Fat (884–887)
Emperor

Carloman

Louis the Stammerer (877–879)
West Francia

Arnulf (896–899)
Emperor

Charles the Simple (898–922)
West Francia

Louis the Child
(899–911)

Louis the IV (936–954)
West Francia

Lothar (954–986)
West Francia

Louis V (986–987)

TABLE III. THE SAXON, SALIAN, AND HOHENSTAUFEN SUCCESSION IN EAST FRANCIA AND THE EMPIRE, 919–1268

Henry I the Fowler (919–936)
Duke of Saxony
King of East Francia

Otto I the Great (936–973)
King of East Francia 936–973
Emperor 962–973

Henry, Duke of Bavaria

Henry the Wrangler
Duke of Bavaria

Henry II (1002–1024)
Emperor

Liutgard — Conrad of Lorraine

Otto II (973–983)
Emperor

Otto of Carinthia

Otto III (983–1002)
Emperor

Henry

Conrad II the Salian (1024–1039)

Henry III (1039–1056)

Henry IV (1056–1106)

Henry the Black,
Duke of Bavaria

Henry V (1106–1125)

Agnes — Frederick of Hohenstaufen

Lothar, Duke of Saxony,
Emperor (1125–1137)

Conrad III (1138–1152)

Frederick, Duke of Swabia — Judith

Henry the Proud — Gertrude

Frederick I Barbarossa
(1152–1190)

Henry the Lion

Constance of Sicily — Henry VI (1190–1197)

Philip of Swabia

Frederick II (1215–1250)

Beatrice — Otto IV of Brunswick (1209)

Conrad IV (1250–1254) Manfred (d. 1266)

Conradin (d. 1268)

TABLE IV. THE CAPETIAN AND VALOIS SUCCESSION IN WEST FRANCIA, 987–1498

Hugh Capet (987–996)

Robert II (996–1031)

Henry I (1031–1060)

Philip I (1060–1108)

Louis VI (1108–1137)

Eleanor of Aquitaine ━ Louis VII (1137–1180) ┳ Constance of Castile

Philip II Augustus (1180–1223)

Blanche of Castile ┳ Louis VIII (1223–1226)

Louis IX (1226–1270)   Charles of Anjou

Philip III (1270–1285)

Philip IV the Fair (1285–1314)   Charles of Valois (c. 1325)   Margaret ┳ Edward I of England

Edward II of England

Isabella   Louis X (1314–1316)   Philip V (1316–1322)   Charles IV (1322–1328)

Philip VI (1328–1350)

Jean II (1350–1364)

Joan   Jean I (1316)

Charles the Bad King of Navarre

Charles V (1364–1380)   Philip, Duke of Burgundy (d. 1404)

Charles VI (1380–1422)   John, Duke of Burgundy (d. 1419)

Charles VII (1422–1461)   Philip, Duke of Burgundy (d. 1467)

Louis XI (1461–1483)

Charles VIII (1483–1498)   Charles the Rash, Duke of Burgundy (d. 1477) ┳ Isabella of Bourbon

Mary of Burgundy

TABLE V. ANGLO-SAXON, NORMAN, AND PLANTAGENET ENGLAND, 871–1485

England

Alfred (871–899)
Edward the Elder (899–925)
Aethelstan (925–939)
Edmund I (939–946)
Edred (946–955)
Edwy (955–959)
Edgar (959–975)
Edward the Martyr (975–979)
Ethelraed Unraed (979–1016)

Normandy

HRolf (911–930?)

William Longsword (927–942)

Richard I (942–996)

Richard II (996–1026)

Danish Line

Cnut (1016–1035)
Harold I (1035–1040)
Harthacnut (1040–1042)

Richard III (1026–1027)

Robert I, Duke of Normandy (1027–1035)

Edward the Confessor (1042–1066)

Harold II (1066)

William the Bastard (1028–1087)

William II Rufus (1087–1100)

Henry I (1100–1135)

Adela — Stephen of Blois

Stephen (1135–1154)

Geoffrey Plantagenet, Count of Anjou (d. 1151) — Matilda (d. 1167)

Henry II (1154–1189) — Eleanor of Aquitaine

Richard I Lionheart (1189–1199)   John (1199–1216)

Henry III (1216–1272)

Edward I (1272–1307)

Edward II — Isabella of France

Edward III (1327–1377)

Edward, the Black Prince   Lionel   John of Gaunt   Edmund, Duke of York

Richard II (1377–1399)

Henry IV (1399–1413)

Henry V (1413–1422)

Henry VI (1422–1461)

Anne ———————————————————————— Richard

Richard, Duke of York

Edward IV (1461–1483)   Richard III (1483–1485)

TABLE VI. THE LATER EMPERORS AND KINGS OF GERMANY, 1273–1519

Habsburg	Wittelsbach	Luxembourg	Nassau

Rudolph I
(1273–1291)

Adolf (1291–1298)

Albert I
(1298–1308)

Matilda —— Ludwig II
Duke of Bavaria

Henry VII
(1308–1313)

Albert II
(d. 1358)

Ludwig of Bavaria
(1313–1347)

John of Bohemia
(d. 1346)

Charles IV
(1346–1378)

Leopold
(d. 1386)

Albert III
(d. 1395)

Wenceslas
(1378–1410)

Sigismund
(1410–1437)

Ernst
(d. 1424)

Albert IV

Frederick III
(1440–1493)

Albert V
(1438–1439)

Elizabeth of
Bohemia and Hungary

Ladislas
(d. 1457)

Maximilian I
(1493–1519)

General Bibliography

Guides to Medieval Studies and Bibliography

Two excellent introductions to the general character of medieval studies and the types of sources and methodology for dealing with them are R. C. Van Caenegem and F. L. Ganshof, *Guide to the Sources of Medieval History* (Amsterdam: North Holland Publishing Co., 1978), and J. M. Powell, ed., *An Introduction to Medieval Studies* (Syracuse: Syracuse University Press, 1976). Among other important general reference sources are J. R. Strayer, ed., *The Dictionary of the Middle Ages* (New York: Scribner's, forthcoming); L. J. Paetow, *A Guide to the Study of Medieval History,* rev. ed. (Cambridge, Mass.: Mediaeval Academy of America, 1931); and Gray C. Boyce, *Literature of Medieval History, 1930-1975: A Supplement to Louis John Paetow's 'A Guide to the Study of Medieval History,'* 5 vols. (Millwood, N.Y.: Kraus, 1981). For current bibliography, see *International Medieval Bibliography* (Leeds: Leeds University Press, 1967-), and R. Rouse, *Annotated Guide to Serial Bibliography* (Berkeley and Los Angeles: University of California Press, 1969).

Source Materials in English Translation

C. P. Farrar and Austin P. Evans, *Bibliography of English Translations From Medieval Sources* (New York: Columbia University Press, 1946), has been continued by M. A. Ferguson, *Bibliography of English Translations From Medieval Sources, 1944-1968* (New York: Columbia University Press, 1973). There are many fine collections of source materials in anthologies. Some of these have been noted in the individual bibliographies above, but mention must be made of Brian Pullan, *Sources for the History of Medieval Europe* (New York: Barnes & Noble, 1966), the best single collection of annotated documents in English translation.

Atlases

The most readily available atlas is Colin McEvedy, *The Penguin Atlas of Medieval History* (Baltimore: Penguin, 1961). More sophisticated is Geoffrey Barraclough, ed., *The Times Atlas of World History* (Maplewood, N.J.: Hammond, 1978). Specialized atlases are also very useful. See, for example, F. Van Der Meer and Christine Mohrmann, *Atlas of the Early Christian World* (London: Nelson, 1958).

Historical Geography

See C. T. Smith, *A Historical Geography of Western Europe Before 1800* (London: Longmans, 1967); Norman J. G. Pounds, *An Historical Geography of Europe, 450 B.C.–A.D. 1330* (Cambridge: Cambridge University Press, 1976). For an important region, see H. C. Darby et al., *A New Historical Geography of England Before 1800* (Cambridge: Cambridge University Press, 1973), and R. A. Dodgshon and R. A. Butlin, eds., *An Historical Geography of England and Wales* (New York: Academic Press, 1978).

Archaeology

See Rainer Berger, ed., *Scientific Methods in Medieval Archaeology* (Berkeley and Los Angeles: University of California Press, 1970), and the ongoing research published in the journal *Medieval Archaeology*. A good example of specialized work is M. W. Barley, ed., *European Towns: Their Archaeology and Early History* (New York: Academic Press, 1977).

The Physical Environment

For climate, see E. Le Roy Ladurie, *Times of Feast, Times of Famine* (New York: Doubleday, 1971), and H. H. Lamb, *The Changing Climate* (London: Methuen, 1966). For human geography, see Emrys Jones, *Human Geography: An Introduction to Man and His World,* rev. ed. (New York: Praeger, 1965), and Derwent Whittlesy, *Environmental Foundations of European History* (New York: Appleton-Century-Crofts, 1949). A brilliant example of working these kinds of data into historical knowledge is Fernand Braudel, *The Mediterranean and the Mediterranean World in the Age of Philip II,* 2 vols. (New York: Harper & Row, 1972).

Demography

See J. C. Russell, *Late Ancient and Medieval Population* (Philadelphia: Transactions of the American Philosophical Society, 1958); idem, "Recent Advances in Medieval Demography," *Speculum,* 40 (1965), 84–101; and idem, "Population in Europe," in *The Fontana Economic History of Europe,* Vol. I, *The Middle Ages,* ed. Carlo M. Cipolla (London: Collins/Fontana, 1972), pp. 25–70. See also E. A. Wrigley, *Population and History* (New York: McGraw-Hill, 1969).

Medieval History: Narrative Surveys

The most complete history of the Middle Ages is J. B. Bury et al., eds., *The Cambridge Medieval History,* 8 vols. (Cambridge: Cambridge University Press, 1911–36); Vol. IV of this history, *The Byzantine Empire,* ed. Joan Hussey, appeared in a new edition in 1966. The most comprehensive recent survey is the series edited by Denys Hay, *A General History of Europe* (New York: Longmans, 1966), which includes volumes by A. H. M. Jones, Christopher Brooke, John Mundy, and Hay dealing with the period 300–1500. Two superbly illustrated collaborative histories are David Talbot Rice, ed., *The Dark Ages* (London: Thames & Hudson, 1965), and Joan Evans, ed., *The Flowering of the Middle Ages* (London: Thames and Hudson, 1966). The first individual history of medieval Europe—and in the opinion of many still the greatest—is Edward Gibbon, *The Decline and Fall of the Roman Empire,* the most complete edition of which is that of J. B. Bury (London: Methuen, 1909–14).

Chronology

A good extensive chronology is that of R. L. Storey, *Chronology of the Medieval World, 400–1491* (New York: D. McKay, 1973). For England there are fine guides by F. M. Powicke and

E. B. Fryde, *Handbook of British Chronology,* 2nd. ed. (London: Royal Historical Society, 1961), and C. R. Cheney, *Handbook of Dates for Students of English History* (London: Royal Historical Society, 1945).

Language

See W. B. Lockwood, *A Panorama of Indo-European Languages* (London: Hutchinson, 1972), and Philippe Wolff, *Western Languages* A.D. *100–1500* (New York: McGraw-Hill, 1971).

Economic History

Extensive, detailed, and uneven is J. Clapham et al., eds., *The Cambridge Economic History of Europe,* Vols. I–III (Cambridge: Cambridge University Press, 1941–61). For the early period, see Georges Duby, *The Early Growth of the European Economy: Warriors and Peasants From the Seventh to the Twelfth Century* (Ithaca, N.Y.: Cornell University Press, 1974), and A. F. Havighurst, ed., *The Pirenne Thesis,* 3rd ed. (Lexington, Mass.: Heath, 1976). From 900 see Robert S. Lopez, *The Commercial Revolution of the Middle Ages, 950–1350* (New York: Cambridge University Press, 1976), and Robert S. Lopez and Irving Raymond, *Medieval Trade in the Mediterranean World* (New York: Columbia University Press, 1955). For the later Middle Ages, see Harry A. Miskimin, *The Economy of Early Renaissance Europe* (New York: Cambridge University Press, 1975). In general, see Carlo M. Cipolla, ed., *The Middle Ages,* Vol. I of *The Fontana Economic History of Europe* (London: Collins/Fontana, 1972), and Carlo M. Cipolla, *Before the Industrial Revolution* (New York: Norton, 1976). All of these works have extensive bibliographies.

Social History

Perhaps the classic work in medieval social history is Marc Bloch, *Feudal Society* (Chicago: University of Chicago Press, 1961). It should be compared now with Georges Duby, *The Chivalrous Society* (Berkeley and Los Angeles: University of California Press, 1977), and *The Three Orders: Feudal Society Imagined* (Chicago: University of Chicago Press, 1980). Excellent samplings of different kinds of social history may be found in Sylvia Thrupp, ed., *Early Medieval Society* (New York: Appleton-Century-Crofts, 1967), and *Change in Medieval Society* (New York: Appleton-Century-Crofts, 1964). A splendid specialized study is Georges Duby, *Rural Economy and Country Life in the Medieval West* (Columbia, S.C.: University of South Carolina Press, 1968). Two fine collections of studies on one aspect of social history, the history of women, are Susan Mosher Stuard, ed., *Women in Medieval Society* (Philadelphia: University of Pennsylvania Press, 1976), and Derek Baker, ed., *Medieval Women: Studies in Church History: Subsidia,* Vol. I (Oxford: Basil Blackwell, 1978). For a particular culture, see Suzanne Fonay Wemple, *Women in Frankish Society* (Philadelphia: University of Pennsylvania Press, 1981). An excellent anthology of documents in translation is that of Jeremy duQuesnay Adams, *Patterns of Medieval Society* (Englewood Cliffs, N.J.: Prentice-Hall, 1969). Excellent examples of modern approaches may be found in David Herlihy, *The Social History of Italy and Western Europe, 700–1500* (London: Valiorum, 1978), and John W. Baldwin, *Masters, Princes and Merchants: The Social Views of Peter the Chanter and His Circle,* 2 vols. (Princeton, N.J.: Princeton University Press, 1970).

Political History: General

Medieval political units did not always coincide with modern political societies. For the character of political life and thought in general, see H. Mitteis, *The State in the Middle Ages* (Amsterdam: North Holland Publishing Co., 1975); Fredric L. Cheyette, ed., *Lordship and Community in Medieval Europe: Selected Readings* (reprint ed., Huntington, N.Y.: Krieger, 1975); Ewart Lewis, *Medieval Political Ideas,* 2 vols. (New York: Knopf, 1954); and Beryl Smalley, ed., *Trends in Medieval Political Thought* (New York: Barnes & Noble, 1965).

For the early Middle Ages, see J. M. Wallace-Hadrill, *Early Germanic Kingship in England and on the Continent* (Oxford: Clarendon Press, 1971); P. H. Sawyer and I. N. Wood, eds., *Early Medieval Kingship* (Leeds: School of History, University of Leeds, 1977); Walter Ullmann, *The Carolingian Renaissance and the Idea of Kingship* (London: Methuen, 1969); and Robert Folz,

The Concept of Empire in Western Europe From the Fifth to the Fifteenth Century (London: Edward Arnold, 1969).

For the later period, see Timothy Reuter, ed. and trans., *The Medieval Nobility: Selected Essays* (Amsterdam: North Holland Publishing Co., 1978); Ernst Kantorowicz, *The King's Two Bodies* (Princeton, N.J.: Princeton University Press, 1957); and Brian Tierney, ed., *The Crisis of Church and State, 1050–1300* (Englewood Cliffs, N.J.: Prentice-Hall, Inc., 1964). See also Antonio Marongiu, *Medieval Parliaments: A Comparative Study* (London: Eyre & Spottiswoode, 1968); Gaines Post, *Studies in Medieval Legal Thought: Public Law and the State, 1100–1322* (Princeton, N.J.: Princeton University Press, 1964); Michael Wilks, *The Problem of Sovereignty in the Later Middle Ages* (Cambridge: Cambridge University Press, 1963); and Frederick H. Russell, *The Just War in the Middle Ages* (Cambridge: Cambridge University Press, 1975).

Political History: Regional

England: Standard and exhaustive, although out of date in some places, is Sir George Clark, ed., *The Oxford History of England,* vols. I–VI (Oxford: Oxford University Press, 1937–62). The series edited by David C. Douglas, *English Historical Documents* (New York: Eyre & Spottiswoode, 1955–), complements the Oxford series with extensively annotated source materials in translation. Current work is listed in the Cambridge University Press series *Bibliographical Handbooks.* Especially useful are the volumes edited by Michael Altschul (1969), Bertie Wilkinson (1977), and DeLloyd J. Guth (1978). A standard work is Edgar B. Graves, *Bibliography of English History to 1485* (Oxford: Oxford University Press, 1975).

France: There is no comprehensive history of medieval France in English. On specific periods, see Robert Fawtier, *The Capetian Kings of France* (New York: Barnes & Noble, 1962); Elizabeth H. Hallam, *Capetian France, 987–1328* (New York: Longmans, 1980); and P. S. Lewis, *Later Medieval France: The Polity* (New York: St. Martin's, 1968). For the countryside, see Marc Bloch, *French Rural History* (Berkeley and Los Angeles: University of California Press, 1970). On towns, see Charles Petit-Dutaillis, *The French Communes in the Middle Ages* (Amsterdam: North Holland Publishing Co., 1978).

Germany: The best general introduction is Geoffrey Barraclough, *The Origins of Modern Germany* (reprint ed., New York: Oxford University Press, 1963). More recent work may be traced in Josef Fleckenstein, *Early Medieval Germany* (Amsterdam: North Holland Publishing Co., 1978), and Joachim Leuschner, *Germany in the Later Middle Ages* (Amsterdam: North Holland Publishing Co., 1978). See also Karl Leyser, *Rule and Conflict in an Early Medieval Society: Ottonian Saxony* (Bloomington: Indiana University Press, 1980); Philippe Dollinger, *The German Hansa* (London: Macmillan, 1970); and Gerald Strauss, ed., *Pre-Reformation Germany* (New York: Harper & Row, 1972).

Hungary: C. A. Macartney, *Hungary: A Short History* (Oxford: Oxford University Press, 1962).

Ireland: A. J. Otway-Ruthven, *A History of Medieval Ireland* (New York: Barnes & Noble, 1968); Kathleen Hughes, *The Church in Early Irish Society* (Ithaca, N.Y.: Cornell University Press, 1968); J. F. Lydon, *The Lordship of Ireland in the Middle Ages* (Dublin: University Press of Ireland, 1972); L. Bieler, *Ireland: Harbinger of the Middle Ages* (New York: Oxford University Press, 1963). See also the ongoing series edited by T. W. Moody, F. X Martin, and F. J. Byrne, *A New History of Ireland* (New York: Oxford University Press, 1976–).

Italy: J. K. Hyde, *Society and Politics in Medieval Italy, 1000–1300* (New York: St. Martin's, 1969); Gino Luzzato, *An Economic History of Italy* (New York: Barnes & Noble, 1961); Daniel Waley, *The Italian City-Republics* (New York: McGraw-Hill, 1969); John Larner, *Italy in the Age of Dante and Petrarch, 1216–1380* (New York: Longmans, 1980); Chris John Wickham, *Early Medieval Italy* (Totowa, N.J.: Barnes & Noble, 1982); Marvin Becker, *Medieval Italy* (Bloomington, Ind.: Indiana University Press, 1980).

Poland and Slavic Europe: A. P. Vlasto, *The Entry of the Slavs Into Christendom* (Cambridge: Cambridge University Press, 1970); O. Halecki, *The Borderlands of Western Civilization*

(New York: Ronald Press, 1952); Francis Dvornik, *The Slavs in European History and Civilization* (New Brunswick, N.J.: Rutgers University Press, 1962); Geoffrey Barraclough, ed., *Eastern and Western Europe in the Middle Ages* (New York: Harcourt Brace Jovanovich, 1970); A. Gieysztor et al., eds., *History of Poland* (Warsaw: Polish Scientific Publishers, 1968).

Scandinavia: P. H. Sawyer, *The Age of the Vikings,* 2nd ed. (London: A. Edward Arnold, 1971), and D. M. Wilson, *The Vikings and Their Origins* (New York: Praeger, 1970), are good introductions to the Viking period. See also Palle Lauring, *A History of the Kingdom of Denmark* (Copenhagen: Host, 1973), and Karen Larsen, *A History of Norway* (Princeton, N.J.: Princeton University Press, 1948).

Scotland: William C. Dickinson, *Scotland From the Earliest Times to 1603,* 3rd ed., rev. and ed. A. A. M. Duncan (New York: Oxford University Press, 1977).

Sicily: Good readable histories are those of John J. Norwich, *The Normans in the South* and *The Kingdom in the Sun* (London: Longmans, 1968, 1970). Steven Runciman, *The Sicilian Vespers* (Cambridge: Cambridge University Press, 1958), addresses the late thirteenth century. For the period of Frederick II, see Ernst Kantorowicz, *Frederick II* (New York: Ungar, 1957).

Spain: See J. Vicens Vives, *Approaches to the History of Spain* (Berkeley and Los Angeles: University of California Press, 1970); J. F. O'Callaghan, *A History of Medieval Spain* (Ithaca, N.Y.: Cornell University Press, 1975); D. W. Lomax, *The Reconquest of Spain* (New York: Longmans, 1978); J. N. Hillgarth, *The Spanish Kingdoms, 1250–1516,* Vol. I, *The Precarious Balance, 1250–1410,* and Vol. II, *The Castilian Hegemony, 1410–1516* (New York: Oxford University Press, 1976, 1978); J. R. L. Highfield, *Spain in the Fifteenth Century* (New York: Harper & Row, 1972); Thomas F. Glick, *Islamic and Christian Spain in the Early Middle Ages* (Princeton, N.J.: Princeton University Press, 1978); A Chejne, *Muslim Spain* (Minneapolis: University of Minnesota Press, 1974); and R. I. Burns, *The Crusader Kingdom of Valencia,* 2 vols. (Cambridge, Mass.: Harvard University Press, 1967).

The Church

The history of the Church touches so many aspects of early European life and thought that its study is indispensable for those who wish to understand something of the history of Europe. There are many histories of the Church available, but those that take the broadest approach and invite the most serious thought are considerably fewer. Probably the greatest history is the multivolume work edited by A. Fliche and V. Martin, *Histoire de l'Eglise* (Paris: Bloud & Gay, 1935–), now in the slow process of completion and translation. Equally substantial is the monumental *Handbuch der Kirchengeschichte,* ed. Hubert Jedin. Of this work, not yet completed, Vol. III, *The Church in the Age of Feudalism,* ed. F. Kempf, H.-G. Beck, E. Ewig, and J. A. Jungmann, trans. Anselm Biggs (New York: Herder & Herder, 1969), is certainly the best single study of the period 700–1123. A comparable work, less consistent and better in its original French sections than in English translation, is *The Christian Centuries,* ed. Louis Rogier et al., Vol. I, *The First Six Hundred Years,* by Jean Danielou and Henri Marrou, and Vol. II, *The Middle Ages,* by David Knowles and Dimitri Obolensky (New York: McGraw-Hill, 1964, 1969). All of the works cited above contain extensive bibliographies.

Among shorter studies, Henry Chadwick, *The Early Church* (Baltimore: Penguin, 1967), and R. W. Southern, *Western Society and the Church in the Middle Ages* (Baltimore: Penguin, 1970), constitute the first two volumes in the fine series *The Pelican History of the Church.* Both are superbly readable and reliable, although selective in their approach. A handy reference is F. L. Cross, ed., *The Oxford Dictionary of the Christian Church,* 2nd ed. (London: Oxford University Press, 1972). A comprehensive recent bibliography is Henry Chadwick, *The History of the Church: A Select Bibliography,* 3rd ed. (London: The Historical Association, 1973). The best atlases are F. Van Der Meer and Christine Mohrmann, eds., *An Atlas of the Early Christian World* (London: Nelson, 1958), and H. Jedin, K. S. Latourette, and J. Marten, eds., *Atlas zur Kirchengeschichte,* (Freiburg: Herder and Herder, 1970).

See also Dom Jean Leclercq, Dom François Vandenbroucke, and Louis Bouyer, *The Spirituality of the Middle Ages* (London: Burns & Oates, 1968), Vol. 2 of *A History of Christian*

Spirituality. On dogma, see Jaroslav Pelikan, *The Spirit of Eastern Christendom* and *The Growth of Medieval Theology* (Chicago: University of Chicago Press, 1974, 1978).

The Jews in Medieval Europe

A good short introduction to the history of the Jews in the world of late antiquity is Michael Grant, *The Jews in the Roman World* (New York: Scribner's, 1973). Volumes III–VIII of Salo W. Baron's *A Social and Religious History of the Jews,* 2nd ed. (New York: Columbia University Press, 1957), deal with most of the Middle Ages and represent the work of one of the greatest modern historians. The range of Baron's concerns is also reflected in his collected essays, *Ancient and Medieval Jewish History* (New Brunswick, N.J.: Rutgers University Press, 1972).

The most exhaustive recent work on the early period is Cecil Roth and I. H. Levine, eds., *The Dark Age: Jews in Christian Europe 711–1096,* Vol. II of Cecil Roth, gen. ed., *The World History of the Jewish People, Second Series: The Medieval Period* (New Brunswick, N.J.: Rutgers University Press, 1966). Among particularly useful detailed studies is Joshua Starr, *The Jews in the Byzantine Empire, 641–1204* (reprint ed., New York: Burt Franklin, 1970).

A good collection of documentary evidence is assembled and expertly commented upon in Jacob Marcus, *The Jew in the Medieval World* (reprint ed., New York: Harper & Row, 1965). A useful depiction of community existence is found in Israel Abrahams, *Jewish Life in the Middle Ages* (New York: Atheneum, 1969).

A fine study of the roots of anti-Semitism is Joshua Trachtenberg, *The Devil and the Jews: The Medieval Conception of the Jew and its Relation to Modern Antisemitism* (New Haven: Yale University Press, 1943).

An immensely important review of the question of the Jews in medieval Europe and the methodology of research into medieval Jewish history is the study of Gavin Langmuir, "The Jews and the Archives of Angevin England: Reflections on Medieval Anti-Semitism," *Traditio,* 19 (1963), 183–244. Most of the works cited above, and particularly that of Langmuir, contain useful bibliographies.

The most thorough study of a single Jewish community in the Middle Ages is S. D. Goitein, *A Mediterranean Society: The Jewish Communities of the World as Portrayed in the Documents of the Cairo Geniza,* Vol. I, *Economic Foundations;* Vol. II, *The Community* (Berkeley and Los Angeles: University of California Press, 1968, 1971). Equally important in studying the impact of Judaism on a very different kind of society is D. M. Dunlop, *History of the Jewish Khazars* (Princeton, N.J.: Princeton University Press, 1954).

Islamic History

A good brief introduction to Muhammad and the rise of Islam is the work of Francesco Gabrieli, *Muhammad and the Conquests of Islam* (New York: McGraw-Hill, 1968). The best biography of the Prophet is Tor Andrae, *Mohammed: The Man and His Faith* (reprint ed., New York: Harper & Row, 1960). Two excellent short introductions are Bernard Lewis, *The Arabs in History* (reprint ed., New York: Harper & Row, 1960), and G. E. von Grunebaum, *Medieval Islam* (reprint ed., Chicago: University of Chicago Press, 1961).

For the *Qu'ran,* see R. Bell, *Introduction to the Qu'ran* (Edinburgh: Edinburgh University Press, 1970). For general information on Islam, see *Encyclopedia of Islam,* latest ed. (Leiden: Brill, 1960–).

Two distinctive and very different approaches to various aspects of Islamic thought are F. I. J. Rosenthal, *Political Thought in Medieval Islam* (Cambridge: Cambridge University Press, 1962), and E. W. Lane, *Arabian Society in the Middle Ages* (reprint ed., New York: Barnes & Noble, 1971). A. H. Hourani and S. M. Stern, eds., *The Islamic City* (Philadelphia: University of Pennsylvania Press, 1970), collects much important recent scholarship, as does D. S. Richards, ed., *Islam and the Trade of Asia* (Philadelphia: University of Pennsylvania Press, 1971).

A good recent study of Islamic culture is D. M. Dunlop, *Arab Civilization to 1500* (London: Longmans, 1971). There is much related material in several essays included in K. M. Setton, gen. ed., *A History of the Crusades,* Vols. I and II, 2nd ed. (Madison: University of Wisconsin Press, 1969). Norman Daniel, *The Arabs and Medieval Europe* (London: Longmans, 1974), is a good introduction to Islamic Christian relations. See also Maurice Lombard, *The Golden Age of Islam* (Amsterdam: North Holland Publishing Co., 1975).

Byzantine History

The standard reference work is now *The Cambridge Medieval History,* Vol. IV, Joan M. Hussey, ed., *The Byzantine Empire* (Cambridge: Cambridge University Press, 1966). The best single shorter history is that of George Ostrogorsky, *A History of the Byzantine State,* 2nd ed. (New Brunswick, N.J.: Rutgers University Press, 1968). Norman Baynes and H. St. L. B. Moss, eds., *Byzantium: An Introduction to East Roman Civilization* (reprint ed., Oxford: Oxford University Press, 1961), consists of essays by experts on various aspects of Byzantine civilization. An excellent recent survey of Byzantine civilization is H. W. Haussig, *A History of Byzantine Civilization* (New York: Praeger, 1971). Joan M. Hussey, *The Byzantine World* (New York: Harper & Row, 1961), is a fine brief introduction.

On Constantinople, see David Talbot Rice, *Constantinople: From Byzantium to Istanbul* (New York: Stein & Day, 1965). On Byzantine art, see David Talbot Rice, *Byzantine Art* (Harmondsworth: Penguin, 1968). On religion, see the chapters by Hans-Georg Beck in Friedrich Kempf et al., eds., *The Church in the Age of Feudalism* (New York: Herder & Herder, 1969), and George Every, *The Byzantine Patriarchate, 451–1204* (London: Society for the Promotion of Christian Knowledge, 1947).

Byzantium's impact upon neighboring societies is outlined in the important study by Dimitri Obolensky, *The Byzantine Commonwealth* (New York: Weidenfeld and Nicolson, 1971).

Various important elements of Byzantine civilization are explored in Steven Runciman, *The Byzantine Theocracy* (Cambridge: Cambridge University Press, 1977); D. J. Geanakoplos, *Interaction of the Sibling Byzantine and Western Cultures in the Middle Ages and Italian Renaissance (300–1600)* (New Haven: Yale University Press, 1976); and Louis Bréhier, *The Life and Death of Byzantium* (Amsterdam: North Holland Publishing Co., 1977).

Thought and Learning

A good general introduction to the early period is M. L. W. Laistner, *Thought and Letters in Western Europe,* A.D. *500–900,* 2nd ed. (Ithaca, N.Y.: Cornell University Press, 1957). Philippe Wolff, *The Awakening of Europe* (Baltimore: Penguin, 1968), deals well with the period 800–1142. Pierre Riché, *Education and Culture in the Barbarian West* (Columbia, S.C.: University of South Carolina Press, 1977), is the standard work on a complex subject. C. S. Lewis, *The Discarded Image* (Cambridge: Cambridge University Press, 1964), is a good short treatment of literary cosmology. David Knowles, *The Evolution of Medieval Thought* (New York: Random House, Vintage Books, 1962), is an extensive history of philosophy. M.-D. Chenu, *Nature, Man and Society in the Twelfth Century* (Chicago: University of Chicago Press, 1968), is a classic collection of studies revealing thought in action, as is, in a different way, Alexander Murray, *Reason and Society in the Middle Ages* (Oxford: Clarendon Press, 1978).

On the universities, see the classic work by Hastings Rashdall, *The Universities of Europe in the Middle Ages,* 3 vols., eds., R. M. Powicke and A. B. Emden (Oxford: Oxford University Press, 1936); Anders Piltz, *The World of Medieval Learning* (Totowa, N.J.: Barnes & Noble, 1981); Lynn Thorndike, *University Records and Life in the Middle Ages* reprint ed. (New York: Norton, 1975); Gordon Leff, *Paris and Oxford Universities in the Thirteenth and Fourteenth Centuries* (New York: Wiley, 1968).

Mathematics, Science, and Medicine

Loren C. MacKinney, *Early Medieval Medicine With Special Reference to France and Chartres* (Baltimore: Johns Hopkins, 1937), and *Medical Illustrations in Medieval Manuscripts*

(Berkeley and Los Angeles: University of California Press, 1965) constitute a good introduction to the history of medieval medicine; each includes bibliographic guides. B. Lawn, *The Salernitan Questions* (Oxford: Oxford University Press, 1963), is a good introduction to the conceptualization of medical and scientific problems in the Middle Ages. C. H. Talbot, *Medicine in Medieval England* (London: Oldbourne, 1967), is extremely wide-ranging and informative. A more extensive bibliography may be found in Edward Grant, *A Sourcebook in Medieval Science* (Cambridge, Mass.: Harvard University Press, 1974).

Standard histories of medieval science are A. C. Crombie, *Medieval and Early Modern Science,* 2 vols., rev. ed., (New York: Doubleday, 1959), and George Sarton, *Introduction to the History of Science,* 3 vols. (Baltimore: Johns Hopkins, 1947–58). Edward Grant, *Physical Science in the Middle Ages* (New York: John Wiley, 1971), contains an excellent bibliography. Richard Dales, *The Scientific Achievement of the Middle Ages* (Philadelphia: University of Pennsylvania Press, 1973), offers a fine selection of documents in translation and includes an introduction and bibliography.

For all of these fields, see David Lindberg, ed., *Science in the Middle Ages* (Chicago: University of Chicago Press, 1978).

Some of the important work of Anneliese Maier is now available in English in Steven Sargent, ed. and trans., *On the Threshold of Exact Science* (Philadelphia: University of Pennsylvania Press, 1982).

There is a fine introduction to mathematical theory and practice generally in Michael S. Mahoney's essay "Mathematics," in *Science in the Middle Ages,* ed. David C. Lindberg (Chicago: University of Chicago Press, 1980). For a good recent survey of the Muslim contribution, see Ali Abdullah Al-Daffa', *The Muslim Contribution to Mathematics* (London: Kazi Publications, 1977).

Transportation and Technology

A. P. Newton, *Travel and Travellers of the Middle Ages* (New York: K. Paul, Trench, Trubner, 1930), is a good general introduction. More recent works are G. Hindley, *A History of Roads* (Secaucus, N.J.: P. Davies, 1972), and Albert C. Leighton, *Transport and Communication in Early Medieval Europe, A.D. 500–1100* (Newton Abbot: David & Charles, 1972).

There are a number of good general histories of technology, a subject long neglected but extremely important in early European history. Two particularly lively studies are Lynn White, Jr., *Medieval Technology and Social Change* (Oxford: Oxford University Press, 1962), and *Machina ex Deo* (Cambridge, Mass.: M.I.T. Press, 1969). White's scholarly essays are now collected: *Medieval Religion and Technology* (Berkeley and Los Angeles: University of California Press, 1978).

See also Archibald R. Lewis, *Naval Power and Trade in the Mediterranean, A.D. 500–1100* (Princeton, N.J.: Princeton University Press, 1951), and *The Northern Seas A.D. 300–1100* (Princeton, N.J.: Princeton University Press, 1958); Vincent Cassidy, *The Sea Around Them* (Baton Rouge: Louisiana State University Press, 1968); Pierre Chaunu, *European Expansion in the Later Middle Ages* (Amsterdam: North Holland Publishing Co., 1978); and James M. Muldoon, *The Expansion of Europe: The First Phase* (Philadelphia; University of Pennsylvania Press, 1977).

Index